Behind
the Stained Glass
Windows

Also by John and Sylvia Ronsvalle

The Poor Have Faces

Behind
the Stained Glass
Windows

Money Dynamics in the Church

John and Sylvia Ronsvalle

A Division of Baker Book House Co
Grand Rapids, Michigan 49516

Published by Baker Books
a division of Baker Book House Company
P.O. Box 6287, Grand Rapids, MI 49516-6287

Printed in the United States of America

Library of Congress Cataloging-in-Publication Data

Ronsvalle, John
  Behind the stained glass windows : money dynamics in the church /
John and Sylvia Ronsvalle.
    p. cm.
  Includes bibliographical references and index.
  ISBN 0-8010-9011-3 (cloth)
    1. Stewardship, Christian. 2. Money—Religious aspects—Christianity.
3. Church finance. I. Ronsvalle, Sylvia. II. Title.
BV772.R63   1996
254.8—dc20   96-1101

To all those men and women
at the local, regional, and national levels
who love the church
and labor so faithfully in God's service

Contents

Foreword

On two occasions—once early on in their studies and once as they were summarizing their findings—John and Sylvia Ronsvalle brought together a group of denominational leaders from a wide spectrum of communions to share our stewardship stories and perceptions.

As persons fortunate enough to be included in this group, we found a warm bond of Christian fellowship and mutual respect. It was striking as we became familiar with the picture of the church the Ronsvalles painted from their research. Each of us said to some degree or other, "This is my church's story!" The parallels are dramatic.

John and Sylvia Ronsvalle are passionate Christians motivated by the pressing needs of a world in pain and committed to the ideal of what the church can be in responding to these needs. While sometimes they are frustrated when the church is weak in living out this vision, at other times they are buoyed by evidences of strong, active faith.

The Ronsvalles have made a significant contribution in identifying some of the points of tension in congregational life, especially in areas related to the stewardship of money and giving. There is a large gap between our belief in a commitment to Christ that results in sacrificial giving for a challenging congregational mission and the rather weak and indecisive ways we often see our congregations respond.

We are convinced that God has given the church the resources it needs to respond in new and creative ways to a needy, hungry, and hurting world. However, to get from here to there, some important issues need to be confronted.

We counseled the Ronsvalles to write this book in such a way as to encourage lay readership, along with the eager use we anticipate by pastors and denominational leaders. We believe the book will make a strong contribution to a needed conversation between clergy and lay leadership about ways in which congregational life might respond to the gospel challenge.

We recommend this insightful work to you. May God use your stewardship of time in reading it for the building of a church that will be stronger, more committed, and joyfully generous.

James Austin, Southern Baptist Convention
M. Douglas Borko, United Church of Christ
Timothy C. Ek, Evangelical Covenant Church
Robert Foster, Church of the Nazarene
David Heetland, Garrett-Evangelical Theological Seminary
Hugh Magers, The Episcopal Church
Herbert Mather, The United Methodist Church
David McCreath, Presbyterian Church (U.S.A.)
Dale E. Minnich, Church of the Brethren
Mark Moller-Gunderson, Evangelical Lutheran Church in
    America
Thomas J. Murphy, Roman Catholic Church
Ronald Nelson, The Lutheran Church-Missouri Synod
Robert L. Niklaus, The Christian and Missionary Alliance
Al Taylor, Church of God (Cleveland, Tenn.)
Robert Welsh, Christian Church (Disciples of Christ)
James E. Williams, Church of God (Anderson, Ind.)

Preface

The book that follows is the result of many years of research. In the mid-1970s, we began asking the question, "How many resources do Christians in the United States have that could be applied to solving some of the great need in the world instead of just coping with it?"

Thus began a journey to document the church's potential for impacting local and global need in Jesus' name. From the beginning we have had great support from the people who help make the vision of empty tomb, inc., a reality, including Milo Kaufmann, Cliff Christians, and Ruppert Downing.

When we first went to Lilly Endowment Inc. with some of our earliest findings in 1987, it was Robert Wood Lynn, then senior vice president, who saw the potential in research based on the data we found. He has continued to be an encouragement to our work, including his helpful comments on this manuscript.

Taking information about Christians' giving potential out to the congregations, we soon learned the reasons that giving was going down did not have to do with a lack of information. Rather, we discovered some dynamics that seemed to be defining the mission of the church. We are grateful to the pastors and congregations who were willing to talk with us and to those brave souls who decided to try to change stewardship patterns in their churches. Their courage was a vital component of the efforts that resulted in this book. Further, several supporters of the local works of empty tomb, inc., were willing to contribute additional money to give us a working budget that would fund our congregational contacts. Their support in furthering those early efforts was critical in helping us take some of these ideas from theory and test them in reality.

In 1992 Lilly Endowment Inc. once again became involved in this project at a very important juncture. We had some preliminary findings about the factors that were affecting church giving patterns. As a result of another grant from the Endowment to empty tomb, inc., we were able to broaden our efforts. We are most grateful to the Endowment, particularly the Religion Division, including Craig Dykstra, vice president, Fred L. Hofheinz, program director—who has worked with us on this project—and James Hudnut-Beumler, then a program director and now dean at Columbia Theological Seminary in Georgia.

With this second grant, we were able to expand our contacts to the national level in a systematic way. We began contacting various national denominational offices to invite their participation on a National Advisory Committee. As one national official explained, he had recently had several such invitations, so we are especially grateful for the gracious response we received from that communion as well as many others. The hope and encouragement the National Advisory Committee provided to us were important ingredients in this project. In some cases, the representative changed over the course of the three years. We list those communions that participated in the project, as well as the members of the National Advisory Committee as of March 1995, with a second person listed for a communion indicating an individual who had previously served on the committee. Their willingness to meet twice, to provide introductions to regional offices, to distribute the survey, and to review the manuscript have all been important contributions to this work.

The Christian and Missionary Alliance: Rev. Robert L. Niklaus, Office of Communication and Funding; Mr. Gordon McAlister, Office of Communication and Funding

Christian Church (Disciples of Christ): Dr. Robert Welsh, President, Church Finance Council

Church of God (Anderson, Ind.): Dr. James E. Williams, Executive Director, World Service

Church of God (Cleveland, Tenn.): Mr. Al Taylor, Director of Stewardship

Church of the Brethren: Mr. Dale E. Minnich, Executive, General Services Commission; Mr. Donald R. Michaelsen, Director, Congregational Support

Church of the Nazarene: Dr. Robert Foster, Headquarters
  Financial Officer; Dr. D. Moody Gunter, Finance Division
  Director
The Episcopal Church: Rev. Hugh Magers, Director of Stew-
  ardship
The Evangelical Covenant Church: Dr. Timothy C. Ek, Vice
  President
Evangelical Lutheran Church in America: Rev. Mark Moller-
  Gunderson, Executive Director, Division for Congregational
  Ministries
The Lutheran Church-Missouri Synod: Rev. Ronald Nelson,
  Assistant Stewardship Counselor
Presbyterian Church (U.S.A.): Dr. David McCreath, Coordi-
  nator of Stewardship Education
Roman Catholic Church: Archbishop Thomas J. Murphy,
  Archbishop of Seattle
Southern Baptist Convention: Dr. James Austin, Vice Presi-
  dent, Stewardship Commission
United Church of Christ: Rev. M. Douglas Borko, Steward for
  Congregational Stewardship
The United Methodist Church: Rev. Herbert Mather, Gen-
  eral Board of Discipleship; Ms. Norma Wimberly, Director
  of Stewardship Education
Seminaries: Dr. David Heetland, Vice President for Develop-
  ment, Garrett-Evangelical Theological Seminary

We must also mention Baker Book House, especially Allan
Fisher and Paul Engle. We went to them with a description of our
plans just as the project began, and their response was a contract
to publish the book. We thank them for their faith in this project
and for the support and encouragement we received from Baker's
staff. We are also most appreciative of the thoughtful editing of
the manuscript by Mary L. Suggs and Wendy Peterson.
    As we pursued these activities on a national scale, we also con-
tinued to oversee the ongoing local outreach of empty tomb, inc.
It made for a busy schedule and would have been impossible
without the willingness of the staff to carry on so gallantly. We
are most grateful to Ann Shanholtzer, Joyce Blissit, Betty Har-
grave, Marcia Gruschow, Harriet Wash, Yolanda Nash, and

Miriam Chenault for ministering to others through their jobs even as they ministered to us, as did DiAnne Hatch in her responsibilities as treasurer. We also appreciate the supporters of empty tomb who have been willing to go with us on this adventure.

Two individuals joined the empty tomb staff as a result of the grant. H. W. "Bill" Tredway and Allison Christians devoted energy specifically to the tasks related to this project, and their help was greatly appreciated. In addition, Faye D. Wilson helped at a critical juncture, and we are grateful for her participation, as well as that of Rosie Shelby-Everett and Nichole Perkins.

We thank the church authorities who were willing to be interviewed for this book. Many had not met us before we requested an interview and yet they were willing to share their thoughts with us in a most gracious manner. In addition, Loren Mead, James Engel, and Dan Conway were willing to give us helpful advice on the manuscript as well.

Several pastors opened the doors of their congregations to us, which has been invaluable to our understanding of congregational dynamics. There are so many that the list cannot be inclusive, but we do thank Gene Peisker, Dave Crittenden, Charlie Julian, Roger Jenks, Mike and Cindy Jones, Steve Aram, Joe Warner, Jim Mahaffey, Scott Estler, Jack Talmadge, Bonnie Davies, Lou Zuck, and especially Jerry King and Jim Thompson for their willingness to meet with us regularly to discuss many of the ideas presented in the book. Many regional officials were willing to explore the vision and ideas we were discussing, in particular Ray Rhoads and Scott Woolridge, who each organized a valuable series of small group encounters.

Dr. Seymour Sudman, Walter Stellner Professor of Business Administration and Deputy Director, Survey Research Laboratory, University of Illinois at Champaign-Urbana, was most gracious in providing us with valuable advice in constructing the survey instrument.

Finally, we received valuable assistance with the statistical analysis of the survey. Professor Stephen Portnoy of the University of Illinois Statistics Department, a Fellow of the American Statistical Association, and a Fellow of the Institute of Mathematical Statistics, served as both a consultant and a friend through the development of the survey. He was ably assisted by

Dr. Kenneth Qing Zhou, then a graduate student at the University of Illinois. Additional assistance was provided by Dr. Douglas Simpson, director of the Illinois Statistics Office, and graduate student Olga Geling, statistical consultant of the Illinois Statistics Office.

As you can see, we received help from many quarters to bring this effort to completion. Of course we ultimately take full responsibility for the content on the following pages. We hope that this book will contribute to a constructive dialogue on the potential of the church in the United States. And even more, we hope it will bring glory to God, through whose grace and mercy we strive to serve.

Introduction

The goal of the study summarized in this book is to provide a description of what church members actually think about money, the role it plays in church dynamics, and the implications these attitudes have for the church as an institution. While these observations may provide insight into the present state of the church, they may also have implications for charting its future course.

A more detailed description of the project undertaken to interact with congregations is provided in the appendixes. In summary, a three-year study titled "Congregation-Level Field Observations and Denominational Giving Reports Stewardship Analysis Project" (referred to hereafter as "the Stewardship Project") was conducted. One element of the project was an ongoing series of reports, from aggregate congregational records provided by the denominational offices to the annual *Yearbook of American and Canadian Churches,* that analyzed church-member giving to denominations. Two findings established a concern about the financial health of churches in the United States. First, per member giving to congregations as a percentage of after-tax income was declining between 1968 and the 1990s in both mainline Protestant and evangelical churches alike. Although composite financial data is not published by the Roman Catholic Church, other reports and surveys suggested that a similar trend was also occurring among Catholics. Second, in the Protestant denominations studied, per member giving in constant dollars earmarked for the "broader mission of the church" beyond the congregation was actually lower in the 1990s than it had been in 1968, suggesting a change in congregational priorities.[1]

The denominational data analysis was accompanied by a series of encounters with congregational lay leadership, pastors, and denominational officials at both the regional and national levels.

At the congregational level, the Stewardship Project offered a plan to reorganize budgeting and mission priorities. The plan was a structured discipline, which a congregation could choose to adopt. It was designed to assist congregations in improving stewardship, stabilizing their operating budgets, and increasing their domestic and global mission outreach. For the purposes of the Stewardship Project, the plan served as a test instrument to catalyze dialogue with church leaders. The congregations contacted by the Stewardship Project staff had generally been recommended by their own denominational structure. The structured budget plan offered a congregation-wide education campaign to discuss individual giving patterns as well as to review the congregation's goals. The plan also offered a disciplined budgeting approach, designed to put the congregation's current financial activities on a more firm footing. This budget reorganization was coupled with a commitment on the part of the congregation to use income in excess of their defined needs to expand their international mission activity through their denominational channels and domestic outreach in the local community.

The interactions with pastors and congregational leaders through the consideration process of the structured budget plan provided the base of field observations. Through the first phase of offering the plan to congregations, there were more than sixty in-person interactions with congregational leadership from 1988 through 1992. Observation notes from these encounters and interviews were reviewed. Interactions were limited to congregations in the states of Illinois and Indiana. The focus of the contacts was also on the historically Christian church, representing a broad range of the theological spectrum of belief within that category.

Preliminary findings from this first phase suggested certain dynamics were being repeated in various congregational settings, quite apart from denominational affiliation or organizational structure of the individual congregation.

The project was expanded through a grant from the Lilly Endowment Inc. of Indianapolis in 1992. The in-person contacts were continued in this phase of what was now formally the Stewardship Project, bringing the total of face-to-face conversations with pastors or pastors and their leadership boards to 203. These in-person encounters were in addition to the 207 telephone conversations conducted with pastors, as well as the interactions with the 96 pastors who participated in small-group discussions led by Stewardship Project staff.

Further, 105 regional officials were contacted, including 66 who were willing to meet in person with the Stewardship Project staff.

A survey was also designed to obtain additional feedback on some of the preliminary field observations. The Stewardship Project survey was conducted as an elite sampling of selected regional officials and ministers rather than a random sample. Fourteen national Protestant officials who were members of the Stewardship Project National Advisory Committee distributed the survey in ten regions of the United States through their denominational structures. Response was high, with 209 of the 280 surveys distributed to pastors and regional officials through the national denominational offices being completed, a return rate of 75 percent. In addition to the regional officials and pastors, a select group of fourteen national denominational stewardship officials, eleven seminary development officers, and ten seminary faculty were also surveyed. Although there was a limited number of respondents for these three categories—the main focus of the Stewardship Project survey being the attitudes of pastors and regional officials—several of the resulting responses from this select sample, which are included on the following pages, suggest further exploration is warranted.

The Stewardship Project survey sampling was not designed to be representative of some large population. Rather, the goal of the Stewardship Project in general was heuristic, attempting to discover and identify what issues are affecting giving patterns and to establish a baseline for further exploration. The value of the total survey lies in the fact that it extends the base of field observations in this very understudied area of current attitudes toward stewardship at the congregational level. The elite sample survey also provided input beyond that resulting from the in-person congregational encounters, which were conducted in Illinois and Indiana.

The complete results of the survey are presented in appendix C. Several of the findings are also referred to on the following pages. It should be noted that the "agree" and "strongly agree" responses are combined when a description of the findings is referred to in the text as "agree." Similarly the "disagree" and "strongly disagree" responses are combined in the discussion that follows. Several general points are worthy of note.

Statistical analysis was done to highlight any differences between various groups. The appendix indicates the variation that appeared in answers between the pastors and regional officials, between the seminary development officers and seminary faculty, among the denominations, and among the regions. Interestingly there were virtually no differences among the answers by region.

Similarly very few responses produced a difference based on denomination. The hypothesis was that there would be little difference by denomination among the responses in general. Given the feedback received in encounters, it was difficult to predict responses to six observations asking whether the denominations' national stands in general, or specifically on abortion or homosexuality, would affect either church-member giving to the congregation or congregational giving to the denomination. In fact, the responses did not display great differences by denomination on these six observations. The hypothesis was that there would be agreement with each denomination's national stands in general, as well as with the handling of abortion and with the handling of homosexuality specifically, although a variation in the level of agreement was predicted. In fact the observation regarding church-member agreement with the national office's handling of the issue of homosexuality was the only response that produced a differentiation among evangelical and mainline Protestant communions among the 123 observations. The observation regarding national stands in general produced a somewhat similar response, although one mainline Protestant denomination registered responses similar to the evangelical denominations.

In the other observations, which produced some difference among the denominations, no clear patterns based on theological perspective or polity were immediately apparent.

What these results suggest is that, on the topic of financial stewardship, the church in the United States has a lot in common among its many members.

Finally, Stewardship Project staff interviewed national church leaders and other authorities on the topic of money and the church. Some of their comments are included on the following pages as well. If a quote is cited with no footnote, the comments presented are from these in-person conversations rather than from a published source. A list of these interviews is included preceding the notes.

The fact that money is an important dynamic in our society seems obvious to the most casual observer. The fact that money plays an important role in the patterns of church life may be less clear. The discussion on the following pages attempts to explore the implications of those dynamics for the state of the church in the United States.

1

The Challenge
before the Church

The Church's one foundation
Is Jesus Christ her Lord;
She is His new creation,
By water and the Word:
From heav'n He came and sought her
To be His holy bride;
With His own blood He bought her,
And for her life He died.

Samuel J. Stone, 1866
"The Church's One Foundation"

The church in the United States is facing a great challenge as the twentieth century draws to a close. Some people refer to the situation as a crisis. Others suggest the creaking ship of Zion is merely navigating the stormy seas of natural social change.

One particular area that shows signs of the stress the church is experiencing is in its relationship to money. Perhaps this idea is not surprising in a consumer society that measures its success not on the level of meeting basic needs but rather by its quantity of accumulation. Although the church specializes in the spiritual realm, its spiritual concerns remain in tension with the temporal. As any pastor knows, lucre may be filthy but it pays the bills.

Part of the challenge before the historically Christian church in the United States—that combination of believers with a historically acknowledged confession of the faith, including Roman Catholic; mainline Protestant, which would include such communions as Congregational (now United Church of Christ), Disciples, Episcopal, Lutheran, Methodist, and Presbyterian; Orthodox; Evangelical; Pentecostal/ Charismatic; Baptist; Anabaptist; and Fundamental communions—is that the role of religion in general is changing in contemporary society, particularly in how it affects the lives of individuals. Formerly certain values were generally accepted. The church was recognized as a positive social institution. The opinions of well-known clergy were quoted along with those of national political and business leaders. Currently no such general acceptance greets the church. Commentators talk about a "post-Christian" era in a pluralistic society. In the minds of many, religion has been reduced to a personal preference, not considered to be on a par with, say, politics, which people acknowledge as having a broad impact on society.

The church itself seems to be suffering from a lack of self-esteem, as noted in the absence of a clear voice or compelling vision with which its members identify en masse. It is not that there are none who are willing to speak. Such religious leaders as Pope John Paul II, Rev. Billy Graham, and Mother Teresa are routinely in the list of the most admired people.[1] But the audience seems to have shifted. In times past, America was a society that tolerated what amounted to a civil religion. This society welcomed perspectives from religious leaders such as these. Today religious leaders find pluralism the popular view. Their opinions can be seen as curiosities or, if stated with too much conviction, be greeted with hostility. There is evidence that the church is turning more inward, more local, with less of a national or international focus. As it does so, it may be less interested in defining its role in the larger society. Stephen Carter suggests in *The Culture of Disbelief* that the legal system has effectively defined religion as a hobby rather than a central operating standard from which the rest of a person's life flows.[2] It is unlikely such a development could occur without some level of cooperation from the church itself, most likely through passivity.

The Impact of the Church

Religion played an important role in the founding of the United States. The vitality that marked the emerging country was evident in the religious practices as well. A reforming spirit and high sense of personal responsibility involved the religious impulse to help define the quality of public as well as private life. Kenneth Scott Latourette, former Sterling Professor of Missions and Oriental History at Yale Divinity School, referred to the "distinctive" nature of the Christianity that developed in the United States in comparison to Europe. He noted that "Christianity had an important part in moulding the ideals of the country," influencing the practice of democracy and combining an emphasis on personal evangelism with the cultivation of a "Christian conscience and resolution" that impacted public policy.[3]

Church structures have been important bases for social services that defined community life. Even now many communities turn to local churches for a variety of reasons, from funeral dinners to service activities ranging from recycling efforts to preschools. The church as an institution has provided primary and high school education and has had successful programs even in cities where public education systems are under siege. Higher education in this country began in 1636 with Harvard University, which was established, the founders noted, to avoid leaving "an illiterate Ministry to the Churches, when our present Ministers shall lie in the Dust."[4] Churches and their related institutions have also been responsible for major social movements in the United States in the past 150 years, from abolition to the civil rights movement, from child labor laws to the support of labor unions and the women's movement, from prison reform to the care of those sick in mind or body.

Latourette suggests the significance of the church in the United States was the "vitality as seen in new movements, in the fashion in which it initiated and maintained missions in the United States and in much of the rest of the world, and in its effect upon the United States and mankind as a whole."[5]

While there is a strong reaction in some circles today to what has been termed the Judeo-Christian ethic in American society, it cannot be denied that this perspective had an impact on the United States. A. James Reichley, in reflecting on the role of religion in the public life of the United States, concluded: "From the standpoint of the public good, the most important service churches offer to secular life in a free society is to nurture moral values that help humanize capitalism and give direction to democracy. . . . From the beginning of American history, religion and the practice of democracy have been closely intertwined."[6]

Stephen Carter also suggests that religion has a critical role to play in a society such as the United States.

> [O]ne therefore sees two chief functions that religions can serve in a democracy. First, they can serve as the sources of moral understanding without which any majoritarian system can deteriorate into simple tyranny, and, second, they can mediate between the citizen and the apparatus of government, providing an independent moral voice.[7]

The types of values taught in the church have been a factor in this functioning democracy. Richard John Neuhaus, in a reflection on John Paul II's encyclical *Veritatis Splendor,* presents the position that freedom cannot exist in a vacuum of truth. He notes that in a society that acknowledges no absolute truths, individual power serves as the only basis for negotiating life: "If what you call your rights is no more than an assertion of your interests, I can counter your interests with my interests. If I can muster greater force, you lose. So much for your vaunted rights. Again, in the absence of truth, power is the only game in town."[8]

One contribution that religion, including the historically Christian church, has made in the United States has been to offer a reference standard by which all people can be judged equally. Thus the struggles facing the church in the United States have broader implications than for Christians alone.

Changes in the church immediately impact the more than 60 percent of the U.S. population that claims membership in a historically Christian congregation. Beyond that group, the general social structure may underestimate the effect changes in the church will have on its own organization. In recent times American society has not been as quick to identify the positive legacy that the historically Christian church has contributed to the cultural formation of the United States. Yet a brief review of the social heritage provided by that religious perspective makes it difficult to deny its impact. One can trace basic values such as courtesy—rooted in respect for one's neighbor as a creature of God—

and "justice for all" to concepts presented in the Bible and preached from the pulpits, no matter how imperfectly implemented at times. As sociologist Robert Wuthnow has written,

> Another way in which religion has often been relevant to our work and our money is by supplying norms of daily conduct. These norms range from simple rules of etiquette, to ethical standards concerned with honesty and equitable dealing in the marketplace, to contractual obligations focusing on property, labor, marriage or parental responsibilities. Religious teachings undergird these norms—associating them with sacred writings, reinforcing them in sermons, and perhaps including them in sacred rituals.[9]

The contributions of the church do not erase the mistakes that have been made in the name of religion. People can point to instances where the institutional church served as an impediment to change, rather than as a catalyst, when history has concluded that change was needed. One can find numerous individuals whose lives were marred on a personal level by individual representatives of the faith enforcing abstract traditions without regard to the specific situation. The church is an institution that focuses on the divine yet is populated with human beings who have not escaped the frailties associated with that condition.

A strong emphasis in this increasingly secular society has been placed on the past negative actions of the church, including repression and misuse of power. Individuals recount personal experiences that conjure up feelings of guilt, anger, and confusion that are produced as evidence of the lack of credibility on the part of the church in general. In addition, events from another century, such as church support for slavery before the Civil War, are used as evidence against the contemporary church.

However, even as the benefits that the church has produced in American society do not excuse the mistakes it has made, in a similar fashion the mistakes made in its name do not cancel the positive influence the church at its best has exerted on American culture. To deny either the church's contributions or its limitations is to develop an incomplete picture of a vital social organization.

A Changing Society

And if the church is going to weather its current transformation in a constructive manner, an objective review of both its
strengths and weaknesses is vital. Society in general ought to be
interested in the course the church is now navigating. Of a more
critical nature, the church itself must resist the secular view that
it is a negative or outdated institution and evaluate its present
state as objectively as possible. A more mature attitude needs to
develop—beyond resistance to the church just because it is the
church, to a fuller, more objective appreciation of the contributions religion in general, and the historically Christian church in
particular, has made.

The present struggle facing the church is made the more difficult because of the broad social changes taking place. Christendom has been the mode for centuries in many of the western
hemisphere cultures, equating religion with the empire's goals.[10]
But that position has been unraveling for the past two centuries.
Governments in Europe that had been closely identified with
Christendom experienced upheaval in the late eighteenth and
throughout the nineteenth and twentieth centuries. Whereas
there used to be consequences for not having even a superficial
belief system, unbelief has become permissible. Between 1957
and 1994, the percentage of the U.S. population that sees religion as having an increased influence on American life dropped
from 69 percent to 28 percent, and those that see it losing influence grew from 14 percent to 67 percent.[11] The church in the
United States is under stress to define itself as an entity in an
increasingly secular culture. As Loren Mead describes it, "Our
task is no less than the reinvention of the church."[12] The challenge is relatively new because not having a religious belief
became a respectable option only in the last two hundred years
or so. Cultures tended to have a religious patina, which is now
no longer required.

Changes within the Church

The threat to the church's role is not only external, however.
What direct assaults on the church through new political and eco-

nomic doctrines could not accomplish may have been achieved by the success the church has experienced. Perhaps a threat, greater than persecution, now facing the church is a condition described by Jesus in Revelation 3:14–18. The real danger to the church may be that it has become lukewarm from within.

Giving patterns in the United States indicate the church is losing market share among its own members. Even many denominations that are growing in membership are receiving a smaller portion of their members' incomes. For the first time in history, a few societies, including the United States, find most of their members with money beyond what is needed for their personal basic needs. "Discretionary income" is a reality for most of the population. And advertising agencies very intentionally have targeted that income, turning "wants into needs."

This increase in affluence becomes significant to the degree that the Bible suggests that money has a spiritual component. For example, in Matthew 6:24 Jesus tells his followers, "You cannot serve both God and Money." French philosopher Jacques Ellul points out that in this text, Jesus personifies mammon "as a sort of god," a force that is competing with God for our souls. Ellul suggests that Jesus' choice of words "reveals something exceptional about money, for Jesus did not usually use deifications and personifications. What Jesus is revealing is that money is a power."[13]

In Matthew 6:21 Jesus also describes another aspect of money, that it is an important indicator of our heart's condition: "For where your treasure is, there your heart will be also." Money is a measure of devotion, the way we spend it indicating something about us—sort of like a spiritual thermometer—according to Jesus. In a consumer society, such as the United States, it may be the most intentional measurement available.

Yet, for reasons that will be explored on the following pages, the spiritual import of money has largely been ignored in the churches. In the new situation of widespread resources, when most people coming to church have income above basic needs, the contemporary church has, for the most part, been silent on the implications of these changed circumstances. Without a clear agenda for this new affluence being voiced from the church, members have absorbed the world's agenda of consuming and accumulating and then brought that agenda back into the void that was present in their congregations.

Today many communions within the United States face a serious situation. Giving as a percentage of income has been declining. Congregations are keeping more of their income. As a result, regional and national denominational offices are no longer trimming the fat from budgets, as one national leader termed it, but have had to start carving into muscle.

Why are these negative giving patterns showing up in the church? "We don't know. That's the real answer," commented William McKinney, dean of Hartford Seminary. "The study of church finances is where church growth research was thirty years ago. It's the most significant issue for the next quarter century."

So the field of financial dynamics in the church is a relatively new one. In a review of the factors that are influencing what church members contribute, the congregation might be an excellent place to begin.

2

Congregations

No matter what we say we do,
This is what we think of You.

Offertory Prayer

Church members have changed from stewards into consumers. A middle-aged church woman reached that conclusion
after six months of trying to raise the mission vision of her congregation. The idea had seemed so clear to her. Once the congregation met its own financial goals, it would raise its sights and
expand mission outreach. But after six months of talking to various people in the church about this idea, enthusiasm was still
limited. Her frustration was evident as she tried to put her experience into words. People are not returning a portion of their
incomes to God, she concluded. Rather, they're paying for services rendered by the church.

The firsthand experience of one pastor supports her observation. He was visiting a couple who had recently worshiped at his
church. He asked them if they would be interested in exploring
membership. Their response took him by surprise. "Oh no," they
explained. "We plan to attend your church for communion, but
we like the music program across town and we send the kids to
a third church because of its dynamic youth activities."

A different pastor likened the attitude of present-day potential members who are visiting churches to the way someone shops
at a grocery store. "If they're challenged or [their] needs are not
met, they'll go where they aren't challenged or [their] needs are
met. They'll go to another church that will welcome them." "Therapeutic" is the term Robert Wuthnow, author and sociologist at
Princeton University, used in an interview to describe the church's

31

value to many members. Church members want "love, to be comforted, patted on the back. Churches are therapeutic and if they're not, 'I can go somewhere else, thank you.'"

The fact that other churches will welcome unhappy parishioners defines the agenda for some congregations. Describing services provided by her congregation, a laywoman noted that if the congregation did not provide these services, people would just go someplace else. A second person agreed: "The music program attracts a lot of people." "The nurseries," joined a third. "A Catholic father said those nurseries are a godsend. He told me, 'I got to sit in church and put my arm around my wife.' The Catholic church in town doesn't have a nursery," she went on.

The Distraction of Affluence

While our frustrated laywoman at the beginning of the chapter seemed shocked at her own conclusion, church leaders apparently recognize this mind-set as a growing trend. At one meeting, a layman suggested people he called "church shoppers" have actually done "the cost-benefit analysis; they've gone through the cafeteria of Christianity." He suggested churches are diversifying to attract different parts of the market since what these people are looking for is "the church that provides the most." He described these types of members as the ones who come in "to see what you're going to do for them today."

Affluence has been a distraction from true religion in the past as well, of course. As early as 1885, Josiah Strong was giving form to the debate of wants versus needs. "Surely, it is right to supply our necessities. But what are necessities? Advancing civilization multiplies them. Friction matches were a luxury once, a necessity now. And may we allow ourselves nothing for the comforts and luxuries of life? Where shall we draw the line between justifiable and unjustifiable expenditure?"[1]

By the late 1920s the situation had progressed even further. H. Richard Niebuhr looked at American religion with a critical eye. Writing in 1929 he observed,

> It remained for America to carry the accommodation of the faith to bourgeois psychology to its extremes. . . . In its final phase the

development of this religious movement exhibits the complete enervation of the once virile faith through the influence of that part of the middle class which had grown soft in the luxury the earlier heroic discipline made possible by its vigorous and manly asceticism. . . . This is not the religion of that middle class which struggled with kings and popes in the defense of its economic and religious liberties but the religion of a bourgeoisie whose conflicts are over and which has passed into the quiet waters of assured income and established social standing.[2]

As insightful as history has proved H. Richard Niebuhr to be, he was wrong when he suggested that the move toward a bourgeois religion was in its final stage. Wade Clark Roof and William McKinney suggest in *American Mainline Religion* that "greater personal fulfillment and quest for the ideal self" were becoming even more important in recent decades than when Niebuhr wrote. "While the quest itself is as old as the American experience, social scientists and cultural historians are generally agreed that in the sixties and seventies this quest was pursued with particular intensity. It was pursued on a far wider scale than ever before, touching almost every sector of society."[3]

Social scientists suggest that major shifts took place that affected not only the wealthy or even an expanding middle class but virtually the entire society. Roof and McKinney point to "rising levels of education, opportunities for upward mobility, greater regional migration and geographic movement, and a high rate of divorce and family instability" as factors that have allowed the focus to shift from a more broadly based community perspective toward "more radically individualistic concerns."[4] One national leader noted that the GI Bill of Rights made higher education available to a much larger portion of the population, impacting first-generation immigrants in particular. Sociologist Richard Inglehart also observed the increase in mass media and international travel, technological innovation, changes in the job market, and the increased number of women in the workforce as major changes after World War II.[5]

Intertwined with these changes was an extended period of economic growth after World War II. Before that time, the best estimates suggest that, even with an expanding middle class, most Americans were struggling to make ends meet. Although the "poverty line" had not been developed then, extending the formula backward suggested that a majority of Americans may have fallen below it.[6] The industrial expansion that characterized the 1950s and 1960s produced in some societies around the globe widespread affluence never seen before. This was also true in the United States.

Thus many in earlier generations did not bring a consumer mind-set to their churches because their life's agenda was to survive and/or cope. However, in the past several decades, incomes have increased dramatically for the majority of U.S. citizens. Consider that in 1921 the average American's annual income was $555 after taxes, and by the early 1990s, it was over $17,000 per person, per year. Those figures do not, however, take into account what inflation did to the dollar during that time. When inflation is factored out, by converting the income levels to the value they would have had in the same year, the comparison is still striking. In constant 1987 dollars, the average American earned $4,188 after taxes in 1921, compared to well over $14,000 in the early 1990s, an *increase* of about 250 percent, apart from taxes or inflation. Incomes have increased about 90 percent just since the late 1950s.

These kinds of economic changes occurred not just in the United States but in many Western countries. What did these changes mean in actual buying power for citizens of these nations? A renowned French bread maker put the situation in terms of his own product: "[T]he French worker, who spent 50 percent to 70 percent of his pay on bread in the sixteenth and seventeenth centuries, and 25 percent in the nineteenth, spends only about 1 percent on it today."[7]

Needs Now Include Wants

As James Hudnut-Beumler, dean of Columbia Theological Seminary in Atlanta, Georgia, suggested, if these economic changes had occurred overnight, church members would have been happy to give a greater percentage of their increasing incomes to the church. However, the broad increase in real per capita income, resulting from the relatively steady economic growth since World War II, came slowly over many years, and so the increase was gradually absorbed in a variety of ways—without the awareness a sudden change would have brought.

Now instead of a few individuals being able to meet their basic needs with money left over, the majority of Americans could include more "wants" in their lifestyles. The new medium of television provided a compelling means for advertising products to absorb these expanding resources. The emphasis changed from saving money for a fearful future to consuming the good life in the present. An approach formerly reserved for the few came within the reach of the many.

These changes were being felt by the early 1970s. A comprehensive study was conducted by the Stewardship Office of the National Council of the Churches of Christ in the U.S.A. With the cooperation of fifteen denominations, in-depth interviews were conducted with 3,450 laypeople and pastors throughout the United States and Canada. In the report of the study, published in 1972, the authors concluded, "As people see it, the main thing blocking church support simply is a surpassing urge for more affluent living. . . . Rival attractions seem to be gaining more of the religious dollar."[8]

These changes in the culture continued to grow in influence during the 1970s and up through the present. For example, sociologists David Roozen and C. Kirk Hadaway suggest that some of the basic concepts of American culture were redefined during this period. They propose that new moral norms and a change in social values were two important factors affecting American society. "The third dimension concerns a change in the meaning of 'freedom.' Once tied primarily to more utilitarian concerns of economic security and upward mobility, the baby boom generation gave it an expressive twist, redefining freedom as choice and self-fulfillment."[9] Penny Long Marler and David Roozen write that "our analyses show that the increasing dominance of religious consumerism, as a form of cultural individualism, is the most important change in the American religious marketplace of the late 1980s."[10] And Roof and McKinney propose that the changes impacted members' approaches to their churches in a powerful way: "Less and less bound to an inherited faith, an individual is in a position of 'shopping around' in a consumer mar-

ket of religious alternatives and can 'pick and choose' among
aspects of belief and tradition."[11]

Giving Patterns

The attitude observed in the 1970s that continued into the
1990s has impacted church-member giving patterns as well. In
the late 1950s average per member giving for one set of Protestant communions was above 3 percent of U.S. per capita income.
By the early 1990s it was about 2.5 percent, a drop of 20 percent. Further, the amount of money being spent beyond the congregation's own needs, for such activities as denominational support, international and domestic mission activities, and seminary
support, was declining. Among one group of denominations that
included 100,000 of the estimated 350,000 religious congregations in the United States, giving to benevolences (those activities beyond the local congregation's operation) was lower on a
per member basis not only as a percentage of income in the early
1990s than in the late 1960s, but per member giving to benevolences was also less in constant dollars.[12]

These giving patterns may be due to the fact that this slow
increase in income was accompanied by a steady education, courtesy of television and other advertising media, about the value of
consuming all the new products being developed to help attract
these increasingly available resources. A massive change occurred
in four decades. Americans switched from an agenda of survival
to a pattern of widespread consumption unrivaled in even the
richest societies in history. And, on reflection, it appears the
church did not escape the effects of this transition. The current
consumer mind-set among church members may well be a function of this changing social dynamic. The new economic condition had become established, with a generation having reached
adulthood in the midst of this wealth.

In early 1992 we asked a group of thirty-four pastors what were
the three most common responses given by church members
when challenged to improve their stewardship. More than three-
quarters of the pastors said that people maintained they could
not afford to give more. Yet, just two months before, we had asked
a group of ninety-two laypeople and pastors combined what was

the main reason they thought people didn't like to think about stewardship. In a response that harks back to the study from the early 1970s, more than 40 percent said "selfishness" quite plainly or they referred to consumerism, advertising, and/or a commitment to materialism. Only 8 percent suggested the economy had anything to do with attitudes toward stewardship.

Similarly, a group of 261 Catholic leaders, both priests and laity, were attending a stewardship workshop.[13] In an informal poll, they were given a questionnaire asking them to evaluate certain factors that might be contributing to the decline in the percent of income donated to the church. Only 24 percent, including 29 percent of the lay parish council and stewardship committee members, agreed with the idea that church members could not afford to give as much as they used to because of economic factors. In contrast, 89 percent of those present agreed with the statement, "People are too preoccupied with the demands of personal consumption," with 87 percent of the lay leaders affirming this was a problem. At some level church members are aware of the struggle going on for their pocketbooks.

Megachurches

Some people pointed to the existence of megachurches as the proof of the stewards-into-consumers idea. The term "megachurch" generally refers to congregations that provide a worship opportunity to thousands of members each weekend in one physical plant. Of course, many Roman Catholic parishes have been doing just that for decades. It is not uncommon for thousands of communicants to attend one of several masses offered each weekend by a single congregation. One person who studies the topic defines megachurches as those congregations that attract at least 2,000 attenders weekly.[14] By this definition, perhaps 19 percent of all Catholic parishes—or more than 3,500 congregations— would be megachurches.[15] However, those congregations that have been termed megachurches are set apart in that they also often focus on entertaining worship services and emphasize additional activities that may include bookstores, restaurants, and multiple basketball courts for church members who want a guaranteed spiritual atmosphere for their activities. Consultant

Thomas P. Sweetser, S.J., suggested one difference between large Roman Catholic parishes and Protestant megachurches is the motivation of the participants. Megachurch members "are choosing to go to church. Many Catholics go to the local church because they feel it is a sin not to attend church." Thus the energy of a Protestant megachurch may not be duplicated in a Catholic parish.

One former priest, now a Protestant minister, summarized the difference in two words: coat hangers. In Catholic churches, he noted, people aren't expected to hang up their coats to stay a while. Rather, one group leaves after mass to make room for the next set of communicants. In contrast, his experience in Protestant churches was that the first thing to expect on entering the front door is a coat rack. The expectation is that people would attend worship and stay for other activities as well.

Whatever the reason, Roman Catholic congregations with members numbering in the thousands are not referred to in the "megachurch" terms that describe some Protestant congregations.

Pastors of smaller, more traditional congregations may feel a level of competition from the presence of these Protestant megachurches in their neighborhoods. Although the stated focus of a congregation such as Second Baptist Church in Houston, Texas, which has 12,000 members, is to provide an atmosphere "that a totally godless, secular person can come to . . . and not feel threatened," the fear is that *current* church members may shift their congregational loyalties to this type of exciting worship center as well.[16]

However, the relatively few megachurches, mostly situated in large metropolitan areas, do not account for the broad perception—and perhaps the related reality—that there has been a change in what church members expect from their churches in general. Pastors in smaller areas, serving tradition-bound congregations, find an attitude change has occurred there as well. To some degree, the megachurches may not be producing a new phenomenon in the church—of church members turning from more traditional disciplines to more of a comfort orientation— as much as recognizing and responding to a change in expectations from church members overall.

Among those polled in the Stewardship Project survey, more than 90 percent of the pastors and regional officials agreed with the observation, "Church members today demand a higher level of comfort and services from their congregations than did previous generations," as shown in figure 1.

Figure 1: Survey Observation #29

Church members today demand a higher level of comfort and services from their congregations than did previous generations.

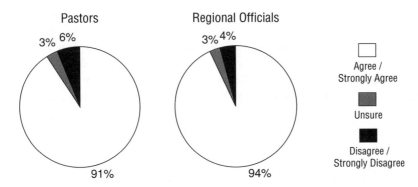

See appendix C for a complete list of the 123 survey observations and responses.
Details in the figures may not compute to 100% due to rounding.

Pastors are feeling pressured to offer more specialized services as they compete to attract new (or transferred) members. As one pastor described his embracing a people-pleasing approach to ministry, "We don't feel we have any choice." A different pastor described the situation saying, "Jesus played with the children and taught the adults. We teach the children and let the adults play."

Another pastor described his attempt to found a new congregation based on a strong commitment to traditional church values. By all appearances, he was quite successful. A new building had been constructed with no debt, the expectation was clear that the tithe, or 10 percent of income, was the accepted level of stewardship commitment, and members did not just maintain their names on the rolls but were also actively involved on a weekly basis. However, congregational membership had plateaued at just

over one hundred. "I'm not going to have any excuses or feel sorry
for myself and my congregation. Workshops are saying, 'Give yup-
pies what they want.' Another congregation across town does and
has a thousand members." They reach people he wouldn't, he
notes; he's counted the cost of another way.

Mobility

The present idea of "church shopping" is often associated with
Protestant churches. However, a consumer mentality may have
begun to appear in the Roman Catholic Church too. With the
availability of transportation and the existence of suburbs
removed from work locations, the idea of traveling beyond the
local community for worship services is not unusual. Now
parishes develop "personalities" and may attract communicants
based on what approach the priest and parish pastoral council
pursue. One Catholic leader suggested many people will shop for
a priest who will say what they want to hear.

One disaffected Catholic was confused at the changes that
had taken place in the church since she was active in her youth.
The woman decided to return to the church because she wanted
her children to have the same religious background she had.
There were two parishes within driving distance, and she found
herself presented with choices. One parish emphasized sacrifice
and social justice. The other seemed to attract upwardly mobile
younger people, with a clear pressure on those attending to dress
well. Having selected the religious tradition for her children, she
still had to choose between perspectives within that tradition.

Of course when people lived in local neighborhoods and walked
to their parish church as a family, these types of concerns would
have not been a problem. You heard what the local priest or pastor had to say. Mobility is one factor that has produced more
options for church members and increased the challenge before
the church. "The private automobile has allowed most people to
pursue a variety of interests and meet a variety of needs with various groups of people, mainly of their own choosing. . . . Most
people today live simultaneously within several social networks
rather than within a simple neighborhood or community."[17] One
result of this greater freedom to choose social networks has been

pressure on churches to attract new members as well as maintain current members who now have more choices. Counting membership has become an important measure of how a congregation is doing.

Felt Needs

Church growth advocates have been strong proponents of the idea that congregations should be adding new members. C. Peter Wagner's name is closely identified with this school of thought. He writes, "Church health and church growth are presumed to be closely associated. If a church is fully healthy, it will grow. Conversely, if a church is not growing in membership, there is probably something wrong with its health."[18] There are two other basic tenets of the movement as well. First, it was proposed that people like to worship, and join churches, with people like themselves. Second, the idea was popularized that every human being has "felt needs," which the church, to be successful, should address.

Interestingly, the idea of "felt needs" apparently shifted from its earliest definition. Authors James Engel, who has been a marketing professional as well as a university professor, and Wilbert Norton wrote one of the early important works on church growth principles. In *What's Gone Wrong with the Harvest?* they referred to the concept of "felt needs" as describing the deep-seated spiritual hunger in every heart that causes humans to yearn for God. In describing the parable of the sower, they explored Jesus' description of the different soils on which the seeds land. "Much of the reason for the nonreceptivity of some soil is that the 'worries and riches and pleasures of this life' choke out the seed of God's word (Luke 8:14). Put differently, Christ is saying that filters are closed and there is no real response to anything said because of the absence of *felt need*" [italics theirs]. Describing the kinds of needs that might be felt in a congregation, Engel and Norton go on to write, "We are referring to the spiritually hungry who are not having their hunger satisfied."[19] Engel and Norton further describe what they mean by the term "felt needs" later in the book.

> The facts of man's created nature indicate that initial and continued growth and fruitfulness involves a progression of decisions

initiated by problem-recognition and followed by a struggle to find the correct way. This is a natural but tortuous process in which the believer is conformed by the Holy Spirit to the image of Christ. The Spirit initiates felt need by showing the gap that exists between "what is and what ought to be."[20]

By the mid-1980s, if not before, the idea of felt needs had been transformed into a more general marketing technique to help churches draw in new members, not always carrying the same emphasis on the spiritual dimension evident in the early writings. No longer focused on the spiritual hunger of potential or current church members, "felt needs" began to be identified as programs or services that congregations could offer to bring in the crowds.

Church attendance in the United States remains higher than in many other Western cultures. A residual historical commitment to the Christian church may encourage Americans to seek the answers to the deeper spiritual hunger present in human beings in these church structures. However, the answers many churches are offering these seekers involve an emphasis on services that address immediate comfort needs. Without guidance and leadership, people may not be aware that there are additional levels to the faith beyond making themselves happy.

By the early 1990s some pastors were beginning to report unexpected by-products from an approach that placed such a heavy emphasis on letting the needs of potential new members set the agenda for the congregation. Apparently a conscious choice was made to downplay some of the harder sayings of the gospel. "The church growth movement and those in leadership positions in evangelism who have adopted this paradigm speak of the 'postponement of ethical awareness' in presenting the gospel to potential converts."[21] This approach was not without long-term consequences.

One pastor described the situation he experienced. A young businessman had joined the church some months before. The pastor visited with him and invited him to a Bible study that would explore what increased discipleship would mean. The businessman seemed somewhat offended. "If you have a bill to pay, let me know and I'll do my part," he responded. "Or if you need a pie for the annual bake sale, I'll ask my wife to make one. But nobody mentioned sacrifice when I joined this church."

How the change in attitude may have affected church giving patterns was evident in one woman's interaction with her grown children. She asked them about their pledge to their church. The children seemed surprised, responding, "We pay when we go." Another pastor observed, "When you bring people in through church growth, they don't necessarily give much. You can tell if they leave and the level of giving in the church doesn't change."

There were those who raised questions about the emphasis on growth that spawned a new movement. William McKinney, dean of Hartford Seminary, wrote in 1979 that a

> questionable assumption is seen in a tendency to view numerical increases in church membership as a sole indicator of local church and denominational health. The question "Is church growth good?" presses one into the realm of theological values. It needs to be addressed from the perspectives of both theology and the sociology of organizations.[22]

One church official developed this idea as he reflected on his own communion's efforts to balance a desire to be more inclusive with a faithfulness to important tenets of the faith. "The Anabaptist tradition has historically emphasized the cost of discipleship and the sacrifice we make (including most of our first leaders who were martyred) to be faithful. In our communion we have attempted to become more inviting (evangelistic) of those who were not born with [denomination] families. We have stopped talking about the cost of discipleship. One example is our disagreement over when to tell newcomers that we are a historic peace church, and that, traditionally, military service is considered unacceptable for our members. Refusing to serve in military service has almost always meant that young men have been ostracized and abused by patriots in their communities. This has been one of the most common sacrifices in our church in the last forty years."

Second Thoughts

While many continue to affirm the value of bringing new believers to the faith, the emphasis on meeting the needs of those new

converts as a way to promote the primary goal of growth is being
reevaluated. Experts are beginning to observe that unintended
side effects of the felt-needs approach may now be limiting the
church's effectiveness. James Engel was one of the early proponents of the idea that the church should be more responsive to
the needs of its potential "market" of the unchurched. He now
has second thoughts. He continues to propose that evangelism
should start where an unbeliever finds himself or herself. However, he also notices a "lack of holiness and power" in the church.
The church, he suggested, is not providing an authentic alternative to society. He affirmed those megachurches that have
developed small group structures fostering discipleship. But while
he believes there's nothing wrong with a "user-friendly" church,
"many haven't moved beyond it. Christianity has become like a
consumer good." Going on, Jim Engel reflected, "I'll be honest
about church growth. I don't believe the basic premise is true: A
healthy church will grow numerically. That's not in church history or the Word of God. While this may happen, the most significant measure of growth must come in kingdom values. A
healthy church will be profoundly countercultural . . . always a
minority group but an extremely compelling group."

Nordan Murphy, retired director of the National Council of
Churches Stewardship Commission, suggested that part of the
problem pastors are facing with their congregations is that "no
one has informed them what it means to be a giving person." And
when people do not understand the dynamics of giving, they continue to protect their resources. Since no one discusses the matter, Murphy is not surprised people view the church as "'It's a
free ride. It doesn't cost you anything.' That's the invitation you
get to the altar. Then you join and they need money and you're
hit with a sledgehammer that you should share the wealth."

Another denominational official suggested there may be long-
term serious consequences of this approach. "We've attracted
people with methods that weren't entirely 'honest' which now
will have the possible effect of further alienating a generation. . . .
'Entertaining' persons into the church is a far cry from challenging
persons to faithful discipleship."

Another church leader, when presented with the finding that
church growth may be having a negative influence on the church,

responded with some surprise. "This is startling, because efforts to bring persons into any system will need to start with a focus on their needs. But if we remain there, the church will be turned inward and away from the gospel."

A nationally recognized megachurch, Willow Creek Church in South Barrington, Illinois, has actively tried to counter the trend for church members to remain at a superficial level. Each weekend, more than fifteen thousand people attend services at a campus run so efficiently that regular attenders and their children wear a photo ID to insure the child is released from Sunday school to the right person. Services emphasize music and drama, and people fill front-row seats, in contrast to the usual four empty pews between the pulpit and the parishioners. While great attention is given to making "seekers" feel comfortable on the weekends, an equal amount of attention is given to guiding them into one of the midweek small groups, where intentional spiritual growth is the goal. The objective is to attract people initially and then challenge them to grow in the more traditional definition of the belief system after that.

While the theory may be successfully applied by a gifted person such as Willow Creek founding pastor Bill Hybels, some of the details appear to have been lost in its translation to the general populace. A workshop sponsored by a religious institution was designed to help pastors market their churches. The leader asked pastors to list possible felt needs in their congregations. After a list of more than fifty topics was on the board—ranging from new widowers to divorced single mothers to empty nest syndrome—the pastors were encouraged to decide on one or two groups on which to focus. No discussion was given in the multi-day seminar as to how to lead those individuals into a deeper relationship with God through Christ. The idea was to get the people into church, and if your congregation came to be known as the "great-for-empty-nesters" congregation in the area, people would come.

Perhaps it was assumed the pastors would automatically know how to lead people into deeper faith, such discipling having been the business of the church for two thousand years. However, recent changes have left the church in the United States, and thus the pastors who serve on the front line, in some confusion about its purpose. The implications of deepening discipleship, as a result, have become increasingly unclear.

Special Interest Groups

The idea that pastors would know how to lead their people assumes the church has an agreed-on sense of direction. That traditional supposition may no longer apply to contemporary congregations. One observation made during Stewardship Project encounters was that congregations often resembled coalitions of special interest groups rather than cohesive communities of faith gathered for a common purpose.

Consider the experience congregations had in trying to implement a structured budget approach designed to increase missions giving. In early interactions with congregations, we made presentations to the leadership board of each congregation considering whether to adopt the disciplined strategy being offered. The congregation could proceed with the budget reorganization approach and educational activities if the leadership board approved involvement. Ten congregations became involved in this way. We then stayed in contact with the congregations through telephone and mail.

In-person interviews were conducted with these ten congregations after six months to see how they had fared with the various activities associated with the strategy to reorganize the budget and to increase missions giving. In the interviews, it became clear that none of the ten leadership boards had yet figured out how to inform the members that the congregation was participating in this effort. "People don't read the newsletters or come to meetings," was a common explanation. And the leadership board reported they had no alternative effective ways to communicate about the ongoing life of the church with the congregation as a whole.

Thus a new stipulation was added in the next phase of congregational encounters. The leadership board must first agree to the congregation's participation and then they would need to conduct a congregation-wide education campaign, putting the final decision before the church as a whole about whether to proceed with the outlined activities. The response of a leadership board chair was enlightening. On hearing the requirement for a congregation-wide education campaign, the response was, "Do you mean we would have to talk to those people? They just go to church here!"

Structured Budgeting Approach

One of the hardest ideas to understand for congregations participating in this structured strategy was that the congregation would be agreeing on a common agenda as part of this new approach. The budget that the congregation developed using the budget design would be inclusive of all activities in the church, with few exceptions. The congregation would agree to limit their spending on their own operations by the total of this inclusive budget; all income received by the church in excess of this budget total would be directed toward increased mission outreach in a prearranged manner. Since the congregation's budget was both inclusive of all activities in the church and capped, the budget would be defined not by what individuals were willing to fund but by an agreed-on direction as defined by the line items. Many leadership boards apparently pass budgets on paper, with little expectation of fully funding them. One laywoman suggested that most budgets are designed as a goal for members to shoot for. In many cases, the congregation's leaders expected to spend whatever money came into the church in ways that people who gave it wanted it to be spent. The business of the church was often decided as a result of who had donated how much for what purpose. A discussion about Christmas trees demonstrated how deeply ingrained this perspective may be.

One congregation that had decided to adopt the proposed budget structure to increase missions giving spent a large part of one leadership board meeting having the idea of a line-item budget explained to them by one of their own leadership board members. The congregation, having developed their budget, had agreed to fund the operating budget line items, limiting the amount of the congregation's expenditures in the coming year to those line-item allocations in the budget. Any new activities of the congregation would have to be attributed to a particular line item in the newly designed budget. Or, since the budgeting approach provided for the congregation's budget to be changed from year to year, the proposed expense could be delayed a year and attributed to an updated line item. The strategy's formula to update the budget annually took into account changes in membership and attendance in their congregation, as well as inflation and real change in the economy. Thus any proposed new activities could be included the next year when the congregation's budget would probably be larger than that of the current year. When the operating budget line items were funded, the congregation would then allocate any money above these operating line items to expand specific missions activities. This approach was in keeping with the commitment they had initially made in approving the strategic budgeting plan, to adopt a discipline that would help expand the missions outreach of the church. The leadership board listened carefully, asked questions, and then reaffirmed its commitment to the idea of bringing greater discipline to its spending habits in order to move toward the goal of increasing its missions outreach.

Immediately after this detailed discussion, a leadership board member asked to introduce an item of new business. The Christmas trees looked shoddy, he noted, and he suggested that a special collection be taken to purchase new ones for several thousand dollars. Another layperson, who had helped make the presentation on the newly adopted line-item budget, asked what line item such a collection would be attributed to, knowing that a spur-of-the-moment purchase of artificial Christmas trees would "bust" the new budgeting approach that had just been reaffirmed. The layman who made the proposal looked confused. It didn't need to go into a line item, he offered; they would have a special collection and only people who wanted to give to the Christmas tree fund would do so. The layman proposing the idea, businessman though he was, could not understand the church having defined goals and limiting appeals to the congregation in order to achieve them.

The Christmas tree proposal seems an excellent illustration of the way many congregations conduct their business. Much of the activity apparently does not happen because thought has been given to the wisest or most effective way to further the kingdom of God but rather because a particular idea happens to catch the fancy of one or more members. The idea of actually organizing budget expectations, and educating other congregation members about those expectations, is not the mode of operation of many congregations. One pastor responding to the Stewardship Project survey wrote, "Too many 'personal' agenda issues reduce the energy needed to promote the broader mission of the church."

Experiences such as these started us formulating the theory that the church in many places was not, in reality, a community of faith gathered around a common vision or purpose provided by the New Testament or even by denominational priorities. Perhaps it never had been and that idea is a rather attractive fiction. In any case, a number of congregations might better be described as coalitions of special interest groups that have gathered out of mutual convenience around a single physical plant.

One of the first congregations that decided to adopt the structured budgeting approach to increase their mission outreach illustrated this idea. It was a congregation of fewer than one hundred members—yet there were eight separate treasurers. When they adopted the disciplined budgeting strategy, it was made clear to the leadership council that the new system would provide for coordination among all the funds of the congregation toward a common goal. Several of the treasurers, however, actively resisted the effort to organize the church's finances. The congregation's involvement eventually foundered.

The presence of a variety of different financial centers in a congregation suggested the presence of special interest groups in the church. However, many times it was difficult to identify any centrally agreed-on common purpose beyond the basic worship experience. For example, Stewardship Project staff found that the basic idea of improving stewardship in order to give more money to missions was by no means an obvious priority for many of the listening leadership boards. Proposing what was thought to be a commonly accepted purpose of the church did not receive immediate support from lay leaders. Further, it was noted that a minister might express a high level of enthusiasm about the broad vision of the church's potential for impacting domestic and global needs presented in the Stewardship Project pastors' workshop with comments like, "This would be great for my church!" The minister would often fill out a form, asking to be contacted to schedule a similar presentation to the individual congregation's

leadership board. However, when Stewardship Project staff called
two weeks later to schedule the presentation, there would be a
noticeable coolness on the part of the pastor. It was that transition—from enthusiasm about the idea in general, to the reluctance to implement it in the congregation in specific—that raised
questions about the type of resistance pastors met when trying
to challenge members to expand their giving in order to act on a
vision for outreach.

The implications of this finding may affect various areas of the
church's life. In a review of factors affecting congregations, sociologist Dean R. Hoge concluded, "Almost as important to church
growth as overall membership's satisfaction is the quality of relationships between members and the consensus about the church's
purpose and mission."[23] The fact that pastors found it difficult
to involve their leaders in a discussion about adopting a possible
new vision that combined financial stewardship with increased
missions may provide important insight into the present state of
the church. As Loren Mead has observed, "Where a sense of mission has been clear and compelling, the church has been sacrificial and heroic in its support of that mission."[24] When a mission vision cannot even be discussed, then the church may not
fulfill its potential for good.

Congregations may actually be organized in such a way that
makes it difficult for them to develop a broad agreement among
members. In organizational structure, the Protestant congregations the Stewardship Project staff encountered generally had
some combination of missions committees, stewardship committees, and finance committees, in addition to an oversight leadership board. In some cases, trustees also handled property concerns and investments. Each of these committees had some
responsibility for money in the congregation. The finance committee was most often concerned about developing the budget
and paying the bills. The missions committee was entrusted with
the task of keeping the larger idea of missions in front of the
church, to inspire people and keep the congregation faithful to
its larger purpose. Any new ideas, however, would be evaluated
by the finance committee, generally in the context of present
financial realities. Since the stewardship committee (often responsible for the annual financial campaign in the congregation

at large) routinely expressed reluctance about asking people to increase their giving, the current giving patterns were seen as the deciding factor in setting mission goals for the congregation.

One pastor shared that in a congregation he served, the roles of the finance committee and stewardship committee were combined. "The finance committee members never got out of their chairs to do anything. And they forbade having a financial campaign organized by anyone else. Their stated opinion was, 'The church should be satisfied with what it gets.'"

In this context, an individual who cared about a particular issue could impact the agenda of the church. Since money was a key factor in deciding whether a particular project would be undertaken, if an individual was willing to fund some activity, there were few arguments to bring to bear about whether the congregation really needed or wanted that particular possession or outreach. As one pastor said, "If they pay for it, we often accept it." Thus the agenda of the churches with which the Stewardship Project staff came into contact often reflected the priorities of individuals in the congregation, and the issues they were willing to put their money behind, rather than a publicly recognized bond that served as an organizing point for the localized group of denominational believers.

Buildings as Incentives

Some congregations find it most convenient to grow broadly and fast by emphasizing the kinds of "felt needs" that most people can agree on. The megachurch with its multifaceted offerings is an attractive goal for many churches, large and small.

In fact constructing new church buildings is actively promoted by denominations and fund-raising consultants as a creative way to build enthusiasm and revitalize congregations. One fund-raising consultant pointed out that the theory used to be that a congregation ought to have a building project every few years. He advised that the idea is now for a church to always be in some stage of a building project to keep people involved in the life of the church.

There is little question that revamping the organ or installing air conditioning or building a family life center (after the sanctu-

ary, fellowship hall, and education/office wing are in place) is certainly more attractive than asking people to lay down their lives for
their neighbors in need who live in the inner city or overseas.
People's responses to buildings and missions differ in other ways
as well. For example, one objection congregation leaders raised
about the Stewardship Project structured budget approach was
that they would have to plan their missions activity. They preferred
to keep their options open and did not like losing control by com-
mitting to a formula that would prescribe how much of the money
beyond their own needs would be going overseas and how much
locally. Yet people overcome such reservations for a building project. The architect and the contractor demand very clear plans that
limit the congregation's options for years to come. It is interesting
that people will accept the disciplined organization required to construct a new sanctuary but are not willing to submit to the same
discipline to carry out the mission of the church. One pastor commented wistfully, "If you can ever catch the spirit from when people
are building a building and get that for missions—some people
have suggested we build a building, just for the unity of it. . . . In
this church, there's no unity, no commonness. My guess is there
are a lot of congregations that are similar. It is not a church with
an identity as a family committed to certain ideals and goals. I've
tried to lift up the ideals. It just doesn't seem to light a fire."

Downward Trends of Giving

The fruits of this pattern of coalitions as opposed to community
are relevant to the present discussion. Trends of giving as a percentage of income in both evangelical and mainline Protestant
churches are in a downward direction, although evangelicals continue to give at a higher rate than mainline denominations. Of the
money coming into both types of communions, more is spent for
the congregation's own operations, putting pressure on denominational structures and often requiring cutbacks in international
and, in some cases, domestic missions outreach. Membership decline in mainline Protestant churches continues. And although
many evangelical churches have continued to add members since
the late 1960s, should that rate of membership growth stall, indications are that evangelicals would be facing denominational fund-

ing crises similar to those that have been highly publicized among mainline denominations. Church members who view the congregation as a provider of services may join for a particular reason and not expect to support the overall structure.

There seems to be little doubt that churches today do not have a strong vision around which to rally their financial giving. In the Stewardship Project survey, 81 percent of the pastors and 94 percent of the regional officials agreed, "Congregations do not have a clear overarching vision with which to challenge their members to improve their stewardship," as shown in figure 2.

In a presentation to one denomination's national staff, the Stewardship Project staff suggested the idea that the church had changed from a community of faith to a coalition of special interest groups. A seminary professor suggested that this was not a new development. "Read Corinthians," he went on. "The church has always been a coalition of special interest groups." However, he did allow, a change has taken place in the church in the United States. The role of church leaders was always to call these various groups into a focus on the overarching mission of the church. This professor agreed with our contention that no overarching vision now challenges the church in the United States. Without such a broad vision, he concluded, what had always been a strug-

Figure 2: Survey Observation #109

Congregations do not have a clear overarching vision with which to challenge their members to improve their stewardship.

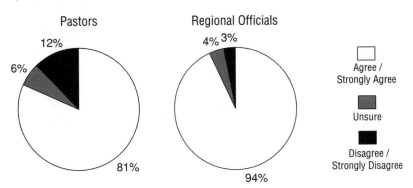

Details in the figures may not compute to 100% due to rounding.

gle for the church had now become endemic in the latter twentieth century.

Of course, as Joseph M. Champlin of Camillus, New York, a priest who has popularized the Sacrificial Giving program among Catholic churches nationally, noted, the fact that the church has a varied makeup has been one of the peculiarly lovely aspects of those who claim faith in Jesus Christ. "The church has always been messy. It is not elitist. The church has always been a messy church with people at various levels of commitment."

An oft-quoted statement of John Wesley supports the fact that the church has long struggled with the challenge of keeping a uniting vision before the faithful:

> It nearly concerns us to understand how the case stands with us at present. I fear, wherever riches have increased, (exceeding few are the exceptions) the essence of religion, the mind that was in Christ, has decreased in the same proportion. Therefore do I not see how it is possible, in the nature of things, for any revival of true religion to continue long. For religion must necessarily produce both industry and frugality; and these cannot but produce riches. But as riches increase, so will pride, anger, and love of the world in all its branches.[25]

Writing in 1929 H. Richard Niebuhr also found the church lacking in a unifying theme that would call people to be their best. He observed,

> The ethical effectiveness of an individual depends on the integration of his character, on the synthesis of his values and desires into a system dominated by his highest good; the ethical effectiveness of a group is no less dependent on its control by a morale in which all subordinate purposes are organized around a leading ideal. And the churches are ineffective because they lack such a common morale.[26]

These observations would suggest churches have been struggling to call people to a common purpose over many centuries.

New dynamics, however, may be in evidence in the latter twentieth century. Craig Dykstra, formerly of Princeton Theological Seminary and currently vice president for religion at Lilly Endowment Inc., suggested the culture has impacted belief systems in powerful ways. "Increasingly people seem to feel that religion is something they make up rather than something given to them by parents or church. The theme song is personal choice. One can choose which religion to participate in, or even whether to be religious or not, with few social constraints. Today there are fewer social sanctions for no religion. Religious authority has been displaced from the community to the individual."

Wade Clark Roof and William McKinney also find this attitude more common. They write,

> Today choice means more than simply having an option among religious alternatives; it involves religion as an option itself and opportunity to draw selectively off a variety of traditions in the pursuit of the self. . . . Put simply, religious pluralism in the modern context is further individualized: each person has a different "version" of religious reality.[27]

Among the survey respondents, almost two-thirds of the ministers agreed with the statement, "Pastors feel pressure to be balancers among the various special interest groups in their congregations rather than strong leaders," with regional officials affirming the idea even more strongly. In pastor workshops, this idea always received strong positive feedback. When the workshop leader provided a description of this finding, the pastors seated in the audience often appeared to be doing the "wave," with heads bobbing in assent.

The lack of a compelling vision to hold the congregation together appears to have had a negative impact on the pastor's role.

3

Pastors

The world behind me, the cross before me;
The world behind me, the cross before me;
The world behind me, the cross before me,
No turning back, no turning back.

"I Have Decided to Follow Jesus"

The change of church members from stewards into consumers has impacted the role of the minister. Pastors have always functioned as the linchpin in a congregation. As interviews continued with pastors and leadership boards throughout the Stewardship Project, the image developed of the congregation as the pastor's "shop." A Catholic leader suggested that the "priest is pope in his own parish," and we saw a lot of evidence that suggested Protestant congregations experience oneness with their Catholic counterparts on this point. As one Presbyterian pastor pointed out, "A pastor cannot do anything single-handedly in a congregation, but a pastor can stop anything single-handedly in a congregation."

To the degree that congregations lack a common vision and, perhaps by default, are becoming more and more coalitions of special interest groups, the question may be asked: What is expected of a pastor in these changing circumstances?

A Unifying Force

The pastor, of course, has always been responsible to be a unifying force in the congregation. In America's past, a generally accepted purpose of the church was affirmed by the larger soci-

56

ety. The pastor provided leadership to guide the congregation along this path while keeping various interest groups, if not happy, at least at peace. This common vision was supported by a general cultural awareness of religion as a broadly defining force for society. "The major faiths might differ in their particulars, but they shared a common morality and civil religious heritage. The consensus lasted into the 1960s, when it began to erode as the nation entered a new period of moral and ideological pluralism."[1] As the common culture eroded, the pastor was left solely with the role of balancer.

No Longer on a Pedestal

Pastors, as the church leaders on the front lines, so to speak, found themselves in an increasingly challenging situation. Relativity of belief that emphasizes privatization of the faith and a noninterference with, rather than responsibility for, the neighbor has confused the issue of where the pastor is to lead the congregation. A Gallup poll, for example, found in 1991 that more than two-thirds of the U.S. population agreed that "there are few moral absolutes." When asked, "What is the most believable authority in matters of truth?" 43 percent cited personal experience, with Scripture second at 31 percent. Parents at 16 percent, science at 7 percent, and media at 6 percent all ranked higher than religious leaders at 3 percent.[2] David Wheeler, a state association officer of the Southern Baptist Convention, felt that attitude change. Whereas it used to be that pastors were on a pedestal, "Now, if you tell people, 'I'm a minister,' it's not as positive. In some cases, it's even a negative."

Loren Mead has written, "No one needs to underline the pressure pastors are under today. As paradigms of ministry change, clergy are also buffeted by financial pressures, insecurity regarding their professional futures, and a diminished public image of their role in society."[3]

Ronald Voss, an Evangelical Lutheran Church in America minister who is active in the leadership of synod stewardship, wondered if the church has retreated from society, living on the leftovers of a previous strong generation.

Others notice a qualitative difference in the life of the church as well. Fred Hofheinz, program director for religion at Lilly Endowment Inc., observed that "we seem to have lost the ability to hand on the transcendent beliefs to the young, lost the way to educate the young with the gospel. Each generation has become less religious."

Meanwhile church members have had increasingly more ways in which to spend their money outside of the church. With these new spending patterns may have come an even more basic attitude change. People formerly viewed themselves as producers, but have switched their self-concept to that of consumers. "The culture leads us to look at money in terms of self-interest," according to Robert Wuthnow. "This plays into consumerism. Look out for myself, the right to enjoy, play a little—it's okay to buy adult toys."

These attitude changes—from an outward responsibility to an inward preoccupation—have been accompanied by the decline of church as a special entity. In *The Culture of Disbelief,* Yale law professor and author Stephen Carter documents that religion no longer claims a unique place in the social structure. Robert Welsh, president of the Church Finance Council of the Christian Church (Disciples of Christ), considered the financial implications of that change. When people give to the church, he said, they think they're "supporting an important institution, but that institution is no more holy than the zoo or symphony. I don't want to be too negative, but I don't think people see church giving as different." Giving patterns tend to indicate a higher portion of income being donated in evangelical Protestant churches than in mainline Protestant congregations, so his observation may not be universally applicable. But research indicates that giving as a percentage of income is declining not only among these two groups but among Catholics as well. So this view may be increasingly more descriptive of the church in the United States as a whole.

Jesus' statement that God, and therefore the church, is, in fact, in competition with mammon for the hearts and minds of church members became a more practical observation as credit card interest payments increased significantly faster than church contributions in the last three decades. So when people began promoting the ideas of "church growth" and "felt needs," many pastors welcomed the strategy as an effective response to the challenge before them.

Keeping Everyone Happy

With increased emphasis on individualism and the related privatization of faith, and not even a consensus on a general civil religion, the pastor is hard put to call the members to some higher agenda. The various power centers in the congregation may not acknowledge a common vision to which they need to submit their individual agendas. The pastor is not recognized as having the moral authority to call people to make changes in their lifestyles or their giving patterns because of an impelling need and agreed-on mission. In these circumstances, what is left to the pastor is to keep everybody happy.

The minister, with decreasing social and institutional affirmation in an increasingly hostile culture, has had to rely more and more on personality. And meeting the individual's identified needs can be a relatively sure way to be liked. Joseph Champlin understood this tension well. "I'm a pastor. I want people to like me. If I mention money, they're going to get angry and leave. They'll go someplace else. The leader needs courage. It's the 'greening of America': anti-institutionalism, anti-authority. I'm a white male. Everybody is angry at me. Why would I want to talk about money?" Champlin understood the pressures, but he wasn't content with that conclusion. "You have to bite the bullet and preach on it. It's like preaching on racism in the South a few years ago."

The Illinois/Wisconsin District of the Christian Church (Disciples of Christ) prepared a report on clergy compensation. The report refers to a resource document, *Who Ministers to Ministers? A Study of Support Systems for Clergy and Spouses,* by Barbara G. Gilbert, published by The Alban Institute in 1987. The report summarizes the resource as follows:

> The author examines the stresses of parish ministers, clergy spouses, and clergy marriages. In ministry "one's economic well-being and vocational position are derived from an occupational system which is almost totally dependent on the approval and good will of the congregation." This creates job insecurity, deters risk-taking, and creates tension.[4]

Paradigmatic shifts that have affected domestic and foreign missions, economic changes that have altered the character of the volunteer pool, and other major trends that have impacted the agenda of the church are discussed in more detail in chapter 13. One idea deserving some reflection in the current context of the pastor's role in the congregation and society, however, is how the pastor deals with the idea of hell and its place in modern theology.

Preaching Hellfire and Brimstone

One pastor suggested that the common mission of the church was irreparably weakened when theologians dismantled the idea of hell. For purposes of the present discussion, it is important to separate the theological debate regarding the merits of threatening people into faith to avoid the prospect of the fiery furnace, or calling them to action because of the impending doom others faced, from the sociological function that eternal damnation previously played in the church. When considering changes in the role of pastor from leader to balancer, the issue of whether a main emphasis on hellfire and brimstone was the most constructive approach to encouraging faith for the individual or action on behalf of others is being set aside. Rather, an important idea to be considered is whether, through a positive means or not, the pastor wielded more authority when hell was a more popular concept. Pastors could urge congregation members to feel responsible for those in other lands by reminding church members that the consequences for those unreached would be not only misery in this life but eternal pain as well. If people would not act out of a compelling love for the neighbor, they could perhaps be motivated by horrible images of the future. Compelling parishioners to a course of action might even have been an expected part of the ministerial job description, rather like the annual stewardship sermon.

Surprisingly the society at large still endorses the existence of hell but now the idea seems divorced from consequences. A Gallup survey, for example, found as many as 73 percent of the U.S. population still believe there is a hell, but more than three-quarters believe they won't go there.[5] It may be that hell has not disappeared as much as it is considered irrelevant. To a great degree, this relativism in society has influenced the church. One evangelical layman complained in an interview about the lack of agreement among members of his own denomination regarding the need to reach people for Christ in light of eternal consequences. A leading laywoman in a mainline congregation questioned the pastor's initiative in promoting an increased global mission emphasis, inquiring whether U.S. Christians ought to be going over and intruding in other people's cultures.

The theological debate of whether orthodox Christianity should include or exclude an acknowledgment of the existence of hell and its implications will continue. But apart from that, it must be noted that the de-emphasis of hell, with no equally compelling alternative, has not only undermined the traditional evangelistic focus of the church but has also removed part of the clergy's job description—to call people to action to avoid consequences—and the implied authority that went with it.

Elimination of Sin

At the same time, relativity and the privatization that reduced every choice to personal opinion eliminated the concept of "sin" as a theme to bring church members to points of decision. Psychiatrist Karl Menninger reflected, "The present world miasma and depression are partly the result of our self-induced conviction that since sin ceased to be, only the neurotics need to be treated and the criminals need to be punished. The rest may stand around and read the newspapers. Or look at television." He goes on to describe the impotence such a mental approach produces among people who feel powerless in the face of "vague, amorphous evil." When the idea of sin has been eliminated, Menninger suggests, there is no action that can be taken in the face of evil. One cannot hope to affect or change behavior. The only alternative is a sense of "despairing helplessness." He therefore does not see a reintroduction of the concept of sin—and its related behaviors of repentance and forgiveness—as a negative development. "If the concept of personal responsibility and answerability for ourselves and for others were to return to common acceptance, hope would return to the world with it!"[6]

"Basic decency was what I was taught and what you were taught," mused one national leader. But things have changed. This leader related the story of a father, who had provided his children with a strong religious education, being told by his daughter, "a very decent kid," that "she was sexually active with her boyfriend. 'Other than you and the church, no one thinks this is wrong.'" The values of the church are not being translated into the way church members conduct their lives. These values being promoted by many church leaders are provided more as guidelines rather than rules for living.

Reflecting on the same topic, Fred Hofheinz commented, "We need a healthy emphasis on both love and sin in the church. But they stopped preaching sin and started preaching love. Both are important. I'm not sure where it happened—somewhere between Eisenhower and Clinton."

Dean Hoge also feels that we turned a corner, perhaps in the 1950s. Religious relativism, he stated, is not new. "For centuries there was relativism. However, there does seem to be more of it in the United States in the last few decades," as documented in his study of Presbyterian baby boomers. Increased education seems to have been a contributing factor. However, to the degree that all religions are seen as spiritual resources, that perception "cuts to the heart of Christianity," he said. "That is part of the problem. Does that mean Christianity is going down the tubes? Not necessarily. It is a genuine issue, however."

Menninger, writing in the early 1970s, asserted that pastors have a special responsibility to help people understand the impact of sin in their lives.

> The clergyman cannot minimize sin and maintain his proper role in our culture. If he, or we ourselves, 'say we have no sin, we deceive ourselves, and the truth is not in us' (1 John 1:8). We need him as our umpire to direct us, to accuse us, to reproach us, to exhort us, to intercede for us, to shrive us. Failure to do so is *his* sin.[7]

But clergy face a difficult situation. Individualism has increased to such a degree that there are few consensus points to which church members are willing to submit their independent agendas. The tension surrounding the pastor's role only increases in such a setting. Even if the practicing minister has not read the sociological studies, he or she knows at a deep level that "member dissatisfaction or conflict within the congregation are clearly sources of decline."[8]

Kindly Shepherd

With no clear reason to urge members to sacrifice their increasingly available physical comforts, the pastor was left with little other than trying for popularity. The role of leader becomes moot if a minister is not guiding church members on a journey that involves either making a major impact in the present world and/or securing personal safety in the next. Between leading and balancing, balancing appears to be more dominant in the expectations of both pastors and church members today.

Perhaps that is why the church growth concept has been embraced so broadly. No longer issuing a call to potential members to become disciples of a faith centered on an outward-focused, agreed-on mission requiring self-sacrifice and discipline on the part of the believer, the pastor could fill the role of kindly shepherd, helping the current or potential member identify a "felt need." As has been noted, this term originally was offered as referring to a deep-seated spiritual hunger that inevitably draws a human being back to the true Source of life. By the time the idea of "felt need" had been popularized, the pastor was urged to help church members identify how the church could provide services to make their life a little more comfortable. Robert Welsh observed, "If someone needs four-year-old day care, we have it. That's easier than meeting the real, deeper need. . . . What people really need is to experience God's grace. And we don't know how to deliver that. We know four-year-old day care."

On the surface, the idea of bringing people into the church by providing services that they want may not be a counterproductive approach. If people cannot come to church regularly because the church does not have an efficient nursery, then providing a nursery is indeed a positive thing to do. The same is true for vans for the elderly, singles groups for the unmarried, and any number of creative, constructive activities being offered for church members.

But somewhere along the line, it appears a change occurred. These services are no longer support structures to provide an environment in which church members can deepen their relationship to God. Rather, these services become an end in themselves, the purpose of the church's existence. The church now seems to view itself as competing on equal footing with the secular world. In the absence of a compelling vision with which to challenge church members to live up to their full spiritual potential as described in the Bible, the church finds itself bringing in people who are asking what the church can do for them.

Apparently it is assumed that the removal of a particular problem in a church member's life, such as the need for trustworthy day care, will then free the member to recognize his or her need for God at a deeper level. Such a connection is not always made. Unanticipated and unrecognized is the effect of the massive education through advertising that has gone on, changing the public into sophisticated consumers who view the meeting of their needs as a right. Without accurately counting the cost and preserving its own unique character, the church seems to have sought to win converts not to a higher calling but to a more comfortable present. The spreading theological relativism of the 1960s and 1970s also influenced church-member expectations. Now some potential members joined the church out of personal conviction—while others were interested in a preferred place on the day care waiting list. Further, given the changes in societal expectations, this thinking was not a cynical avoidance of the traditional personal experience but rather was seen as fulfilling the church's stated expectation of new participants.

Dispensable and Replaceable

In the many encounters and interviews conducted through the Stewardship Project, it became clear that pastors have entered the ministry for a variety of reasons. Pastors, asked why they chose the ministry, would often describe a spiritual experience or a specific call or share that they wanted to emulate a respected minister. In practice, their initial noble impulse has been overwhelmed by their responsibility to run the congregational organization smoothly.

With the shift in congregational priorities going from a nationwide spiritual purpose manifest through the local congregation to private individual comfort, the pastor who does not produce the results desired by the congregation faces certain consequences. One regional denominational leader pointed to a consumer attitude that even extended to church members' attitudes toward the minister. Pastors are generally willing to extend themselves on behalf of their congregations and, more and more, people are willing to take and not give back. It is almost as though people look to the pastor to produce all the glorious results they expect from the church, with decreasing effort on their own part. "We're not growing or whatever. We'll get someone who will take us where we want to go" is the way one official described church members' attitudes toward their clergy. The official noted that his denomination was experiencing a record number of forced terminations, which he attributed to the consumer attitude that has come to view even the pastor as dispensable and replaceable.

Other types of pressures brought to bear on pastors whose priorities differ from the status quo are varied. When one pastor indicated he had stopped challenging his church, we asked him why. He was "tired of fighting," was the response. What "weapons" would a congregation use? Withholding a salary raise or expulsion from the congregation, he replied.

We personally knew two former pastors who no longer were in the ministry because of stands they had taken during the civil rights movement. In their cases, a great cause required personal sacrifice. Are such weapons still being used when no broadly recognized prophetic stand is clearly at issue?

One pastor described his increasing commitment to prayer. He told his congregation he would not be available on two mornings a week, because at that time he would be concentrating on prayer. Several members of the congregation were upset about the fact that the pastor would be unavailable. Did they actually tell the pastor not to pray? Not in so many words; rather, the pastor felt the disapproval from increasing comments about unfulfilled expectations, such as, "When we visited Grandmother at the nursing home yesterday, she told us you had not been to see her for two weeks." The pastor felt the comment was a clear criticism of the time priorities he had set.

A key pressure technique also seems to be passive resistance. One pastor suggested that it can be difficult to find people willing to serve on key committees at nomination time if people are unhappy with the pastor's performance. Also, there may be a marked lack of participation in scheduled meetings. Rumors are also a handy approach: One pastor reported that he was informed that an eighty-three-year-old matriarch of the church was telling select friends the pastor "was trying to force her out of the church," apparently because he did not give her the deciding vote on several issues.

The methods, however, may not always be passive.

One pastor reported having eggs thrown on his car. In another case, a congregation did not fix a leaky furnace in the parsonage, apparently so displeased with the pastor that asphyxiation did not seem like a bad alternative to the pastor's continued ministry with them.

Paying the Pastor

A minister was told if he pushed for additional staff, his salary would not be raised. He replied, "Let it be known to you, money will not control me." Even though he had led the stewardship efforts that had doubled the congregation's income, with an increase of more than $100,000 in one year, he still had to, in his words, "fight for every raise." And when he left that congregation, the church cut the minister's salary again as they started over with a new pastor.

Pastors indicated in interviews that salary raises are generally an awkward point between the pastor and the congregation. As one pastor observed, "Every time I've received a raise, I've had to fight for it." Another pastor described a learning experience he had in a church. His congregation decided, when setting the budget, that there was not enough money to provide the pastor with a cost of living raise. "Nine times out of ten," this minister explained, "the pastor will have no reaction—'That's what you've decided, what can I do?'" But this time he decided to say something, so he asked the board whether they were trying to tell him to leave. Oh no, was their reply, it's just that people won't give. He responded, "Why don't you ask them?" The pastor went on,

"They were surprised because people didn't want to go through the hassle of training a new minister and paying for a move. They told me, 'Nobody ever told us before they'd leave if we didn't raise the salary.' I asked them, 'Didn't people leave?' They responded, 'Sure, but they never told us why.' They admitted they guessed the salary might have something to do with it, but they also wondered if the pastors just didn't like pastoring their small church."

Even in the best of circumstances, the budget discussion surrounding the raise seems based on whether the congregation is pleased or not with the pastor's performance in the past year. There may be denominational guidelines to set the level of the pastor's salary, yet congregations can find ways to resist their implementation, often over stated concerns about being able to fund the entire budget. A variety of pastors interviewed had not had raises the previous year. In two cases, pastors were asked to take salary cuts in order to keep the congregation going. Another technique was to ask a pastor to find another church when his salary reached a certain level on the denominational scale. Then the church would hire a less-experienced candidate whose salary would be at a lower prescribed level.

In the Stewardship Project congregational budgeting structure, a formula updates the budget from one year to the next, based on changes in membership and attendance and changes in the U.S. economy. The pastor of one of the original participating congregations called the year after his congregation had ended their involvement, asking for this budget update formula even though his church was no longer involved. He commented that the formula had provided the first salary discussion in his congregation that centered on some reasoned standard for considering his salary, other than on whether he had made the congregation happy or not.

Clearly, the level of salary paid the pastor is one aspect of the relationship between the minister and the congregation that affects the level of demand the minister places on the congregation.

At least one pastor, recognizing the trend, decided to adapt. A denominational office received a proposal from a pastor who wanted to set up a network of no more than 150 households who would contract with him in advance for services. Weekly worship would not be held, but a monthly or annual fee would guarantee such attention as pastoral care during major life crises, religious instruction if desired, and other pastoral services. The pastor would be available on a per fee basis for those who had not signed up in the network, with a hospital visit costing $25 while waiting with a family during surgery would be $100. Funerals and weddings would be provided on a fee basis as well, although those who had signed up as part of the network had these services included. The denomination declined to endorse the pastor's approach.

A Voluntary Organization

The pressures on the minister are aggravated by the fact that the church is a voluntary organization. Especially since there are fewer social consequences for not being a church member, people are in church because they want to be—even if it is just out of habit, as one lay leader explained to his pastor who had inquired why he still came when others had stopped.

This voluntary nature is part of the church's glory in North America. Douglas John Hall points out that unlike European churches, the North American church has had to maintain a high level of energy to convince people to participate and to help fund its ministries of necessity. "Still, by comparison with European forms of Christian establishment, the churches in North America have been independent, separate, and voluntary organizations whose members have themselves been directly responsible for their maintenance."[9]

At the same time, as in any voluntary organization, people can leave if they are not happy. Or in some cases, the worse scenario is they might stay.

In making a presentation to one congregation, Stewardship Project staff met with the leadership board. The pastor later explained that he was in a power struggle with some of the people who had been present at the meeting that night. They had apparently attended to see what kind of proposal was being brought before the congregation. These people had stopped attending for a while and withheld their financial support from the congregation. When the pastor continued to serve in the church and services were still held, the dissidents became concerned they would lose their influence if they were totally uninvolved. So they had started coming back to meetings, to monitor events, and to resist the pastor as they could. Because some of these people still held leadership positions, the pastor was stymied from moving ahead in the congregation, and a tenuous status quo seemed the only option.

One large congregation opened an escrow account and deposited money in it, to be kept there until the time when they could force their current pastor out of the pulpit.

"Small wonder," wrote Menninger, "that some preachers have become conformist, banal and dull. When some statement or action by the minister offends a group of the sinners, they cry out that morality is none of the church's business. They subtract funds from its support as punishment."[10]

A fear of church splits is often based in experience. Ten congregations accepted the structured budget approach designed to increase missions giving in the first phase of the project. Four of these congregations had had membership splits some time before they became involved with the project. Two church divisions had involved disagreements with denominational policy, and significant portions of the membership had left the main body to form a different congregation. In the other two cases, individual personality differences had led to the founding of new congregations.

The fear of a split can impact a church in strong ways. One pastor was intrigued with the possibilities of the Stewardship Project structured budget approach. Project staff made a presentation to the leadership board with more than fifteen people present, and the general response was positive. In the following month the pastor talked to the individuals on the board and, in wise fashion, counted the votes needed to pass a resolution for adoption of the structure. He went into the next meeting confident he had the necessary majority. At that meeting a young businessman was present who had not heard the initial presentation the previous month. This businessman had joined the church less than two years before and was asked to serve on the leadership board because of his secular professional qualifications and enthusiasm. He was seen as bringing fresh energy to a long-established church. The meeting began with some preliminary discussion among those who had been in the church for many years. After listening to the conversation, the businessman announced,

"To discuss the issues involved in this project will split the church." Discussion ended, and the resolution to participate did not even come up for a vote. Neither the pastor's leadership nor the long-term members' interest in the project were an adequate counterweight to even a relatively uninformed threat of a potential church division.

Another factor that affects the pastor's ability to function on a local level is that the congregation, as a voluntary organization, may be the last area of control as many of its members feel overwhelmed by the changes in society. Surveys point to a public that is anxious about crime and the economy. Therefore churches, different people suggested in interviews, are accessible institutions that provide a sense of security to their members. For example, a layman attending one workshop offered that church members were giving less to their churches because they were angry about the high amount of taxes they had to pay to the government. They couldn't protest their taxes but they could control their church budget. Another pastor commented that the church might be the last social institution in small towns, where stores have closed and schools consolidated.

M. Douglas Borko, of the United Church of Christ Stewardship Council, said people feel like "the whole society is falling apart. The church is the last place, the last bastion where people have a say." He observed that people who feel disenfranchised in a dramatically changing society can still exert power and feel they are important in the church.

Robert Wood Lynn, current scholar in residence at the Bangor Theological Seminary, referred to "the enormous disabling anxiety people have about their own religious institutions." An example might be the particularly poignant concern among churches in rural communities observed by Herbert Mather of The United Methodist Church General Board of Discipleship. When a community loses its school through consolidation, it can put additional stress on the church. "Some of the smaller churches feel they are holding on to the last institution in a community. They feel they're holding on to a major institution and 'then they want us to send money away to the denomination.'"

The preservation instinct can be strong. One pastor shared how a woman told him she made a point to sit on committees solely to make sure that nothing would change. Thus the church is subject to a variety of emotional dynamics not directly connected to its own stated purposes.

It seems clear that the minister, as leader of a voluntary organization that sits in a pluralistic culture increasingly committed to a private religion, subject to the relative merits of what everyone else thinks, is pressured to keep things primarily on an even keel.

And while the pastor figures out how to hold all these trends together at the local level, he or she also is responsible for the connection to the denomination.

4

Pastors and Denominations

We give Thee but Thine own,
Whate'er the gift may be:
All that we have is Thine alone,
A trust, O Lord, from Thee.

William W. How, 1858
"We Give Thee But Thine Own"

One of the strongest responses from pastors on the Stewardship Project survey was agreement with the fact that "denominational officials expect a pastor to be able to secure support for denominational programs from the congregation as a whole."

To the degree congregations have come to resemble coalitions of special interest groups with no central binding purpose, this expectation presents an increasing problem for the minister. The pastor may have a difficult time securing broad congregation-wide support for any proposal—including denominational support—from a congregation joined together by little more than a Sunday morning worship contact point. This stress is particularly evident in the changing relationship between congregations and their denominations.

Changing Relationship to Denominations

The denominations that exist in the United States today generally fit into one of two categories. The denominational structure either continues a structure brought to the United States by immigrants from another country, or the denomination was formed to help congregations that originated among settlers in the United States to coordinate their cooperative efforts, often focused on frontier or global missions. Denominational purposes, therefore, were rooted in an outward focus of the congregation.

72

To the degree that congregations in the United States are turning inward to promote a comfort agenda, this trend would have implications for relationships with the denomination. For example, there is evidence that global missions coordinated by denominational offices, as well as general activities, may be receiving decreasing support from the congregational level. This trend is evident across the theological spectrum, including in what might be termed evangelical denominations that have traditionally emphasized global missions as a high priority. In addition, the long-term cultural loyalty to a denominational structure closely associated with immigrant roots may be losing ground to an emphasis on immediate gratification of spiritual needs, regardless of denominational source.

Yet pastors indicate they are still expected to bring the congregation in line with the denomination's agenda, particularly in terms of financial support. Ministers who were interviewed in the course of the Stewardship Project sometimes expressed a pull on them to balance the congregation and the denomination, in addition to the pressure on them to keep all subgroups within the congregation happy.

The tensions can be very real. The comfort agenda that has become increasingly important in many congregations may have implications for the portion of congregational income available to support the regional and national levels of the church. As individual lifestyles have adjusted to increased affluence, congregational expenses to maintain a certain level of comfort have also gone up. As Hugh Magers, director of stewardship for The Episcopal Church, noted, "Those churches also have a significant need for the comfort of the people in them—68 degrees, padded pews. . . . Rich people live comfortable lives and it's costing more and more. It grows financial pressure on the congregation out of their desire for comfort."

A leader in an evangelical denomination provided a similar analysis with a slight twist. In discussing why the support of denominational programs was dropping at the congregation level, he said, "Don't you think it might also be major building projects? The level of expectation in our communion has gone up over fifty to seventy-five years. There's a demand for better facilities. It's the 'gospel lift' people talk about: When the gospel sets in, things tend to improve. More staff, more facilities add economic stress and strain on the congregation to provide better facilities."

That "gospel lift" was observed as early as the 1700s, in the church John Wesley was dealing with, and has influenced the church throughout its history. If that "gospel lift" tended to produce widespread increases in the portion of growing incomes donated, then the tendency to improve local facilities might not result in a decline of national denominational support. But church-member-giving research indicates that, while expectations have risen, the portion of per capita income donated has declined. The trend, therefore, is for congregations to keep a larger portion of their total receipts in the local congregation and to pass less on to both the regional and national levels. For example, one study of two denominations concluded, "As the demand for additional services, classes, and specialized programs has grown, so has the need for additional staffing—both ordained and non-ordained."[1] Another study found that the number of ministers per one hundred members increased for such activities as "counseling, music directors, and so on." The researcher, Robin Klay, comments on the turning inward of the congregation:

> This is ironic given biblical teaching about proper responses to poverty and the obvious needs of Christian churches in such regions as rapidly evangelizing Africa. However, it is not surprising to economists, who find that as incomes rise people typically spend an increasing share of their incomes on luxuries.[2]

The Task of Mission

The minister's task may have been easier when the denomination served a purpose that was clear to the congregation. For example, if the congregation was convinced of its moral responsibility to carry the light of the gospel to other countries, funding for the denomination's efforts was perceived as a necessary element of the church budget. Now a shift has taken place. Denominations also live in the same complicated society that everyone else does. As a result, the task of mission has sometimes taken on as much diversity as cable television has channels. Consider for instance, the Presbyterian Church (U.S.A.) held a convocation in Chicago in October 1992. The goal was to identify the mission priorities for the church. The result was a 256-page document summarizing the priorities in 143 reports, each from a separate subgroup. On closer review, the results were not as diverse as they at first appear. The largest discussion group involved more than one-quarter of the participants, who divided into eleven subgroups. Each subgroup focused on the task of suggesting the five top mission priorities for the General Assembly of the church. Interestingly, in the eleven groups, eleven identified evangelism, ten identified education, and at least eight identified global mission, with one additional group using terms that might also be interpreted as referring to that idea.[3]

An increasingly accepted piece of business wisdom is "do a few things very well." And yet when the pastor interprets the denomination to the congregation, there are not three or five clear directions, but perhaps as many as 143 aspects of that organization to explain and promote. Unable to understand the denomination in its present diversity, congregations see the requested financial support going to a vague institution. In those circumstances the denomination may appear to be, or even to function as, a "regulatory agency."[4] Without a clear understanding of the services provided by the denomination, the term "taxes" was sometimes used by pastors and lay congregational leaders alike to describe denominational financial requests in Stewardship Project interviews.

One younger pastor expressed some frustration about his denominational ties. He compared his situation to that of an independent congregation up the block that had three church buses and often brought in popular singing acts. His church could do the same, he offered, if they did not have to forward such a large portion of their funds to denominational headquarters.

Another young pastor wrote a column in his church newsletter, countering an idea apparently floated by a lay member that the congregation "secede" from the denomination "and save thousands of dollars" in denominational support payments.[5]

Financial Support to Denominations

Mainline Protestant congregations may have emphasized the need for financial support because of their losses in membership and declining income to national offices. One pastor lamented that the only information the denomination wants to hear from him is his statistics on money and members. "Why don't they want to know if we're arguing more or less or if people are being spiritually fed?"

Data shows, however, that mainline Protestant denominations are not the only institutions affected by declining giving patterns. Denominational structures are feeling pinched across the entire spectrum of the church. Reports indicate that foreign missions among mainline, evangelical, Roman Catholic, and Anabaptist communions are suffering cutbacks. Denominational staffing at the national and regional levels is being cut. In the face of these developments the pressure mounts on the pastor to produce more funding from the congregation to support the denominational structure.

As one regional denominational staff member confided, "If I'm going to be honest, we at the regional office have become basically fund-raisers with the congregations." With the pressure to keep operations going—sometimes to keep a job position funded—regional officials were not in a position to provide support to pastors struggling to hold together congregations undergoing a transition from stewards to consumers. Ray Coughlin of the Archdiocese of Chicago voiced a similar perspective, "Most dioceses do not have a support structure to help pastors to raise funds."

James Hudnut-Beumler suggested that laypeople may not have been given the information they need to make intelligent spending decisions. "The church has not made the case that people need to give a lot of themselves through the vehicle of the church. They have also not made the case that using the other funds entrusted to you for all sorts of consumer purchases is not necessarily good. I've never heard a sermon that said, 'Put off buying a new car for another year, and put the money into Africa.'"

Whatever the reasons that led to present giving patterns, the impact of the decreasing levels of support is being felt in many circles. And these patterns are affecting the way congregations and their denominational offices relate. Mark Moller-Gunderson, executive director of the Division for Congregational Ministries of the Evangelical Lutheran Church in America, noted that the partnership between national denominations and congregations seems to be eroding: "I think economic factors are driving the church in a major way. It is hard for any planning process to catch up with the money crunch. The course is so accelerated, I'm not sure how to get in front of it. I don't know if anyone else does either."

Money and Denominational Services

Of course, in many cases, denominational officials are concerned about maintaining programs that provide valuable services both to the congregation as well as to society and for global need. No doubt there would be a great complaint if many of the services were not present. Yet communication has broken down between the congregation and the denomination so that church members take the services for granted and yet can resent denominational requests for support. "Support, people seem to think, for these programs, and especially for people who staff such programs, comes from nowhere—the manna experience relived," observed Thomas J. Murphy, archbishop of Seattle, somewhat wryly.

Many of these denominational programs began in the 1950s, when the economy was expanding, the suburbs were sprouting, and to be American was to be religious. As affluence became taken for granted and societal attitudes increasingly emphasized individualism, denominational support plateaued, raising new questions for how church structures would respond. James Powell of the Southern Baptist Convention Cooperative Program office summarized it well when he said, "You know as well as I, when money is slack, people ask, 'What's the problem? How do we fix it?' When money is plentiful, everything's fine. But when it's slack, the question arises, do we take the old battleship and change it to a cruise ship?"

Increased Pressure on the Pastor

To revamp the denomination is one course of action. Another is to increase the pressure on the pastor at the local level to produce increased contributions. One national official, responsible for overseeing officials in the field, felt "this denomination's short-term goal is to stay in business as a denomination, versus most of us in the field, whose goal is to come to terms with the faith issue and not just pay the bills."

William McKinney, of Hartford Seminary, agreed that many denominations are looking for new ways to tell pastors what the denominations have been saying all along: Figure out how to raise money. "But things haven't *really* changed—and pastors are smart enough to know that." His view was borne out by one pastor who commented, "In spite of what they say about time, talents, and money, it's fund-raising."

Two young up-and-coming pastors were among those who participated in a workshop. The discussion question was, "What would be two or three positive consequences in your congregation if money were not a problem?" Their conclusion after small group discussion? "Staff and buildings." No matter how much denominational rhetoric the regional and national offices had put forth about the broad mission and broader purposes of the church, increased staff and larger buildings were the expectations that were communicated to the local level.

That may be a contributing factor as to why pastors do not preach those sermons about putting off a new car in order to send money to denominational missions work overseas. Perhaps tellingly, only a third of the pastors in the Stewardship Project survey agreed with the statement: "Most pastors feel they would receive strong support from their denominational structure if they were to challenge perceived selfish patterns among their congregation members," as shown in figure 3.

This finding becomes more important in light of another survey response. When asked to respond to the statement, "Congregations have effective ways of pressuring the pastor to stop if the pastor challenges them on a difficult topic," almost 60 percent of the pastors agreed.

The response of one pastor on hearing another minister's experience was enlightening. The story was related that a regional official had received a call from a person representing three families in a congregation. In a follow-up meeting, the families informed the regional official that they were the biggest givers in the congregation and they were unhappy with the minister there. Further, the families informed the regional official that they would withhold their contributions until the current minister was removed. The regional official promised to look into the situation and he did. After conferring with the pastor and with other

Figure 3: Survey Observation #5

Most pastors feel they would receive strong support from their denominational structure if they were to challenge perceived selfish patterns among their congregation members.

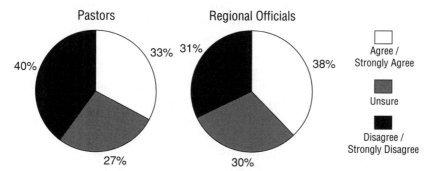

Details in the figures may not compute to 100% due to rounding.

laypeople in the congregation, the regional official decided that the current pastor was fulfilling the demands of the gospel, within the guidelines of the denomination. At this point the person telling the story said, "So do you know what he did?" The pastor listening responded eagerly, "He told the pastor to back down and please the three families, right?" The storyteller was a little taken aback by the confidence with which the listening pastor responded. In fact the regional minister told the pastor he would back the pastor but that the pastor had to realize that his budget would be drastically decreased. The pastor continued his ministry in the congregation, the angry families withheld their funds, and in some months the budget was at previous levels through contributions from additional families.

The dynamics that seem so clear in this true illustration will be explored in greater depth in chapter 11. The immediate point of interest is that the listening pastor was sure that the denomination saw the support of high-level donors as more important than a pastor leading the congregation in the demands of the gospel. With only 33 percent of the pastors responding to the Stewardship Project survey confident of the denomination's support if the pastor were to lead strongly on the issue of lifestyle, the listening pastor may not be all that unusual.

Another story indicates that some denominations may be so preoccupied with their own institutional concerns that they are not in a position to support their ministers. One pastor described a congregation where his diploma was spat on and some of his other personal possessions were attacked. We asked whether the denomination had warned him about the situation he was going into. No, he explained, they had told him that it would be an opportunity to use his pastoral skills. The pastor continued without any trace of bitterness or irony. To their defense, he suggested, the usual signs were not there to warn the denomination. Although several laypeople had contacted the denominational office to report difficulty in the congregation, the contacts were regarded as rumors because the congregation's financial commitment to the denomination was current.

Regional offices, struggling to make ends meet economically, and coping with various other factors, may feel that they are not in a position to support the pastor in unusual individual circumstances.

Meanwhile, the pastor in those circumstances confronts not only individual issues but also the broader organizational dynamics. The pastor is in a position to help strengthen the connection between the congregation and the denomination. When the denominations were the brokers for generally affirmed cooperative efforts among the congregations, such as frontier and international missions, or when they represented first- or second-generation ties to the mother church in another country, or when they represented very distinctive, core beliefs that were a rallying point for the members, the purpose of the denominations was extremely clear on a local level. Now, in many denominations, no overriding vision binds congregations together within, let alone to other congregations. Without a clear purpose that draws the congregation's attention outward, the church has turned inward to accommodate the increasing individualism among parishioners, and the denomination's services become more vague.

So the denomination has a challenge to reach out to its congregational constituents. And its frontline interpreters are the beleaguered pastors who are having an increasingly difficult time holding together the varying demands for increased comfort being promoted by interest groups within the congregation.

Denominational Loyalty

The weakening of the strong denominational purpose may have impacted the pastor's loyalty to the denomination as well. In systems where the congregation "calls" the pastor (hires the pastor directly), denominational advice is sometimes sought, but on a daily basis there is a real sense in which the pastor's tenure depends on his or her relationship with the congregation. And so the minister's job security lies there to a great degree. A pastor for whom everything is going smoothly at the congregational level is not likely to leave until he or she wants to. And a positive reputation will have a positive impact on the next assignment.

In systems where pastors are appointed through the denominational structure, pastors popular with their congregations can be moved against their will, but in such cases, the new appointment would usually be to a more prestigious congregation, meaning more members, higher salary, and likely a better parsonage or housing allowance.

Pastoral assignments have been a traditional link between the pastor and the denominational structure. Even in nonappointive systems, national or regional officials may have access to information, or can provide important recommendations, to attractive congregations. As William McKinney observed in the late 1970s,

> The expectations a denomination has of its local churches can have considerable impact, since denominations have some sanctions to ensure conformity. The sanctions include the withholding of professional leadership from deviant congregations, influencing placement of clergy, and other forms of organizational pressure.[6]

However, on a practical level, a congregation and pastor who find themselves compatible can find ways around the most well-intentioned efforts of a denominational office. For example, sociologist R. Stephen Warner described the hiring of a pastor in one congregation. Having been unhappy with the previous pastor, several of the laypeople were very involved in finding the right minister as a replacement. When he was found, they still had to contend with the affirmative-action procedures of the denomination. "So four of them agreed to conduct what was reportedly to all parties a *pro forma* interview of a nonwhite clergyman who, though his name appeared on the job-seekers' list, had expressed no interest" in pastoring that church. The congregation, having gone through procedures described by one committee person as "farcical," hired the pastor they wanted in the first place.[7] Thus determined congregations and pastors can comply with the letter of the law without allowing themselves to be limited by it much.

Pastoral Career Goals

Although it is often overlooked, pastors, too, have career goals and plans. Like their parishioners, they are concerned about the schools their children attend and the homes in which they live. Some pastors still live in the parsonage provided by the congregation, although there is now a trend for ministers to be given a housing allowance and to buy their own homes. Not all pastors are seeking to move up the career ladder, although some have deliberate timetables that cause them to explore the idea of moving every three to five years, as part of a career strategy, until they have reached a certain level of congregation. In order to pursue such an agenda, the minister must have a good relationship with the congregation being served at each stage of the plan.

And as the pastor ages, the pressures to find a comfortable and secure position may increase. Said one, "I have a 'tape' in my head that I don't want to be where I'm not wanted. And I can't find another church easily. I'm over 55, no kids at home. So it's hard for me. I literally don't know what I would do if I left here. So that's a pressure on a lot of pastors, another form of power."

Another pastor noted the difference between the pastor's working environment and that of many congregation members. He pointed out that in a church, the pastor's immediate family knows everyone the pastor is working with, unlike a business setting where an individual's work life is separate from home. The pastor's family can become friends with, and certainly interacts with, the people that the minister is trying to lead. One retired minister described how he had planned to "go out and change the world. . . . Then I had six kids and gave the world six hostages to hold against me."

Thus the pastor's attention is preoccupied with the life of the congregation. Meeting increased resistance at the congregational level to issues that might cause discomfort to potential new members and experiencing increased demands from groups that want to be happy within the church, the denomination becomes one more interest group for the pastor to balance.

In addition, the pastor may no longer see the denomination as a strong ally. There are some indications that a pragmatic, rather than loyalist, view of the denomination is widespread. In the Stewardship Project survey, almost three-quarters of the pastors disagreed with the statement, "Most pastors feel that identifying large donors for solicitation by denominationally affiliated entities may be helpful to their career." (One pastor even wrote on the survey, "I resent this question.") Thus pastors do not see cooperating with denominational campaigns as assisting their career plans. Nor do they see such cooperation as a pleasurable part of their duties, as indicated by the 86 percent of the pastors who disagreed with the statement, "Pastors like to provide their congregational membership mailing lists for use in solicitation by denominationally affiliated entities." Figure 4 provides these findings.

In the days when working one's way up to larger churches also provided a series of appointments in the denominational structure, the pastor's career plans and the denomination's goals were intertwined. Craig Dykstra and James Hudnut-Beumler refer to this

Figure 4: Survey Observation #3

Pastors like to provide their congregational membership mailing lists for use in solicitation by denominationally affiliated entities.

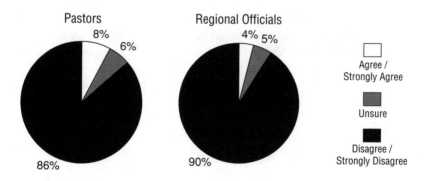

Details in the figures may not compute to 100% due to rounding.

period of church structure as the "corporate" model. "Corporate trustees were paralleled by the ministers and laypeople, almost always men, who came to headquarters several times a year from the largest and wealthiest congregations to serve on the boards and councils of the denomination."[8] However, there was a concerted effort on the part of some denominations to break apart this traditional "old boys network" in an attempt to make the denominational structure accessible to more members of the church.[9]

One interesting theory suggests that the affirmative action movement may have dealt a heavy blow to pastors' denominational loyalty. A retired national leader of one denomination noticed deep bitterness on the part of pastors who had "played the denominational game" throughout their careers. Their career path involved accepting a series of churches, always moving toward an appointment in what are commonly termed the "tall steeple churches"—long-established, large membership, and big budget congregations influential in their communities as well as in the denominational structure. Apparently certain denominational committee appointments were traditionally associated with having arrived as a senior minister in one of those churches. As denominations worked to be sure the appointments and elections were responsive to affirmative action rather than the "old boys network," many of those positions were no longer guaranteed to one of these "old boys." One pastor in a highly prestigious church went through a humiliating experience where no one would run against him for the position that his current pastorate would normally have guaranteed. The election was delayed until someone could be found. The opponent won. The influential pastor was reported to be deeply hurt. The situation is a difficult one. Many of these influential pastors find themselves trapped by historical change. While they support affirmative action in theory, they find it difficult not to resent being deprived of the perks they feel are theirs by right of thirty years or more of faithful service. The rules changed in transit for these individuals who have surfaced as the most successful in the denomination. The denominational structure that was creating this atmosphere of change was no longer the same entity that the pastor had been loyal to for the past three decades.

5

Congregations and Denominations

All ye who are of tender heart, forgiving others, take your
part, sing his praises, Alleluia!
Ye who long pain and sorrow bear, praise God and on him
cast your care,
O praise him, O praise him,
Alleluia, Alleluia, Alleluia!

Francis of Assisi, c. 1225
All Creatures of Our God and King

Changing Relationship

Pastors who feel the denominational structure does not reward
them as it should may feel alienated from that structure. This
type of hostility may be a contributing factor to the changing relationship between denominations and congregations, since these
recently disenfranchised ministers continue to serve in influential and prestigious congregations. An official in another denomination described a significant number of congregations in the
denomination as being "at risk." These tended to be smaller congregations that had traditionally supported a full-time pastor but
were now decreasing in membership due to various demograph-
ics, both urban and rural. The denominational staff spent considerable time developing support systems for them. Meanwhile,
the "tall steeple" congregations in that denomination organized
into a fellowship of sorts among themselves. In conversation with

the national office, this fellowship made it clear that these larger congregations felt they were not receiving enough attention from the national staff. In essence, the fellowship representatives proposed the national staff decide whether the denomination was interested in providing the level of service these large, thriving congregations felt they deserved. If not, these congregations were ready to contract independently for the services the denomination had traditionally provided.

Another manifestation of this trend of discontent might be a group like Churches United in Global Mission (CUGM). Founded by Robert Schuller of the Crystal Cathedral in California, the CUGM is a coalition of large congregations from a variety of different denominations. Their purpose is to create and provide mission activities that these churches agree on, independent of any denominational structure to which the individual congregation might be connected.

Another service provided by denominations has been educational materials that present both Christian doctrine and denominational perspectives. In the 1972 National Council of Churches study that included interviews with more than three thousand ministerial and lay leaders, education was a key role of the denomination. "From the vantage point of the local churches, members see the denomination's main task as training and supplying ministers, along with coordinating mission support on fields beyond the congregation's purview and supplying program and training curricula."[1]

Yet more congregations are using independently produced study materials, as confirmed in the Stewardship Project survey. When asked whether they agreed with the statement, "Congregations today, compared to forty years ago, use more independently produced, rather than denominationally produced, Sunday school materials," more than three-fourths of those surveyed agreed there was a shift in congregational practice.

Several denominational leaders reported the increased use of independently developed materials for Sunday school as well as stewardship training programs. This situation has broader implications for the congregation-denomination relationship, since another purpose of such denominational Sunday school materials is to communicate not only historical verities of the faith but also unique perspectives contributed by denominational history. The importance of this history, though, may be lessening at the congregational level. This change may be partly due to a more free-floating movement of constituents among some of the communions, with an emphasis on convenience replacing tradition. Officials in two different evangelical denominations noted that a significant percentage of their pastors were from outside the historical culture that had traditionally produced their leadership.

In another case, while the denomination's leadership remains loyal to traditional tenets, the congregations themselves are moving away. Dale Minnich, executive of the General Services Commission of the Church of the Brethren, noted that the Brethren's traditional peace stance is strongly affirmed year after year by delegates attending the denomination's annual meeting. However, nationally only about 10 percent of the young men in Brethren congregations filed as conscientious objectors when the draft was in effect, and the peace stance had become controversial at the local level.

The increased emphasis on individualism in society, and the related expansion of demands on congregational programming, as well as the decreasing long-term loyalty to the denomination on the part of pastors, have been some of the factors turning congregations inward. As a result, denominational coffers may not have experienced a priority level of funding from small congregations worried about survival or large congregations preoccupied with church growth principles. The traditional approach to denominational funding has been a defined level of support from the congregation as a whole. The denomination may assign an expected dollar amount for each congregation to provide to the regional and national denominational offices. In other cases, the denomination recommends that an amount or a percentage of the budget be forwarded. Even in systems where an amount is assigned, however, there has been a decreasing level of compliance in providing the money.

Large Direct Donations

Several denominations have begun to consider whether large donors who are underchallenged at the congregational level might not want to become more directly involved in making contributions to the denominational level. As one national official asked, why wouldn't parachurch organization techniques of direct mail and large donor solicitation work for denominations as well?

And so various denominations decided to emphasize direct appeals to individual congregation members in general or specifically to those who were capable of making large gifts. In some cases, the denomination launched a special campaign and enlisted the minister in identifying potential large donors. In other cases, the denominations opted not to bother the pastor with the need to identify large donors, using other means of finding contacts within the congregation.

To a certain degree, agencies within various denominations moved to direct appeals and away from the unified budget concept before the central denominational administration did. A variety of subgroups carry on appeals for camps, seminaries, the foundation, and retirement homes. So the trend against unified budgets—where contributions from the congregations come to a central office and then are divided among various departments—is not only resulting from external paradenominational groups but also from agencies within the denomination. One denominational agency reported increasing levels of support from individuals, as much as 25 to 50 percent for certain mission projects. The central administration, watching all this activity and experiencing the decreases in formula congregational support, is tempted to follow suit.

Regional and national officials justify the trend toward direct solicitation of potential large donors with the idea that many big givers don't contribute large amounts at the local level because they don't want to overwhelm the congregation with a big gift that exceeds budget needs or encourages a dependency attitude in other members. This concern may be based in fact. One pastor told of a lady in her church who would write a check at the end of the year to make up whatever deficit was in the budget. The pastor felt it hurt the stewardship of the other members, creating a "welfare mentality." A church member of considerable financial means and capable of making large gifts may feel that faithful giving on his or her part would have a profoundly negative impact on the giving habits of other church members. The fact that the congregation has limited its vision to maintaining its present operations does not provide the room for such a large gift to be absorbed and yet challenge other members to be faithful givers. Thus it seems logical to denominational officials that such gifts could be incorporated at the regional or national levels.

The danger in such a direct approach to individual congregation members is that the denomination can be perceived as an organization separate from the congregation, not one that deserves support because of its integral relationship to the congregation. To the degree that denominations adopt the approaches of parachurch organizations, the members at the congregation level may begin to perceive them that way.

Certainly denominations do not like to think of themselves on a par with independent parachurch religious organizations. One consultant shared an experience in which he met with national leaders from several denominations. Being unfamiliar with some of the dynamics the leaders were facing, he made a remark that included denominations in a group with "other parachurch organizations." The response he received to that characterization was strong and negative, allowing him to understand that, however an outsider may view the structures, denominations do not see themselves as entities independent of the congregation.

Designated Gifts

An increased desire at the congregational level to designate gifts rather than send general contributions is perceived by the denominations as supporting their desire to take a more direct approach with local donors. Among those surveyed, a large majority of the pastors and the regional officials agreed with this statement: "Most church members want to know 'what their money is buying' when sent out of the congregation" (see figure 5). If people want more information about what their money is accomplishing, the thinking goes, one might ask them to contribute directly to the denomination for specific items.

Denominational officials who were interviewed were very aware of this reality. A study in The United Methodist Church polled Annual Conference church leaders on various topics. One of the highest responses was to the statement, "People would

Figure 5: Survey Observation #54

Most church members want to know "what their money is buying" when sent out of the congregation.

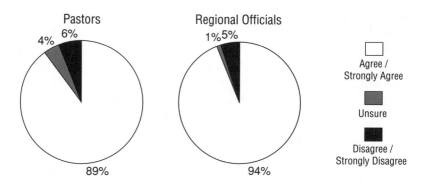

Details in the figures may not compute to 100% due to rounding.

rather give to specific causes than to a general budget." A total of 98 percent of those responding agreed.[2] Hugh Magers, of The Episcopal Church, suggested that 65 to 75 percent of the people who are the largest contributors in that denomination "*must* see that lives are being changed and saved" as a result of their donated funds. Their focus may be vague—health or education in general—or very specific in the number of those experiencing salvation and conversion.

A regional official who was interviewed strongly resented the designated giving trend that was becoming more popular at the congregational level. He expressed strong support for the unified budget and spent time promoting the concept in congregations within his regional jurisdiction. Imagine his dismay when he received a call from an enthusiastic young businesswoman who sat on the mission committee of one of the largest congregations in his area. The committee was reviewing its mission budget for the coming year, she explained, and she had been assigned the task of contacting the regional office for information about the services they provide. She noticed that the regional office had not submitted the mission fund request form that the committee had sent to all the agencies it supported. Would he like to tell her what they were doing, so her committee could evaluate their line item as they were doing with the local home building project and the battered women's agency? This particular congregation had certainly developed an alternative view to seeing denominational support as a tax.

Thomas J. Murphy, presently serving as treasurer of the National Conference of Catholic Bishops, also observed that church members expect some return for their investment. Human nature being what it is, he went on, people want to know what they're getting in return for their dollars contributed. The archbishop pointed out that the church has a lot to offer. "It provides quality education to countless young people, offers assistance and help to the elderly, helps infertile couples and others to adopt a child—and these are but some examples of how people have the opportunity to experience their Church and their faith touch their lives—and they are grateful to that institution."

Improved Communication

Communication about the good that the denomination accomplishes may be a key component to improved relationships between national, regional, and local levels of the church. In an atmosphere in which competition for the charitable dollar is skyrocketing, denominations may not be effectively getting out the word to their constituents. Herbert Mather of The United Methodist Church General Board of Discipleship observed that many people are saying, "'I want to give my money where it helps people.' In The United Methodist Church, we've not told the stories that have established trust. Connectionalism is seen only as whether you pay apportionments [denominationally assigned financial support from the congregation to the denomination structure]."

That link of trust is critical for congregations to continue to support their denominational structures. Some propose that a lack of communication has produced a distance between denominations and the congregations that have supported them. In a study of one denomination, Richard W. Reifsnyder observed,

> Historically, Presbyterians have often sought to resolve their doctrinal differences by focusing on mission, but there is less clarity on what the fundamental mission of the church is. The consen-

sus that the church was to spread the gospel so that people would become believers in Jesus Christ, establishing worshipping communities and building churches, has waned as the frontier has disappeared, both nationally and globally.[3]

Others suggest that the more progressive religious professionals tended to congregate in denominational offices, creating a perspective gap particularly between those in national headquarters and those in congregations.[4] For whatever reason, in some cases, particularly among mainline denominations, "Many members of congregations feel that their judicatories and denominations are using rhetoric about mission to secure support for activities that the members themselves do not understand to be mission. The nerve of trust has been cut."[5]

Motivation to Contribute

Denominational officials face the additional tension that while they recognize congregation members have a right to expect accountability of their institutions, the denominational leadership has a responsibility to lead congregation members into the deeper truths of the faith. One of those truths is that an important aspect of Christian discipleship involves giving not to get but giving in response to experienced grace. How is that concern balanced with accountability? Denominational offices have faced increasing competition from nonprofit charitable organizations, both Christian and secular, who emphasize specific ends.

Nonprofit charitable organizations often have as their goal a meeting of a particular need. In contrast, denominations not only provide services to their congregations but also feel an obligation to provide those services in a theologically sound context that provides spiritual growth for their members. With the luxury of emphasizing needs, many nonprofit charities have pointed to what donors receive for their contributions, setting a general expectation that donors then bring to the church. Not everyone sees the focus mainly on the needs being met as the best approach. A psychologist who is beginning to explore motivational aspects of nonprofit organizations reached a similar conclusion in his preliminary work. Paul Baard suggests that "enticing" donations from church members with acknowledgments or other rewards might actually undermine the higher motivation "to further the cause" that initially leads many donors to contribute.[6]

There may be spiritual implications as well. "One of my primary criticisms of charitable organizations is that they don't understand the global nature of someone's life," said Ron Blue, president of Ronald Blue and Company, an independent financial planning company based in Atlanta. "They don't understand the barriers in people's lives to giving and so they appeal to their special interests rather than encourage them to develop disciplined giving. It's not spiritually beneficial to the donor to ask for money based on how a project appeals to people."

On a more practical level, a denomination adopting parachurch techniques may find they violate the congregation-denomination relationship. A national official, who had observed the success of various nondenominational parachurch organizations in terms of direct mail, decided to pursue a direct appeal approach. This particular denomination maintains a higher than average level of congregational support and a strong commitment to the denominational structure. Still, this denomination was experiencing the same trend of stagnant revenues and was exploring additional approaches. So the official sent out a direct mail appeal to the membership of the denomination's congregations, asking for contributions for the denominational office. The official explained that it was not long before he heard from some very angry pastors. They made it quite clear, he reported, that the pastors were not interested in having the denomination compete with the pastor in terms of congregational support. The official stopped the direct mail campaign, realizing there would be serious implications for the denomination-congregation relationship were he to continue to pursue it.

Nor does it appear that direct solicitation and making use of designated giving is the first choice of many denominational officials. Regional and national leaders who were interviewed often expressed frustration at the pull away from "unified giving," that is, a general financial gift made to the denomination to be applied as thought best by regional and national officials.[7] They realistically point to the difficulty of administering designated gifts because of the paperwork, and also because of the disparities involved. It is difficult for them to watch popular missionaries in one area, for example, have ample funds, while just as effective but less charismatic missionaries in another area are struggling to make ends meet. Administrative services to the congregation, including pastor pension planning and health care, legal oversight, pastor assignment coordination and resource materials, are often not dramatic features of denominational functioning, yet they need to continue to be funded through unified giving by the congregation. Many church members do not connect the unified denominational requests with the services that help their congregation and pastor to function smoothly in a secure environment.

History of Denominational Support

In the 1920s through the 1950s, unified budgets developed as congregations made a shift from designated giving to the more general concept of denominational support. One 1929 study found pastors complaining about the number of benevolent boards that developed and the resulting demand on the pastor to encourage church members to support them. "The pastors, in turn, began to feel that they were being used as money-raisers rather than as spiritual leaders of the people, and many of them came to regard the providing of funds for the work of the benevolent boards as a pastoral burden rather than as an opportunity to lead people into ever-broadening sympathies and an ever-widening service." The pastoral protests became so marked that denominations moved toward a unified giving approach to benevolences.

> Not a few of the great boards gave up their immediate contacts with constituencies, long conserved and cultivated, and unification and consolidation of benevolences became the order of the day. . . . The faithful few or the many, who had come through the years to visualize specific situations and needs, now had their eyes turned to a "budget" to be raised.[8]

This "unified budget" approach allowed the congregation to focus on its local activities, trusting the denomination to allocate the general income from the congregations for the larger mission of the church. As Robert Wood Lynn has written,

Simultaneously, the inherited formula of the every member canvass and the stewardship message undergirded impressive growths in congregational budgets. By the 1950s most old-line congregations took for granted the discipline of a unified budget. That act reflected denominational loyalty and also reinforced the power of national denominational agencies.[9]

The system worked well as long as there was general agreement on the value of that larger mission. Now this unified system in being dismantled.

Back to Designated Gifts

In our interviews, a variety of denominational people mentioned the marked increase in designated gifts. Rather than sending the majority of the money from the congregation to the regional and national offices to be used as seems best, more and more of the money is being designated for special purposes. A denomination may be able to benefit from this specialized interest. One official commented, "To some extent we ride the current events—but that's part of the game."

However, the trend toward designation can hurt the ongoing programs of the denomination. James Williams, executive director of Church of God World Service (Anderson, Ind.), describes increasing pressure from various sources to cater to those special interests. "People say, 'The money's out there.' I've lived with that tension for years. Others will ask, 'Why don't you bring in more money?' And I say, It's increasingly tougher to raise money for ongoing activities—people assume the ongoing will go on. They want the exciting and new. The challenge is to interpret the ongoing."

James Austin, vice president of the Southern Baptist Convention's Stewardship Commission, reflected on his communion's experience with designated giving compared to a unified budget. "In 1925, we began a unified giving system called the Cooperative Program. Up until that time, our people were societal people: People who wanted to give to foreign missions gave to the Foreign Missions Board; people who wanted to give to home missions gave to the Home Missions Board. As I hear other denominational leaders talking, it seems people are facing a return to that system, a system that did not work. We were in debt—all of our agencies were in debt—and the longer you live as an individual society, the deeper you get in debt. That's because people's emotions are high when there is a hurricane, and they go low when the sun is shining. When we founded the Cooperative Program, thank the Lord, things began to get on an even keel financially. We became able to do the mission work we had talked about for eighty years and to start fulfilling the purpose for the founding of the SBC—'eliciting, combining, and directing the energies of the whole denomination for the Redeemer's cause.'"

Denominational officials generally agree that there must be a balance of providing a broad theological context for giving as well as effectively communicating the very real good that is being accomplished through denominational channels. Mark Moller-Gunderson of the Evangelical Lutheran Church in America commented, "For a long time, 'pure' stewardship was giving from the heart and 'dirty' stewardship was giving to a need. There's room for both. It's not necessarily an either/or situation."

Yet many denominational officials, at both the national and regional levels, are feeling the very real pressures from declining giving income. The situation became even more critical with the decline in investment and interest income in the late 1980s and early 1990s. If a denomination had endowment funds or other investment income to provide large portions of their operating budgets, this income may have decreased rather suddenly with the stock market decline in October 1987, declining interest rates, and the recession of the early 1990s. It was then that they may have especially noticed the slow decline in congregation support for their programs, a decline that began in some cases as long ago as the early 1960s.

Perceived Competition

The trend of making direct donations to denominations may affect pastor-denomination relations. Pastors may perceive the denomination's direct involvement at the congregational level as competition. Sixty percent of the pastors surveyed agreed with the statement, "To some extent, pastors perceive denominationally affiliated entities as competitors for their congregation members' money." Meanwhile, 89 percent of the responding regional officials agreed. How the pastor sees the denominational appeals is a critical factor in congregation-denomination relationships.

Ray Coughlin, director of development for the Archdiocese of Chicago, sees pastors as the most influential denominational representative in the congregation. "They talk to the people weekly. They have a finger on the pulse of what is going on. They are the ones who are holding the hands of the dying and guiding our children." The difficulty that Coughlin and others noted is that many pastors are preoccupied with local problems. The idea suggested by a number of different denominational officials was that pastors see themselves struggling for survival. "Firehouse mentality" was the phrase that Coughlin used. "Pastors are sweating out payrolls and operating expenses, keeping schools open, in debt to the archdiocese. They are scratching to make ends meet, and then the Archdiocese Annual Appeal or a special collection for a global crisis like Rwanda comes along and pastors say, 'The cause is wonderful. I believe in it. But I can't ask my people to respond to that until our parish needs are cared for.'

"Many pastors have a misimpression that out-of-parish causes take money out of their own baskets—they see these appeals as a great big vacuum cleaner sucking money out of the congregation. They're wrong. Catholics are rarely single-minded in giving."

Joan Sanford of The Christian and Missionary Alliance also recognized this pastoral concern. "One fear I've heard from some pastors: If they push missions too hard, will it hurt the local operations? Studies tend to show the opposite."

Yet many pastors seem to act out of this concern. One retired church official winters in Florida and returns north the rest of the year. In the Florida church he and his wife attend, the denominational materials are distributed in the pews and discussed from the pulpit. In their northern church, they've received no information. "Pastors are not using the tools available," he says. When he received a letter from the pastor of the northern church, it announced that each member owed $17.47 for denominational commitments. He told us he wanted to respond, "What is it *for?!*" When he did ask questions about the details, he was told, "The budget can't be met unless giving is raised." He commented, "While that's true, it's not very exciting." The retired official feels the pastor of the northern church is an effective preacher and a caring person, but her communications with the congregation suggest she is no good at stewardship.

Another national denominational official helps organize a national missions symposium every summer. Thousands of lay-people pay their own way to learn more about the denominational mission outreach. More than once, this official reports, she's received angry comments from laypeople who wonder why their pastors have not given them this mission information. "Why haven't they?" we asked her. "Perhaps because pastors are threatened in terms of money," she mused. "They should know better but they see missions in competition with raising the budget."

Mixed Messages

There may be a certain degree to which the denomination is sending confusing signals as well. William McKinney observed that the message coming from the denomination may be difficult to interpret. On the one hand, the pastor is told to encourage congregation members to give not to a need but out of a spiritual commitment. Stewardship, pastors are instructed, "is not money or money alone—giving money is a way to express loyalty out of appreciation." So pastors work to educate people to the more general principles of stewardship and denominational support. Then the denomination announces a new campaign, perhaps a new national capital campaign, and the message is, "You ought to give because we spend it well." This type of approach puts denominations on the same footing as other fund-raising appeals from other organizations. The pastor, and the members the pastor is interpreting the denomination to, may become "befuddled," suggests McKinney. "Do I give in response to grace or because it's an effective institution?"

Al Taylor is director of stewardship for the Church of God (Cleveland, Tenn.). He said he can understand the frustration at the congregational level. "With few exceptions, the general and state levels of the church communicate continually, 'We have these needs—what are you going to do about them?' This is a violation of Paul's admonition to give not of necessity."

Other denominations are beginning to recognize the situation Taylor described. Mark Moller-Gunderson, executive director of Congregational Ministries for the Evangelical Lutheran Church in America (ELCA), remembered the merger of other denominations into the ELCA in 1987. "The first message from the new denomination was 'We have a $12 million deficit.' Then 'an $8 million deficit.' In retrospect," he commented wryly, "this was not the best approach."

Taylor suggested that the denomination would do better to remember how and why it was formed in the first place and to spend its time reminding congregation members of that history. "We forget how it happened and we come back with this need and that need and more need, and people get angry: 'We created this organization to meet a need, and instead we hatched more needs.' We're misrepresenting this work to them."

Many pastors are not shy about voicing their concerns about repeated requests for denominational financial support. Such input caused one national official to clarify the message he sends to congregations. He realized the denomination needs money not only for institutional survival but also to accomplish the purposes for which it was originally designed. A pastor may complain, "This denomination stuff has got to stop. You're spending money like water. It's got to stop, so we're not going to give." At that point, the official explained, "We have to back them into a corner and say, 'How are you going to do the Great Commission?'" The official went on to describe all the layers of accountability the national office has at different levels from the local congregation to the annual regional gathering in that communion. With the issue of accountability settled, he repeated, "You have to ask, 'How are we pursuing the Great Commission?' Every pastor is going to have to answer that."

The declines in financial support for denominational structures have raised questions about their institutional survival. And some national officials who urge congregations to increase the level of support realize their motives can be misunderstood. "At the regional and general levels, we are not afraid we are going to lose our jobs, although that's what we get accused of," explained Robert Welsh. "We're afraid that we're going to so collapse the ministry of the church that what's left won't be church anymore.

I could care less about the job but without the program and the witness, can we call ourselves church anymore?"

The Inward Trend

The trend for congregations to focus more on their own needs and less on a larger mission is a natural organizational development. As sociologist Reginald Bibby has noted, "Observers have drawn attention to the reality of routinization, whereby groups tend to become turned inward, focusing upon themselves as organizations, rather than on the original purposes that brought them into being."[10] Yet this natural development is in direct contrast to an important purpose of a religious congregation. Loren Mead describes this role: "Congregations remain one of the key places where self-centered citizens may be transformed into disciples ready and eager to become bearers of good news to the needs of the world."[11] The denomination provides vital assistance to the congregation in fulfilling this responsibility, according to the editors of a seven-volume study of Presbyterianism and the mainline Protestant experience in the United States. They concluded, "As critical as the congregation may be, it will never be able to capture the fullness of the biblical conception of the body of Christ or to carry out the mission of the church in its breadth and depth"[12] on its own.

One irony is that many pastors who are concerned about growth of their congregations are willing to allow the congregation to turn inward, away from the larger mission of the church, regardless of the enormous amount of biblical teaching to the contrary. This movement is in contrast to the findings of one study that observed,

> An emphasis, or an increased emphasis, on evangelism may lead to growth. Similarly, churches that emphasize world mission have higher growth rates. . . . Thus leaders interested in growth must also think carefully about how to change the identity of such churches from an inward focus on members' needs to an outward vision for the needs of nonmembers.[13]

Pastors may not have anticipated the extremes to which the inward trend may go. One reporter called for some information about church-member giving. A discussion followed about the turning inward and data trends that suggested not only denominational structures but also congregations may be eliminated at some distant point in the future if current giving patterns continue unchanged. His response was surprising. "Oh, I've already written stories about that. That's the privatization-of-religion idea. People get themselves a twelve-step program, maybe attend a Bible study once in a while, and put a religion together for themselves."

This trend certainly puts denominational offices in a bind. The denomination's income is shrinking, which causes a scaling down of programs. Offering fewer services, the denominations have greater difficulty explaining why the congregations ought to continue to support the structure. The denominations risk the wrath of pastors for going directly to church members. Yet their key interpreter at the congregational level is the pastor, who may be finding greater difficulty in rallying congregation-wide support for the denomination.

If national officials did not have enough to do with working out the relationship between the pastor and the denomination, two additional developments are complicating the issue.

Defining Local Missions

First, some congregations maintain that they are doing more mission work locally and therefore have less need for the regional and national structures. Several national denominational officials feel this change in attitude is impacting their relationship with local congregations. After years of encouraging people to be involved in mission "in their own backyard," congregations now ask the national office why the congregations are being criticized for keeping money to do just that.

Part of the difficulty is the definition of what constitutes mission at the local level. While money going to the regional and national offices is automatically defined as being directed to the broader mission of the church, local mission definitions can become fuzzier. There would be no question about the traditional soup kitchen and homeless shelters being included as "mission" versus "operations." But what about additional staff to service current members? What about a day-care center that mainly serves members of the church? Or what about air conditioning to make the church more comfortable and therefore perhaps attract seekers? These types of discussions have financial implications. Some denominational offices ask the local congregations to send a percentage of income as the congregation's support for the regional and national programs; however, certain types of line items can be subtracted from the congregation's total income figure before calculating the percentage that should be sent on to the denomination.

One national official also serves as an officer in a local congregation. He described it as "fascinating" to sit next to the congregational treasurer as the treasurer tried to "beat the denominational formula" in figuring "what was in and what was out" of the income total and thereby lessen the amount passed on to the regional and national levels.

In addition, some congregations are taking a more direct hand in organizing their broader mission outreaches, filling roles that have previously been assigned to denominational structures. National officials at the Southern Baptist Convention Cooperative Program office have noticed an increase in congregations wanting to organize their own short-term mission trips. It may seem odd to an outside observer that congregations would want to go to all the trouble to organize their own trips when Southern Baptists have at their disposal the largest Protestant international mission network in the United States. Yet James Powell of the SBC Cooperative Program office observed that, while there used to be some concern about this trend, he is now convinced that these trips are worthwhile because of how excited the participants are when they come back.

That there is a movement from national and regional support to the local level is generally acknowledged. How much of the money being kept at the local level is maintaining and expanding the internal operations of the congregation and how much would actually be considered local mission outreach in the traditional sense of that term is more difficult to discern.

Competition

The second important complication of the national officials' work is the increasing competition between the regional and national offices. As the amount of money coming from the congregation to all levels has lessened, each level of the church has had to rethink its role. Sometimes the regional levels have rethought themselves into expanding services and keeping more of the congregational dollars.

Robert Niklaus, of the Office of Communication and Funding of The Christian and Missionary Alliance, in discussing national and regional staff positions observed, "A Christian Education director, a youth director—the regional offices are providing some of the same services the national traditionally has. There's a trend toward districts being more active."

For the Church of the Brethren, this type of division of labor is a relatively new development. Until around 1960 all of the congregational support went directly to the national office. The districts were staffed with volunteers who mainly worked with the congregation to improve the Sunday school efforts. About ten years ago districts began to have paid staff. They worked in the area of pastoral placement, church planting, and developing support for the camping system. Now giving to the districts exceeds giving to the national office, with a decreasing awareness of the role of the national office at the congregational level.

The Lutheran Church-Missouri Synod is experiencing a similar trend. Congregational giving goes first to the regional office and then a portion is sent on to the national. However, the portion passing on to the national has been declining in recent years. Ronald Nelson, assistant stewardship counselor in the national office, has made a point to visit various district offices as part of an effort to clarify roles. He has found his efforts resulting in the building of helpful relationships between the national and district offices. "Because of budgetary constrictions, the national office will be limited," he said. By developing a clear working relationship with the districts, he's in a better position to decide whether his office should respond to an inquiry from a congregation or refer the person to the district office.

Many regional and national officials acknowledge that the pastor's role is critical. One regional development officer explained why he had completely revised his annual appeal plans: "To make it successful, you have to involve pastors immediately."

James Williams of the Church of God (Anderson, Ind.) was even more forceful on this point. "In our movement, the pastor is either the faucet or the bottleneck. If we can't get to the congregation, generally it is the pastor who is keeping us out. When we get in, the pastor sees us as partners. If you try to go around the pastor, you've defeated yourself." The Church of God national office trains lay volunteers by saying, "Go to the pastor. If you can't get cooperation there, you can't get anywhere."

Cultivating Large Donations

Some denominations, faced with a lack of support from the pastor, choose to go around the pastor anyway. One consultant hired by a denominational mission agency indicated he disliked going to the pastor first because pastors inevitably tell him that a particular individual congregation member is "not a good candidate" for a large gift. This consultant said he does visit with the local pastor but usually after he's made the call on the potential donor. In one situation, the pastor was quite sure one of his members was not ready to be approached about a special gift, when the consultant had already visited the congregation member in question and received a check for several thousand dollars.

Some denominations have recognized that relationships with large donors can be cultivated. Seminaries have long taken this approach, organizing special president's weekends, as well as designated giving options for wealthy donors, such as the construction of buildings or funding scholarships. Apparently some denominations are beginning to undertake similar activities to increase individual giving to denominational campaigns. In one case, an archdiocese plans an elegant dinner, including a talk by the archbishop. In another case, a denominational mission agency plans a special weekend in a pleasant location, during which donors of large gifts are able to interact with visiting missionaries.

Interestingly, it does not appear that the same type of cultivation of the pastor's interest and support is taking place on the part of denominations. For example, two denominational mission agency officials were lamenting the decrease in congregational financial support. When asked how many of their pastors had visited a mission field in the last five years for even a brief firsthand experience, one denominational official replied less than 1 percent and the other suggested that it was probably less than 5 percent. When an additional group of denominational mission officials was asked whether cultivation events similar to those offered to donors of large gifts were offered to pastors, all shook their heads no.

In interviewing pastors and lay leaders, we formed the impression that they felt that denominations took their support for granted. Indeed, it appears that stewardship was less of a problem in the past because it was more of a cultural norm. The denominational structures were created and adapted by congregational representatives to further their desires for cooperative efforts. Whether it was foreign missions or outreach on the frontiers of the United States, relief work globally after one of the World Wars, Sunday school education, or Bible distribution, the denominations had been shaped to meet the need. In addition to the clear purpose, there was general societal support for the issues being addressed by the structures. People gave because it was the right thing to do. In that setting, denominations were seen as experts, and congregations and pastors accepted a role of providing the base for the denomination to continue its obviously important activities on the larger scale. With the erosion of a clear common vision, little is obvious to the congregations about the denominations anymore. That shift may be evident in the declining financial support.

Perhaps this would be a good point at which to review, very briefly, how the collections and oversight of money have been organized among the various communions in the United States.

6

Organizing Money and the Church

Jesus calls us; o'er the tumult
Of our life's wild, restless sea,
Day by day His sweet voice soundeth,
Saying, "Christian, follow Me."

Jesus calls us from the worship
Of the vain world's golden store,
From each idol that would keep us,
Saying, "Christian, love Me more."

Cecil F. Alexander, 1852
"Jesus Calls Us o'er the Tumult"

One ironic success of the ecumenical movement is that many church members have adopted a view that one congregation is likely as good as another. While this idea has positive consequences for Christian cooperation, it has had serious implications for the idea of loyalty to the specific denominations that have often been the proponents of ecumenism. As denominational identity lessens, church members may more freely attend a congregation that is affiliated with a denomination different from the one in which the member was baptized.

Dean Hoge feels there may be a permanent loss of denominational identity in the mainline churches that will not be turned around by techniques. William McKinney referred to the "new voluntarism" as a key dynamic. "People don't feel bound to the inherited religious practices of their parents. That same voluntarism has come into church finance."

106

One consequence of people feeling free to switch denominations easily is that new members—or even pastors—do not have a sense of history to guide their activities. Robert Niklaus, of The Christian and Missionary Alliance, was happy that the denomination was growing but he noted that a number of the new pastors were not from an Alliance background. Funding has remained sufficient, mostly because of increased giving by longtime members. As the growth rate has continued, and with it the attendant expenses, the denomination has begun to notice the consequences of having so many pastors and people from a non-Alliance background. "We're paying the cost. It's catch-up time. Now we're trying to communicate what part giving plays in their lives"—a perspective deeply ingrained in those with an Alliance history.

David McCreath, coordinator of stewardship education for the Presbyterian Church (U.S.A.), remembered the strengths of the ecumenical movement. "The church was in confrontation with the world. It didn't matter what communion you were then. There was a strong ecumenical sense, with the chief supports being the World Council of Churches and the National Council of Churches. There were not tight boundaries." Yet he said he had noticed a change in attitude. "More recently, for three or four years, there's an emerging attempt to reclaim what it means to be a Presbyterian church, especially among the ministers. There's an attempt to recover Reformed theology."

Similarity in Organization

There is a striking similarity in congregational organization, regardless of denomination. The organization outline generally provides that the pastor works with a lay-constituted leadership board. The relative influence of this leadership board often depends on the pastor's personal style and the personality of the congregation.

Some traditions authorize their leadership board to make decisions and conduct ongoing business on behalf of the congregation. Others, such as Southern Baptist, American Baptist, and Church of the Brethren, are congregational in nature, with decisions that can be handled by the leadership board in other communions being brought before a meeting of the entire congregation. The differences in congregational structure may not be as marked as these distinctions would suggest. For example, one Southern Baptist pastor that we interviewed indicated that Southern Baptist churches do not have leadership boards. When pressed, however, he noted that they do have a board of deacons that often makes decisions about the ongoing business of the church rather than taking every detail to the congregation as a whole. On a functional level, the deacons or advisory council in a congregation often conduct much of the ongoing business of the church in the same manner that those with formally constituted leadership boards do.

Committees

Most congregations also have a committee system to conduct the business of the church. In Catholic parishes, a finance council is mandated by the Revised Code on Canon Law. There may also be a lay parish council that advises the priest. In Protestant congregations, a group of committees usually answer to the leadership board, or the congregation as a whole, depending on the polity. This group routinely includes a committee to handle pastor relations, to oversee religious education, to assist in planning the worship experience including music, to determine missions, and to direct finances. There may also be a separate stewardship committee, responsible for raising the budget formulated by the finance committee, although in some cases the finance committee also takes the responsibility of raising funds for the budget. Even though the general provision is for the finance committee to submit a recommended budget to a larger body for approval, the process seems to be pretty much decided at the finance committee level. Thus the finance committee is always a powerful position in the congregation.

Missions and Finance Committees

A key factor in attempting to understand money dynamics in the congregations of America is the separation that exists between the missions committee and the finance committee. The missions committee appears to have the responsibility to outline the broader vision of the church. However, it is the finance committee that decides how much of that vision is practical for the congregation. The power of the finance committee in the current structure of most congregations must be understood in greater detail if present giving patterns in the church are to change.

Because finance involves numbers and figures, very often business people, and traditionally men, are recruited for membership on that committee, with little regard as to whether or not their Christian commitment qualifies them for implementing the goals of the congregation. Interactions with many finance committees during the course of the Stewardship Project indicated that the mission of the church could only be as large as the budget would allow. Many finance committees worried about such typical issues as "the bottom line" and "ending the year in the black."

The missions committees could be open to new ideas and even work to garner enthusiasm for the ideas in the congregation. Yet those ideas might not make it past the finance committee into the budget, with the finance committee acting on its main concern that all the bills be paid. With little financial stewardship education going on in many congregations and an aversion to asking people for money, current giving patterns often limit any missions vision in the church.

The experience of one missions-minded lay leader illustrates the type of dynamic that can result from the separate agendas of the finance committee and the missions committee. Appointed to the finance committee because of his leadership in other areas of the church, he began to campaign for a larger percentage of the operating budget being directed to missions. After much debate, the higher goal was passed. The issue was debated again when there was turnover on the finance committee the next year. Although the denomination's background was firmly rooted in missional intent, there was increasing resistance on the part of the finance committee to having to educate the congregation members about the need for increased giving to cover both the basic operations of the congregation and the increased percentage to missions. After much discussion, the missions goal as a percentage of the operating budget stayed on the books.

As the layman's term ended, the nominations committee came to him with a proposal. They had seen, as he had, that there was a need for members throughout the congregation to better understand the importance of missions. Would the layman use his considerable talents to chair the missions committee for the next term? They understood it would preclude his renewing his tenure on the finance committee but they felt he had a valuable contribution to make in this new responsibility.

Even the most humble servant would have been flattered by their request, and the layman agreed. Soon into his term on the missions committee, he requested that he receive the finance committee minutes. He was told, however, that each committee's minutes were distributed only to the members of that committee. He lost contact with the finance committee's agenda and he could not later pinpoint at which meeting the decision was made to decrease the missions percentage in the operating budget.

The path of least resistance is to keep the congregation's budget as close as possible to the same level it was the previous year. One pastor noted a little cynically that the ideal budget in his church would be less than the year before, an idea that has consequences at some point in the future. That is not to say that finance committees in all congregations do not have a broader vision for the church's ministry. However, the encounters through the Stewardship Project suggest that church leaders often set the criteria for finance committee membership largely based on being good with numbers. As a result, finance committees may bring a more practical than visionary perspective to the task.

Mark Teresi was formerly with the Planning Office of the Archdiocese of Chicago and currently is the executive vice president for development at Mercy Home for Boys and Girls. He indicated that financial planning is in a separate category from mission vision among Catholics as well as Protestants. "Do people on the Archdiocesan Finance Council even have a clue about stewardship? They're making serious business decisions, strictly looking at the numbers. Even in a parish structure, the finance committee is separate from the pastoral leadership committee. In our whole system, dollars are separate from mission, and our structures reinforce that. Then we put the needs in front of people in the pews, and I can see why they're not compelled to give—they're making a financial decision, not having a mission experience."

Finance committee members may well be willing to acknowledge that the higher calling of the church appeals to church members at some level, as the following story suggests. In this case, according to a frustrated laywoman, the finance committee in her congregation knew precisely how attractive the goals of the missions committee were to church members at pledging time. Each year in this congregation, the finance committee led out the stewardship campaign by describing the compelling local and global needs the missions committee had outlined for attention. The laywoman appreciated this type of educational effort. What frustrated her in this case was that the missions committee line item was always the last one funded each year. So the actual dollars for the missions committee were not usually available until December, when there was enough income to fund the other line items completely. And if donations were not sufficient that year to fund all line items, it was the missions committee that first absorbed the shortfall.

As one pastor who responded to the Stewardship Project survey commented, "The building fund is in competition with the general fund, which is under continual requests for help from the youth fund. Meanwhile, the missions fund silently suffers like a lawyerless orphan at an estate settlement."

An Ongoing Challenge

One thing all the committees have in common, however, is that money to run the church in America has always been a challenge to raise. The earliest congregations often reacted against the enforced tithe systems that were present in England and Europe. Even so, some colonies did have laws on the books that provided for the public support of ministers in the community. In Virginia, for example, every male over sixteen had to provide a certain amount of tobacco to the local minister as a result of a Virginia Assembly action in 1621–22. The parsonage routinely had a tobacco room, and the pastor's annual income was directly linked to his business acumen in selling it.[1]

However, as it became clear that the colonies were moving away from the idea of recognizing one denomination—or even one religion—as the official faith of the developing country, state support became problematical.

The resulting necessity for voluntary giving may be one reason the church in the United States has maintained a relatively high level of commitment from its members. But asking for money is not presently something churches like to do any more than their religious ancestors did. So a variety of approaches have been tried in the past.

Robert Wood Lynn has made a study of attitudes toward money in the American church. He suggested there have been controversies not only over how much to donate but also as to why to give. He has concluded, "There has never been a consensus in American Protestantism as to why or how or how much church members should give." Further, he suggested the whole area has been a source of deep clergy-lay tensions. "Clergy have found themselves subject to lay resistance. In the early nineteenth century, one explanation for this resistance was described as 'covetousness.' The issue became so heated and convoluted that in the early twentieth century, the fashionable rule of thumb was that laypeople would raise the money and the minister was to only preach one stewardship sermon a year."

Very early on, subscription lists were one popular approach. Author Luther Powell suggests the lists were a logical successor to taxation, substituting the force of the state with the social pressure of peers who would review the list. Church members would commit to providing the pastor so much money, or just as likely so many bags of flour or pounds of butter in the coming year. This list would be distributed publicly, thus maximizing social pressure to fully subscribe the pastor's needs or pay for the new building under construction.[2]

When communities began to change from a strictly rural economy, it was still not uncommon for these support lists to be published annually, listing the financial contributions by family name and amount. This practice continued in a variety of European American congregations into the mid-twentieth century. One middle-aged national leader remembers reading the posted annual list in the Reformed church where he grew up. Two national Catholic leaders also recalled that parishes would publish annual lists at the end of each year, as recently as the 1950s.

The publication provided for some humor, when, for example, one anonymous gift on the list might be claimed by thirty different church members.

Although the United States went through a shift from rural to urban during the twentieth century, with a shift to cash contributions becoming more usual than in-kind gifts, nevertheless, in-kind gifts continued well into this century. Herbert Mather remembered from his childhood that the pastor was often paid in "gunnysack contributions." When a church member butchered or canned garden produce, the results were shared with the minister. "Even in my first pastoral assignment, which was in 1960, I was paid $4,600 annually and without the gunnysack contributions, it would have been impossible. Even if you bought paint, for example, it was provided at a huge discount. It was a way for the businessman to show his support, even if he was from a different denomination. That was small town America in the 1930s, '40s and '50s."

In addition to subscription lists, the sale and rental of pews was another income source for congregations. The sale of pews had been controversial throughout the nineteenth century. One denomination, the Free Methodist Church, broke with the Methodist Episcopal Church over issues of freedom including slavery, the rights of women, and very explicitly the exclusion of the poor through the sale and rental of church pews. This approach to church funding was continued into the early twentieth century, at least until after World War I, although there was mounting public pressure against the practice throughout the late nineteenth century.

It appears that loose plate offerings, as opposed to pledges, were not widely used to fund the basic operation of the congregation until the early twentieth century. Before that, benevolences and the mission of the church were funded through these more spontaneous collection plate offerings, and the operation of the congregation was financed through some system of pledging. The tithe was implemented in some traditions but generally as a voluntary guideline instead of the enforced legal system that had supported the church in England and Europe.

Support for the voluntary missions offerings that supplemented pledges to the church operating budget was high. According to one source, after World War I benevolences averaged 30 percent of congregational activity among some denominations between 1919 through 1922. However, pastors reportedly felt overwhelmed with the task of being the main source of missions education for the congregation, in addition to the other pastoral responsibilities they had. As noted earlier, these complaints were one reason the unified budget system was introduced in the mid-1920s. By the late 1920s, data indicates benevolences had declined as both congregational expenses and building campaigns increased.[3]

Pledges and Commitments

The strong emphasis on pledging to meet the operations of the congregation apparently sowed seeds of deep resentment among church members that perennially appear in many churches. In interviews at the congregational level, the reaction to making a formal written commitment suggested a deep hostility on the part of some to the structure associated with a pledging system. One pastor strongly advised the Stewardship Project representatives to talk of "commitments" rather than use the word *pledging*. The church, she explained, had had a bad experience some thirteen years before and now refused to hear the term. One regional official responding to the Stewardship Project survey commented, "An older woman remarked in a meeting where I encouraged a Stewardship EMV [Every Member Visit], which includes statements of intention or pledges: 'God loves a cheerful giver. If I have to pledge, I won't be cheerful! So, I think we should not do it!'"

Other pastors suggested that church members resist making a financial pledge because they regard it as a debt to be paid. A completely new alternative, however, has not been found. Instead, there are variations on the theme. Some commercially available programs try to make the idea fun. The well-known "Pony Express" program introduces the title "Trail Boss" for the campaign coordinator, and congregation members drop off a bag of pledge cards in a "saddlebag" that is passed from household to household.

Others avoid the idea of a contractual commitment. For example, many congregations in the evangelical tradition now use the "Faith Promise." First developed by The Christian and Missionary Alliance founder, A. B. Simpson,[4] this approach asks the church member to pray about a possible commitment he or she feels led to make. The card that is filled out indicates that the person will contribute the money as the Lord provides for the person to do so. Thus the obligation in the arrangement is removed, and the emphasis is placed on a commitment made in faith.

Public commitments and social pressure to give may have eroded as congregations have made a transition from tightly knit groups to more heterogeneous communities. As Craig Dykstra noted, "Fewer and fewer people since the 1950s live in and stay in communities where they know each other." With the passing of such communities, the accountability associated with them has also seemed to fade.

Ethnic Congregations

A Filipino pastor, associated with a mainline communion, explained in an interview that he did not make use of stewardship resources available through that denomination. The pastor was asked what alternative stewardship approach was used in his church. He indicated that everyone in the congregation was aware how much money everybody else made. Thus when a need arose, whether for the ongoing operation of the church or a special need, there was a meeting after the service. No one left the gathering until that need had been funded. The wealthier people in the congregation knew that they were expected to cover a larger share of the need and most often volunteered, although occasionally social pressure was applied.

His next comment may provide insight into the present state of stewardship practices in many second-, third-, or many-generation European American congregations. The Filipino pastor lamented that the young people in his congregation did not share these community-held values. They were working in businesses that their elders were unfamiliar with, and thus the older people had no way of knowing how much money they made. Further, the younger people refused to tell their elders about their salaries, stating, "It is none of your business." The pastor noted sadly that if this trend continued, the congregation would have to start availing itself of stewardship techniques promoted through the denomination to replace the accountability that had been present in the community up to that point.

The same level of accountability appears to be present in Korean congregations. A young Korean pastor who came to the United States expressed shock at the lack of acceptance of the tithe as a basic standard of discipleship in the European American congregations he encountered. Even though he shared a denominational heritage with these congregations, there was little common agreement on financial stewardship standards. It had not occurred to him, he reported, that support of the church was optional.

As an Indian pastor described stewardship practices in India, it sounded similar to how the pastor of a rural church in the United States described stewardship practices of a generation ago in her congregation. In India, the elders visit each home monthly to pick up the church member's contribution, writing a receipt for the money that the church member gives to the elder. The pastor of the rural U.S. congregation explained that, in the past, the elders in her church would visit each family during the fall, asking them how much that family would be contributing to the operation of the congregation in the coming year. In both cases, leaders of the congregation met face-to-face with the church members to discuss their level of commitment.

African American churches also seem to have relied on a high level of community accountability to provide for the operations of the congregation. Experts suggest that African Americans had an added dimension to the local congregation, viewing it as a mutual aid association in addition to its role as a place of worship.[5] Giving has tended to be more public in those settings. In some congregations, a list of financial gifts, by name and amount, may be published each week in the bulletin. Offerings are not always taken by ushers; rather, the entire congregation may be asked to proceed in an orderly fashion to the front of the church, where the ushers stand over the offering plates. In some cases, the tithers are asked to stand and bring their gifts first, before the general congregation comes forward. After a prayer is said over those gifts, the tithers return to their seats as each row of remaining individuals goes forward. Thus social awareness once again plays a role in increasing the church member's accountability.

It appears that congregations that reflected some type of ethnic identity approached stewardship from a viewpoint of community accountability. James Williams, of Church of God (Anderson, Ind.) World Service, noted that his communion's giving patterns have not reflected as strong a downward trend as others apparently have. He attributed that situation in large part to the size of and attitude within the church. "Our size is always a factor. We are family. I can call almost every pastor by first name and can sign my letters 'Jim.' In all the states I can go and not be a stranger."

Al Taylor, director of stewardship for the Church of God (Cleveland, Tenn.), a Pentecostal communion that began in 1886, noted that his church worked hard in the past to maintain its boundaries. During the height of the charismatic movement, when many different people experienced the "charismata" attributed as gifts from the Holy Spirit, such as speaking in tongues and powers of healing, Al Taylor said many congregations in his communion would not accept these people because the gifts were not accompanied by an emphasis on personal holiness. The denomination is just over one hundred years old. Taylor observed that as the church moves into the third and fourth generations, there is an increasing emphasis on numbers of members. But, he went on, "Growth in attendance doesn't necessarily mean 'growth.' Pastors say, 'I can't afford to lose any people.' I say, if they've been here long enough to be trained and aren't stewards, let them go—you haven't lost anything. Let them go someplace else and take a free ride."

Taylor was familiar with one large church where the names of all tithers were published—not the amounts, just the names. A new pastor came in and stopped the practice, and the number of tithers shrank. When the next pastor came in, he reintroduced the practice of publishing tithers' names, and the list grew again. Taylor felt it was not the public recognition but the weekly accountability that really reinforced the giving. "Tithing and giving are equivalent to a regular rededication of oneself to God, somewhat akin to an altar call."

Where congregations changed to reflect the more heterogeneous and anonymous makeup of their communities, stewardship began to rely more on techniques rather than mutual accountability.

Although it appears that ethnic communities—whether European American or African American or Asian American—have a great deal in common in their attitude toward the support of the local congregation, that shared understanding does not necessarily extend to denominational structures. While some officials reported that Asian American communities tend to focus on their home countries to the exclusion of financial support through the U.S.–based denominational global mission channels, others reported strong support from Asian and Hispanic congregations for their mission outreach.

In the case of African American congregations, there are state associations for the African American Baptists, even as there are for Southern and American Baptists. However, unlike European American–based congregations, there appears to be little provision for African American Baptists to report their congregational finances to their denominational entity. Calls were made to national officials of a major African American Baptist denomination. The goal was to obtain records to be included in an analysis of church giving patterns, including the records of thirty other denominations in composite form. After several calls, the appropriate official was located. He replied that financial records are usually not available beyond the congregational level, even to the national denominational body. Other researchers report a similar finding.[6]

This highly localized attitude has implications for denominational structures that work to be inclusive. The American Baptist Churches in the U.S.A., for example, made a concerted effort in the post–civil rights era to involve African American Baptist congregations in their denominational structure. The recruitment effort has been successful on one level. By 1990, 18 percent of its congregations, and 39 percent of its membership, were in African American congregations that affiliated with the structure in the last few decades. However, support levels for the national American Baptist Mission Support denominational fund indicate that the African American membership provided only 3 percent of the income received by the national office in 1990.[7] The data suggests a different perception of the congregation-denomination relationship than has been common in many European American denominations. Noting the differences, American Baptist officials point out that African American churches are often aligned with more than one denomination and have often focused their mission dollars on local church mission projects rather than national structures.[8]

Officials in two other denominations were struck by the finding that stewardship expectations might be different among congregations with distinct ethnic identities. Comparing notes, both denominations, with strong mission emphasis as a key purpose of the denominational structure, found that they had actively increased the composition of their constituent congregations to 20 percent of other than European American ethnic identification, but that the congregations in that 20 percent gave no more than 2 percent of the denomination's income at the regional and national levels.

The Roman Catholic Church is posting membership increases in the United States. At the same time, there is some evidence that giving patterns may be stagnating or even declining. One former diocesan consultant suggested that membership growth may be coming in ethnic groups that are not educated about giving to the church structure on a voluntary basis. An example would be immigrants from Latin American countries where the Catholic Church has been the communion with the highest membership, and voluntary individual giving was not strongly taught.

On a local level, some ethnic congregations demonstrate a vitality and accountability in stewardship that is often not evident in other congregations. At the same time, it cannot be assumed that ethnic congregations share a commitment to the broader goals of the church-at-large, as represented in denominational structure support.

Crisis Fund-Raising

Because of the difficulties in raising funds, pastors have fallen into a stewardship approach that appears to have widespread application. A major strategy in use is crisis fund-raising.

One pastor said, "I actually enjoy the wolf at the door. It's the only time my people don't yell at me when I bring up the topic of money." Often in interviews, the pastor suggested people almost preferred this approach to pledging. Rather than an organized campaign, some pastors reported that people will often say, "Just let us know what the church needs, and the money will be there."

Crisis fund-raising can also be frustrating, though. One pastor spent several weeks educating the congregation about a denominational mission opportunity. When the offering time came, the offering was considerably below expectations. Soon after, the organ needed some work. The pastor found himself almost angry when brief announcements on two Sundays brought in more than enough for the repair work.

The attractive aspect of crisis fund-raising is that it works. The negative aspect is that it apparently reinforces some destructive giving patterns in the church. For example, crisis fund-raising educates church members that their money is their own until it is wrung out of them by some appealing need. People who are encouraged to respond to crises resist a transition to proportionate giving. Church members who have come to expect the next crisis may then distrust the church leadership's suggestion of proportionate giving, suspecting that another campaign or special offering will be announced after pledge time.

In addition, crisis fund-raising encourages a survival/maintenance mentality in the congregation. E. Earl "Scoop" Okerlund, who has served in various capacities of the national office of the Evangelical Lutheran Church in America, feels that "so many churches are in the survival mode. Keeping the church open is the goal." If paying the bills is the goal of stewardship, and it is not clear that the church has a constructive agenda beyond its approved operations, then it does not make sense to give the church extra money. Rather, the routine is to wait until the end of the year and see how much is needed to balance the budget and make sure all the bills are paid.

Pastors and regional officials responding to the Stewardship Project survey strongly confirmed that this approach is very common. More than 80 percent of both the pastors and regional officials agreed that "In most congregations, the goal of stewardship is defined as meeting the budget," as shown in figure 6.

One encounter gave a clear example of this mind-set. A leadership board had endorsed adoption of the Stewardship Project

Figure 6: Survey Observation #97

In most congregations, the goal of stewardship is defined as meeting the budget.

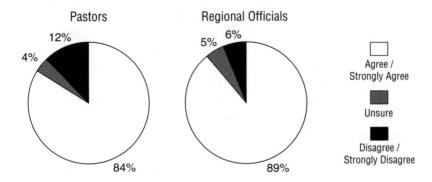

Details in the figures may not compute to 100% due to rounding.

budget discipline to increase missions giving in principle. Since they operated with congregational polity, Stewardship Project leaders were asked to come to a congregational meeting after worship on a Sunday. An outline of the project was given. The goal, the leadership board members pointed out, was to become organized so that the church would not have to focus on raising its budget but rather could focus on expanding its mission outreach. The floor was then opened for discussion. One lady rose and was quite incensed. "I don't know why we are talking about organizing the church. I've belonged to this church for thirty years. And each year in December, the church is short three thousand dollars, and each year in December we call an emergency congregational meeting and that need is met."

This mind-set does not appear to be a peculiarly Protestant dilemma either. John C. Haughey writes, "My observation of the Catholic community now is that it has developed the bad habit of connecting its collections merely with paying its bills."[9] Thomas Sweetser sounded a familiar theme: "Many are not thinking of giving back to the Lord. They are thinking more of funding the services provided by the congregation. Many Catholics think in terms of funding the program. They're paying for services."

In an informal poll of a group of Catholics who attended a stewardship workshop, the 102 pastors and pastoral team members and the 104 lay parish council or stewardship committee members were asked whether they agreed with various reasons why people were not giving. There was a strong response to the statement, "In the Catholic Church, giving as a percentage of income has declined because Catholics have not been educated/motivated to give in proportion to their means." Ninety-six percent of the priests and 91 percent of the laypeople agreed. There is a perceived need for moving beyond paying the bills to a more disciplined approach to giving.

Yet merely paying the bills is a dominant approach for many congregations. Dale Minnich of the Church of the Brethren General Services Commission indicated that especially those churches declining in numbers of members may be vulnerable to this thinking. "There's a growing pressure on individual congregations' budgets. A survival mentality results. Outreach gets squeezed. Global missions, without directly telling the story to church members, gets squeezed the most." Minnich went on, "One factor for some of it is that they are not catching the vision of the wider work. 'How inexpensively can we get this church run—if we increase 2 to 3 percent, surely that's enough.' What results is a tight budgeting mentality rather than what we feel called to do."

Piecemeal Fund-Raising

Piecemeal is another element of stewardship as it is currently practiced. Piecemeal fund-raising also teaches people that paying the bills is the goal of stewardship. Several national leaders interviewed suggest that people have not increased the portion of their income given because their money is not needed. Associating giving to the church with paying specific bills educates the church member that it is not necessary to give beyond the level at which all the bills of the church are paid.

In several workshops with leadership boards, the leaders were asked why they thought church members did not increase giving to the church. One response that was repeated in different settings was that people do not want to give the church one dollar more than it needs. Why not? "Because the church will just spend it." This answer has some serious implications for stewardship attitudes. Apparently people perceive the church as spending whatever comes in, rather than setting goals and funding them in an orderly fashion.

Al Taylor indicated he understood why congregation members might feel that way. "The fear is the next time they hear from you, you will have hatched more needs and bigger needs. People are getting worn out quickly. Giving is unto Christ. People don't know that—they think they're giving to the preacher. The preacher was given to them by Christ, as it says in Ephesians 4:11. Christ can do anything with the offering money. He's chosen to run his church with it. But he could burn it up. In the Old Testament he did it all the time. We're only horrified by that idea because we have bought into materialism."

Sometimes laypeople take matters into their own hands. Stewardship Project staff learned of more than one instance where the congregation had money stashed that only a few people knew about. In every case there was not a hint of illicit use of the money. Rather, the involved individuals thought they were protecting the church from itself.

For example, one congregation was asked to provide a complete listing of accounts as part of their participation in the Stewardship Project structured budget approach. The leadership board asked the treasurer to prepare the statement. Several weeks went by and the statement was not forthcoming. Another request was made and still the treasurer had not complied. Finally, after more time and a very clear directive, the treasurer produced a list of accounts. Imagine the surprise of both the pastor and the leadership board when they found an extra ninety thousand dollars invested in certificates of deposit that had not appeared on regular income and expenditure statements. It turned out that the treasurer had been depositing extra money over a period of time for a rainy day. The pastor, in describing the situation, could only think about the mission activities that had not been undertaken for lack of funds.

The person who handled the funds in another congregation arranged an internal loan from one account to another at the end of the year. When asked why, he explained that he was sure people in the congregation would not give if there were a surplus, so the loan allowed the financial statement to indicate a deficit.

One regional official estimated that 30 percent of the congregations in his area had resources in funds that only one or two people in the congregation knew about. The danger is that those people may not pass on the information to all those responsible for directing the congregation. Loren Mead, author and founder of the Alban Institute, has consulted with congregations all over the United States. He remembered one call he received from a pastor who asked him, "You help pastors starting out in new places, don't you? There's money here but I can't find it." Mead recruited a person to assist the pastor. They eventually found eight trusts, which had been established at different times in the past with gifts to the church, in four or five different banks. No one currently on the church leadership board knew about all of the funds, each of which had its own oversight rules. The banks were uncomfortable that no one from the church was managing the accounts, which by that time had grown to about six million dollars.

Of course many congregations would like to have such problems as hidden accounts. The more usual situation is that the pastor and leadership board do know what funds are available, and those funds are just not enough to cover what is needed to be done. To raise the money, church members are usually not challenged to give a portion of their incomes in response to grace; rather, they are asked to fund specific line items, sometimes one at a time.

A church member could well feel the church is constantly talking about and spending money when one reviews a list of typical requests throughout the year. In addition to the annual commitment campaign, it is not unusual to have additional requests for Sunday school offerings, annual women's group offering and fund-raising events, youth work trips, youth choir fund-raising events, special music programs, special mission projects (including the Christmas and Easter offerings), weekly flowers for the altar (as well as at Christmas and Easter), love gifts for special speakers or staff who are leaving, the radio program. These types of special offerings are in addition to crisis requests that may develop for emergency capital needs, new building projects, end-of-the-year shortfall or cash-flow crises, retired religious staff needs, or relief requests for national disasters. One Catholic leader suggested that people often do not know what the "second envelope offering" is being collected for, whether the diocese or the Pope or some other activity. Another source suggested there might be as many as thirty-two of these special offerings a year. It is not at all unusual to arrive in a Protestant congregation and find an additional envelope in the bulletin with an announcement about a special collection.

Perhaps in response to these many requests, church members have developed, to a startling degree, a desire for the church not to have more money than it needs. One regional official commented about the mysterious way church budgets are met. "I'm amazed at the corporate animal that is able to meet the exact amount." He recalled one congregation that had a special Sunday offering with a goal of $27,500. The actual cash offering that Sunday was $27,350—only $150 short. The official said that he could not help feeling that someone must have been cheating to have come so close to the goal without going over. In another instance, the congregation knew that there was $30,000 in reserve. The special campaign to raise $100,000 actually resulted in pledges of $73,000, missing the goal by just about the amount in the reserve account.

When piecemeal and crisis fund-raising are in operation, the atmosphere is not conducive to telling church members that giving to the church ought to be a response to God's grace in their lives. It is hard for a pastor to promote a view of grateful response when there is a distrust, ingrained by crisis fund-raising, that the church is not capable of handling money beyond that needed to pay the bills. The simplest arithmetic indicates that church members moving from present giving levels of about 2.5 percent to proportionate giving of 5 percent or the classic 10 percent would produce a great deal more money than the church presently needs to operate its budget. The church has not communicated a larger compelling goal that would absorb any excess funds, such as global missions or domestic frontier missions used to provide. The church has not shown itself able to plan a strategy to provide for its own needs even while planning to impact domestic and world need funded through a faithful response from the mem-

bers. Rather, the church has presented itself as emphasizing one
need after another.

The church has generally represented stewardship in a topi-
cal fashion, meeting this budget need or that special offering or
this emergency. The focus is on the need to be met, the services
rendered by the congregation, or the item that appeals to the
donor's fancy, rather than on a grateful demonstration of the grace
the donor has experienced, and the church as God's agent for
changing a hurting world. So church people respond as they are
asked to respond, piecemeal to a variety of disparate causes, and
the church stays at maintenance levels.

In summary, denominations face a different situation in the
latter twentieth century than they have previously. As congregations place a higher priority on issues of comfort rather than mission, as denominations strive to be more inclusive, and as privatization of religion replaces traditional cultural community
standards, denominational structures in the United States are
under stress.

Many of the changes have resulted in declining financial support from church members. Regardless of the structure or theological perspective of the national denomination, evidence indicates that church-member giving as a percentage of after-tax
income is declining across the board. The mainline Protestant
communions that are losing membership, evangelical denominations that are growing in membership, as well as Catholic dioceses all report financial stress.

How can this be, when "all the church talks about is money"?

7

Money as a Topic

Take my lips and let them be
Filled with messages for Thee;
Take my silver and my gold,
Not a mite would I withhold,
Not a mite would I withhold.

Frances R. Havergal, 1874
"Take My Life and Let It Be"

"We do not discuss money in this church." The gentleman in the suit was chair of the finance committee. The Stewardship Project staff, at the invitation of the pastor, had come to make a presentation about giving patterns and to discuss the congregation's potential for increasing its mission outreach. This gentleman seemed agitated throughout the evening and finally spoke up during the question period. "What gives you the right to come in here and talk to us like this?" he went on coldly.

At the time, his response to a presentation about increased faithfulness through giving came as a shock. Having seen the slide set at a regional meeting, the pastor thought the presentation would be good for his church. He believed the people were capable of a great deal more than they were doing and he saw that they were merely going about the business of the congregational operation with little excitement. The Stewardship Project staff had shared the pastor's hopeful attitude and were a little taken aback by this challenge. There was some fumbling for an appropriate response until the pastor came to the rescue. "They're here because I invited them. I wanted them to raise the topic of your stewardship potential because you won't discuss it with me."

127

"Of course we won't," the finance committee chair responded crisply. "We had a bad experience with money seventeen years ago, and we have not let anyone discuss it since."

At first blush, it's easy to wonder what their finance committee meetings were like if the "M word" was never discussed. Obviously the finance committee chair did not mean that dollars and cents were never talked about in these meetings. What could this gentleman be saying then?

Additional experiences began to suggest a distinction in language, one that would prove critical to an increased understanding of money dynamics in the church. When the finance committee chair was saying that money was not discussed in his church, he did not mean nobody talked about paying the bills. Churches often talk about money in terms of how much is needed to meet a particular crisis or to end the year in the black. So we now propose that when church members—or even worse, potential church members—utter the dreaded phrase, "All the church ever talks about is money," what they mean is they *feel* like the church talks far too often about paying some bill or collecting special offerings.

In reality we found a definite prejudice in the church against talking about money as a spiritual concept, about its discipleship aspects, its lifestyle implications, and church members' own individual giving patterns. As John C. Haughey has written, "It's not like faith to be silent, but in the presence of money it has learned to accept a monologue."[1] Thus a finance committee meeting could consist of three hours of talk about balancing the budget and yet entirely avoid the topic of whether church members are authentically responding to God's grace in their lives through their giving patterns.

Stewardship Sermons

This resistance to a more general discussion of money appears to be quite strong, based on experiences shared by pastors in interviews. For example, one pastor described being told in his first interview with the congregational leadership board that the congregation expected one money sermon a year. Another pastor was inspired to preach what he thought was a powerful stewardship sermon in March. One of the congregation leaders made a special effort to inform the pastor that he had given a fine sermon—except that it belonged in September, not in the spring.

A third pastor was enthusiastic about stewardship. A tither himself, he felt that it was his responsibility to keep the possibility of good stewardship before the congregation. He would therefore preach stewardship sermons when he felt it appropriate, regardless of the time of year. He would do this in spite of the fact that an older man, who faithfully sat near the front of the church each Sunday, would stand up at the first mention of money in the sermon and walk out the long aisle in full view of the entire congregation. This gentleman explained to the pastor that he felt money was a topic totally inappropriate for the church.

Bishop William McManus said that he thinks it is "very distressful for some young priests to deal with money. These young priests don't seem to know that the Gospels and talking about money are compatible."

Thomas Sweetser, S.J., of the Parish Evaluation Project, works with a variety of Catholic parishes as a consultant. He felt that the pastor is the key person in a congregation to come to terms with stewardship. "It's the pastor, nobody else. It has to be the pastor who can pull it off," he commented, "no one else can." Yet his experience has been that people get angry if someone tries to put a specific figure on what is appropriate to give. Their likely response will be, "What right have you got to tell me?" Sweetser feels that the authority of the church has been eroded to some degree, and more and more Catholics are making up their own minds about a number of issues. They may see the church as offering guidelines, but there is a lot of individual formation. As a result, the church feels reluctant to tell people what to do in the area of finances.

Wesley K. Willmer, vice president of university advancement at Biola University and board chair of the Christian Stewardship Association (CSA), spoke about a similar trend among evangelicals. "We often put ourselves first and God second. It's a historical problem. Pastors are not trained, so they seldom know what to say and [when they do know] are afraid to say it." Willmer feels that Christians, including evangelicals, have been separating areas of life, with little connection between faith and money.

When asked what pastors might be afraid of when talking about money, Willmer suggested they might hear, "My money is none of your business." He has heard people coming out of church services complaining that "the pastor has no business saying anything that has to do with my money."

Robert Wood Lynn pointed out that, historically, laypeople resisted the leadership of their clergy in the area of money. Thomas Sweetser and Wes Willmer suggested that the trend continues into the present. This resistance may be an important reason why, as Robert Wuthnow observed, the church is not speaking clearly about stewardship. In a national survey, he found that fewer than half of those church members surveyed had heard a stewardship sermon in the past year. "And even among those who attend religious services every week, a bare majority (57 percent) have heard such a sermon." This finding seemed strange when pastors are generally expected to preach at least one stewardship sermon a year. He suggested that perhaps people stay home on Stewardship Sunday. "Or perhaps clergy find it so awkward to talk about stewardship that parishioners don't realize it when the topic is being discussed."[2]

One minister confirmed that there may be a communication problem between clergy and laypeople. She came to a congregation that was having financial problems and so in the previous year had preached three sermons on stewardship. She confessed she was surprised, therefore, when her leadership board asked her to preach a stewardship sermon in hopes that people would help pay the bills. Taken aback, she asked these regular attenders, "Well, how many stewardship sermons do you think I've preached in the last year?" "None," they responded. As she told the story, the minister noted she was embarrassed at the sermon she preached the next Sunday. "I felt crass. I felt like I was talking to a junior high class," she said. Her sermon thesis was basically "If you want this church here, give your money." The offering was up by quite a bit that Sunday, and several people thanked her for the good sermon.

Other pastors report that businesspeople tell the pastor they have to deal with money matters all week; they come to church, they inform the pastor, to deal with more spiritual issues.

It appears that ministers must walk a careful line between "My money is none of your business" and "Give money or the church will close" balanced with "The church is always talking about money." Ministers must do this with little or no formal stewardship training.

Resistance to the Topic

Pastors who want to address the topic of money are not unique in finding opposition. Laypeople also were surprised at the resistance they met when trying to introduce the topic of money and giving patterns to other members of the church. In one congregation, a committee was formed to implement the Stewardship Project structured budget approach and the related education efforts. The main focus was to raise additional money for missions. In fact, the approach was titled "The National Money for Missions Program"; so most of the members of the committee thought it was logical to call the committee the Money for Missions Committee. Time was spent in the first meeting discussing the objections of one committee member who thought the word *money* was inappropriate in the title of a church committee; besides, would people rule out other types of stewardship if they included that word? Another name was found so the committee could be about its business.

Interestingly it may be more difficult to talk about money on a personal level in church than anyplace else. According to the survey conducted by Robert Wuthnow, 82 percent of those who attended religious services every week never or hardly ever discussed their personal finances with friends, 88 percent had not talked with fellow workers about it, 93 percent had not had such conversations with members of the clergy, and 95 percent had not talked to fellow congregation members.[3] The experience of one lady who talked with Stewardship Project staff seemed to provide a painful example of how true this finding is.

This quiet woman wanted to share with longtime friends in the congregation some of the ideas she had learned through a workshop about giving patterns and missions-support potential of the church. However, her friends refused to read the materials she gave them. The woman expressed that she was hurt by their unwillingness to even read materials she found exciting. In reflecting on her experience, she had what she called an "awful thought" in response to their reaction. What if she stood up in front of the congregation and tore every hymn out of the hymn-book that spoke of commitment? She guessed she would end up with half the hymns torn out. What would be the reaction of people in church, we asked. Another person present suggested they would "haul her off to the loony bin." She smiled and thought a moment and then decided they would probably criticize her for destroying church property.

The church might be a more hostile environment toward money than society in general. A regional official came across a letter in his office files from a professional who had been hired some years before to train selected church women in conducting a regional stewardship survey. Apparently the ladies being trained had been told they would be contacting a certain number of people, because they became quite upset when the consultant told them they would have to call on more. Although the consultant was making very good money, according to the regional official, the letter indicated she would rather quit than be subjected to the attacks she received from these ladies, the likes of which she'd never experienced in the nonreligious world!

Money is perhaps the only sacred topic left in Western culture, as Jacques Ellul suggested when he wrote,

> [F]or modern man money is one of his "holy things." Money affairs are, as we well know, serious business for modern man. Everything else—love and justice, wisdom and life—is only words. Therefore we avoid speaking of money. We speak of business, but when, in someone's living room, a person brings up the topic of money, he is committing a social error, and the resulting embarrassment is really expressing the sense of the sacred.[4]

Nordan Murphy thought this point well illustrated by the fate of Howard Stern's political campaign in 1994. It seems shock radio personality Stern—who has thought nothing of sharing all kinds of information over the airwaves, including details not only of his own sex life but also that of his parents—withdrew his bid to be governor of the State of New York because he felt that a financial disclosure statement was too personal an item to be discussed in public.[5]

Indeed, a pastor related an experience in counseling a couple on the verge of divorce. This couple shared such intimate details that a less-trained professional might have been embarrassed. Yet no reconciliation was evident. The pastor, therefore, suggested they talk about the couple's finances and any tensions that might be present there. The couple finally had something to agree on: They informed the pastor most firmly that the counseling sessions would end immediately if they were forced to share anything as personal as their money.

Perhaps, as Daniel Conway, secretary for planning, communication and development of the Archdiocese of Indianapolis, mused, there are broader spiritual implications to the present situation. "In a way, if the devil were thinking about this, probably the smartest thing he could say would be, 'Let's create a taboo about talking about money in the church.' Then financial issues would never be compared to Christian life. We'd never ask what do the creed and the Beatitudes have to do with the stuff of life in America in the 1990s."

What the Pastor Knows

This silence can have implications for the pastor's ability to minister. Although more than three-quarters of the pastors and regional officials responding to the Stewardship Project survey agreed that "the pastor's knowledge of what individual members give to the church can be a helpful assessment tool of individual members' spiritual health"; more than three-quarters of them also agreed that "most church members do not want the pastor to know how much individual members contribute to the church." Knowledge of giving may be a helpful spiritual tool, but it is not one readily available to most pastors (see figures 7a and 7b).

The issue of the pastor knowing or not knowing what people give is controversial, both at the lay and the ministerial levels. Some pastors resist knowing because, they say, they are afraid that it will influence their treatment of parishioners. In one Stewardship Project workshop, a pastor challenged his colleague on this point. "Do you feel you can treat parishioners fairly when some share personal moral aberrations with you? Why, then, would information about their giving practices have an inordinate influence over you?"

Another pastor of a large church had a more immediate reason. "As a pastor, I have access to figures on individual giving. I

Figure 7a: Survey Observation #7

The pastor's knowledge of what individual members give to the church can be a helpful assessment tool of individual members' spiritual health.

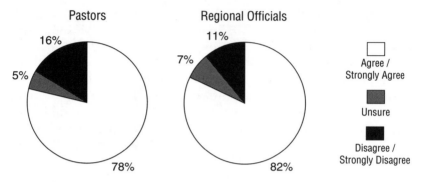

Details in the figures may not compute to 100% due to rounding.

Figure 7b: Survey Observation #49

Most church members do not want the pastor to know how much individual members contribute to the church.

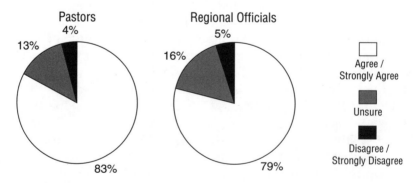

Details in the figures may not compute to 100% due to rounding.

stopped looking at it years ago because my stomach couldn't take it. I see where both members of a couple are working, their kids are grown, and the house is paid for, and they feel if they are giving five dollars a week, they are doing well. There are too many of these."

Other pastors indicated that their denominations do not have a formal position on the subject, and yet they were given the impression at the seminary level that it was inappropriate for them to know what people give.

Several national leaders of Protestant denominations said that the pastor not knowing what was given is deeply ingrained in their culture. "It's not written down," said Robert Welsh of the Christian Church (Disciples of Christ). "It's in our bloodstream."

Elsie Holderread of the Church of the Brethren national office observed, "It's almost a dogma of the Church of the Brethren" that giving remain anonymous. James Austin, vice president of the Southern Baptist Convention Stewardship Commission, commented, "I don't think anybody in our churches knows what anybody gives. People resent anybody knowing. One campaign designed by the national offices asked people to openly witness about their giving, and that was real hard for them." Hugh Magers spoke of a "prejudice in The Episcopal Church that no one should know except the treasurer. There is anger about the idea of clergy knowing."

In his experience, Magers said he believes that the clergy who do know what people in their congregations give are better teachers on stewardship. And yet it is not easy to provide that kind of leadership. "Terrible pressure is brought to bear that no one know," he said. "Episcopalians will tell you astounding things about their sexuality but not talk at all about their financial life."

James Williams agreed. "When pastors tell me they do not know about the giving level of people in their churches, I push them to the wall and ask, 'Why not?' They'll say, 'I couldn't stand up and preach if I knew.' 'Oh, no?' I respond, 'I've had people come in and tell me all kinds of stories that would make the hair stand up on my head—if I had any—all sorts of immorality. Does that mean I can't preach on it?' This issue is an important spiritual topic."

Williams and many of the other church leaders who were interviewed felt that giving levels are an important indicator of church members' spiritual condition. But changing the secretiveness of the culture is not easy. Robert Welsh described the training experiences he's had as he worked with pastors. "We go out saying the pastor *should* know, and laypeople don't agree. And the resistance is so strong the pastors begin to believe they shouldn't know. Pastors may say, 'I have someone making hundreds of thousands of dollars and giving one dollar, and I don't need to know.'"

This controversy has been going on throughout the history of the church in the United States, according to Robert Wood Lynn. He has begun to wonder if pastors do not feel comfortable knowing because of the implications of what they find out: "Is it a judgment on their own work?"

Timothy Ek is now vice president of The Evangelical Covenant Church. As part of his denominational leadership, he said, "I am emphasizing through seminars that pastors should know what people give. That's bucking the implicit and explicit trend in traditional seminary education, where we were taught that the pastor should not know." He remembers being a seminary student in the late 1960s and early 1970s. A professor of practical theology taught that the pastor should not know because knowing what people give will influence you. Pastors who know will kowtow to the rich and ignore the poor was the theory.

These many years later, Ek definitely does not agree with that perspective. When he tried to live out that perspective as a pastor, he found it was not practical. For example, he found out that many of the biggest troublemakers in the church did not give to the church financially. He concluded as a pastor that if people were not investing their money in the congregation, he was not obligated to listen to their complaints about how the congregation operated.

A more theoretical aspect of the ministry also helped to change Ek's mind. "As a pastor, I can be trusted to know deep violations of the Christian walk. People can trust me to be a friend, to extend Christ's forgiveness. Therefore, I can also be trusted with this knowledge about giving. It is a key area, because of the weight of Jesus' teaching on this topic. Jesus recognized that commitment to 'things' challenges his lordship. I think what people give is a sign of spiritual maturity. It's important to stop and ask our-selves, both as individuals and as a church, how much do we give to missions and how much do we keep to help ourselves?"

Interestingly, the topic, though extremely controversial in Protestant churches, has not been an issue in the Roman Catholic Church. The priest has always had access to that information. Ray Coughlin noted that many priests are simply not interested in the information. Yet he does not believe parishioners mind. "Catholics like the fact that their giving is between them and their priest."

Various Protestants are trying to demystify the area as well. James Powell commented, "As I look back on my years as a pas-tor, I could have preached a lot more effectively if I had known—rather than [supplying] an 'oatmeal gospel,' where I hoped that everyone will take a spoonful."

Ron Voss, both an Evangelical Lutheran Church in America pastor and active on the synod committee for stewardship, gets a weekly report of the giving of the members of his congregation. "Like a doctor needs a complete physical profile, including tests, your giving is part of your spiritual profile." Asked about the fear that some pastors may handle the information poorly, Ronald Voss observed, "The information always has to be used with dis-cretion and wisdom. A couple of pastors may misuse it, but that should not preclude most clergy using the information in a responsible way."

In spite of a professed desire on the part of many pastors not to know what people give, the ministers inevitably develop impres-sions that lead to operating assumptions. David McCreath, national staff for the Presbyterian Church (U.S.A.), spoke of a workshop he attended for pastors with three to five years of expe-rience. The workshop leader asked the pastors present to line up between two pieces of furniture. Then the leader asked the par-ticipants to move toward one piece of furniture if they thought the pastor should know what people give to the church and toward the other if the pastor should not know. As the pastors gathered, most went to the side saying the pastor should not know. Then the leader asked the participants to move toward one of the pieces of furniture if they would be willing to identify potential large donors for a special denominational campaign and toward the other if they would not be willing. Now all the pastors crowded around the space reserved for those who said they would be willing to identify potential large donors. How, McCreath asked the pastors, could the pastor know whom to identify if the pastor did not have an idea who were generous givers to the church? The pastors suggested that they could sort of guess, based on conversations with or behavior of various parishioners, or perhaps they could review donor lists to the United Way or the local art museum. McCreath pressed the workshop participants further. "If these church members don't care that these secular groups know how much they give, why is church different?" The pastors explained, "That's a matter of faith."

After this illustration, McCreath reviewed the position of the staff at the national office. The general consensus was that the pastor should know what people give. They summarized their position as, "Yes, your giving is between you and God. It *is* personal, but it is not private."

Consequences of the Pastor's Lack of Knowledge

On a practical level, pastors generally do form opinions about who are givers and who are not. Those opinions are often based on general impressions instead of facts. One pastor shared about a complaining member of the leadership board. This individual tried to counter many of the creative moves the pastor wanted to introduce in the congregation. Through a series of events, the pastor received a copy of the congregational contribution list. He found himself shocked that this loud complainer gave virtually nothing to the church. It was at that point the pastor realized that he had put up with the complaints because he had *assumed* this individual was a large donor.

The pastor's lack of knowledge can also have other consequences. A middle-aged pastor remembered his laborer father as a faithful giver to the church. From his earliest childhood, the pastor remembered his father emphasizing the importance of faithfully giving 10 percent of the household income to God through the church. The family sometimes had to eat thin soup yet they never failed to tithe their income.

There was also a wealthy man in that church who only rarely attended and gave even more rarely, often on special occasions. The pastor remembered one particular worship service when his childhood minister announced with great joy that this wealthy man had decided to donate such-and-such amount for a special capital project at the church. As the minister went on with praise for this special gift, the pastor telling the story said he looked at his laborer father and saw pain on his face. The one-time capital gift that created such excitement, even though it was probably a small portion of the wealthy man's income, was smaller than his father's annual tithe. Yet the sacrifices of his father to insure year-round faithfulness in their family giving had gone entirely unacknowledged. The pastor telling the story said he knew his father was not giving to get credit. Yet the minister's lack of knowledge about the giving patterns in the church led to at least one faithful giver in the congregation feeling deeply hurt.

Other pastors report that they have met active resistance when they tried to find out what people gave. In one congregation, the financial secretary kept the records and refused a direct request by the pastor to share the information. As one pastor observed, "I'd have to be sure of my authority before I asked for the records, because I would not want it to be the secretary's decision."

The topic of money is sometimes actively separated from the clergy's ministry among the members. We live in a culture, however, that is preoccupied with money. We respect people who have it and write whole television series about how they make it and spend it. While church members hear one sermon a week on average, they are exposed to about sixteen hundred commercials every day,[6] on billboards and bus seats, in newspapers and magazines, on matchbooks and clothes with designer and product logos, on radio and television, each offering advice on how to spend their money. What is the church's responsibility for guiding them through this cacophony of opportunities?

Spiritual Aspects of Money

Jesus spent a great deal of time establishing that our relationship to the material world has strong spiritual implications. Wesley Willmer says that seventeen of the thirty-eight parables are

about possessions. His review of the number of times various topics were mentioned in the Bible indicated that *believe(ers), (ing)*
appeared 272 times, *prayer* 371 times, *love* or *loving* 714 times,
with *possessions* and *giving* appearing 2,172 times.[7]

Howard Dayton, founder of the Crown Ministries small-group
Bible study network that focuses on financial discipleship, suggested, "The reason Jesus talked so much about money is that it
competes with God for lordship of our lives. Our relationship to
money has an impact on the level of intimacy we have with Christ,
as suggested in Luke 16:11 ['So if you have not been trustworthy in handling worldly wealth, who will trust you with true
riches?']. True wealth is having a deeper relationship with Christ."

Stewardship Training

Into this money-dominated arena, the minister arrives vastly
unprepared. Sitting in a northern Indiana church building, the
pastor expressed surprise and embarrassment that two laypeople
did not show up to meet with the Stewardship Project staff, who
had driven five hours to meet with them. (Over time we learned
not to take such "no-shows" personally and developed low attendance expectations if the pastor had used the word "stewardship"
to invite people to a meeting!) In the conversation that followed
with the embarrassed pastor, he talked about his frustration with
his congregation's attitude toward money and the church. Asked
what training he had received to guide his congregation from
their starting point into a more constructive attitude, the minister replied he had not received any relevant training at seminary.
He was trying to cope as best he could.

Today the fact that pastors do not receive stewardship training in seminary seems to be general knowledge. However, several years ago it came as quite a shock. After that first conversation, Stewardship Project staff began to ask pastors, "What did
you learn in seminary about stewardship?" And the answer,
repeatedly, was "Nothing. Everything I know I've picked up since
then."

Given the hostility with which a visiting presentation on giving patterns had been greeted by that one finance committee
chair, it was clear the issue of money was not an easy one to

broach in congregations. With no training, how could pastors change this deeply embedded pattern? And given the resistance on the part of congregations, why would pastors even try?

A Difficult Topic

Money is a difficult topic for Americans in general, including church people. Americans seem to enjoy the effects of money, but the topic itself remains awkward in this culture. For example, some visitors from the People's Republic of China reported it was interesting that Americans are offended if asked, "How much money do you make?"—a perfectly usual question in China.

This reluctance to discuss money is not rooted in a Christian perspective, given how often Jesus brought up the topic in the parables. Yet these attitudes are often expressed in churches, as evidenced by a comment quoted in an article about one successful congregation: "'We never get a money sermon,' one member boasted."[8] Scoop Okerlund recounted, "I've had pastors tell me with *pride*, 'I have never preached a sermon on money.' I now ask them, 'Don't you care about the spiritual well-being of your people?'"

Howard Dayton voiced a similar perspective. "The church has not appreciated the spiritual impact of money on the believer, and so the church has immature believers."

Indeed, there is an acknowledgment in many circles that money is *the key* reality in our culture. Director Spike Lee appears as himself in the documentary *Hoop Dreams*. The top high school basketball players in the nation have been gathered at a Nike basketball camp. He tells the students not to be misled—the schools are interested in them for their basketball talent because the schools make a lot of money from winning teams. "This whole thing is revolving around money."[9]

And yet pastors and church leaders are proud that "We've never had a sermon on money." How relevant, then, can the church be in this culture?

In practice, functional gnosticism describes the way Christianity is presented in the United States. As the businesspeople informed the pastor, the church is seen as a haven from the practical, dirty reality of everyday life. Douglas Johnson and George

Cornell, in their conclusions drawn from the more than three thousand interviews conducted with church leaders in the early 1970s, note, "As the study brings out, however, lay people don't demonstrate an active congruity between their high religious attestations about giving and their substantive participation in it."[10] Haughey writes on the topic, "A split consciousness deals with financial and material resource issues with one part of its consciousness. . . . The fact is most of us are working both sides of the street and doing so as if each of us were more than one person." He points to "the epistemological schizophrenia, or even the hypocrisy in this kind of behavior."[11]

The Pastor's Problems with Money

The fact that the clergy share the broader cultural view of not talking about money has direct implications for the financial health of the church. The problem is recognized in other areas of the church as well. "I believe every pastor who knows the Bible knows Jesus talked about money," said James Powell. "The pastor will say, 'I should preach more on it; I don't.' We expect God to take care of the situation without any effort on our part. We expect people to just know."

Another reason pastors find it difficult to discuss money may be that they are as vulnerable to a consumer culture as their members. National leaders in three different denominations, ranging from mainline to evangelical, suggested that in their personal lives a majority of pastors are in financial arrears. One of the national denominational executives believes that many of the pastors have never been trained to handle money, so they have trouble handling their personal finances. Robert Wood Lynn suggested the situation is even more complex. The pastor's lack of enough money for personal needs has been a problem in every generation, he said. Of course, this situation is aggravated by a lack of training in the area. Another subject for concern that is only starting to receive attention, he noted, is that some Protestant clergy leave seminary carrying education debts. His concern was echoed in an article titled "Re-Engineering the Seminary": "A recent survey by the Center for the Study of Theological Education at Auburn Seminary found that 22 percent of 1991 M.Div.

graduates had borrowed $10,000 or more by the time they graduated."[12] Pastors just starting out often receive low salaries and if they have a large debt as well, they find it difficult to manage their personal finances. One pastor commented, "You can be depressed by economic debt for a long time." In that communion's ordination service, there is a question that goes something like, "Are you in so much debt as to compromise your ministry?" "There's always a chuckle," this pastor explained, "because you should say 'yes' but you have to answer 'no' as the right answer."

Given this combination of factors, a pastor finds it difficult to lead parishioners into the responsible use of personal money when his or her own checkbook cannot balance.

If a pastor is having difficulty managing personal finances, it may well have implications for his or her public ministry. David Schmidt, a marketing and management consultant who has worked with churches and parachurch groups, observed, "The pastor has to model stewardship based on personal experience. It's really an integrity issue." A Southern Baptist assistant regional minister, David Wheeler, agreed: "I don't think people will give unless the pastor leads as an example." But there is no guarantee that people will give if the minister does. Several clergy reported that, when the church financial secretary prepared a giving tree indicating how many households gave in various dollar ranges, these ministers were in the top five or six households. This often discouraged the pastors, since they were confident their salary would not place them in the top five or six households of the congregation.

While there is no guarantee that people will give if the pastor does, there does seem to be a perception that the majority of people will not give if the pastor does not. Logically the pastor is not going to feel comfortable urging percentage giving or increased giving if the pastor is resistant to the idea on a personal level. However, some pastors have developed creative ways of thinking about the topic. Nordan Murphy remembered how many pastors had told him, "I'm already giving. I'm giving time—more than forty hours, more than anyone in this church." That time seemed to absolve these ministers from giving more of their incomes.

Al Taylor explained how a similar attitude developed in his communion. When the denomination was starting, pastors received a portion of the income of the church, rather than a fixed salary. Since a tithe of the church's income was sent to the denominational office, many pastors regarded that tithe as their personal contribution, since they would otherwise have kept the money as salary. However, when the churches grew large enough to pay a salary to the ministers, many pastors continued to view the church's tithe to the denomination as their giving. In discussing this idea with pastors, Taylor will say, "You're telling me, a layman, everything you've told me about tithing is not true. Do you believe the Scriptures? If not, how can you preach salvation? If so, don't you need to be blessed by giving a tithe of your resources?"

When people enter the ministry, they know they will not be making as much money as they might have made pursuing other career paths. They have chosen a different road than the majority of their parishioners. It may be difficult for the pastor to turn around and feel comfortable with the very topic of money he or she has, in effect, rejected through his or her professional choice. Also the pastor may have unresolved feelings about money, his or her own family's relationship to it, and the feelings and relationships of the members in the congregation. Interestingly in a study conducted by Dan Conway, although 85 percent of the pastors expressed dissatisfaction with the seminary education they had received on these practical topics, fewer than 25 percent expressed interest in continuing education in this area of study.[13]

Attitudes about Money and Spirituality

Though most pastors seem to reflect the same distaste as laypeople for the topic of money, differences were noticed in the Stewardship Project among their attitudes toward giving. On several occasions, pastors referred to the publication of a list of annual donations by amount rather than by the donor's name as part of a stewardship campaign, reporting they were surprised to find themselves among the top givers. The study that involved more than three thousand interviews with church leaders in the United States and Canada during the early 1970s found a similar pattern. The report noted a difference between clergy and lay members as they think about money. Laypeople were less likely "to equate financial support of the church with a sense of closeness to God," as judged by their rating of the idea in a list of church-related factors. In contrast, pastors placed it second, "suggesting that they are more keenly conscious of the deeply interwoven, interacting links between man's material and spiritual commitments."[14]

James Hudnut-Beumler referred to the view of German sociologist and economist Max Weber as he considered the worldview clergy may bring to their ministries. "The greatest obstacle is that pastors, along with nuns and religious order brothers, actually think differently about religion than people in the pew. There's a differing mentality, a divide. Max Weber argued that there were normal people and there were 'religious virtuosi.' For the 'virtuosi' God is so real and religion is so important, they must commit their lives to it. Most clergy fit into that category at some point in their lives. For some lay leaders—those who become involved in regional/national boards, missions activity—what they do in the name of Jesus is more important than their jobs as well." That "divide" need not limit the minister's ability to lead, according to Hudnut-Beumler. Being aware of it, the pastor can make a point to build bridges. "If leaders want to lead people to see things their way, not just tell people how they [the leaders] see the world, then they need to get into conversation and, through the process of dialogue, get to a more coherent view of what it means to be a Christian."

In a consumer culture, the expectation that the minister and family do not have the same aspirations as the rest of the membership is a special strain. Ministers have traditionally lived a different lifestyle. Francis Asbury, the early Methodist bishop, had a "mite" fund for the support of the church's preachers. Maximum subscriptions were one dollar, reportedly because he thought it best for pastors to remain too poor to marry, thus to be free to concentrate on their higher calling in life.[15]

Author Julio de Santa Ana suggests a division was present in the church as early as the second century between "ordinary believers," who sought to "compromise between the demands of faith and the styles of life around them," and others who responded "with no concessions to context, thus trying to maintain the fundamental demands of faith."[16] By the time Emperor Constantine declared Christianity to be the official religion of the empire in A.D. 313, the church was on two tracks: those who sought rigorous faithfulness to the demands of the gospel, and those who were willing to accept a degree of compromise with the dominant social order. Without the entire church agreed on the level of intensity needed to pursue the overarching agenda, there was also a compromise in how the mission of the church was to be defined.

> The struggle to eradicate poverty as such ceased to exist, and was replaced by ways of alleviating the suffering of the poor. . . . This solution to the problem was to be decisive in the Church's response to the challenge of the poor and poverty in the centuries which followed. The intention was to relieve the suffering of the victims of injustice rather than to present a radical witness to the justice of God.[17]

The Pastor's Salary

Combining a general sense of rejection of the world with a societal attitude that keeps the spiritual and temporal separate leaves a difficult path for clergy to follow. The added difficulty is that clergy bring to the task all the human hopes and dreams and desires as those cherished by people in the pew. For some pastors this is not a serious problem. The church pays well and/or a spouse has a good job. For many others, the denominational structure provides for pension benefits and health care. Yet many pastors commented on the stress of balancing lifestyle concerns with the role of spiritual leader of the flock. This can add to the minister's burden of leadership.

The expectation that the pastor's role requires a humble lifestyle may stem directly from Asbury's early proposition in U.S. history or from an even older view that those set apart to lead the church often experience life from a different perspective than the general church population. In either case, the attitude that pastors are somehow exempt from lifestyle aspirations continues to be prevalent in many circles.

Certainly the pastor is expected to be of high moral character. The statement in the Stewardship Project survey registering the strongest response among the pastors was "In instances where immoral behavior occurs on the part of the pastor, such behavior has no significant effect on the level of giving in the congregation." Ninety-four percent disagreed, as shown in figure 8.

Pastors are expected to live a cut above in personal morality, and that appears to extend to their attachment to worldly goods. Yet this latter expectation is not without its struggles.

One successful pastor was confused by a flash of anger he experienced when his son, two weeks after college graduation, obtained a job that offered a higher salary level to start than the pastor expected to make throughout his career. This was true even though the father had received several years of education beyond college.

One minister responding to a survey conducted by a regional office of the Christian Church (Disciples of Christ) commented, "Even if you're not struggling to pay the bills, you may feel tension if you are expected to dress, entertain, educate your children, et cetera, like the more affluent parishioners."[18]

Hugh Magers, in his capacity as director of stewardship for The Episcopal Church, has worked directly with clergy in their attempts to come to terms with stewardship. He observed that

Figure 8: Survey Observation #31

In instances where immoral behavior occurs on the part of the pastor, such behavior has no significant effect on the level of giving in the congregation.

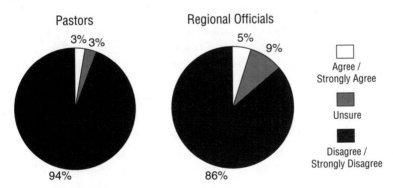

Details in the figures may not compute to 100% due to rounding.

salary of the clergy in his denomination routinely is about 60 percent of the congregation's average income. Yet the pastor is expected to socialize with the membership. This disparity, he suggested, can make clergy feel angry. However, since anger is not seen as an appropriate emotion for a spiritual mentor of the flock, the pastor may turn the anger inward and become depressed, perhaps resulting in an apathetic attitude. Magers suggests in his workshops that ministers confess their anger and forgive their members for their lack of sensitivity to the pastor's situation.

One pastor reflected on the congregation's expectation of the minister to be free of anger. "That's an interesting phenomenon. They want the pastor to be human so they can relate. Yet the pastor shouldn't get angry." This pastor has observed that these high expectations on the part of the congregation are often combined with a familiarity with the pastor that he's not supposed to mind. "They'll say the pastor shouldn't grow a beard when they'd never think of saying that to their physician or lawyer."

Although the contributing factors may be described at the macro level, the issues are very real and practical at the micro level of ministers' lives. Phil Williams, who is currently the director of the Ecumenical Center for Stewardship Studies, has been a pastor as well as worked in a national denominational office. He feels young pastors are under tremendous pressure. "I ask, 'How are the kids? Getting ready for college?' And they will respond, 'I sure hope they can get scholarships.' They can't all get scholarships."

Pastors live very much in the world, although trying to demonstrate how not to become too much of it. One pastor described the difficult task of explaining to his son why their family was not going with several others from the church on a vacation to Disney World.

Another pastor receives regular invitations from members to go golfing on weekday afternoons at the club the pastor can't afford to join. The members apparently assume he has the free time to go. When the pastor refuses, they offer to pay the fees for the day, which, he said, makes him feel a little like a charity case, quite apart from the irritation he experiences about the assumption that he has no other commitments during the week.

In a conversation we had with Tim Ek and Phil Williams, Ek noted, "Our pastors with congregations under one hundred members wouldn't be able to feed their families without a working spouse. Yet some churches with one hundred members try to have two full-time staff because there are fewer volunteers to do the work of ministry." It might be possible to raise the pastor's salary in that setting, if people were willing to give the money. But sometimes parishioners don't want the pastor earning a large salary for reasons other than the difficulty of raising a budget. Ek remembered one situation where there were objections to his salary being increased. "The person who tried to keep my salary low didn't want me to earn any more than he did." "We are imprisoned," Phil Williams agreed. "Then we feel guilty because we feel we ought to make do on less. The impact is that we can't really open the conversation with the congregation. We're captive to the culture. We can't get free because we can't discuss it."

Roman Catholic priests are also feeling the same pinch as their Protestant counterparts. In the past, the Roman Catholic Church may not have had stewardship problems because of the sheer numbers of parishioners attending mass in each parish. Even small amounts from lots of people provided the funds for the operating budget, including the priest's salary, and contributions to the diocese were high as well. Ray Coughlin pointed out, "The Catholic Church has, in the past, relied on huge masses of people. Even if parishioners gave one or two dollars, it was great, and, in turn, the archdiocese assessment was high." Mark Teresi affirmed the idea that in the past there was no need to emphasize individual giving, as illustrated by the comments of one older priest: "The new pastor has a hard job. My pews were always filled. Numbers generated the funds."

In large part, costs were kept low in the Roman Catholic Church through the sacrificial labor of priests and religious who taught in the schools and provided support services. Many of these people had taken vows of poverty. The decline in membership among these religious orders has led parishes to hire more lay workers.

Certainly time has produced a variety of changes in the way the church conducts its ministry. Archbishop Thomas J. Murphy observed, "When I was growing up as a kid, people supported the service of the religious and priests who were the primary ministers to the community. Since Vatican II, more and more professional and volunteer laypeople are serving the Church as well. The Church has become far more sensitive to the justice issues involved, which include just salaries and a living wage. There is the ongoing concern for the needs of lay employees, as well as a sensitivity to the retirement needs of religious and priests. These are important issues, in addition to the ongoing care and maintenance of the physical plant."

Protestants went through a similar process, recognizing the need for health insurance and pensions for ministers who serve their entire careers on low salaries. David McCreath pointed to several factors that influence the relationship between pastors and their congregations. "Congregations are, on the average, smaller than they were a decade or two ago. In addition, health care, pensions, and minimum salaries for pastors are taking a proportionately larger part of congregational budgets. Pastors of small congregations feel it is difficult to talk about financial stewardship because it looks so self-serving. It feels like they are asking for their own salaries."

Robert Wood Lynn pointed out that the worry about the pastor as a "money-grubber" is an old stereotype that has been repeated throughout history. The situation has been made more difficult by current trends. Mark Moller-Gunderson observed that pastors in smaller congregations find a certain awkwardness about the topic of stewardship, since as much as 80 percent of the budget goes for the pastor's salary and benefits. Ronald Nelson of The Lutheran Church-Missouri Synod suggested a similar situation existed in his communion, where pastors feel it is inappropriate to talk about money because they benefit from the church's income, and that is not "acceptable." Nelson pointed out that those who break that cycle of silence and talk about money openly find people will, in fact, give.

Interestingly not all pastors in the Stewardship Project survey shared this feeling about the awkward connection between salaries and raising the budget. In response to the statement, "Many pastors find it difficult to preach about financial stewardship because their salary and benefits are such a large part of the budget," just over half agreed. In contrast, almost three-quarters of the regional officials felt the statement was true.

When the size of the pastor's congregation was taken into account, 59 percent of the pastors in congregations of 100 or fewer members agreed with the statement, and 58 percent of those in congregations of 101–250 agreed. Meanwhile, in congregations of 251–500 members, 45 percent agreed; in congregations of 501–1,000, 43 percent agreed; and in congregations over 1,000, 45 percent agreed.

Some of those pastors who do worry about the connection between asking church members for money and having their salary paid may be confusing two issues, according to one church leader. "I've heard about 'feathering their own nest' over and over," said Nordan Murphy, retired director of the NCC Stewardship Commission. "I don't think congregations see it that way. When we hear the pastor preach stewardship, we think institutional. It is more likely the pastor doesn't want to deal with the topic in general, so this is a rationalization."

Still, pastors may find themselves having to interpret the need for the number of paid professional staff serving the congregation. Given that many church members today can remember thirty or forty years ago when the church, whether Catholic or Protestant, was filled with staff (or volunteers) working at very low wages out of great commitment, it may be hard to understand why it takes so much money to pay these people today. Church members may not connect the fact that two-income households have reduced the free time available for members to volunteer at the church. Or that pastors with families find it more difficult in a culture of widespread consumerism to ask their children to live as simple a lifestyle as pastors' children did in the past. Or, living longer than previous generations, pastors find it more difficult to face retirement with no pension. Or that the numbers of priests and religious have diminished to the degree that laypeople with families must now do some tasks that were previously subsidized through the community structures of religious orders. Not taking all of these realities into account, people wonder why it takes so much more money to run the parish than it used to.

All these factors combine to increase the pressure on the pastor. An emphasis on more just salaries for the lay and religious

workers, as well as the decline in attendance in some neighborhood parishes, has meant some Catholic congregations and dioceses are facing the same types of financial strain that their
Protestant counterparts have experienced. One Catholic priest
commented, "Just salaries put an albatross around the neck of
every parish priest. 'Raise salaries,' but no one told him how to
do it."

Interpretation may be a key. Thomas Sweetser, S.J., of the
Parish Evaluation Project, said that large church staffs may be
one reason church members are reluctant to give more money.
The large staffs that include many laypeople may appear to be a
problem. However, Sweetser suggested that these staffs might be
less bothersome if church members understood that the purpose
of the staff is to help the parish carry out its ministry and to call
other people to service.

Mark Teresi believes that pastors have a responsibility to understand the role of stewardship quite apart from their individual
salaries. "They need to get beyond that they're asking for themselves. Some don't see themselves as a vessel, an instrumental-
ity of God, to generate their parishioners' response." In that context, the emphasis is on the spiritual need of the parishioner to
give, not the need for the congregation to pay its bills.

Even though the true issues may well have more to do with a
deeper understanding of discipleship and grace, it is the practical
fact that many churches are having trouble paying their bills that
is bringing the topic into focus. As Timothy Ek pointed out, "Des-
peration is a good teacher. Pastors are feeling the challenge to
address the issue. So hopefully it will provide them a chance to
talk about their hot button issues in this context of stewardship."

The issue is all the hotter for pastors because they have received
so little training on the issue of money and the church. Further,
the types of people being recruited for seminaries have also been
changing. Perhaps a brief review of who is going into the ministry and what type of preparation they are given would be in
order.

Pastors and Seminary Training

8

Were the whole realm of nature mine,
That were a present far too small;
Love so amazing, so divine,
Demands my soul, my life, my all.

Isaac Watts, 1707
"When I Survey the Wondrous Cross"

Who Goes into the Ministry?

It may be possible to trace both the reluctance to discuss money and the difficulty some pastors have in handling money to the type of people being recruited for the ministry, as well as to the type of training that clergy receive in seminary. The culture has changed, so that recruitment of clergy has become more difficult. "Money buys many," suggests Ron Voss. "Law, medicine, and business get some of the most gifted people. The people with less leadership ability go into education, government, and the ministry." As a result, he suggests, the candidates going into the ministry may not have the ego strength to take on the difficult role of leadership, particularly in the area of money. Robert Wuthnow voiced a similar view, saying, "We're just not getting the best and the brightest."

One review of the academic preparation of a group of master of divinity candidates found that this set of individuals scored an average of 502 on the Graduate Record Examination (GRE) in

153

1988. "This average is somewhat lower than the averages for most other humanities areas, but it is higher than the averages for examinees planning to enter the helping professions of social work, guidance, or education."[1]

John P. O'Neill of the Educational Testing Service commented on the changes that have taken place in seminary candidates. "In the immediate postwar years, it used to be that Phi Beta Kappas were more proportionately going into the ministry than other professions." Now data for 1981 through 1990 indicates male religion majors have lower GRE scores "than men who matriculate in other programs. Meanwhile, you have a very able body of women who are entering the ministry."[2]

Cultural Change

Part of the shift in seminary candidate characteristics is due to changes in the culture. The Catholic Church, for example, has to think more aggressively about promoting vocations. "The church is facing the challenge of making the priesthood look like an attractive alternative for younger men," according to Ray Coughlin. "Role models are needed. We must market the good things that the priesthood's got going. . . . There are so many different directions for our young men that the priesthood is not an option."

Another cultural change is that seminaries can no longer assume that people attracted to the ministry understand the church environment they will be entering. James Hudnut-Beumler, dean of Columbia Theological Seminary in Atlanta, Georgia, said that the seminary's curriculum was being revised to account for the fact that many people coming to the seminary "were coming to us without the benefit of basic theological training—not knowing the books of the Bible, the great ways of thinking. Faculty and supervising ministers were telling us that the seminarians who come to us don't know the story; they are biblically and theologically functionally illiterate." The other factor is that many of these students had not grown up attending church. Having come to belief perhaps as late as college, the students were not familiar with the culture of the church. "If you had twenty-two years of Sunday school and years of worship, you got it slowly and seminary was finishing school."

A survey of graduate theological education conducted by the M. J. Murdock Charitable Trust found a similar pattern. "Many students come to seminary not far removed from un-Christian environments. They do not have the spiritual maturity that once was assumed and expected of seminary students."[3]

The type of student coming into the seminary may be, in turn, a result of the situation many seminaries find themselves in. As a consequence of the larger cultural changes going on, recruiting and training ministerial candidates has become more complex on a practical level. Economic factors have changed admission procedures at some seminaries. Both an article in *The Atlantic Monthly* and the Murdock Charitable Trust study came to a similar conclusion. As the article notes, "Those who accredit Protestant seminaries, as well as those who administer and teach in them, reluctantly admit that the institutions are considerably less demanding of applicants than they were in the past." Further, many seminaries are expanding their range of services, to attract a broader market of students, with ministerial training now being only one purpose of the seminary.[4]

This trend is not limited to the Protestant institutions. For example, a major survey was conducted of women religious in the United States. The author of the report was Sister Anne Munley of the Immaculate Heart of Mary. She is a sociologist at Marywood College in Scranton, Pennsylvania. She referred to a potential problem in "the heavy reliance of orders on the individual members' gifts and preferences as the basis for deciding which ministries they enter." While 97 percent of the leaders responding to the survey indicated the experience of individuals in the order determined new ministries, "corporate discernment or the requests of leadership" were identified as significant in how such decisions are made by just over half the respondents. According to an article on the report, she indicated that the "concern for individual rights and well-being" will have to be balanced with "a greater sense of the corporate."[5]

The Seminary Program

Faced with the challenge of preparing future pastors for their ministries, seminaries have a daunting task. Theological preparation seems critical to many faculty. The role of the practical aspects of running a church are less clear, to the degree that there appears to be a prejudice against practical aspects of ministry at the seminary level. This lack of agreement about the purpose of theological education is generally recognized. In the M. J. Murdock Charitable Trust study, three separate focus groups—one with national and regional Christian leaders, another with seminary presidents and deans, and one with seminary faculty—each produced the finding that there is a sense of distance between the seminary and the local church. The national and regional Christian leaders' summary was, "The seminary and church are more competitive than collaborative."[6]

Dan Conway observed, "The person going into ministry feels the dichotomy, and everything in seminary reinforces that. In the seminary curriculum, management, money, human resources are all incidental things you have to pick up. They're electives, not the substance of Christianity. Patristics, Scripture are the important things. Nobody says, 'How do you integrate God's Word with balancing the checkbook?'" In Conway's opinion, the future pastor ought to be given the same amount of general knowledge that the executive of any comparably sized voluntary organization has. "The point for clergy is that they are not getting anything in seminary, and they are being told in a thousand nonverbal ways, 'It's not important.' It would be one thing if the seminary said, 'You need it but we can't teach you.' Rather, the message is, 'Theology is real, and practical pastoring is not.'"

Nordan Murphy concisely summarized how the training of pastors affects their later ministry in the area of stewardship. "No one ever told them that part of their mission was to train people to be giving people."

A variety of national leaders described the struggles they had in trying to introduce stewardship courses at the seminary level. A common objection was that the seminary only had the students for three years, and there was no time to add one more course. Other observers reported that stewardship was not viewed as an academic topic, and seminaries feel they need to maintain their academic integrity. As one described it, "They just don't think it is important. They're dealing with 'important theological issues' and they don't understand the role of stewardship yet. 'Laypeople will take care of it'—there is a tradition that's been passed down in the church, and that's enough." One regional official responding to the Stewardship Project survey had also pastored. He commented, "NO stewardship training in seminary. It was like reading Greek would help pay the light bill. There is a lot of magical thinking in seminary class planning."

The Atlantic Monthly article, which reviewed seminary training in 1990, raised an even deeper concern. The separation of the practical and the theological may be made all the wider because of a possible separation between the spiritual and the academic for the faculty of some seminaries. "The beliefs and practices of seminary teachers are increasingly important in theological education now that it is becoming clear that a brilliant faculty of agnostics may produce some interesting scholars and scholarship but will do little to help shape men and women for careers in the ministry." The article points out that schools with a conservative view often ask faculty members to sign statements of faith. In other institutions, however, such an approach would be seen as an affront to academic freedom, leaving room for a wide variety of approaches in courses taken by ministerial candidates.[7]

It may be, as James Waits, executive director of the Association of Theological Schools in the United States and Canada, suggested, that seminaries have been impacted by the advent of religious study centers at secular universities. "Over many years, seminaries have focused on scholarly academic theoretical questions, and there has been an absence of work related to practical church life. The advent of religious studies departments, fostering the secular study of religion, has provided a mind-set of the scholarly associations. These have become the reference point for seminary faculties, a scientific approach to religious studies. It doesn't mean that seminaries have given up the church, but they've been affected by the mind-set of this approach."

That mind-set may have had an important effect on how clergy approach their roles, particularly in terms of translating academic resources for interpreting the faith into the practical aspects of ministry. Craig Dykstra, formerly of Princeton Seminary and now vice president of religion at Lilly Endowment Inc., commented, "If there's a problem in theological education—and I think there is—it's the fragmentation of it. How large ideas inform living situations is not evident to people coming out of the seminaries, and that's the failure."

Theology has not always been that way, according to Dykstra. "Augustine was a bishop, a very busy church administrator. He composed philosophical and theological writings because he needed answers to the questions of his time. 'Whom do we pray to?' 'The Trinity.' 'What's that?' Or, 'What shall we teach one another?' 'Christian doctrine.' One of his major treatises is a direct response to a young pastor who said, 'When I stand in a congregation, what should I say to them?' And he said, 'Tell them this.' It is rhetorically powerful, narratively beautiful. For another example, Calvin's *Institutes* were answering pastors who asked, 'In light of all that's happened, what should we preach and teach?'

"We live in a technological society. In the late nineteenth and early twentieth centuries, profound questions about the existence of God have been asked, about the nature of faith and about how we should interpret the Scriptures. These are difficult problems, which sometimes leave seminarians simply confused. Some end up feeling that seminary did little more than convince them they were not competent to interpret Scripture, at least by the standards expected. In reaction, some even say to themselves, implicitly if not explicitly, 'If I can't interpret the Scriptures rightly, why bother to do so at all?'"

In that context, pastors may be unprepared to answer basic questions from church members such as, How should I spend my money?

William McKinney, dean of Hartford Seminary, also noted a distinction at the seminary level between the practical and the academic. "I don't think most seminary faculty think they're about activating the church. They're about writing books. We're not in the business of success." Further, seminaries may see themselves as playing an important role in safeguarding some of the less popular traditions of the church, he suggested. Asked why seminaries had not developed the area of stewardship even as U.S. society—and most church members—became more affluent, McKinney replied, "Alongside the affluent society, you also have the focus on those left behind, those who were never there. That was a shift in traditional Protestant seminaries to identification with the 'left out.' Liberation theology, if not dominant, is strong.

In that context, fund-raising becomes hard. Faculty condemning capitalism and money, then go to a CEO and ask for one million dollars—it's a hard sell." The "communities of reference"—a conscious choice to identify with the poor—of many seminary faculty members may have left them unprepared to develop a theological approach for the majority well-to-do. "It's not that we're bad," McKinney reflected. "Rather it's entropy—the way we've been is hard to change."

His comment was underscored by Kenneth D. Meyer, president of Trinity Evangelical Divinity School in Deerfield, Illinois, affiliated with The Evangelical Free Church of America. In a speech to the M. J. Murdock Charitable Trust, he noted, "The curriculum for the M.Div. in most of our schools has had little change in twenty years. At Trinity we changed two courses between 1975 and 1990. Yet think of the changes that took place in the church during that same period."[8]

Al Taylor had a more practical theory about the lack of stewardship training at the seminary level. "There is a suspicion if we teach people to give to the local church, they won't give to the seminary, and pastors fear if they teach people to tithe, they'll give offerings elsewhere. I tell the pastors, 'Help the man in the pew; help him solve his financial problems, and your problems will be solved.' The problem solved in the pew helps the congregation solve its problems, which helps the denomination. You give pastors all this training at the seminary, and the first problem they run into in the congregation is money and you haven't taught them a thing about money."

Even when stewardship is taught at seminaries, the topic of money may still be avoided. "I want to focus the area of study on faith and money, not the broader sense of stewardship. Some people who use 'stewardship' mean the term so broadly as to include all Christian ethics," observed Robert Wood Lynn. David Heetland, vice president for development at Garrett-Evangelical Theological Seminary, described one course of study on stewardship that produced complaints from a few students: Topics such as the environment were being covered, but the faculty did not discuss money.

Students, however, are not always excited about the topic either. Heetland offered a course in stewardship, assuming students would eagerly sign up because of the real frustration he had heard from practicing pastors about their lack of financial training. However, only three students signed up, and two were international students. "I did little promotion for the course because I thought everyone would be dying to take it." Hugh Magers received complaints from students, saying he was talking too much about money in a stewardship course he taught for two years.

One indication that the area of money is seen as distant from the core curriculum is the attitude cited toward development officers. Faculty may complain that these officers of the seminary, including the president, do not raise more money, while at the same time they deride the mundane activity of paying the bills and exalt the more vital area of theological education. William McKinney noted that development officers are not usually members of the faculty, nor do they engage in regular dialogue with the "serious" faculty. "If you create a radical separation between the academic and the institutional, what we teach students is to keep the deacons and the finance committees separate, which is poor theology."

Part of the difficulty may be a lack of agreement about what the ministerial candidates are being trained for. The Murdock Trust study found that "there is a gap between the education provided and the pastor's duties as performed. The churches expect the seminaries to send them well-rounded graduates who can fulfill these responsibilities successfully. Seminaries expect their graduates to learn administrative, leadership, and nurturing skills in the church." A table in the study provided the top five expectations of pastors found among laypeople, pastors, and seminary professors. The differences are illuminating. While the top priority for the laypeople was that the pastor be strong in "spirituality," defined as "a model of Christian loyalty, devotion and biblical applications to daily life," that priority was number four for pastors and did not appear in the professors' top five. For the pastors, the top priority was relational skills, which ranked number two for laypeople and, again, did not register with professors. For professors, the top priority was theological knowledge, which ranked as five for both the lay and pastor respondents.[9]

One national leader observed that people in seminary are being trained as preachers rather than leaders. Other descriptive terms used in interviews, perhaps reflecting the priorities of the pastors in the Murdock study, were "facilitators" or "social worker with theological degrees." Given the difficulty in talking about money in this culture, leadership may be a key quality necessary for ministers to succeed in the area of stewardship. Describing a dialogue he hopes to have with some pastors of growing churches, Ronald Nelson of The Lutheran Church-Missouri Synod said, "We want to ask, 'What characteristics does the pastor have to make the churches grow?' We speculate it's fearlessness—not being afraid of anything: of losing a position, of people's opinions, of failing."

Mark Teresi worked with a group of priests on a project during his graduate school days. He developed a corporate model pastor network. In business, when using this model, executives talk with each other regularly to find out what others have tried and to compare notes. The priests in this model took almost a year to become willing to be vulnerable and talk with each other about their successes and failures. The network concept was not familiar to them. Teresi noticed a strong difference in the business and religious environments he was bridging. "In the corporate world," he observed, "leaders who succeed have a higher failure rate. Business executives *know* they'll make mistakes. They need to get together to learn from each other. For ministers, it's the nature of the position—we, the lay folks, train them to be that way. People approach them, and they're supposed to know all the answers. If you're supposed to be the final word on life's important issues, it's tough to be vulnerable."

Don McClanen of the Ministry of Money observed that seminaries, with their emphasis on academic training, may have "become a stumbling block, unintentionally a stumbling block rather than stepping stones to spiritual formation and spiritual vitality." Nordan Murphy agreed. "I don't feel people comprehend the gospel in their training. We're so theoretical about everything. Historically correct, theologically correct. I don't know how much is done in matters of the heart, especially regarding generosity."

John Haughey expands on this idea in *The Holy Use of Money*:

That we can and do think in terms of social systems today makes it all the more necessary that the historical-critical method of scriptural exegesis not be the sole moment in the process of interpretation or use of the Scriptures. To make this the only moment or process of interpretation results in a positivism that reduces the value of the text to a mere trickle of the power it could unleash.[10]

Bishop William McManus observed that some younger priests leaving the seminary have been reluctant to take leadership in the area of financial stewardship as they enter the ministry. Part of the reluctance, he feels, may be that some priests in the past, priests who became known as "money pastors," had set a bad example of how stewardship was taught. But he also believes that there is an emphasis on leaving practical matters with the laity while the priest focuses on the spiritual. "I think it's shortsighted. If it is left to the laity, then they will take a business approach and remove all spiritual elements from giving. What we older priests need to say to the younger is, 'You're missing a great opportunity to train people in justice.'"

In discussing the curriculum revision at Columbia Theological Seminary, James Hudnut-Beumler commented, "Even if you gave people all the pieces, students weren't putting it all together. For example, at the back door of the church after the sermon, someone hits you with, 'What about in Leviticus where it says, "Kill homosexuals"?' And the student might respond with, 'You must understand it was written in a time . . .' and provide a historical critique. In fact, if the student had listened further, what the person might be saying is, 'I deeply believe in this Bible and my son told me he is gay and I love him—what do I do?'" Hudnut-Beumler added, "Ministry is not the disciplines; it is the artful juggling of those disciplines into a life lived in a better way."

Many of those interviewed suggested that at least part of the solution to the lack of practical training at the seminary, including the area of stewardship, was to provide for educational opportunities once the seminarians have been in the field. Many times, what seemed irrelevant at a time when term papers and final exams were the dominant crises becomes all too real as the leadership board turns to the pastor for guidance in raising the budget. David Heetland believes that there is an opportunity to meet pastors at that point of need. "I was asked to do a continuing education course in stewardship by a seminary," he said. "They told me, 'If you have twenty people show up, you'll be lucky.' Forty came, and most were out in the parish. They mirrored the frustration of the need for practical development training. There is a teachable moment, and we need to do both—incorporate the information into the seminary and offer continuing education."

To some degree, seminaries are beginning to look in more depth at the issues involved in the practical aspects of training future clergy. "One of the agendas we've identified in theological education is the formation of theological teachers," offered James Waits. "What are the special needs of seminaries in contrast to religious studies departments in a university? One of the significant points of discussion has already been initiated: What should be the nature and character of training seminary faculty?" Waits said that the ecclesiastical oversight statement of the Association of Theological Schools (ATS) provides that the denomination, as the consumer, should have a significant role in determining the seminary curriculum. He also pointed to both a review of the seminary accreditation process, which may take some of these issues into account, and a series of North American conversations on the "viability of ministerial formation" that ATS will be cosponsoring in the context of a global initiative of the World Council of Churches. "We will ask church people what are the needs of the church in ministerial formation and talk about where we are in theological education."

As seminaries regard how to introduce more practical aspects of church ministry into theological education, Archbishop Thomas J. Murphy of Seattle strongly feels that stewardship ought not to be a separate track. Rather, he sees the topic as integral to basic theological education and so should be interwoven where moral theology, creation, and a variety of other topics are discussed.

Waits, writing in the report of a study of attitudes among Catholic and Protestant clergy about stewardship, proposed,

> It is intriguing to think of the teaching of stewardship as a potential unifying theme for the theological curriculum. . . . As an integrating theme within theological education, the subject of stewardship offers the occasion to reflect upon both the missional and theological elements of church life.[11]

A few seminaries now have core courses in stewardship. Hugh Magers was proud of the fact that he convinced one seminary to allow scholarship students to include "tithes" as a line item in the budgets they are required to fill out. Since then, three other seminaries have followed suit.

The fact that seminaries may be starting to focus on how to improve the practical aspects of their training may be encouraging on one hand. However, such changes will not soon benefit currently practicing clergy. These are the individuals in the field who probably came to seminary with the culture's attitude that the spiritual and the monetary are divided. Further, the discussion above would suggest this attitude would have been reinforced through their years of specialized training. This divided mind may deeply influence the way the minister approaches the task. Dan Conway is currently in the Planning, Communications, and Development Office of the Archdiocese of Indianapolis as a lay staff member. He reflected on the decision he had initially made to explore the priesthood. "There is something of a *fuga mundi*—a certain sense of rejecting the world to go into ministry. When I made the decision to go to seminary, there was something about it. The expectation was that I'd be in business. So there was a rejection."

Conway was the project director for a study of stewardship attitudes among two hundred Protestant and two hundred Catholic clergy. While the ministers were generally happy with their choice of vocation, only 25 percent of the Protestant clergy and 31 percent of the Catholic priests found administrative duties "extremely satisfying" or "very satisfying," and only one-third of either group found financial duties either extremely or very satisfying.[12]

This finding underscores an observation from the Stewardship Project encounters. As important as money is in the culture in general, and in the congregation in particular, pastors are none too comfortable with it. Their unease may be due in part to the fact that few pastors have received formal training about how to deal with money.

It may be valuable then, before proceeding with the discussion on how money affects the dynamics of a congregation, to briefly consider what money is as an entity that affects church life so deeply.

9

What Is Money?

That word above all earthly pow'rs,
No thanks to them, abideth;
The Spirit and the gifts are ours
Thru Him who with us sideth.
Let goods and kindred go,
This mortal life also—
The body they may kill;
God's truth abideth still:
His kingdom is forever.

Martin Luther, 1529
"A Mighty Fortress Is Our God"

What is money that the church has to struggle with it so?
It is quantifiable and transferable time and talent. Money is who I am as represented by my stored time and talent. It is a system of exchange. It is also like Aladdin's lamp, which can be rubbed and has the potential of being translated into all kinds of new realities. "Because money is the symbol for acquiring many goods and services," writes Philip Slater, "it assumes for many people the character of a magic wishing ring—the gateway to all our desires."[1] Money is also the inheritance of parents' time and talents.

And from another vantage point, since money is the product of labor, money is ultimately a form of God's time and talent, stored in the creation of the world and made available for human use.

Greed, then, can be equated with idolatry, as the apostle Paul does in Colossians 3:5. Greed is worship of self; of the created rather than the Creator; of what we possess through our own and

165

our ancestors' time and talent, stored in

currency; of the potential of whom we c

opposite of honoring the Source of al

endowed with by the Creator—both ir

our individual abilities—and instead

"In this sense, materialism is a reli

author and now teacher at Eastern

sylvania. "Everything is for me, a self-oriented

often doesn't have room for values. And any stated values will be

ignored, as in Phariseeism."

Robert Wood Lynn said he was greatly helped by Luke Johnson's book on New Testament attitudes toward possessions. Bob Lynn's distillation of these ideas was that humans, as a result of the Fall, have an insufficient sense of being and so compensate by having. In Isaiah 44 the compensation takes the form of the construction of actual idols. "We have our own version of that—not of constructing idols but of being anxious about being. One way to compensate is to get money and spend it on anything that enhances our sense of well-being. Our handling of money has to be rooted in our theological sense of what grace means and the gift we now have in Christ who is all we ever want to have . . . being free to recognize and able to overcome our anxiety about not having."

Don McClanen has worked with many different people in regard to their attitudes toward money. He sees money as highly emotion-laden. He also talked about the role that money can play in our lives. "Money is the tangible god at hand. Augustine said 'Our hearts are hungry until they find God.' The easiest way to find a god is through money, which can quickly give you power, prestige, and security."

Hugh Magers, however, points out that money may not be able to deliver on its promises. "We have needs for security, safety, inclusion, identity, and community, and the culture tells us they are provided by financial security. There's no such thing as security; the death rate is 100 percent."

The spiritual implications of money have been largely ignored in a society that has focused on merely accumulating it. Money represents our boundless potential, and the advertising that is so prevalent in our society plays to that idea.

Money was not always central in every culture, according to psychologist Paul Wachtel. He proposes that it would be wrong to attribute similar meaning to references made to money in ancient, including biblical, texts. Rather, he suggests that money for much of past history was "confined largely to a rather limited realm of luxury items. . . . People grew primarily what they needed, not what would 'sell,' and when they traded it was for particular items that filled quite specific needs."[2]

Hugh Magers sees money tied up with self-esteem issues in this culture. "In the gospel, we understand Christian behavior and realize that a lot of stuff we used to do we don't have to do because now we're free. But the culture tells us esteem comes from spending money, consuming. If a fifty-two-year-old man is worried about his sexuality, he can pour cologne on himself. Or if he needs status, buy a car." Magers thinks the gospel has an alternative to offer. "The gospel is *metanoia*, which is the opposite of paranoia; spiritual conversion and renewed thinking instead of defensive isolation. So stewardship is really good news. But with the Good News, something has to die."

Part of what has to die might be the power that is assigned to money by so many people, including church members. Magers heard about one seminary class where a man burned a one-hundred-dollar bill "and the students went up the wall. Some of the seminarians said, 'Oh, we could have given it to the poor,' and the professor responded, 'You know the last person who said that.'"

Ronald Nelson observed, "The money or wealth that people give to the church is a distillation of everything they are. It's the time they've spent earning it. No system does not connect with wealth."

Nordan Murphy said, "I've always felt our money is a symbol of who we are. We invest our blood, sweat, and tears and work hard to get it. And what we think of it reveals who we are. If we're generous or stingy—our internal self is there. The old concept of 'your money is you'—when you give it away, you're giving away part of yourself."

Giving and Lifestyle

In this context, when people give money away, they are not just parting with a possession—they are actually affecting their future potential. The culture would suggest they are diminishing their possibilities, while the Gospels would suggest they are expanding them. In the hugely successful movie *Forrest Gump,* the likable and extremely simple lead character almost literally stumbles into great wealth. His response is to give large portions of it away to a hospital and to his church, citing his mother's advice, "Now Momma said there's only so much fortune a man really needs and the rest is just for showing off." His actions prove to be controversial. It was a war buddy, Bubba, who had suggested the idea that led to Forrest's great wealth. "And even though Bubba was dead and [his current partner] Lieutenant Dan said I was nuts, I gave Bubba's mama Bubba's share," Forrest explains.[3]

Church members also struggle to make sense of a world that tells them they are "nuts" to lessen their own unrealized potential by giving their money away. And they struggle, by and large, in the midst of a church that is silent on the subject.

An encounter in a Stewardship Project workshop illustrates this point. One leader in a church was really struck with the presentation about church giving potential. She expressed frustration with the lack of financial support present in her own congregation. Why did she think people give less than they used to? she was pressed. After some thought, this middle-aged professional woman responded, "Peer pressure. I have no difficulty telling my son he does not need a pair of thirty-five-dollar stonewashed jeans or a forty-dollar perm. But I went right out and bought a VCR after a neighbor left my house, because I felt so out of the conversation we'd had over coffee."

"Keeping up with the Joneses" has become an important part of the post–World War II culture in the United States. The idea was reviewed in a Sunday comic strip. A very Raggedy Ann was standing in the window of her patched shack, while her counterpart Raggedy Andy sat in his worn chair reading the paper. Raggedy Ann, looking through binoculars, exclaims to a frowning Andy, "Oh great. Now Ken and Barbie have a camper and a pool set and a dream kitchen and a . . ."[4] Even toys in our culture are provided with accumulation options to keep up with the expanding American dream!

Of course the problem of church members being faithful with their resources is not new. During the last century, church leaders were challenging their followers to come to terms with the increasing resources resulting from the Industrial Revolution. In 1828 Lyman Beecher exhorted listeners to double the amount of their giving in response to the great opportunities before the faithful and reminded them, "Next year, our tongue may be employed in celestial praises; and our substance be in other hands."[5] By 1885 Josiah Strong was calling for a change on a par with an earlier reformation. "What is needed is not simply an increased giving, an enlarged estimate of the 'Lord's share,' but a *radically different conception,* of our relations to our possessions."[6] Things had become so bad that Washington Gladden, writing in 1905, cried out in despair:

> So in these days there are hundreds of thousands who have not been debauched by the worship of Mammon, but it is the religion of the multitude. Men do believe in him; their faith is sincere and unwavering; they are ready to prove it every day, by their works. They have no doubt of his power, of his supremacy; all things are possible, they think, to those who secure his favour. That he holds in his hands the real good of life for man, and that there is no real happiness for any unless they propitiate him, is the first article in the creed of the great majority. . . . It is only within the last one or two centuries that the way to the altars of Mammon has been cleared for the multitude. In slavery and in feudalism the opportunities of gain were confined to a very few; now that freedom is the heritage of all, this craving has become the common experience of mankind. Like every other natural passion it is a good servant but a tyrannical master.[7]

Thus the challenge of materialism has long confronted the church in this country. However, if Washington Gladden and the others were concerned about conditions in their own times, what might they say about the post–World War II general affluence that abounds now?

In this kind of economically comfortable environment, it seems logical that church giving would be affected. An interview was held with the highest per capita missions giving church in a missions oriented denomination. The beautiful building sat in a wealthy suburb. One of the Stewardship Project staff expressed surprise at how the particular suburb had changed so dramatically. The assistant pastor agreed, noting that a family would probably feel awkward in that community if they did not have a three-car garage and the vehicles to fill it. The interviewer was a little taken aback. Given the historical commitments of the denomination this congregation was affiliated with, the interviewer responded, "But that is not true in the church, right?" The assistant pastor shook his head, "No, it's true in the church too. And," he went on, "I should tell you, while we're the highest giving church per capita to missions in the United States, we're not the highest in the denomination. That would be a church in [an Asian country], and they are sending missionaries to the United States." One wonders what U.S. congregations could accomplish for the kingdom if they were able to overcome the secular lifestyle that peer pressure has caused to seep into the church.

From a spiritual point of view, the accumulation of possessions may have become confused in the minds of some. Jesus criticized the Pharisees for giving their alms in such a public way as to generate a public response. In the same way, do some church members flaunt nice clothes and cars as an external expression of how they have been blessed by God? Do their churches give them any guidance on the matter?

One woman described how she and her husband work to try to keep their lifestyles in perspective. As part of their effort, they send a check to overseas ministries for the same dollar value they spend on their children's birthdays. The woman said she tries to find friends to talk with about these kinds of issues, but what she would really like would be a discussion in her church to give her some guidance.

Consumer Values

This silence in the church may have broader social implications as well. In a consumer society, the church is one of the few groups that have a vested interest in promoting anything other than the pursuit of affluence, spending, and accumulation. Yet with no countering voice, these goals can be destructive. Consider the ruthlessness that has developed in our culture of accumulation. The United States raised a generation who viewed as heroes the main characters in such prime-time soap operas as

Dallas and *Falcon Crest.* Children are killed for their designer clothes and shoes in the cities. Young people enslave their peers with drugs as a means to make money.

Values are relative in our society, as shown by one Louis Harris survey that found 66 percent of the five thousand high schoolers polled said they would cheat if it would help them pass an important exam.[8] A reporter presented a conversation he had with an aspiring young rapper in Indianapolis, who explained the content of his music: "'We've got some sides of our town where you grow up with nothing and at sixteen, you still have nothing,' he says. '... [Y]ou can see a kid who's sixteen drive by in a BMW. And you're thinking, not only do I not have any car, but my shoes are torn to hell. Man, I could kill somebody for that car. I would kill *that person* for that car.'"[9] Without a strong alternative vision coming from the church, accumulation begets a new set of relative standards independent of human worth.

In theory, religion ought to be providing a profound countercultural view for those in a consumer society. "Religion touches resources in us and gives us capacities that are the answers to the problems we see on the streets," observed James Waits. "We haven't found the way to articulate the alternative and make it available to people."

The conflict between culture and the church is clear to church leaders. What is less clear is the church's willingness to wage the battle. "The materialism of our culture is the dominant issue, and the church has not combated materialism with its own set of values," said Wes Willmer. When asked why the church was not presenting a viable alternative, Willmer went on, "People in the church often feel that if they take the biblical teaching on stewardship to heart, they would have to give up a lot that they don't want to do without."

Part of the difficulty is defining what is wealth today, in order to figure out what side of the discussion a person is on. Robert Welsh said, "I don't think most people who are affluent feel affluent. We feel we are in debt and someone else is affluent." Timothy Ek voiced a similar view. "People in the Depression knew what it was like to live without things. For my kids, poverty is not having Nintendo. I would prefer uniforms at school. I think having to wear all these preppy clothes is a plot by kids' clothes manu-

facturers so you have to wear just the right things to go to school,"
he added only slightly facetiously.

Faced with this confusion of definitions, many pastors find it
more convenient to keep talk of financial stewardship to a minimum. This avoidance on the part of the spiritual leader of the congregation can send mistaken cues to the people listening in the
pews. "When the pastor stands up once a year and speaks on tithes
because it is expected, the person hears, 'They want my money,
and they don't know I'm hurting,'" proposed Howard Dayton.

The Wealthy

Church leaders should know that the false promises of the culture will not meet people's real needs for self-esteem. Yet it seems
hard even in the church for ministers to recognize the pain experienced by the wealthy, people who have succeeded on this materialistic culture's own terms. "The wealthy are outcasts," stated
Don McClanen. "They have the one addiction—the accumulation of power and control—that is not only okay, it is even hero-
worshiped."

McClanen compared the accumulation of wealth to other
addictions. "Sooner or later, the other addictions are found out
through disease or exposure. Sex violators, crack addicts, or alco-
holics are looked down on. The one not looked down on is the
one who accumulates wealth, who robs the poor and robs God—
who rob themselves. These people are elected to leadership in
the community, the church, the seminary. Everyone kowtows to
them. It kills the spirit, it kills the heart of the wealthy person
and all those under the influence, and we all are. We are all idol-
aters and want it as much as they want to keep it."

It appears hard for many pastors, struggling with their own
lifestyles and perhaps a load of debt, to help wealthy people out
of what might be termed a gilded trap toward deeper discipleship
and toward a more constructive use of their wealth in keeping
with their faith commitments. As a result, the topic is often
ignored.

And in the long run, the silence is just plain bad development.
The spiritual implications of money should not be pursued as a
fund-raising technique. However, the church not educating its

members to their religious responsibilities in terms of their resources and to their opportunity to respond to God's grace in their lives does have budget implications. Several leaders, when asked why people were not giving to the church, responded, "They haven't been asked."

Ron Blue, who works as a financial planner helping wealthy people explore the possibilities their resources have for helping others, responded, "They don't understand that their money is needed." Once again, he cannot be talking about a "paying-the-bills" mentality, since most churches spend a great deal of time talking about what bills need to be met. Rather, compare two sets of figures: in a recent year, two billion dollars was received by more than six hundred Protestant overseas ministries—denominational, interdenominational, and independent combined—to further both the word and deed mission of the church, compared to more than forty billion dollars in soft drink sales in the United States. From this information, it is easy to conclude that people understand the role of soft drinks in their lives much better than they have grasped the need for a caring church to reach out internationally in Jesus' name. Not having a positive agenda coming from the church for the general affluence in this society, church members can find advice from countless other sources that will be happy to absorb those resources.

Government Programs and Charitable Giving

Although funding the church has always been a struggle, in the past it appears that the church had a message that made people not afraid to sacrifice. The great missions movement of the nineteenth century found many young Protestant laypeople packing their bags and departing for shores unknown. In the Roman Catholic Church, the nineteenth century saw incredible energy in establishing the church in the United States. "Catholic immigrants gave what they had," observed Fred Hofheinz of the Lilly Endowment Inc., "which was their children. As nuns and priests, they worked for free and built an incredible school system. I went to a Catholic school, and my parents paid nothing; I was taught by nuns who were receiving little compensation. I sent my kids to schools with lay teachers, and I paid plenty. I gave money, my grandparents gave their daughter. Both of these are a different kind of stewardship."

In times past, with less money, people gave their lives. As affluence spread throughout the culture, giving money became an increasingly convenient option. Are people giving resources to the church on a par with their grandparents, who sometimes gave a child? Since the late 1950s, the portion of income the church has been able to command has been declining, pointing toward a change in attitude about the need people feel to give to the church. Several leaders interviewed suggested that one major impact was the increasing role of the government, accompanied by a more secular mind-set and a diminishing role for the church. Robert Wuthnow suggested, "There was a shift in attitude, which was even encouraged by church leaders. 'We can't do it all through voluntary means. We can build some universities but not all,' and so public universities and community colleges were built. 'We can build hospitals but not take care of all the sick; we can take care of orphans and widows but not all,' and so entitlements developed." He saw an important consequence of this trend. "As part of this attitude shift, many of the most thoughtful people in this society thought the church is not where it's at—it's in Washington, D.C. To make society a better place, don't care about the church—go to Washington and lobby."

This change in attitude had implications for charitable giving, according to Wuthnow. "In churches, charitable giving is not [seen as] something that everyone should do. Should I give time and money or write my government to get it accomplished?" Furthermore, the church not being seen as the central agent of change meant that a variety of other charitable causes could be seen as equally valid. "In other cases, too, pastors were giving their parishioners kind of outs. Congregations used to have the monopoly on giving. If people were giving 10 percent to their congregations, there was a way to hold people accountable. Now the religion industry is diverse, and clergy know not all giving is going through the church. Clergy will say 5 percent to the church and 5 percent elsewhere is okay. But you can't stay on top of charitable giving when it doesn't go through the church."

Wuthnow sees the change related to the shift in the role of government. "I don't know for sure. I think there's also a psychological shift that's related to increased taxes. As the Great Depression taught us to think, 'Government is going to do it for us. The voluntary associations won't do it.'"

Joan Sanford of The Christian and Missionary Alliance reflected on the same idea. "I wonder how much of a factor the whole cultural shift has been. Our parents used to say, 'Work hard, you get the good life.' Now we say, 'We deserve the good life.' In past times, the church was more active in the public sector. Now it's the government. How much has been relinquished to government?"

Others also noted that the church does not now play the same public role as it has in the past. The "leisure and materialism that are now possible with two-family incomes impact the church, who can volunteer, and the choices church members make about spending money," said Don Michaelsen, formerly of the Church of the Brethren national office and now with the United Church Board for Homeland Ministries. "The church, because it doesn't assert itself in a way that calls attention to itself, gets less of the dollar and less involvement. People don't attend as much as they used to. They're doing things on Sundays that their parents and grandparents wouldn't have done."

Without a strong sense of direction coming from the church, it is easy for church members to absorb the culture around them and to be overly influenced by it. The Church of God (Cleveland, Tenn.) is a Pentecostal communion with a strong emphasis on personal holiness. The denomination began in the late nineteenth century in the mountains of Appalachia. Isolated for many decades, it has more recently been growing in other areas of the United States as well. This growth, accompanied by the general increase in affluence in the culture, has presented new issues to the denomination, particularly in its relationship to financial discipleship. Al Taylor described the situation not only for his own denomination but also for many other Christians who experienced the change from the Depression through the booming 1950s. "It was easy to condemn as sinful anything we couldn't afford. When we could afford it, it became a challenge to subordinate it to Christ. Unless we are strongly discipled in the Word, we have not the strength to do it."

A Public Voice

One reason the church may not be as publicly visible could be the lack of what formerly was termed a "public theologian." "The church in the United States does not have an adequate public voice," offered James Waits. "Religion in the U.S. has been so pressed by increasing pluralism, affluence, and materialism that religious values don't have the weight and influence that I think is needed to address deeper problems in contemporary society. I think religion is the answer to many problems in society. But the church in the U.S. has not developed a coherent public voice to address those problems."

Writing in the late 1970s, James H. Smylie lamented the loss of prominent mainline Protestant figures such as H. Richard Niebuhr, Reinhold Niebuhr, and Paul Tillich:

> the shakers and shapers of mainline Protestantism and of the national ethos—not parochial, but international figures. These men are now dead. Although they influence us through their numerous writings, we no longer live with the same confidence since their strong voices have been stilled.[10]

However, as we have seen, it may be that the very culture to which such leaders addressed themselves has also disappeared. It was possible for these church leaders to speak to the entire culture when the society recognized a set of shared values to a greater degree. Wade Clark Roof and William McKinney reflect on the increasingly clear distinction between the churched and the unchurched: "A common civic faith united Americans in ways that transcended many of their subcultural differences. But with a weakening custodial role for religion in American life and less cultural conformity, the two sectors of the population have become more divergent."[11]

Certainly, there is no lack of brave, articulate people continuing to voice a clear call for moral righteousness in contemporary times. John Paul II has been willing to address what he has termed the "culture of death" in forthright terms. Named *Time* magazine's "Man of the Year" in 1994, the pontiff has been willing to speak boldly on social moral issues. Further, the Catholic bishops have "emerged as a collective conscience for the nation . . .

[a]ddressing themselves not just to Catholics but to all Americans."[12] Billy Graham continues to call individuals and the country to faith and righteousness in nationally and globally televised meetings. And former president Jimmy Carter combines the role of an international statesman with a deep religious faith that is recognized by those who hear him.

The difference may be not in the quality of the visionary people who are willing to speak but in the condition of the audience that is unable to hear them. American society honors the individual over community, promoting private opinions at the expense of shared values. In such a setting, one voice, no matter how compelling, can be lost amidst the babble of diversity.

As a result, people refer to the United States as being in a post-Christian era. Hugh Magers wondered if church members feel the church has not lived up to its commitments. "People fear that the values that hold society together are vanishing and that the church isn't doing its part to hold up its end of the bargain. I think a lot of folks bought into church because the church sustained these values. It has not to do with the church, but with society. If ever we were a Christian society, we aren't now. But people feel betrayed somehow. When we have a case of sexual misconduct of the clergy, even if we take the minister out and 'lynch him,' it doesn't change people's anger. That says to me we're tapping into something pretty deep, pretty profound. This concern about the basic values in society may be a root source of a lot of the fear."

Or as Loren Mead has suggested, "Much of the bitter anger in the theological and political conflicts in our denominations comes from the depths of persons who have a sense of loss of the church they loved."[13]

Not Keeping Up with the Culture

In spite of all these dramatic changes going on in society, the church appears to be stuck in a pre-1950s mind-set, especially in helping people come to terms with the moral implications of the affluence that has become real for more people. Until about 1950, the majority of the United States was struggling to meet basic needs. Pastors at that time were generally facing congre-

gations where many of the members were economically challenged. Part of the minister's role was to comfort these members,
helping them cope with the burden of their economic circumstances and giving them hope for a better future. At that point,
especially beginning in the Great Depression, the needs were so
great and so broad, that when the government responded to them,
it was a relief in many circles. People were bound together in
social movements, having their need in common. Government
could serve as a mediating force between the masses of people
who were struggling to establish themselves and the minority—
expanding though it was—of people who had more than they
required for their basic needs.

At the same time affluence was spreading ever more broadly
in U.S. society, individualism was replacing a community consciousness. After about 1950, it was now the majority who could
meet basic needs and still have money left over. As marketing
promoted an expanded definition of what "basic needs" were,
many people were willing to go into debt to secure their immediate comfort. Government became not an advocate for the majority but a protector of the minority, who were now those struggling to establish themselves economically. And the church did
not offer a positive agenda for the affluence that the majority of
their church members were obtaining.

Many times clergy still seem to approach their congregations
as though the majority were hurting financially. Advertising
doesn't believe this to be the situation, since they target people's
resources for such categories as home video games and entertainment systems, more cars per household, and phones for every
member of the family. Ministers have not made the shift that the
culture has—to realizing while there may be the few "extraordi-
narily wealthy" in their congregations, the vast majority of people
sitting in their pews are "ordinarily wealthy," to use terms popularized by Don McClanen. What should the role of the minister
be when the congregation members filling the pews are generally some of the most comfortable people on earth?

Dan Conway remembered a phrase from church culture. "It's
an old saw: The priest settles the unsettled and unsettles the settled. Stewardship education should unsettle the settled." The

value of practical fund-raising, he noted, is to draw the best out of us even when we don't feel particularly generous.

Andrew Greeley, priest, novelist, and sociologist, expanded on that theme. "There's a tradition that emphasizes both comforting and challenging. We do a reasonably good job with comforting—marriage, death. The difficulty is challenging. To challenge, stir up excitement, recapture the energy that is so clear in St. Mark's Gospel. This is a frantically busy culture, overcommitted. In the midst of that the church should be stirring up religious excitement so it would transform everything they do. That's the biggest challenge."

William McKinney noted that the church in the United States is facing a different challenge than it did in the 1950s. "The [sociologist] Will Herberg argument was that to be a Protestant, Catholic, or Jew in the U.S. was to be fully American. New groups on the scene bought into that thinking as much as the established churches did. Through the 1950s, the structure remained intact: To be a Methodist, for example, was not only okay, it gave you a place in the whole picture. If anything, that structure had an uptick in the 1950s, in the 'era of good feelings,' and it still worked. When the crisis hit in the 1960s, people wondered whether that structure ought to remain intact. Those who were really part of the structure suffered most. If sexual morals are up for grabs, what does that do to your church giving patterns?"

When asked what he thought was the greatest challenge facing the church in the United States, James Hudnut-Beumler responded, "The key challenge is getting over the '50s. I say that because this was the time when a lot of our local churches were founded. It was a time when our denominations were rich and constructed their programmatic structures around these resources, and they thought the financial support would continue to rise."

Hudnut-Beumler pointed to a larger than usual group of people establishing themselves, a "concentrated cohort effect," that resulted because so many people had served in World War II. Having delayed their marriages for six or seven years, they then joined others just coming into the child-bearing years. "These people experienced 'church' as a new building, built by themselves. They established the board structures and Sunday school;

they were in on the creation of all this organization. Furthermore, their kids were young, didn't take drugs, nobody died of cancer, no divorce—this was the good life. And a large group of ministers, rabbis, and priests began their ministries during these unusual times. This was a convergence of factors of affluence. To treat the post–World War II decade as normal and everything since as evil, rather than recognizing that period as a lucky point, is a mistake. It has a warping factor on the church today. We conceive of ourselves as in crisis rather than focusing on who is the church of Jesus Christ in the 1990s."

Many would agree that the decades following the relatively calm and booming 1950s were turbulent. During times of change, institutions are tempted to preserve themselves and to remain the same. The church is also vulnerable to this approach. One retired national denominational official suggested that the denominational structures found it difficult to change because they are run by the people who have the most at stake—the clergy. He referred to the system of organization of pastors in his denomination as "the tightest union in the country." Ordained pastors decide who is allowed to join their ranks and who is not. "Laypeople are beginning to notice," he suggested, and may be taking steps to change that.

Loren Mead commented on the role of pastors in running denominations as well. "Ministers are in a real conflict of interest. They write the rules how the institution runs, by and large, and the institution is largely an employment system for the clergy. The professional group in the church that has the most at stake is the clergy. There is a crucial need for spiritual growth here. Clergy have to pay the largest price in order for denominations to change, not only by losing authority but also there will be fewer jobs."

Although Mead acknowledged that in many Protestant structures laypeople have more votes in the governing structure, laypeople may not have as much experience as the pastor, who goes to the annual meetings year after year, who learns the ropes, and who can advise the laypeople when they ask the pastor, "What should we vote for?" The rotating system in lay leadership means the laity loses power to the clergy, he added. "It's not the intention but it is the consequence. A system of leadership has an overwhelming interest in continuation of the system. When you build the system on what you think is important, it winds up serving you. That's not meant as an accusation but rather is an observation."

Mead reflected on the seemingly opposite ways the church can be seen. "As I see it, the church is a major industry. It also happens to be the same place the next generation is going to learn about Jesus Christ. The clergy we've got that are part of the problem are also our greatest resource. We're in a bind. Some believe there's a 'real' church and the local institution is something different. I don't agree. I think that thing I go to on Sunday *is* the church."

The Local Church

One consequence of the church yielding a large portion of its public role to government programs (whether domestic entitlement programs or the ambitious Marshall Plan designed to implement global economic recovery) may have been that what remained for the church was an emphasis on the local institution. Fred Hofheinz observed that dollars spent on the local congregation return to the church member in services. However, the church may not be seen as helping the church member come to terms with passages such as Matthew 25, where Jesus raises the issue of feeding the hungry, clothing the naked, welcoming the stranger, and visiting those in prison. "There's a sense in which a gift to the church is a gift to myself. When I give to the homeless shelter, I don't get anything from that."

Bishop William McManus made a similar distinction. He views each church member as having a duty to support the local parish: "That's justice." However, he does not see that as the sum of financial stewardship. "The concept of alms has been lost. People think when they give to the church, it's alms. I tell them, 'You're kidding—you get it all back: air conditioning, four priests, eight staff, a musician.' Almsgiving traditionally is where the person gives and receives nothing in return from the one benefited."

There may be a lack of credibility in church structures now, suggested Mead, because of their institutional aspect. "If I give 10 percent to my local church, a lot of it goes to things not very important to me. There is a very important industry to support.

It used to be clear the institution supported vital missionary concerns. It's not clear now. There's a collapse of trust, I think."

Church members may then confuse what it means to be a Christian, thinking that support of the local institution is where the answers are to be found. Consultant David Schmidt noted, "We have more and more people in our pews making financial decisions without an adequate, biblical worldview. The culture rushes in with a lot of other good messages for places to put their money. The result? Lifestyles get upgraded but giving doesn't." He referred to the lack of understanding of the broader implications of what faith involves, particularly in the area of money, as "a major tactical issue."

A Broader Vision

If the church is silent on the topic of money, little discipling is taking place. The trend, then, would be away from the broader issues of the church to more local institutional issues that are less likely to challenge increasingly comfortable lifestyles. Loren Mead continued his earlier comments. "I don't think it's a big problem getting people involved on the local level. I do think the attraction of the mission far away has gotten lost in the local focus, however, to the detriment of the church. That is why I think the larger denominational structure, the judicatory is essential. If the church is going to recover a sense of larger mission, the regional judicatory is essential. That's why I'm concerned. I don't see people getting a large vision except from someone directly connected to them. Localization is a megatrend observed by people like [sociologist] Robert Bellah. The trend toward individualism is part of the same thing. I worry about a church that is only locally focused, and I worry about the regional structures being sustained. The denominational structure, particularly the regional judicatory, has to rethink what its role is. Local churches badly need a broad vision. The regional judicatory can buy into this role, can offer vision. In order to carry on the gospel and be teaching the next generation, we need to think how do we do church from the ground up? And how does the regional judicatory fit in?"

A similar theme was sounded by Patrick Brennan of Loyola University in Chicago. In a November 1993 speech at the National Catholic Stewardship Council meeting held in Nashville, he reflected on the value of small groups, for example, in helping church members deepen their faith. He commented: "The church is in the middle of a deep process, whether we want to be or not. . . . Are we willing to create and embrace structures that fit our mission? Our mission, as we work through this deep process and recover our mission, our mission is no less than this: It's the mission of Jesus Christ. The mission of Jesus Christ was to reveal, to usher in the reign of God. . . . It's the essence of the evangelical mission of the church: to invite people to the Kingdom of God."[14]

Others, such as Loren Mead, have been issuing a similar call. The task is to build for the future even as we cope with the present reality of how the church conducts its business. "Meanwhile, we have to deal with this institution of the church," he declared. "I grew up in the church, segregated in a town where the clergy believed in segregation. And I grew up getting a different message. Where did that come from? People are hearing messages that are not being sent. That's why I want the church to exist. So my grandchildren will have a place to go to hear messages I don't understand."

The Money Message

But what message they will hear, particularly about money and the church, remains to be seen. Trying to develop a constructive approach to the topic has plagued the church for centuries. Robert Wood Lynn recounted, "There were early nineteenth-century objections to preaching about money. People would say that the reason for corruption in the medieval church was that they joined the spiritual and money, that religion and the devil were split between the religious and the material."

The struggle with the role of money might be demonstrated by a one-page sheet distributed by Brian Kluth, president of the Christian Stewardship Association. The handout summarized four typical attitudes toward giving. First, he suggested that "Poverty Theology" views possessions with disdain and considers them a curse. In contrast, the "Prosperity Theology" views possessions as the "reward of the righteous." Perhaps most people fall into what he termed the "Commonly Practiced Theology," in which "the pursuit of household possessions and family pleasures is acceptable" and in which possessions are "a right." Suggesting that none of these represent a wholly biblical perspective, Kluth offered a "Stewardship Theology," in which "possessions are a trust given by God in varying proportions," and possessions are "a privilege."[15]

With so much confusion on the topic, it is not surprising that many ministers avoid the subject. However, not talking about money does not lessen the power it wields. As Howard Dayton observed, "People do not appreciate the spiritual impact money has in our lives." People may set their goals by secular standards and yet encounter an age-old problem. "There is no meaning in a 4,500-square-foot home," offered Hugh Magers, "but a lot of people don't know that until they own one."

Church consultant Thomas Sweetser said that helping people sort out the spiritual implications of money is one of the ways the church should be helping people. "People are searching for meaning and happiness," he noted, "and the church could give that. Giving is part of my spirituality, but the connection is not being made. There are vocations of all kinds, but we don't ordain many of them. People are generous, but we haven't allowed them to be spiritual in their finances." Sweetser suggested that the topic of stewardship will be more effectively dealt with to the degree that people begin to recognize how it ties into their spirituality.

Yet it may be no easy task to help people sort out these issues. David Schmidt believes the task is no less than to "de-enculturate" people from their present attitudes toward money. "Drop by drop, wring enculturation out of people's value system. Progress comes from increased exposure to God's agenda. People can't let go of something unless they have something to replace it. What could be better than a clear vision of God's redemptive purposes?"

Magers feels the vision is already available. Solving the stewardship problem of the church is not a matter of figuring out how to pay bills. It's helping people understand the real order of the universe. "'Lay up for yourself treasure in heaven.' *We* human beings are the treasure. We can use our resources to nurture folk into heaven. We have an opportunity to establish a deep appropriation of the faith. Instead of being in a world with starving babies, we have the opportunity to help there be well babies and to support a friend for eternity."

Making the connection with such a vision, helping people sort out what they currently think and what might be a more spiritual perspective on money, is the task before the church. Not succeeding at the task does have immediate practical implications. David McCreath put the issue in context. "My favorite stewardship text is the first sentence in paragraph 2 of the first chapter of the Presbyterian *Book of Order:* 'Christ calls the church into being, giving it all that is necessary for its mission to the world, for its building up and for its service to God.' So if the church is not doing evangelism and ministry of other sorts, and Christ has given the church the resources, then it is a question of stewardship."

Giving as Part of Worship

How is the church handling the task of helping people understand stewardship in new ways (as a possibility to spiritually reorient ourselves rather than to merely pay bills)? According to various leaders, too often inadequately. Loren Mead said, "We're teaching people that the church is useful because of what it does rather than what it is."

Even the way money is collected in many communions seems to separate finances from the spiritual. "In some of our churches, many are subdued when it comes to the offering," said Al Taylor. "The attitude is, Let's get it over with and get on with worship, and that's wrong. The offering is part of worship, and if it is not included in that sense, people are robbed of that blessing."

David McCreath also highlighted this problem. "We're talking about reclaiming the place of the offering in worship. The mechanisms for paying are disconnected from worship. People can respond to letters or use electronic fund transfer or send a check directly. People may be giving well, but they are sending it directly to the church, or they give once a month. We need a different approach. Also, we now strongly encourage that the offering plate be passed to the pastor, to indicate that no one is exempt. That says, 'Money is an important part of faith.' Most do not pass the plate to the pastor because the pastor will say, 'My spouse sits in the congregation and gives.'"

The need for a constructive attitude toward the relationship between stewardship and worship has other implications as well. The idea that worship and faith involve giving is a key element in helping people grow into a deeper understanding of compassion, according to Robert Wuthnow. He described the goal as "mature compassion. The problem is to take the primordial sense of caring and mature it as adults. First, we can care for friends, spouse, children. Churches sometimes reinforce that primordial caring by treating members of the congregation as 'family,' and the concern is not often spread very far. Yet what churches can do well sometimes is to teach people a more mature understanding that is much less heroic, utopian, and more practical. You understand a little bit of money, a little bit of time *does* make a difference. You give a little and the church gives a little, and it gets spread around." He commented on studies he has done with teenage volunteers. Those teenagers who were involved in some sort of service generally matured into adults who had learned how to care about others in meaningful ways. Teens who did not become involved were often not realistic about addressing needs around them, having only a utopian or vague sense of what it means to help others.

These ideas would suggest that giving, then, is important not only because it pays the bills but also because it has the potential to transform church members into caring people, a goal consistent with the tenets of the faith.

In addition to how giving and worship are related, another basic question to ask is, If church members are going to be asked to contribute, how much should they give? This, too, is a topic that is open to debate.

Coming to Terms
with Money

All to Jesus I surrender,
Humbly at His feet I bow,
Worldly pleasures all forsaken,
Take me, Jesus, take me now.

Judson W. VanDeVenter, 1896
"I Surrender All"

The Tithe

When discussing how much to give to the church, one common standard is the tithe, or giving 10 percent of one's income. The term itself may not be the most useful one available. Two Catholic leaders independently identified *the tithe* as a Protestant term. The history of the tithe goes back much further, however, to when there was only one communion. At the Council of Mascon, for example, in A.D. 585, there was talk of reviving the "ancient practice." A system of tithes was used in Europe for centuries, before and after the Reformation, in both the Catholic Church and the emerging Protestant churches, sometimes with injurious results. Active resistance to the forced payments of tithes began after the Reformation. A series of events referred to as the "tithe wars" occurred in seventeenth- and eighteenth-century England, when people rebelled against officials who collected the tithe with force of arms.[1] One might assume that two hundred years had cooled the memory of that event, but not so according to one Episcopal priest, who explained not long ago that he could not promote the tithe because people in his congregation still had bad memories about those wars.

187

There is by no means a clear consensus on the tithe as an accepted standard of stewardship or as an aspect of discipleship. By the early 1970s, Douglas Johnson and George Cornell, writing the report from the survey of more than three thousand lay and ministerial leaders, pointed out that the tithe was seen as a minimum standard among only 27 percent of the laity and 20 percent of the clergy.[2] Although some denominations, such as the Church of the Nazarene and the Southern Baptist Convention, have always promoted the tithe as a standard, and others, such as The United Methodist Church, have more recently endorsed it once again, opinions on its usefulness as a guideline for giving are mixed.

Concerns about the Tithe

One area of concern is that the tithe may give a wrong impression about what it means to be a steward of God's resources. Ron Blue objects to the tithe: "First of all, I think 10 percent is too small. I fight the concept that God owns 10 percent and I own 90 percent. God owns it all."

The Catholic bishops came to a similar position when they approved the pastoral on stewardship in November 1992. Archbishop Thomas J. Murphy of Seattle chaired the drafting committee and shared some of the thinking that went into the final version, which makes minimal reference to tithing. "If you earn two thousand dollars a week and give two hundred dollars to God, what did you do with the other eighteen hundred dollars?" David McCreath of the Presbyterian Church (U.S.A.) described a similar conclusion reached by that denomination's Stewardship Education department: "In the past, most of the energy has been directed toward church receipts—give more to the church. Now that is only part of the goal. The question is being raised, What happens to the 90 percent that people keep? We haven't quite figured out how to approach that discussion, since most of the stewardship materials are geared to fund-raising campaigns."

The discussion in some quarters seems to be shifting from the obligation to pay 10 percent of one's income to "whole-life stewardship." This point was made by Bishop William McManus. "The Lord was concerned that some tithers didn't have much concern for the 90 percent of their income that they kept for themselves. In my wild Irish imagination, I suspect the famous Dives, the rich man who ignored the beggar Lazarus at his gate, was a tither; he ended up in a rather hot situation. Tithing could be misleading," he continued. "'I tithe' is like buying salvation. Jesus, however, expects total stewardship, including concern for the other 90 percent. Extravagant consumerism, contempt for the environment, insensitivity to the plight of others are not good stewardship."

Others raised concerns because of the rigidity with which tithing can be promoted. One Baptist leader worried that the tithe was increasingly being promoted through legalism rather than calling people to a grace-filled response. Craig Dykstra suggested that tithing introduces concepts that don't get an easy hearing in the present culture. "Duty, obligation, responsibility, discipline—these notions now seem unintelligible to many people. The tithe doesn't make sense outside a coherent tradition that gives it intrinsic meaning. It seems merely an arbitrary rule, and in a highly individualistic culture, arbitrary rules don't command allegiance or obedience. Any guideline or rule like 10 percent giving has to have a relatively coherent worldview around it in the context of which it makes sense. If it is going to be meaningful, 10 percent giving must be seen not as an arbitrary or externally imposed expectation or demand but rather as a helpful marker to reach some larger end, some larger vocation."

Indeed, tithing seems to many to be a law rather than a guideline. Robert Welsh of the Christian Church (Disciples of Christ) pointed out that tithing was taught in that communion in the 1950s and 1960s. It is no longer taught, he suggested, because "the Christian Church (Disciples of Christ) is antilegalism about anything, and the tithe reeks of legalism. The shift in attitude is that we are called to be stewards of all, not 10 percent but 100 percent. It's seeping in."

Those who consider the past may be surprised about the role of the tithe in the church in the United States. "It's an ancient custom, debated and fiercely argued in the nineteenth century," commented Robert Wood Lynn. "Equally dominant in the nineteenth century was proportionate giving. There's great confusion about tithing of what? Gross? Net? There's genuine perplexity regarding whether it is a law of Scripture. There's a reasonable argument to be made against the tithe as a law, as it is superseded by the New Testament."

William McKinney had a more practical concern. "It may well be the wrong strategy for churches to emphasize the tithe. It's not a decision that should be made on theology or faith alone. There's too much at stake." He suggested it would be important to have research to show the role the tithe can play before changing current stewardship approaches.

Loren Mead's objection is that "tithing is something we've grabbed on to, not theologically but rather to preserve an institution. It's become a method of financing." The Jesuit writer, John Haughey, suggests there is a confusion about the holy use of money. There are dangers, he writes, in promoting the tithe if it does not sit in a larger context. He notes that many of the "robber barons" at the turn of the century built wealth on the backs of their labor force and did not think it odd to combine this bad behavior with the public application of their wealth in founding museums, libraries, and institutes.[3]

Robert Wuthnow does not seem to think tithing is likely to succeed as a strategy. He described the giving patterns of church people in the United States as far different than the logical approach suggested by the tithe. For most Americans, his research suggests, "It doesn't factor in to give to charitable causes except on the spur of the moment. The logic is, it is virtuous to give. Americans pride themselves on volunteering and giving. It is virtuous to give *voluntarily*, not a certain amount or with legalism. It is no more virtuous to give 10 percent than 1 percent for many people. It's the *giving*, freely, joyfully, not the amount. If the average household gives three hundred dollars and household income is thirty thousand dollars, oh well. One could almost object to the idea of tithing on cultural grounds. It may be accurate biblically. But as far as culture, people don't think in terms of tithing but rather giving a little bit."

Supporters of the Tithe

Yet some staunchly defend the practice of tithing as a spiritual discipline applicable to the church in the United States today. Christian Stewardship Association president Brian Kluth is one of those people. He has taught stewardship concepts among many denominations in the United States and overseas. He described sitting in a small hut in India and having to respond to a question as to whether tithing was indeed part of God's plan for the believer no matter what the circumstances. He recalled hearing the testimony of many Christians in India that tithing is a vital part of their Christian faith. "And if it is true among Christians who live in impoverished situations, how much more should it be true in the lives of American Christians? My sense has been that I must be willing to trumpet the truth of God in a loud cry in the midst of everyone's excuses. Teenagers, college students, young couples, those with small kids, those putting kids through college—everyone has excuses. I can speak with confidence, having spoken on stewardship in Latin America, Africa, the former Soviet Union, Asia, and across the U.S., that when people give to God first, their testimony has always been the same—God is faithful. I even know a young mother who said, 'I wrote the check to God first and it meant I had no food to feed the children. But God brought groceries into my house. I will always honor God first knowing the father-heart of God will take care of me.'"

Of course, a variety of denominations continue to point to the tithe as a minimum standard of giving. One national leader of the Church of the Nazarene said he was surprised to hear that some denominations were coming back to the tithe, since his denomination had never left it.

One interesting line of reasoning on the tithe as a principle for contemporary Christians is offered by Al Taylor. He points out that Abraham tithed to Melchizedek the priest centuries before the law was introduced by Moses, and therefore the idea is outside the law. Further, since Jesus is a priest in the order of Melchizedek, the tithe remains as a timeless means of both worshiping Jesus and also bringing material possessions under spiritual direction.[4]

Tithing may also be a useful statement for people who feel more comfortable having clear guidelines to follow. One young suburban mother explained, "It would be nice to have a sense I was doing the right thing and not feel guilty all the time about what I have." The giver's attitude is important. There is general agreement among church leaders, in theory at least, that God is really the owner of everything people have. In that context then, suggests one writer, the tithe can be seen not as a bill to be paid but rather as a symbolic and acceptable offering of the whole.[5]

In the Church of the Brethren, "We have discovered tithing as an official position in the last seven or eight years," according to Don Michaelsen, who worked in the Congregational Support department. "We had decided it was too legalistic. Now we see it as a spiritual, voluntary discipline that's helpful. It's not the upper limit. It's a concept that's well-known and people can get on the same wavelength. Tithing now has better press than pledging in our denomination."

Bishop William McManus allowed that tithing can serve a purpose. "Tithing is good because it provides a clear target, which is always wise. I'd never speak against tithing but I'm not really for it. Rather, it should be a percentage of income. Get people to pledge a percent of gross household income. Point out that people have fluctuating income, and what they give can go up and down as a percentage of that income."

Through its General Convention, tithing was accepted as a minimum level of giving in The Episcopal Church, according to Hugh Magers, director of Stewardship. "Tithing is a minimum standard, and we have a plan to be tithing in three years. For twelve years, this has been the position." Magers has worked to promote the idea of tithing within the denomination. For example, the General Convention statement was worked into a vestry (congregational leadership board) and diocesan executive committee statement, that reads to the effect, "We all tithe or give proportionately with a goal in three years to tithe." The goal has been to have all these church leaders sign it. Has it worked? Well, Magers observed, sometimes it's gotten a vestry to move to "we agree we ought to give God something at least sometimes."

Having struggled with the issue, Magers has also taken another tack. He will point out to interested clergy that ministers who tithed had higher salaries, since they tended to teach stewardship to their congregations more effectively. They also had larger budgets. He explained that he pursues this line of thinking in terms of enlightened self-interest that may appeal to pastors.

There has been a change in attitude toward proportional giving in the United Church of Christ, according to M. Douglas

Borko of that denomination's stewardship department. Through the 1970s, stewardship focused on giving fixed amounts. Since then it has begun to focus on proportional giving. Asked if that approach has succeeded, he was somewhat rueful as he noted, "The Stewardship Council has done a good job, perhaps to the detriment of financial development and fund-raising. It's been theological. We didn't do fund-raising. We've had fund-raising materials, but we were doing theological education and not asking for money."

Stewardship Education

Most church leaders agree there is a need for theological work and education in the area of financial stewardship. The issues might include the spiritual source of the problem, the role of law and grace in coping with the resulting human condition, what individuals should be taught about how they can respond, a review of that ideal response in light of reality, and how the ability to respond might be translated into practice.

As far as the source of the problem, when asked why people did not give more of their incomes to the church, Andrew Greeley suggested several reasons and then concluded, "Of course, you can't rule out selfishness."

Some of those interviewed were willing to go back to the beginning. In various interviews, we asked, "From your perspective and experience, if pastors in this country were to try to lead people to deepen their desire to help those in need, both domestically and globally in word and deed in Jesus' name, what is the biggest problem or greatest obstacle or difficulty they would face?" Dan Conway reflected on the issues involved and then responded, "That question goes to the heart of Christian life. As a believing Catholic, I'd have to say original sin. What's the greatest difficulty in getting people to be Christian and live as Christians? There's something about us that needs healing and God's grace. And no matter our best intentions, we're not going to get it right. There is something flawed about us. As Saint Paul writes, 'Why do I do things I don't want to do?' We need forgiveness and grace; despite our best intentions, we're never going to get it right."

It's a condition described as "hardening of hearts" by James Engel. "Can it happen to Christians? Sure. The Book of Hosea talks about plowing up the hard ground of my heart." Jim Engel would suggest that the solution lies not in pursuing programmatic solutions but rather in what he terms "seeking the mind of God."

Don McClanen, the founding energy behind the Ministry of Money, which helps people come to terms with their resources, sounded a similar theme. Why aren't church members willing to give more? "The fall. The fall and the selfishness, the fall into selfishness, into sin, pride, greed, idolatry. There's a vast chasm, a dichotomy between what God called us to be and the fall into sin, pride, idolatry, greed."

From a slightly different angle, sociologist Robert Wuthnow also identified the problem in broader terms than institutional factors. "But underneath that financial crisis is a spiritual crisis—the inability to connect work and money and other vitally important areas of life with spiritual and with financial giving; the compartmentalizing so that the spiritual has nothing to do with economics." Wuthnow believes that church-member giving patterns won't be changed as the result of more effective techniques. "The church won't boost giving unless it begins a ministry to a whole range of economic concerns. You can't mount a once-a-year campaign if people don't feel they are cared about—how they are coping with work, stress, and credit card debt, for example."

Giving from the Heart

While theological work in the area of financial stewardship is needed, there's another necessary element as well, according to Don McClanen. "You can work the pants off money, but if you're not deeply into Christ and the Spirit, all the talk, theology, biblical study, suffering of the world won't make any difference. It's a spiritual problem. Money cries out for transformation. As long as we talk about making stewardship more effective, it won't work. What we're talking about is the transformation of the heart. It doesn't come just with theology. It comes through conversion. It comes with an open, wounded, gentle heart of compassion, conversion, transformation. In doing justice, there's joy here, there's freedom. To work with money is to work with freedom. That's the key word here—*freedom*."

Freedom and the related theme of grace raise an issue that has long been debated in the church. Before the New Testament, there was the Old, with its emphasis on law and structure. The Christian faith is built on the grace that resulted from the atonement of Jesus Christ. Yet is there still a role for the law in bringing people to a deeper sense of grace? Evangelical Lutheran Church in America pastor Ron Voss thinks so. "One thing I say, some of us should feel legitimately guilty about what we put in the offering plate. Relative to the wealth that has been placed in our care, few of us give sacrificially. We are greedy and giving God the leftovers. The law has a legitimate role to bring us to the righteous God at the foot of the cross, where we meet a gracious loving Christ. It is the love of Christ that we are responding to, that motivates us to be great givers and deep lovers. The correct tension/balance between law and gospel should be maintained in all teaching/preaching ministry. It all goes to getting people back into the Word, and then their response will develop."

Jim Engel explored a similar idea. "I wonder if we don't overemphasize instant forgiveness and take God too lightly. We forget God is a righteous God too. That's dangerous, of course; we can quickly get over into the law and not understand grace. But maybe we need an emphasis on, for example, Amos: 'You fat cows of Bashan.'" With a smile, we asked him if that might be a book title on the topic of stewardship. He laughed, "You'd sell twelve books to people who thought it was a dieting book."

Grace

This area of theology, attempting to move from the law into a sense of the grace that ought to define financial giving patterns, has apparently been difficult for the church in the United States throughout its history. Robert Wood Lynn commented from his historical studies, "I don't think American Protestants have come close to a scriptural view of God's grace in stewardship. We are a law-ridden people, and the law is becoming more and more important as a means to move us. Why haven't we given more for

140 years? I don't think the American churches have been able to understand the full meaning of the gospel for this area of stewardship. We've been denying this for an awfully long time. It raises the whole fundamental meaning of the gospel. It is not only duties and obligations; it is also grace that can set us free. Then discipline can follow."

Lynn suggested that it is enormously difficult to talk about grace and the subject of financial stewardship, partly because it is so seldom talked about. "Grace is the central reality out of which we can begin to understand what we are to do with these resources. We have to get a conversation started on faith and money. We must not let this be interpreted as another spiritual assault where people are reminded they are selfish and greedy. We already know that. We need a setting in which we can talk about the meaning of money in our lives and discover how much it dominates our lives. We can use this as an occasion to understand again the whole meaning of the gospel. We cannot use grace in order to raise money. But rather we are going to the topic of grace to use this as an occasion to rethink what is the meaning of the gospel for this time."

That grace has to be a key factor in any renewed understanding of financial discipleship was echoed by Loren Mead: "There is no behavior we can adapt that will justify us. A behavior can avoid the problem that we have to live by grace. Faith is more demanding than tithing or helping the poor. Pointing to only a behavior can cut the nerve of the demand of the gospel that we go a lot deeper." Such behavior would result from a deeper understanding of grace, but that understanding must be developed first.

How does one explore the topic of grace, particularly in the context of growing in discipleship and a more responsible use of one's resources? Waldo Werning has been a pastor, writer, and director of stewardship for The Lutheran Church-Missouri Synod. He believes that at least part of the answer will be learned in the context of small groups. "In the twenty-first century, we should be going back to small groups. We have to gain the model in Ephesians 4. In verse 1, there is the call. In verse 7, it says we are graced by Christ—*everybody* is graced. Verse 12 explains that pastors and teachers are to equip people for *their* works of service. Grace—it means recognizing it and using it. Verse 13 answers the question how long should we pursue this: until we grow up in the faith and become mature."

The pursuit of grace. There is, of course, the danger that searching for grace can become a task, which seems just the opposite of experiencing the grace that is offered by God. Andrew Greeley anticipates that struggle: "The trick is not to go out searching for grace but to recognize the grace all around us."

Giving as a Response

Rather than harnessing grace to produce improved giving patterns, discussion seems to be moving in the direction of developing an understanding of grace that will then impact how we consider what to give. What conclusion might a church member who understands grace come to about giving? Ronald Nelson feels that a general consensus exists. "What is the basic thing we'd agree on? Give to God because of what he has done for you."

The idea of giving as a response was a key tenet of the pastoral on stewardship approved by the National Conference of Catholic Bishops. Its title, *Stewardship: A Disciple's Response*, summarized the findings. Archbishop Thomas J. Murphy of Seattle commented about the pastoral's perspective: "Stewardship follows as response. It should be rooted in the Eucharist, in discipleship, in baptism—stewardship is meant to be followed as a way of life. There is the reality of the need for more resources in the church. What is needed, however, is a long-term faith response, not a quick fix."

How to elicit that long-term response from church members who are mired in everyday realities is one of the great challenges facing the church.

Spiritual Disciplines

It is possible that a revamped theology of stewardship can result in a bountiful harvest in the community setting of the congregation, but some are concerned that such a theology also be applied in the individual lives of the church members. One traditional element of the Christian walk has been self-discipline, sometimes pursued in an intentional way. For many communions, for example, daily Bible reading and/or times specifically set aside for prayer have been part of the routine recommended for the believer. In today's busy society, however, and in a church that has been emphasizing the services it provides rather than the growth of the individual, these disciplines have not been as commonly promoted. These disciplines have largely been kept alive in certain subgroups of the church, particularly among religious orders in the Catholic community.

Some years ago a book by Richard Foster titled *Celebration of Discipline* reintroduced the disciplines to a lay audience, both Catholic and Protestant. However, these disciplines now have to compete with a busy and demanding culture. Timothy Ek noted there is a great disparity between the time church members are exposed to Christian values and perspectives compared to the number of advertisements they see each day. "And the church hasn't helped to develop disciplines to guide people. People don't do personal devotions. We set up models for failure. We tell them, 'Pray and it will change.' But we don't tell them it's real work. We need to let them know it's not easy, to give them the practical nuts and bolts of learning not only to think like a Christian but to act like one too!"

In this context, Bishop William McManus provided a perspective in which stewardship could flourish for the individual. "We must respond to Christ's words, 'People will know you're my people by the way you love one another.' That's it. Well, it's unlikely that love will develop if it's not focused on prayer that centers on a personal relationship with the Lord Jesus."

Dan Conway also indicated that he sees stewardship as a spiritual discipline that must be actively cultivated. "There's a sense in which we recognize that stewardship as a goal is illusive. Therefore, we organize ourselves to move toward it. The connection is to original sin or to our disposition to fail in our good intentions as in chastity or patience or in any of the other virtues. Saying we want to do these things is not enough. We have to practice and develop habits. Good, ethical fund-raising provides a way to overcome our natural disinclination to develop this virtue."

Jesus Christ talked of the relationship he wanted with his followers. He saw money as a serious competitor with him for our hearts and minds. He went so far as to say that we humans will serve either God or money and told us we will have to make a choice, since there is no way to hold a balance between the two. Consider the characteristics of these two potential masters. Money promises to serve the one who owns it, through purchasing power, offering prestige, and providing security. And yet, as such classics of literature as Dickens's *A Christmas Carol* suggest, money often proves to be a hard taskmaster, enslaving its subjects in loneliness, isolation, and distrust. In contrast, Jesus asks no less of his followers than that they lose their lives for his sake. Nevertheless, he calls those who follow him his friends and will one day serve them at the banquet in heaven.

Promoting Stewardship

Often the theological approach to stewardship is beautiful and inspiring—and far removed from the person in the pew. For example, sociologist Dean Hoge talked about stewardship materials he has seen. The approach often is "I've been given a lot by God; I need to respond." Will that work for most church members? "I don't think so. It's more common for people to think, 'What did we give last year?' There's a lot of momentum in the system. We're getting into motivational science, and that's not a very exact science. We need to label the ideas more clearly. It's either altruism or reciprocity. In my view, I don't think there's anything else. If you read most of the fund-raising manuals, it's really reciprocity—if people are giving a large gift, fund-raisers believe the donors are buying something. Consider large gifts to the symphony, with the published list of large donors. Would these donations dry up if they didn't list the names? Who's going to risk that experiment? No one. Generally there is group reciprocity—my name is on something. That's why you see plaques. If it was only between me and God, we wouldn't put a plaque on the donated item because the New Testament is slightly against it."

William McKinney also thinks that those who are responsible for stewardship need to reconsider the target audience. "We make decisions on a vision of the 'good church member' and the tithe works there. But what percent of church members actually think that way? You can run a church based on purity, but there are a lot of Corinthians out there."

Promoting stewardship from within an ideal setting could also interfere with the church member's ability to experience grace, according to Waldo Werning. "The expectation of a 'good' member—we need to get rid of that terminology. In the church there are only growing or nongrowing Christians. When you talk about human expectations, you are introducing unspoken rules. The goal should be the spiritual growth of the individual, not raising a budget."

Reciprocity

As if the whole area were not complicated enough, Ronald Nelson raised a further intriguing idea. In some circles, the "reciprocity" idea has been exploited, with church members promised that if they give God ten dollars, God will return it tenfold. This form of fund-raising has proven distasteful to many stewardship professionals, to the degree, Nelson proposed, that they ignore there is some biblical basis for the idea. He commented, "There are the verses in Malachi 3 [verses 8–12: bringing in the tithe will result in God pouring out his blessings]. This struggle has always been in the church. The 'give to get' idea has been pushed down so much, if you say God will bless you if you give, it is almost like heresy."

Nelson drafted a seven-page rebuttal to the position that the idea was unbiblical, quoting from Scripture and denominational doctrinal documents to demonstrate the basis for it. "A pastor wrote to me, 'The only way to get the wealth of the world to the church is through good givers—the "water" will flow through you.' We refuse to believe we should be rich. Yet how else can the church do mission unless they have resources with which they have been blessed by God? We talked to people who are good givers, and they told us stories of how they gave and then found they were able to give more. Every one of them said they have been blessed because they gave."

Requests

A key challenge for the church is to find out how these generous people began giving when so many other church members simply aren't. Developing a clear theological understanding of the role of grace that leads to response (with a recognition that giving deepens one's intimacy with Christ)—allowing people to give financially because they are experiencing true riches—is an important element. Several of those interviewed, however, suggested that there is another key component that is too often overlooked. Frequently, church members have just not been effectively asked.

There may be some who are familiar with church operations whose response to this idea is to protest that the church is asking all too often, as the list of giving opportunities provided earlier would suggest. Rather, these leaders are suggesting another issue. That is, too many people have not been directly asked to include the church in their household budget as a regular portion of their income. Thus they put in the offering plate loose bills or what is convenient after their other expenditures. The unwillingness to ask may go back to the fact that money is such a difficult reality for many Americans. As noted before, churches may be talking about paying their bills, but are they really asking people to change the way they think about their spending habits and to consider giving a portion of their income to the church as part of their response to grace?

Consultant Thomas Sweetser disagreed with the idea that Catholics are not giving because of some problem they may have with their church's positions on certain issues. "I don't think it's a problem with teaching. It's the way we ask people to give. It's the way we ask for money. Many people give week to week, from what they have in their pockets."

One practitioner suggested that concrete details can have an influence on the level of personal stewardship as well. Church members may be asked to fill out pledge cards during a service, but no pencils are provided in the pews for them to use. Another example would be asking people to give proportionately but never taking the time during an informal section of a worship service to walk them through a proportional-giving chart. Such practical aspects of asking for money can be important factors that help translate a theology of stewardship into the daily lives of church members.

Ron Blue has seen that people need a plan but planning for the future is difficult for many. They often close in on themselves in their attempt to prepare for the unknown. "People don't give because they don't know they can give. Good stewardship by planning for the future may inhibit their willingness to respond to more immediate charitable requests. People don't plan to give. My message is, if you're afraid of losing it all, the best thing to do is give it all away now where it can be used in God's kingdom."

Money's Dark Side

Don McClanen's Ministry of Money has done a great deal of work in the area of the nature of money and our relationship to it. One helpful "poster statement" from the Ministry of Money suggests vocabulary that presents the dark side and light side of money:

Dark Side	Light Side
Fear	Grace
Guilt	Joy
Insecurity	Justice
Greed	Gratitude
Vengeance	Generosity
Violence	Magnanimity
War	Peace

In an interview Don McClanen provided some interesting background on the development of the above list. In 1981 he wrote to Dr. Karl Menninger, author of *Whatever Became of Sin?*, thanking him for the chapter on avarice. He also sent him a copy of the "Light and Dark Sides of Money," then under development. McClanen related that the doctor wrote back in response, "I think your question, 'How do we help people shift from greed to generosity?' is one of the great moral questions of the age. I would add, 'How do we get them to shift from vengeance to magnanimity?'" The letter from Karl Menninger continued, "Greed is one of the diseases that doesn't 'get well'; it can be incurable. People with mental disease who come to our Menninger Clinic are likely to get well—even without professional skill applied—but greed is not that way."[6]

McClanen reflected on the doctor's comments, "At that time, the list only went down to 'greed,' and he said we should go further. He told us we should explore vengeance. It can happen with poor people, but it gets exacerbated with wealth. Money feeds the dark side of power, prestige, control. 'Vengeance is mine, says the Lord.' Yet when you probe someone about their money, their response is often vengeful. Unspoken, the message can be, 'I'm going to get you. This is my private domain! You stay out of it!' The dark side leads from one to the next. But there is a light side, the gentle side. It's a mystery why the church is confused about what the Bible has to say about money. The light and dark are mixed in our heads and hearts, and that contributes to why the topic is so emotional and conflictual."

One example of money's dark side, which has pastoral counseling implications, is the fear that so many elderly people have about facing the future. Church members who have been faithful for years somehow find little comfort in that faith as they face the threatening prospect of having to accumulate enough resources for future long-term care. This area of pastoral counseling has not been developed, perhaps once again because of the awkward silence in the church on the subject of money and its role in our spiritual lives.

Giving from a Fixed Income

There is also confusion in the church's mind about the discipleship nature of giving rather than accumulating. Often, pastors and lay leadership boards explain that the majority of people in the congregation are on fixed incomes, and therefore an intentional stewardship effort would be inappropriate. The concern, presumably, is that older people would feel bad if they can't respond from their fixed incomes.

After one such meeting, the pastor pointed out to the Stewardship Project staff that a lady about whom concern had been expressed was already giving 10 percent of her income and would probably welcome such a response from more members of the church. In fact the pastor had become concerned about her level of giving and suggested in a visit that she consider decreasing the amount she gave. She let him understand that her giving level was between her and God, thank you very much!

The popular thinking that people on fixed incomes ought to be exempt from stewardship expectations has at least three inconsistencies. First, many of the elderly are much better givers than younger people. One regional official suggested, in terms of church giving patterns, that it takes three younger families living on 110 percent of their incomes to replace one elderly member who lived on 90 percent of his or her income and was saving 10 percent. If younger people were engaging their elders on the topic, a dialogue might result in which at least some of the elderly could pass on constructive attitudes about giving.

Second, an honest dialogue about the role of money in our spiritual lives might comfort the elderly in ways they are presently not experiencing. Many of the elderly feel isolated. Were they to be included in a congregation-wide dialogue on money, their lifelong experiences and testimonies about the faithfulness of God would be something many of them could contribute. Also, an open discussion might allow them to share some of their concerns in a public forum about their long-term care. Congregations may find a role in supporting their elderly in new and creative ways.

Third, and perhaps most cynical, there is a major preoccupation about the ten trillion dollars that will change hands in the next decade as the older generation dies. Who currently controls these trillions of dollars except the very individuals who, the conventional wisdom goes, should not be challenged about stewardship while they are alive? Somehow, the very people who need to be protected are also in control of the largest amount of money so far that will be passed from one generation to the next. One pastor commented that he guessed at least some of the people on "fixed incomes" in his congregation had higher incomes and fewer expenses than he did. He noticed some of them taking regular vacations and wintering in warmer climates. He referred to the "strong sense of entitlement" among a number of these elderly people.

Apart from that inconsistency, church leaders ought to be concerned not only with how these individuals plan their future distribution but with their spiritual health while they are still alive. If stewardship has spiritual implications, is the church being faithful to these people if it emphasizes only the responsible application of their financial resources after they are dead and no longer need them? Practicing dependence on God in the present may make it easier to depend on God in the unknown future.

The Question of an Inheritance

Some suggest that the answer to solving the problem of declining per member support as a portion of income is to capture for the church much of the ten trillion dollars that is going to change hands as older members die.[7] One baby boom church leader reacted with some hostility to all the planned giving talk along this line he had heard, exclaiming, "They're trying to steal our inheritance!"

This potential conflict of interest between the baby boom generation, now beginning to think about retirement, and the church—which sees the ten trillion dollars as a potential resource for its work—may escalate in the future. And as humor columnist Dave Barry pointed out, the baby boomers have begun to think about that future:

> It was also a good year, spiritually, for us aging baby boomers; after far too many years of being obsessively and selfishly absorbed with our own lives, we are finally starting to reach the point where we become obsessively and selfishly absorbed with our own deaths. This has led to a number of inspirational best-selling books about the afterlife—*Embraced by the Light, Saved by the Light, Garfield Sees the Light,* and *The Susan Powter Post-Mortem Work-out.*[8]

For most, however, between now and death is retirement. A series of articles in *USA Today* reported on the future of the government's Social Security as well as various pension plans. The conclusion was that a person used to a fifty-thousand-dollar annual income would be wise to retire with one million dollars in assets in the near future.[9] For many baby boomers, who may have passed the halfway mark in their careers with no major saving plan in place, the thought of parental inheritance might be seen as an absolute necessity for their retirement comfort. Considering that there are approximately seventy-six million boomers, born between 1946 and 1964, this group could need anywhere from twenty to seventy-six trillion dollars for a comfortable retirement, only ten trillion dollars of which they can hope to inherit. In that context, if the church puts an insensitive overemphasis on the money that will change hands in the next decade, it could further alienate a generation of people that have had fewer denominational and loyalty ties to the institution than their parents. Any approach to estate planning in the church probably ought to keep all the generations informed and consulted and not target only the oldest group.

The issue is certainly complicated. Various church leaders point out that, with little education on the topic, many people will die with no wills, thus leaving others to determine which people receive what portion of the estate. The ten trillion dollars that is going to change hands could make a positive impact for the work of the church, if the energy is invested now in a massive information campaign focused on the people who have built up a large amount of resources and are now reaching the higher mortality range. Estate planning can be a constructive tool, helping elderly people to be responsible stewards of their resources both in the present and the future.

Even here, a pastor may be aware of congregational tensions that escape the attention of the regional officials, who may see only the numbers on the calculation sheet. One minister moved to a Midwest congregation, having pastored in the Southwest for many years. In his previous parish, he had included estate planning in his ongoing stewardship efforts. The feedback had always been positive. When he introduced the idea of such a workshop in his new congregation, however, he was accused of wanting "to get his hands on" their money. Estate planning education, no doubt, needs to take place in an atmosphere of trust.

Few would argue that the church ought to ignore the fact that many people have accumulated large sums of money through faithful living and that these individuals will need to distribute that wealth at the time of their deaths. Creative and sensitive work should be done in sharing information not only with those in the older generation but also with the baby boom and younger generations. Church leaders often suggest the best approach is in the context of being managers of God's resources. The parable of the talents, where the successful servant invested the money entrusted to him and the unfaithful one buried it, might be particularly apt. The question may be asked, however, that while there is a great deal of attention being focused on acquiring these resources from those passing from this scene, is there enough thought being given as to how the church can best make use of those resources should they be donated?

Endowments

Several pastors shared stories about congregations being overwhelmed by a large gift, with no clear plan how to use it. Internal arguments about the use of the money preoccupied the church. In some cases, the congregation began using a portion of the gift to make up any shortfall in operations. Soon the church was also compensating for a falling off in general contributions, with an increased reliance on the bequest. In these cases the large gift of money did not strengthen the local community of faith.

Endowments are one approach some churches have taken to absorb large gifts. An endowment is an investment account where, generally, the principal cannot be expended but the income from that principal can be spent for the program of the church. Many times, an endowment is established by a congregation for a specific purpose, such as only for capital needs of the congregation. The income can be a helpful resource. Yet again there is debate as to the impact the presence of such an account can have on giving patterns in a congregation. In the Stewardship Project survey, responses of both pastors and regional officials were decidedly mixed, with some respondents agreeing that the presence of endowment income in a congregation will not impact giving, while others disagreed.

Those who dislike endowments do not seem neutral on the point. Don McClanen referred to endowments as "the embalming fluid for dead institutions." Ron Blue, commenting on whether it was wise for congregations to establish endowments, said, "I think endowments can be absolutely destructive to good thinking. Once there is no ongoing need to tell people what you're doing, the power of the institution is in management only. There is little need for creative thought and entrepreneurial thinking. The job of the leader becomes a management task only. Endowments inhibit creativity."

Philanthropic leaders of the past took issue with emphasizing the distribution of assets after death rather than during one's lifetime. Josiah Strong warned his hearers that it was easy to accumulate wealth with the intention of later sharing it. "That is the pit in which many have perished. If a man is growing large in wealth, nothing but constant and generous giving can save him from growing small in soul."[10]

Industrialist and philanthropist Andrew Carnegie had practical reservations about those who would leave their wealth rather than administer it well during their lifetime. He pointed out that in many cases, the desires of the deceased are not carried out. "The cases are not few in which the real object sought by the testator is not attained, nor are they few in which his real wishes are thwarted. In many cases the bequests are so used as to become only monuments of his folly. It is well to remember that it requires the exercise of not less ability than that which acquired the wealth to use it so as to be really beneficial to the community." Carnegie went further, suggesting that those who leave large estates merit little praise: "Men who leave vast sums in this way may fairly be thought men who would not have left it at all, had they been able to take it with them."[11]

That it was not only in Carnegie's time that the wishes of the deceased can be thwarted is illustrated by a recent report. A millionaire collected 2,500 impressionist and postimpressionist paintings, leaving them in his mansion with the stipulation that they never be displayed elsewhere. "But wills are made to be bent: To raise cash, 84 Barnes works are now at the Philadelphia Museum of Art on a world tour" and a CD-ROM is being published, which will make 330 of the paintings available to anyone with a computer and the cash to purchase a copy of the disk.[12]

E. Earl "Scoop" Okerlund wondered whether a key to the effective use of endowments is their focus. He commented in an interview, "Any congregation says, 'If only we had one million dollars, we'd be okay.' They're kidding themselves. A pastor in Pennsylvania went to a congregation with a three-hundred-thousand-dollar annual endowment income. There was no personal stewardship being practiced. He advised the congregation they ought to give the endowment income away to further the mission of the church, and develop personal stewardship for the local institution instead."

Because of the problem a sudden large gift can create, the ELCA is advising congregations to develop a bequest policy—detailing how large gifts can constructively be applied—before such a gift is received. "The temptation," Scoop Okerlund continued, "is to worship bricks and mortar, making the church a museum."

One pastor speculated that ministers want endowments as a backup to their faith: "I trust God, but if it doesn't work, I want money in the bank." He commented, "As pastors, we have to come to terms with that. If we really believe this is God's church, why are we worried where it will be ten years from now?" Another pastor with an endowment said he felt it presented an ethical dilemma for him. "The trustees never turn me down when I make a proposal to them. It's almost like a slush fund, really. The problem is that if the general fund is hurting, I feel bad going to the people in the congregation when I know the endowment is growing."

A thoughtful letter in response to an article on endowments raised several points to be considered. The writer suggested that there are "ethical and philosophical issues involved" in endowments. Among other things, an endowment may "signal that a charity doesn't know what to do with the funds it is given, or that its mission isn't particularly urgent. . . . To stay frugal and innovative, a non-profit needs a financial prod. . . . An endowment is a way of escaping financial discipline by giving a non-profit an income regardless of its performance."[13] While a church should be funded out of faithfulness rather than considered for its performance, one earmark of the vitality of the church in the United States has been its active recruitment and involvement of members for the furtherance of the kingdom's goals.

The constructive use of large gifts is a topic Loren Mead also reflected on. He thought it interesting that seminaries might offer ministerial candidates only one administration course and in that course routinely teach that endowments are bad—even while seminary development officers are going out to the congregations to obtain money for seminary endowments. Recognizing that seminaries have raised tuition and fees as much as is likely reasonable, an income source such as an endowment is becoming more necessary for the seminaries. The distinction between the seminary and the congregation, however, is one he observed as possibly inconsistent.

To counter the difficulty of an endowment hampering stewardship, some suggest that endowments provide for a particular purpose in their charters, such as capital needs or mission outreach. Mark Teresi suggested that endowments can be positive or negative. An endowment can allow a local priest to create something like a fiefdom. Not needing financial assistance from the diocese, the pastor is free to pursue a variety of programs. He also cited one parish that established a capital endowment. Having the building taken care of, the priest emphasized applying current giving for programs, with positive results.

Herbert Mather also immediately thought of two examples where endowments produced exactly opposite results. In one case the congregation used its substantial portfolio for a truly dynamic ministry. In the other case the large amount of money in the bank became "a huge albatross" that limited the congregation's effectiveness.

Earmarking large gifts for missions may prove to be no safeguard, however. One minister described his unhappiness with his congregation. The minister felt that the building needed more attention. The laypeople did not agree and would not cooperate with the pastor to increase the maintenance budget from current giving. He described how he therefore used his authority to appoint like-minded individuals to the endowment committee. Once the necessary votes were in place, he arranged to have the endowment structure changed so that half the income went to building maintenance instead of 100 percent to missions. There is no guarantee that future generations will honor present commitments.

At best, endowments with a carefully thought-out agenda may be useful. To the degree they de-emphasize current stewardship responsibility and instead place the emphasis on money no longer needed after one has died, endowments may limit the spiritual growth of current members. Of course, it is possible they could produce a situation like the established churches in Europe, with ongoing budgets but little vitality. A mitigating factor may be whether the congregation has a larger vision to which the endowment resources can be applied or whether the congregation is one of the many operating on a maintenance/survival level, in which case the endowment may merely mask the need for the congregation to reflect on its basic reason for being.

Once again, this topic leads back to the area of how Christians can most constructively relate to money. In the case of endowments, from a purely institutional point of view, any accumulation of funds that ensures the operation of a church building is a good decision. From a larger perspective, is the future of the church actually an institutional question? Is a large building with few active participants really the church as it was meant to be? Before one can decide how best to proceed in regard to endowments or church programs, it is necessary to return more directly to the interrelationship of God and money and the church.

The Need for Clarity of Purpose

The lack of a positive agenda in the church contributes to making money a confusing entity. One pastor interviewed stated that "money needs to stop being a god and start being a tool." Yet a tool is used for a specific purpose. And without a commonly acknowledged, overarching vision, people are not sure their money is needed. Further, much of mission education in recent decades has been about what was done wrong in the mission ventures undertaken in other cultures. Why, then, would people want to give—to continue to risk the same kinds of mistakes? People can avoid repeating mistakes in missions by turning on the television and being told several minutes out of every hour how they can be popular and successful spending their money in other ways.

When the church is confused about its purpose, it cannot help people make constructive use of their money. Several of those interviewed suggested that, because of a lack of broad mission commitment, giving to the local congregation actually works out to be giving to ourselves. Church members have come to see the congregation as a place to meet their own needs, not as an agent of change in a hurting world. One leader noted that if he wants to see something accomplished, he makes a contribution to a parachurch group that is specializing in that area. The emphasis on the comfort offered by the church may also be limiting its image as the most effective agent for applying our money to the needs around us.

Controversial Positions

Many point to controversial denominational positions as a primary reason for current downward giving trends. Per member giving as a percentage of income has declined in denominations that have conducted highly publicized debates on the revamping of personal moral standards, for example. However, it should also be noted that giving as a percentage of income and the portion going beyond the congregation have been declining as well in denominations that have not had this type of debate but have continued to affirm traditional standards.

Certainly the discussion of personal morality has involved some national offices in intense interactions with their congregations on occasion. Few recent positions have resulted in such an intense response as a preliminary draft on human sexuality prepared by the Evangelical Lutheran Church in America (ELCA) in 1993. Ministers had been promised they could review the draft before it was released. However, a national news organization obtained a copy before the report was mailed to the ministers. The resulting article reported, among other points, that one paragraph in the draft could be interpreted as not condemning homosexuality. The news article was picked up across the country. While the ELCA headquarters normally received three thousand calls a day, it received twenty-two thousand calls in one day after the article was published.

In some cases those conflicts may have financial support implications for specific denominations. In the Stewardship Project survey, few questions resulted in marked denominationally defined results. One statement, however, that produced a marked result was, "Most congregation members in this denomination agree with the national office's handling of the issue of homosexuality." The division of responses was the only one in which what might be termed evangelical denominations were on one side of "unsure" and mainline Protestants were on the other. The evangelical denominations agreed with the statement, and the mainline Protestants disagreed. This response could have implications for church-member support of denominational programs, in that more than 80 percent of the pastors and regional officials disagreed with the statement, "Whether congregation members agree or disagree with the national office's handling of the issue of homosexuality will have no effect on the congregation meeting its denominational commitments." There was not a marked difference among the responses by denomination.

On the issue of abortion, there was not as strong a differentiation between denominations. Evangelical denominations registered clear agreement with the statement, "Most congregation members in this denomination agree with the national office's handling of the issue of abortion"; while the mainline Protestant denominations tended to register weaker agreement bordering on "unsure." Again the statement was offered, "Whether congregation members agree or disagree with the national office's handling of the issue of abortion will have no effect on the congregation meeting its denominational commitments." In regard to this issue, 70 percent of the pastors and 71 percent of the regional officials either disagreed or disagreed strongly with the statement, again without a marked difference among the responses by denomination.

Anger Not the Key Factor

Yet congregational withdrawal from denominational support is not sufficiently explained by controversial topics. Evangelical denominations are also experiencing a decrease in per member support from their congregations, even though congregation members apparently agree with their denomination's handling of controversial topics. The turning inward of the congregations that is evident across the theological spectrum appears to be related to other factors than mainly controversial national positions.

Mark Moller-Gunderson, while acknowledging that some issues elicit really strong responses from congregation members, also indicated that conflict with national policies does not seem to be widespread enough or consistent enough to explain giving patterns. When the national office staff asks people about the declining support for the denominational structure, he explained, "We don't get a 'mad' response. We don't get a 'sad' response. We get a blank stare."

Research backs up his experience. The study involving three thousand church leaders in the early 1970s found a very small percentage who had ever withheld money because of disagree-ment with a particular church program or position.[14] Two other studies came to similar conclusions, that feelings about denom-inational stands did not explain the trend of congregations keep-ing a larger portion of their incomes for themselves.[15] Yet another study, a careful analysis of denominational income from Presby-terian congregations during periods of controversy, led D. Scott Cormode to conclude, "The reasons must be found elsewhere to explain why congregations have increased local spending to over 86 percent of expenditures while deemphasizing denominational mission's portion from over 10 percent to less than 2.8 percent of total receipts."[16]

One denomination had a highly publicized policy debate over a period of years, a debate having no immediate connection with issues of traditional morality. Having had internal conflict for sev-eral years, the national leadership assumed that the controversy explained the decreased giving experienced by the regional and national offices. To confirm their theory, the denomination launched a series of focus groups around the country. The offi-cial said they were surprised at the results. In the various regions, the denomination's internal strife did not register as a reason that church members were no longer giving as much as they had been. Rather, the major finding was that the members indicated they didn't know why they were supposed to give.

A similar situation apparently exists in the Presbyterian Church (U.S.A.). David McCreath said there does appear to be some anger around specific issues such as homosexuality or abortion. "Rather than anger, what we sense in the generalized attitude is indifference. Parishes say, 'What's the use of the presbytery, the synod, the General Assembly?' Folks used to say, 'We're Presby-terian, we know the church, we'll give Presbyterian.' Now it seems like they are saying, 'I won't be involved. The General Assembly [the national representative structure] is dealing with issues out there, and I'm concerned about here.' So people are indifferent." After thinking about his answer for a moment, McCreath then amended it slightly. "I said we don't experience much anger. Rather than anger or fear, it's more uninvolvement with struc-tures. A lot of the reason for the indifference is that a lot of the interpretation has been very rational. We have not dealt with the affective side; and money follows affections, not thought. Rarely do you respond from the purely rational. Indifference is what is there. It would be nice if people were angry, because then we could talk about something."

The Roman Catholic Church has a considerably different structure. Yet Thomas J. Murphy also saw that a perceived distance between church members and the institutional structure in a diocese can produce communication challenges. "I see people become angry when they offer financial support to diocesan structures and programs and they perceive little responsiveness to their needs. Providing access to people is important. In our own archdiocese, tremendous goodwill has been generated by providing toll-free phone lines to reach the archdiocese. Likewise, convenient parking access at the chancery lets people know you want them to be in contact with you."

Bishop William McManus also did not feel that anger is a key factor. "Are they angry at the Pope or is it clergy scandal or are they tired? I don't think it's anger. I think some are following an old-fashioned American adage: If you can get it for free, don't pay for it. If coffee is free at a meeting, I'll have a cup. If not, I'll say I'm having too much caffeine. But I'd never not pay for it. I'd feel like a terrible cheapskate.

"Parishioners know that if they call in the middle of the night crying for a priest for seriously ill grandma, the priest will come, but they don't connect financial support with the church. No priest would check out a parishioner's giving before going on a sick call." Then he reflected briefly and added with a slight smile, "Perhaps the priest may be tempted to check contributions before a lavish wedding. Some people spend six thousand dollars on a wedding; they want to take the church apart and mess it up with rice, all for an offering of twenty-five dollars. A priest might be tempted to say no to the whole affair." Nevertheless McManus was fairly sure it would be uncommon for a priest to act on that temptation.

The Need for a Theology of Money

A constructive theology of money and its "holy use," as Haughey terms it, needs to be developed. Why hasn't it been? After we observed the current patterns, one idea presented itself. The academic work in seminaries has depended heavily on major European theologians, such as Aquinas, Luther, and Calvin. Note that all these writers existed in state-supported churches. The issues they were so ably facing do not reflect the challenge of voluntary support confronting the American church in the late twentieth century. Calvin himself notes the distinction of purpose he was pursuing in his *Institutes* and how it focused on topics other than the role of good works, a category within which voluntary giving falls. After a few examples of biblical texts on the issue of good works, Calvin writes:

> These few Scriptural proofs, indeed, I have set forth as a mere taste. For if it were my purpose to go through every one, a large volume would have to be compiled. All the apostles are full of exhortations, urgings, and reproofs with which to instruct the man of God in every good work [cf. 2 Tim. 3:16–17], and that without mention of merit.[17]

There are issues facing the church today that Aquinas and Calvin and Luther did not encounter and had little need to address. These challenges will have to be addressed by contemporary thinkers who can benefit from the wisdom of the past and integrate it into the different shape of the present. Movements in the church throughout its history produced voluntarily supported structures. However, the reality of the church in an entire country, such as the United States or Canada, being based on voluntary support was inconceivable at the time of the Reformation and is unique in the church's experience—the practice not having been seen on that scale since Christendom became synonymous with the empire in A.D. 313. Therefore, the church in North America, including the United States, may be in a position to make a contribution that has not been developed before: the voluntary response to grace that translates into disciplined use of plentiful money.

The task will not be easy. The church has often found it more comfortable to accommodate itself to the larger culture than to develop an authentic alternative. Adolf Hitler apparently counted on this fact when he began his public career in Germany, as indicated in a conversation with Hitler in the early 1930s remembered by Hermann Rauschning. Rauschning quoted Hitler as saying,

> What's to be done, you say? I will tell you: we must prevent the churches from doing anything but what they are doing now, that is, losing ground day by day. Do you really believe the masses will ever be Christian again? Nonsense! Never again. That tale is finished. No one will listen to it again. But we can hasten matters. The parsons will be made to dig their own graves. They will betray their God to us. They will betray anything for the sake of their miserable little jobs and incomes.[18]

Of course, stories of heroic clergy and lay alike, people who were actively involved in the resistance to the movement sweeping Europe, ultimately helped to prove Hitler was not entirely correct. One outstanding exception was Dietrich Bonhoeffer, the Lutheran pastor who disproved the theory that all clergy would compromise themselves in order to maintain their personal comfort. In 1995, on the fiftieth anniversary of his execution at the hands of the Nazis, magazine articles and community memorial services provided vivid opportunities to reflect on the best and brightest that shone forth the Christian witness.

Yet the difficulty of the church to provide an authentic alternative to the larger culture was also highlighted by someone as committed to the church's cause as H. Richard Niebuhr. In 1929 he sounded a critical note when he observed that churches often follow the general population, especially during times of social unrest, such as during war or internal social changes.

> Under these circumstances it is almost inevitable that the churches should adopt the psychologically more effective morale of the national, racial, and economic groups with which they are allied. Hence they usually join in the "Hurrah" chorus of jingoism, to which they add the sanction of their own "Hallelujah"; and, through their adeptness at rationalization, they support the popular morale by persuading it of the nobility of its motives.[19]

One would hope that H. Richard Niebuhr was encouraged by the moral leadership that was offered by many clergy and church members alike during the early years of the civil rights struggle, for example.

Yet as we look back on those times that called forth heroic responses in others, we may wonder what are the equivalent issues in our own times and whether we are facing them as bravely as those who inspire us from the past. Philip Slater reflects on William James's call for the "moral equivalent of war":

> It's fascinating to me how often this phrase is quoted by news commentators and academics as if James had merely expressed a yearning for such an equivalent—as if the search were still on. But in fact James *found* the "moral equivalent of war" and had quite a bit to say about it: "May not voluntarily accepted poverty be the 'strenuous life,' without the need of crushing weaker peoples? Poverty, indeed, *is* the strenuous life—without brass bands or uniforms or hysteric popular applause or lies or circumlocutions; and when one sees the way in which wealth-getting enters as an ideal into the very bone and marrow of our generation, one wonders whether a revival of the belief that poverty is a worthy religious vocation may not be 'the transformation of military courage,' and the spiritual reform which our time stands most in need of."[20]

While one may debate whether a call to poverty is the only authentic Christian response, there can be little doubt that faithfulness with our material resources is expected of every follower of Jesus Christ. We live in a world where it is estimated that thirty-five thousand children under the age of five die daily around the globe, most from preventable poverty conditions and many in areas where no church has been planted to tell them of Jesus' love. We can be confident that such conditions are not God's will: Perhaps one idea that would not be debatable in any part of the church is that Jesus loves the little children of the world. The financial cost to end most of these child deaths, it has been proposed, is about $2.5 billion a year, which is the amount Americans spend on chewing gum. Reflecting on these facts, it could be fairly stated that we live in an occupied society, one that is under the sway of Mammon. Ministers and laypeople alike feel the pressure this conqueror exerts. Even talking about the issues produces anxiety, fear, and, ultimately, silence. Under these cir-

cumstances, where do our opportunities for the moral equivalent of war lie?

The front lines may lie within our own congregations. The
issues need to be identified in order to be clearly faced. Without
a clear theological framework or constructive use for money that
focuses the congregation outward, congregations have turned
inward. One side effect is the resulting internal-control dynamics that define the missions of many congregations, to which we
turn our attention in the next chapter.

11

Control Dynamics

I am weak but Thou art strong;
Jesus, keep me from all wrong;
I'll be satisfied as long
As I walk, let me walk close to Thee.

"Just a Closer Walk with Thee"

The 80 Percent

Conventional wisdom suggests that 20 percent of the people in a congregation give 50–80 percent of the budget. In practice, more than 90 percent of the pastors and regional officials responding to the Stewardship Project survey agreed with the observation, "In most congregations, 20 percent of the people give 50–80 percent of the budget."

What may be less clear are some of the consequences of that fact. For example, what have the 80 percent been taught about stewardship in such a setting? And why are the faithful 20 percent so willing to contribute so much?

One hypothesis that grew out of the Stewardship Project observations is that the less-involved 80 percent have been educated to think that their participation is not needed at a greater level. Consider this: The Stewardship Project observations suggest that most congregations function as though the goal of stewardship is to pay the bills of the congregation. The 80 percent see, year after year, that the bills are paid with only a token effort from them. The question then is, why would they respond to a call for increased stewardship? Currently, with most churches defining successful stewardship as maintenance of the current program, stewardship for the 80 percent seems to them largely irrelevant.

220

In the absence of a large vision that justifies sacrificing the immediate pleasures touted by society, the 80 percent will remain underchallenged. These uninvolved church members have many other things to spend their money on, and they aren't begging to increase their giving.

One building consultant suggests congregations pursue building projects to make a larger number of the 80 percent feel needed. Unfortunately, in this context, constructing new edifices in many cases continues the definition of giving to the church as giving to oneself. It also reinforces the idea of giving for services rendered rather than of loving others in response to God's grace.

Vision

Ron Blue believes that vision can be one way the church can improve stewardship and that a large vision might raise more people's sights than a new building campaign. "I'm not sure the church has proved worthy of 10 percent of people's incomes. The church is missing needs of people and may be self-serving." Describing some of the clients he has, people who are successful at making money and are thinking about how to apply some of their bountiful resources to further God's kingdom, he commented, "The Great Commission is a great vision. People are looking for results. People want to put their charitable dollar where they'll get leverage, where it can have multiple consequences." Fran LaMattina, a partner in Ronald Blue and Company, continued, "My own experience is that churches grow and then begin major building programs—and attendance declines. People want to put their money into vision."

One regional leader commented that Christians should look closely at the motives behind building a new structure. "You build a two-million-dollar building, and one dime of each dollar goes to missions. If you had to cut missions from 10 percent of your budget to 3 percent to build, you shouldn't have built that building. People use buildings manipulatively. 'We need to do buildings so we can attract people—it's evangelism.' If we're going to be scriptural, 90 percent should go to missions from our churches and 10 percent should be reserved for us, then see how much we raise." Few if any churches have taken this leader's approach; so it is not clear if this perspective would actually aid in promoting better stewardship.

Feeling Needed

Mark Teresi suggested that in many congregations, the 50–80 percent of the people who are not currently giving much "might respond if they were personally approached, but they're ignored. And the 25 percent who are left are made to feel responsible as they carry the remaining 75 percent."

Several pastors shared stories that illustrate that some people in the 80 percent are willing to give when circumstances arise and they are needed. The general scenario involves a sudden decrease in congregational income. The decrease may be due to the death of a big giver or a disagreement in the church. In the circumstances described by one pastor, several key families left the congregation in response to serious disagreements with the denomination. This pastor was surprised that the church's income level had recovered within six months. Apparently other families in the congregation were in a position to give larger amounts but had not given while others were providing the bulk of the church's income to meet the bills.

Many churches find they have a difficult time motivating the vast majority of members to give increased portions of their incomes. The question to consider is whether the definition of stewardship as maintenance or survival may contribute to the lack of response on the part of those church members who are currently underchallenged. If paying the bills is the goal of stewardship, and the 20 percent are willing to pay the bills, why should the 80 percent increase their giving?

The 20 Percent

The relationship of the 80 percent to the operation of the church may seem logical once it is pointed out. What came as more of a surprise, and may be perceived as more controversial, were dynamics in congregations that suggest the 20 percent who currently support much of the budget may not want improved stewardship. How could that be?

Power

In Stewardship Project workshops, a list of observations that resulted from congregation-level encounters was presented. After we stated the idea that the 20 percent may not want improved stewardship, the audience was asked to reflect on the question, "Why might that 20 percent resist efforts to expand good stewardship to a larger portion of the congregation?" After a brief silence, someone in the group inevitably suggested either "loss of control" or "power." While there may be other explanations as well, the loss of influence feared by the current leadership of the church is an area that deserves more attention.

A study exploring lay attitudes on church support was interesting in light of these responses. Laypeople in Catholic, Lutheran, Methodist, and Episcopalian congregations were asked to fill out a survey with forty-two questions. Factor analysis divided seven categories of people connected with the church into two groups. The first group factored out as "The People," including governing board/parish council, majority of church membership, and yourself. The second group was defined as "The Leaders," including pastor, other staff, powerful individuals, and diocese/synod/conference.[1] Interestingly, powerful laypeople in the congregation, and not the governing board/parish council, were seen as on a par with the minister and staff rather than as of "The People."

Both firsthand encounters and stories shared in interviews led to the observation that lay leaders in many churches are comfortable with the current level of involvement on the part of other church members and would not welcome the vitality that would come with spreading stewardship out among more people in the congregation. That is not to say that these lay leaders would not like more income for the church. But if it is a choice between maintaining the status quo and involving more people in the church, the status quo will generally win.

A regional official described how an attorney he knew moved to a town and planned to join a church. The attorney missed church the first Sunday. He decided to make the acquaintance of the church treasurer by visiting the layman at his office. During the visit, the lawyer asked the treasurer if he could leave his offering with the treasurer, and the treasurer assured him it would be fine. The lawyer was surprised, however, when he handed the treasurer the check and the treasurer looked shocked. The treasurer handed the check back to the lawyer and said, "I'm sorry, I can't accept this. No one in the church gives this much money." The lawyer was confused and, in talking with the pastor of the congregation later that week, asked the minister what he should do. "Just bring the check to next Sunday's service and drop it in the basket. Everything will be fine," the pastor assured him. So the lawyer did just that. During announcement time, the pastor noted that there had been a change in the position of church treasurer.

Another regional official responded to the idea of the 20 percent resisting improved stewardship by saying, "That explains a congregational meeting I was at last night!" A hole in the sanctuary roof required that a kitchen pot be kept on the altar during rainstorms. The leadership board discussed the repair need for some time and held an informal poll as to how much each leadership board member could contribute toward the repair. The group came up short of what was needed to repair the hole and, therefore, decided to postpone the job. The visiting regional official was somewhat surprised and said he could not resist intervening. "But why don't you have a campaign and invite some of the other members of the congregation to help pay for the roof?" he blurted out. The chair looked at him coldly and said, "We've already decided we can't afford it," and the meeting moved on to the next topic.

One pastor attending a workshop strongly responded to the idea that those in control might discourage giving. "I'm intrigued but distressed. A person in the church I'm serving increased her pledge, but another member of the church said she shouldn't. Where I am today, this is a problem."

David Wheeler of a Southern Baptist Convention state association agreed with the idea that the 20 percent may very well be influencing the congregational agenda. "Core groups want to have power and will resist any effort to diffuse it." Church leaders, he noted, are probably also successful in their businesses and will bring that style of controlling leadership into the church. Those who control the money in the church feel that influence accrues to them. "It's a principle of authority," he said. "They believe money gives them authority. Unfortunately it is this preoccupation with authority and pride that has been the source of sin." Thus the 20 percent may not understand leadership in the church calls for a different kind of leadership, a servant leadership, not only to wield appropriate authority but also to nurture discipleship in 100 percent of the constituents—including the 80 percent who are now often uninvolved. This type of approach may not be at all natural but will perhaps have to be cultivated very intentionally.

Limitations on the Congregation

It also appears that many congregations are limited by what the biggest givers are able or willing to do. A national official described a congregation where one wealthy member always made up the balance of the budget at the end of the year. As a result, this individual had an important veto on what goals were set by the congregation. A new pastor came to the congregation and enthusiastically urged the congregation to broaden its mission. In the congregational meeting, the key individual hesitated but could not resist the pastor's enthusiasm, and so, with his approval, the budget was set for a higher amount that year. The same dialogue happened the next year, with more hesitation on the part of the wealthy individual, yet the budget goal was again raised. In the third year, the large donor protested and said, "Wait, we can't do that! I can't afford to make up that much money." The pastor smiled and said, "Good, because we don't want you to. We've reached a place where we need everyone, including you."

In some cases the intentions of the large donors may be positive, as with the gentleman who did not want his congregation to end the year in the red. In other cases, though, the individual may be pursuing a personal agenda and feel that the size of the contribution gives the donor certain rights. If an individual is presently one of the largest givers, depending on the level of giving, that person may not want new participants to advocate proportionate giving or even tithing, thus raising the level of contribution that will be required to maintain the same level of status.

Several pastors reported on an unexpected reaction to one information technique. Without indicating any names, the church financial officer prepared a "contributions tree." The number of gifts were listed by category on an annual basis; for example: household gifts of $3,000 and above: 1; household gifts of $2,000 to $2,999: 2; household gifts of $1,500 to $1,999: 5; and so on. There usually were two or three families who would say, "I thought we were the highest givers," and would promptly increase their pledge. This type of competitive feeling might also produce a resistance to encouraging good giving patterns. Other people might respond generously and raise the levels of current giving categories, resulting in other large givers feeling pressure to respond.

Fear of Increased Responsibility

Occasionally workshop attenders suggested that there may be another reason why presently good givers resist increased stewardship education. Rather than asserting a particular agenda, the large giver may fear that the only ones who will respond to an increased stewardship emphasis will be those already giving. The 20 percent have demonstrated a concern for the congregation through their present giving patterns and this group may fear that raising the financial sights of the congregation will fall on largely deaf ears—except their own.

The Exercise of Control

This idea sounds as though it may have some basis. Yet it is not consistent with the point noted earlier—that many of those not presently giving significant amounts are often willing to step up to the challenge when a need becomes clear. Quite the opposite, both the building campaign theory that many of the 80 percent can be challenged to give to bricks and mortar and the reported experience of other families replacing absent donors suggest that the 80 percent will respond, under the right circumstances. If that is true, then to the degree that the 80 percent are not responding, the current 20 percent have not found effective ways to challenge them to increase giving, and the control dynamics may provide a partial explanation.

These dynamics are by no means clearly acknowledged or discussed. Precisely because they have not been explored, the dynamics can have a great deal of power. One pastor's eyes clouded as he heard the control dynamics proposed in a workshop. "They had me convinced it was my problem and not theirs," he said. He went on to note that he had begun to think about leaving the ministry, since his lay leadership made him feel responsible for their poor stewardship. The power dynamics suggested by the Stewardship Project observations gave him a different perspective, he said, one that fit more with his experience and his sense of his own gifts.

Another pastor tried to explain what happened as a result of such dynamics in his church. Under the pastor's leadership, the church had decided to work toward raising general giving for missions while organizing their current finances. The pastor, young and enthusiastic, considered the response of the well-established church to think about expanding its mission outreach a victory. Some time later, a powerful laywoman in the church came to see him. She asked him to keep her secret and shared she was planning to offer some property to the church for a new parsonage. The pastor was thrilled and agreed to keep her plans confidential.

Encouraged by all the positive developments in the congregation, the pastor went to a meeting of the congregational leaders to begin organizing the new missions giving plan. Instead of a planning meeting, however, a woman began raising questions about why the church had become involved in such a plan in the first place. Although the leadership board had passed the proposal and the decision had been made to go ahead, this individual initiated a discussion not of how to proceed with the next step but whether to be involved in it at all. In talking about it, the pastor reflected that the woman raising the questions was a good friend of the key laywoman who wanted to sell some property to the church. She asked a variety of questions that made it clear she had not read the available materials. As she talked, the pastor noticed that other people did not rise to the defense of the project. He described the feeling that grew inside him as, "They were circling their wagons and I was on the outside."

In talking about the event later, the pastor mentioned that the woman with the questions was the one other person in the congregation who knew about the impending property proposal. Perhaps, he mused, she worried that a new focus on missions would lessen enthusiasm of the congregation to buy her friend's property. When asked whether he brought out that concern during the meeting, the pastor explained that he had been sworn to secrecy. Also, since it involved the parsonage, he would not have wanted to appear concerned about his own needs. So he did not feel he could bring up in front of the group the matter of the property and how it might relate to the congregation's ability to give more to missions. The result was that he tried to answer the questions raised that night by the woman and some others who joined in. Other members of the group listened in silence. A key lay leader who had volunteered to assist the pastor with the missions project did not come to the meeting. The pastor commented later, "He never told me why, and I never asked him." It did not come to a clear vote that night. Rather, the pastor asked if people were trying to tell him they had changed their mind. The indecisive response he received from a number of people told him they were. The next day, the pastor wrote a letter withdrawing from the project.

As one regional official suggested, "When we talk about money and the church, we're talking about power politics—an incredible dimension we don't understand."

The Perception of Pastors

This area merits further exploration. Seventy percent of the pastors responding to the Stewardship Project survey disagreed with the statement, "Occasionally, a particular church member will be discouraged from increasing his or her contribution because one or more key leaders in the church may fear the increased influence that may accrue to that particular church member." Similarly, strong disagreement was voiced among the regional officials, national officials, and seminary development officers. Only half of the seminary faculty disagreed.

In the same vein, almost four-fifths of the pastors disagreed with the idea, "In congregations where 20 percent of the people give most of the budget, this 20 percent may not want improved stewardship among other members because the large contributors fear a loss of the control and/or influence they now exert in the congregation." The resistance to this idea registered by those responding to the survey was not associated with size of congregation, since resistance was evident among all categories of congregations. Although some people in discussions wondered if the dynamic might be more evident in smaller congregations, a higher, though still small, percentage of pastors in congregations of one thousand or more agreed with the theory than those in congregations of one hundred or less.

How do these survey responses correspond to the Stewardship Project encounters with leadership boards, as well as the strong positive response from pastors attending workshops? One pastor responding to the survey commented, "The 20 percent of my congregation who are great stewards give out of deep conviction and thankfulness and are open and willing to be challenged to grow and give more and are willing to challenge others to discover that joy of thankfulness."

There appears to be a contradiction. Most of the survey respondents suggest that the 20 percent would not discourage increased stewardship participation from more members of the church. Yet the encounters of the Stewardship Project staff at the congregational leadership board level, and in interviews with pastors, highlighted control dynamics that produced just that effect.

To proceed with this discussion, let it be clearly stated that we acknowledge the church includes many noble and generous people who give of their time as well as their money to further the work of the kingdom. We were impressed and encouraged by the sincere concern of many of the lay leaders we met. These people are often willing to work unceasingly and without recognition. They form the foundation on which the activities that are the church are built. It might seem heartless, therefore, to suggest, in the face of their great commitment and sacrifice, that any—because we would certainly not say all—of these authentic examples of Christian discipleship behave other than in the best interests of the entire congregation.

When we first began interacting with congregations, we did not have this perspective. Rather, we were confident that church members would willingly give 10 percent of their income if they only had enough information about the good it could accomplish. So we ventured out with facts and figures in hand to empower church members to reach their full potential for faithfulness.

Someplace along that road, we ran into a brick wall—not once, in one congregation in a particular communion, but repeatedly in a variety of settings with groups of people from quite different traditions. As we compiled the notes and tried to understand what patterns might be producing similar effects in different settings, one common thread seemed to be a resistance on the part of at least some current leaders to take constructive action that would involve more of the congregation in responsible financial stewardship. We began formulating and testing this theory, receiving a lot of affirmation from in-person encounters with pastors and frustrated leadership. Thus it seems only responsible to raise the idea here so that it might be more fully explored. If only a few lay leaders fit the pattern, the church can be locked in a maintenance/survival mode that limits its ability to be faithful.

As we reflected on why those responding to the Stewardship Project survey might generally disavow the power dynamics idea, one hypothesis arose. It might be that pastors have heard such strong complaints from current leadership about nongivers in the church that it seems impossible these people, at some level, would not want generally improved stewardship. The pastor may have sat in so many meetings where people bemoan the lack of giving in others that, at first blush, it doesn't make sense that these same people would not want improved giving habits to be spread among a broader group of people in the church. If asked, both pastors and laypeople would no doubt express a wish that more people contributed to the budget.

Possible Explanations

The fact is that church leadership boards, presumably made up of members who are in the 20 percent category, are open to increased help with paying the bills. However, because the Stewardship Project structured budget approach could lead to a rearrangement of the congregation's goals (much in the same way that a major project such as a building campaign might) leadership boards reacted to the perceived change in power structures that would result. Loren Mead suggests that a surefire way to start a conflict in a congregation is to move a piece of furniture.[2] How much more likely is it, then, that leadership boards are comfortable with the present dynamics going on in the church and are not ready to open themselves to the unknown agenda that a new large contributor might want to introduce?

Another possibility is that the resistance from many leadership boards to active stewardship programs may result from the leadership board not being, in fact, constituted of the 20 percent who are the largest givers in the congregation. In an earlier chapter, we explored some of the consequences of a pastor knowing or not knowing what people give to the church. There is another aspect of this issue that may be relevant to congregational control dynamics. In particular, the pastor who does not know the financial giving levels of the church's members runs the hazard of appointing low-percentage givers to key leadership positions. In this case, the leadership board could be made up of people who do not give financially to the church. Once there, those in leadership may then have a vested interest in not challenging the church financially because they themselves do not want to increase the portion of their incomes that they give. Ninety percent of the pastors disagreed with the statement, "The most vocal church leader is usually the largest financial contributor." As one pastor wrote, "I was having a lot of opposition from one member. She kept saying we needed more commitment and more giving, but every time we got more people involved and raised money, she loudly objected. The longer it went on, the more I diagnosed a spiritual problem. Eventually I looked at her giving record. The total for this person who called for commitment and giving? Zero!"

Also, individual pastors have indicated that on occasion, when they have had reason to find out giving levels, they are surprised at the names of some of the large donors, who apparently have given to the church for reasons other than to exercise control. If this is the case, then one must conclude that the leadership that does show signs of wanting to maintain the congregation in a certain pattern, including resistance to stewardship efforts, may or may not be among the 20 percent of big givers in the church.

However, findings from a variety of research suggest that the most active members in the church, presumably including those on the leadership board, are also the most likely to contribute to the church. Consultant Thomas Sweetser's work with Roman Catholic parishes found a close connection between involvement in the church and contributions. "We use a random sample of registered Catholics in the parish we are working with and obtain a cross section of those people. Those that are active give more. That is the strongest correlation."

This relationship was also highlighted in the American Congregational Giving Study, conducted in 1993, comparing data obtained from congregations in the Assemblies of God, the Evangelical Lutheran Church in America, the Presbyterian Church (U.S.A.), the Roman Catholic Church, and the Southern Baptist Convention. Results from this study confirmed that "members who are actively involved in congregational life give more." In addition, a Gallup poll commissioned in relationship to that study also found a positive correlation between higher giving and higher congregational involvement.[3] This idea would support the thesis that congregational leadership represents a large portion of the more generous givers in the congregation.

It is likely, then, that many of those serving on congregational leadership boards are among the larger givers in the congregation. It is this same leadership that has exhibited resistance to the general discussion of money in the church, as well as exerted pressure, as reported by many pastors, to avoid the difficult topic. Therefore it may be that, while the surveyed pastors and regional officials disagreed with the idea that the 20 percent may resist improved general stewardship because of a perceived loss of control, these pastors and regional officials have not recognized a strong pattern in the congregations with which they are involved. Given the complaints about the uninvolvement of the 80 percent, it seems obvious that the current leaders would truly want increased participation and financial support from the uninvolved. Yet, if the 80 percent are routinely not contributing to the budget, the question may be asked: Why not? Is it not possible that current dynamics, patterns that are so taken for granted that they may not be recognized unless set in a broader context, may be discouraging these people from contributing? If the congregation does not have a compelling enough vision for which the present comfortable status quo might be sacrificed, why should the 20 percent open themselves to dynamics introduced by other potential large givers?

This idea has been proposed before. In the report of the survey of more than three thousand lay and ministerial leaders, Douglas Johnson and George Cornell observe:

> Members predominantly indicated their eagerness to share in planning and developing the congregation's activities. Yet in many instances, this responsibility largely has been taken over by a key few, an inner circle of clergy and close associates who run the budget and program, generally on the assumption that the mass of members are apathetic and disinterested. But the data in this study refute that notion, emphasizing that most members are concerned and want a hand in shaping and carrying out the church's undertakings. They may feel unneeded and unwanted, but they care, and would like to act it.[4]

One pastor's experience in a related area of the church budget might be helpful. The pastor called the Stewardship Project office to talk about a committee situation that confused him. The congregational leadership introduced some educational materials and budget reorganization into the congregation, based on the format of the Stewardship Project structured budget approach. Congregation members had responded with an increased level of giving. The pastor was delighted as he entered the January finance committee meeting but quickly became confused when the committee members announced, "It will never work. People won't give without a crisis." The pastor pointed out that people were, indeed, giving and that the budget-to-date had been met. Nevertheless, at the next finance committee meeting, the committee members again announced, "It will never work. People won't give without a crisis." The pastor again pointed out the income numbers in the reports. This same dialogue continued for three more months. By May the pastor, in frustration, told the committee that it was the first year the church had not had to write out a spring crisis letter and that people were giving without a crisis. The pastor then called our office to ask if we could explain the committee members' behavior.

We talked for some minutes, trying to consider what might be causing these committee members to insist on a dismal picture even in the face of happily contradictory evidence. Might it be that the finance committee had been trained for so long to deal with financial crisis that they had no other agenda for their committee? They resisted the facts because at some level they may have feared that without a crisis their committee served no purpose. Not having a positive agenda, the committee held fast to the currently negative one. The pastor immediately responded to that idea. The change in the congregation's attitude required a corresponding change in the finance committee's attitude, one they were not yet prepared to imagine.

In the same way, those presently in leadership in the congregation may feel uncomfortable with changes that will come with the involvement of additional people in the congregation. No doubt, any new member would be most welcome to serve as an usher, sing in the choir, teach a Sunday school class, volunteer in the nursery, or help with any of a number of necessary but not always exciting tasks that keep the congregation operational. That same attitude may extend to increased contributions. Of course new donors are welcome—to help pay the bills. Yet in the same way the nominations committee probably has a certain acceptable group from which to draw the finance committee, trustees, or endowments committee nominations, a stewardship effort that might result in unpredictable responses upsetting the current maintenance status quo might be frowned on.

As one pastor described it, "They're open to people who will come and be one of them, adopt the agenda to come to church and help pay the bills and fill the slots and perpetuate the congregation because the community needs the congregation. They can meet the needs for institutional survival and ministry. But change the worship service, and right away I met resistance."

Anti-Growth Attitude

A seven-volume study on the Presbyterian Church came to a conclusion that might be applicable to more than one church when it stated, "One of the striking features of the PC(USA) is a pervasive anti-growth attitude and ideology. Apathy and hostility to growth are characteristic of congregations, as well as of governing bodies."[5] The Presbyterian Church, however, is by no means unique. Church growth proponent C. Peter Wagner has observed,

> Whereas almost every church will verbalize a vague desire to add new members, in many cases the congregation and its leaders are not at all willing to pay the price for growth. . . . Growth disturbs the status quo cherished by many. New church members tend to complicate patterns of interpersonal relationships, so their number is kept under control by existing members.[6]

As noted earlier, growth as the one measure of success of a congregation is not necessarily a positive goal. However, an equally negative behavior can keep churches from attracting new believers into the kingdom. The following story is an alarming illustration of this attitude.

The pastor of a conservative church was preparing for the morning's sermon when there was a knock at the door. In walked two key church leaders. Although he usually spent the time in prayer, he invited them in because they insisted they needed to talk with him before church began in fifteen minutes. Then they announced, "We want you to stop talking about inviting other people into this church. There are too many new people now. We don't know half the people who come here, and there are new people in leadership positions." The two leaders then went on to point out they were large givers to the church, and the pastor faced a hefty mortgage payment that would be threatened without their contributions. They told the pastor very clearly that if he preached an evangelistic sermon designed to bring in more people that morning, they would leave and not come back.

One would hope that other church leaders would not react in such an extreme way, but subtle pressures might actually be more difficult for the pastor to identify and resist.

Two pastors were sharing in a conversation that turned to the issue of pressures on the pastor that result from changing the status quo. "In a congregation," one offered, "everything's settled. It's like a spider web. And all the tensions are evenly distributed." For the pastor to try to change the framework is to risk being either tangled up or hit by a snapping thread. "To think that the church is an institution where altruism reigns is a mistake. Sometimes people who can't function in other settings—for good reason—wield power because we are merciful and believe in healing. So it is an extremely complex system." The other pastor agreed, noting that while in smaller churches there may be individuals who wield the power, in the larger churches there would be social groups who have a vested interest in maintaining the status quo.

It is true that groups can wield power as effectively as individuals, as illustrated by an experience one minister shared in an interview at his church. The pastor was aware that a particular group held the power in the congregation he was serving. However, he was to find out how deeply the patterns were set. There was interest in making the church building more accessible; so a proposal was made to install an elevator. A young man in the congregation was approached about heading up the committee. He took his job seriously, visited a variety of churches with elevators, obtained various estimates, and kept the congregation informed. After some months a place in the building was proposed as the location of the elevator, and a letter went out to the congregation. Enough money was received during the first five months of the campaign that a final bid could be selected. A general meeting of the congregation was called to determine the details. At that meeting several people who were in the traditional power group protested the speed at which the decision was being made. Other people who had been involved with the project over the previous eight months asked why these individuals had not spoken up before. The pastor remembered the power group's response as, "We didn't think you'd raise the money. Why get people angry at us when it would never happen? But now that you have the money, we want a say." Eventually, after some extended conversation, a compromise was reached, and the elevator was installed in another location of the building—which resulted in the loss of Sunday school space. The pastor said other members of the congregation, those he described as being "on the fringe," came to him later and shared, "This stuff's been going on for years. We were put in our place four or five years ago, being told, 'We don't do it that way.'"

Consider these "fringe" members' comments in light of a description offered by Paul Baard, a psychologist who is beginning to explore motivations in church member participation: "Another type of motivation, amotivation, describes a sense of futility, of either feeling incapable of meeting a perceived expectation or failing to see any relevance of an activity to personal interests or objectives."[7] This attitude, Baard suggests, is typical of the uninvolved church member. If many of those who are uninvolved have tried at some time to be involved and met active resistance from those currently in control, their occupation of the fringe might be the safest place.

With pastors moving from location to location, understanding and dealing with power dynamics may be a particularly frustrating aspect of the ministry. As one minister observed, "One dynamic plays into that—that they know they'll be there long after the pastor. So it is critical for a member to come up with a solution, because they'll be there after the pastor is gone."

Not all congregations have such a controlling group or individual. Or perhaps sometimes those who control are authentically benevolent. One pastor who had experienced both difficult and constructive controlling groups was comparing two congregations he had served. In the current congregation he contended with what he termed a "CEO," who was, the pastor explained, "excellent at defeating things without opposing them." However, this minister had served a congregation some years before in a community that was quickly changing from an isolated rural village to a suburb. The leaders of the church gathered and agreed that they really preferred that new people not come into their community. Nevertheless, the way they interpreted their faith was that they should be open to newcomers. Therefore the leaders built a modern building with their own hands and gave up the reins of power as new people joined the church. Five years later they were a successful suburban congregation.

One further thought on the encounter the pastor had with the finance committee that was upset that there was no crisis. The committee might have also been uncomfortable with the idea of increased money coming into the church because the pastor, or other leaders, might develop ambitious ways to spend it that would involve an even greater financial response on the part of the congregation. New staff or a new building addition might suddenly seem possible if there were a surplus of funds in the congregation's coffers. No doubt, the surplus would not cover the entire cost but would likely be just enough to raise the sights of some of the expansive thinkers in the congregation. Known misery, it seems, is more comfortable than the unpredictable misery of the unknown.

The Image of Need

Some congregations go to great lengths to preserve the image of the congregation as being in need. The voiced reasons vary from the fact that people won't give if there is a surplus to the congregation's inability to provide for a rainy day. As noted earlier, for whatever reason—and the intentions were always good—on more than one occasion it developed in Stewardship Project encounters that congregations had funds tucked away that only one or two individuals knew about.

There is a pastoral role for clergy to be developed, as congregations move from maintenance organizations to communities of faith participating in the broader mission of the church. The challenge before the pastor is to guide the sheep through the difficult path of deepening discipleship rather than maintaining a sometimes self-destructive status quo. In order to be an effective guide, however, the pastor needs to have a clear understanding not only of the direction in which the church ought to be headed but also of the dynamics at work that prevent the congregation's travel along the path. These would include the money dynamics Jesus spent so much time discussing in his parables.

The Shepherd of the Flock

The minister must be like a shepherd who guides laypeople into an understanding of how money affects behavior. Gene Peisker, an ELCA minister, shared an experience that made the biblical imagery come alive for him. He and two friends decided to drive up a mountain in Montana. On the return trip, they came around a bend in the road to find the rushing stream they had crossed on the way up. On the opposite side, perhaps one hundred sheep were standing at the water's edge, rigid, with their legs locked and their feet dug in. Packed closely together, the huddled sheep made an immovable mass that would not enter the flowing stream. Just then, Gene and his friends heard a soothing voice and soon saw a shepherd coming toward them, picking his way through the closely packed sheep. The shepherd spoke in a low voice as he slowly moved through the band, working his way to the water's edge. Stopping briefly, he analyzed the situation. The shepherd then bent down, picked up a lamb, and confidently strode into the water. For a moment, nothing happened. Then a large ewe began to work her way out of the band. Overcome by a higher calling that outweighed her own fears, she waded into the stream after the shepherd carrying her lamb. Not long after, the other sheep followed in the ewe's path, and soon the entire flock was safely across.

"I am the good shepherd; I know my sheep," Jesus declares in John 10:14. The pastor's role, modeled on the Good Shepherd's concern for the flock, can be crucial in helping laypeople overcome long-standing patterns that inhibit reaching the goals they profess. Every leadership board in every congregation in the United States would be delighted to have more contributions coming into their churches. However, do they want that income enough to be willing to experience the discomfort that comes with dislocated patterns? The pastor's understanding of his or her flock may be a critical factor in whether the congregation can achieve its goals, in spite of its own fears. The minister is in a position to constantly keep the higher calling of the faith before the congregation, including the congregational leadership—a calling that outweighs the learned fears church members bring to the table.

Of course, it also behooves the pastor to be sure that the direction set is consistent with the best interests of the sheep. Pastors are human enough to be subject to personal agendas; it is not impossible to imagine a pastor being tempted to pursue a building project because of how good it would look on a résumé rather than weighing whether the congregation needed the project at this juncture. The role of minister is all the more difficult because the pastor must be constantly checking his or her own motives.

To change the giving situation will require good leadership on the part of the minister. One pastor in a congregational polity insists that every member of his leadership board tithe. He reported strong resistance from very capable people, who would no doubt bring great gifts to the ministry of the church but who were unwilling to tithe through the church. The pastor pointed out that tithing was more than an abstract concept in the congregation and that he could not afford people in leadership who were not clear in their personal commitments, since they might give mixed signals to the congregation.

One national leader of a mainline denomination described a friend's approach to the matter. "At one of the first leadership board meetings at his new church, he announced, 'My wife and I will tithe my salary to the church, and I expect members of this leadership board to do the same. And I will check the records.' His position is, if they are going to be leaders, there is accountability."

Endorsing the Goals

Dean Kelley created a stir in 1972 with a book titled *Why Conservative Churches Are Growing*. His idea that high-demand congregations provoke a committed response from their members continues to be debated. Nevertheless, some of the points he makes sound logical. For example, he suggests that groups ought to have people in leadership positions who endorse the goals and purpose of the organization. But, he observes, while that is taken for granted in secular or civic groups, it is often seen as exclusionary or inappropriate among churches. He points out that a group organized around, for example, the abolition of the death penalty would not include among its members advocates of the death penalty; these people would be encouraged to form their own association. To involve people with opposite views within the first group would be to reduce any possibility of being effective.

> Many there are, apparently, who confuse a church with a lodge or social club (and most lodges and social clubs are more particular about whom they admit than some churches are). By admitting new members for the pleasure of their company and the welcome addition of their contributions, the church is reduced to the condition of a lodge or social club which has little to bind its members together except fellowship—and a fellowship all too easily disrupted by disagreement or difficulty.[8]

From this point of view, although the church needs to be welcoming new members and seekers at all stages of the spiritual journey, it is nevertheless appropriate to provide certain standards for those who would be in leadership, which may include whether a member has come to terms with the role of money and giving in one's own life.

Giving as an Indicator of Spiritual Health

Pastors who do not know how church members are translating their faith into their financial giving lose an important source of information about their church members. As noted earlier, in the Stewardship Project survey, a strong majority of both pastors and regional officials agreed, "Most church members do not want the pastor to know how much individual members contribute to the church," even while they agreed, "The pastor's knowledge of what individual members give to the church can be a helpful assessment tool of individual members' spiritual health."

In one pastors' workshop, a pastor commented that he did not know what people in his congregation gave because the people had made it clear they did not want him to know. The next pastor indicated he thought stewardship was a deeply spiritual matter. The first pastor interrupted and, as if seeing the point for the first time, said, "Listen to what you said. It's a spiritual matter, but the pastor is not involved." Apart from ministering to individuals, whether the pastor knows or does not know can have an influence on the type of lay leadership the congregation receives.

One pastor resolved the dilemma of not wanting to know—and yet not wanting to appoint an unfaithful church member to a key position—by having the financial secretary prepare a list of potential nominees, one of the criteria being faithful givers to the church. Another pastor recognized that changes in giving patterns might indicate problems in the home or with the church. Therefore, this pastor asked the financial secretary to forward the names of any individuals whose giving patterns declined markedly.

The fact that money can be an indicator, perhaps like a thermometer, of a person's spiritual or even physical condition suggests that it is a helpful tool for pastors as shepherds of the flock. Once a problem is identified, the minister can call on the many counseling and pastoral skills that have been accumulated through reading and experience to help the congregation member. What some of those counseling issues might be are discussed in the next chapter.

12

Needs for Pastoral Counseling

> O, grant that nothing in my soul may dwell, but thy pure
>   love alone;
> O, may thy love possess me whole, my joy, my treasure,
>   and my crown!
> All coldness from my heart remove;
> My every act, word, thought, be love.
>
> *Paul Gerhardt, 1653;*
> *translated by John Wesley, 1739*
> *"Jesus, Thy Boundless Love to Me"*

In chapter 10, the idea was introduced that pastoral counseling needed to be broadened to include the area of money. Pastors may receive fairly extensive counseling training, particularly
if they obtain degrees beyond seminary. Yet because of the taboo
nature of money in general, they may well feel unprepared to assist
parishioners with their struggles in the financial area of their lives.
As a result, pastors may even have mixed emotions about challenging their parishioners to greater faithfulness on this topic.
One priest described his reaction to successfully presenting a stewardship challenge: "They were young people with kids, and they
had leaped to the tithe. I felt guilty as a priest that I had asked
them to make such a sacrifice." He hesitated for a moment and,
reflecting on his own response, commented, "That's strange."

Of course, most pastors may psychologically prepare for success but, based on experience, realistically expect some failure.
Psychiatrist Karl Menninger found avarice, as he termed the pre-

242

occupation with wealth, a difficult condition to address. He took comfort, however: "It is reassuring to remember that even Jesus didn't always cure this affliction. I have wondered whether theologians are impressed by the contrast of this failure in dealing with 'a certain rich man' and the many successes in healing that are reported."[1]

If ministers are going to counsel their church members about their faith and money, they will no doubt need to identify some of the issues involved and prepare themselves for the challenge. What might be some of the topics they are likely to face?

Marriage Relationships

The area of marriage counseling is already within most pastors' line of duty. However, more and more, it would seem that money is playing a key factor in this most fundamental of relationships. Pastors must be prepared to guide their members through these uncharted waters, as pointed out by the divorcing couple who felt their finances were the only aspect of their marriage too personal to discuss. Ron Blue noted, "There is one other area of barrier or opportunity in stewardship education—husband/wife communication about finances. It is not at all unusual to find one is a giver and one is a spender. A lot of work needs to be done in that basic area of relationships."

The healing or dissolution of a marriage may depend on the couple's ability to deal with the issue of money. As one magazine noted in covering a well-publicized divorce, "Custody fights aren't always about children—they're often about money."[2]

Hugh Magers recognized this when he was serving in a congregation. In marriage counseling, he advised those for whom money seemed to be a problem, to tithe. He counseled them that in two years, they would be out of their difficulties. What was the response? Magers allowed that most of those to whom he suggested this approach thought he was "crazy." However, he received follow-up calls from two different couples who said it worked for them.

Ministers may find preparation for this type of counseling not only involves their profession but also their personal lifestyles. Can a minister whose own finances are out of control or who has not worked out the family dynamics that revolve around giving a substantial portion of income advise others to do so? These may be key issues as strained marriage relationships continue among church members as well as in the larger society.

Financial Insecurity

Another area that may involve pastoral counseling was also mentioned earlier. Lifelong church members find little comfort in their faith as they face the insecurity of retiring and the possibility of long-term care that may be necessary. How can their faith be so far removed from this practical concern? How can pastors help their parishioners feel the strength of their beliefs and support them in facing the unknown future before them?

The area of economic insecurity, though, is not limited only to the elderly members of the congregation. Herbert Mather of The United Methodist Church Board of General Discipleship visited a large congregation in that denomination. He was struck with the fact that the young successful members expressed a great deal of anxiety about their ability to give because of the insecurity of their professional lives. Corporate downsizing and the accompanying increase in self-employment mean more people now in their peak earning years are also facing uncertain futures. In that context, long-term care for parents in addition to education costs for children are economic concerns that preoccupy people who sit in church each Sunday.

Even those with plenty find themselves filled with anxiety about enough. Robert Wuthnow found in a survey that well-to-do people worry about finances even as do the poor. "And the main reason for this, of course, is that financial obligations expand as people's wants and standards of living expand."[3]

In our culture, so preoccupied with the power of money, it seems that having enough money is absolutely necessary to control the future and provide for long-term care or increasing comfort demands (that are somehow tied up with personal identity) or providing education costs for children. But people's anxiety is high even after they have taken logical steps and planned in a reasonable fashion for these needs. They still fear that what seems like a lot now may not be enough then. As psychologist Paul

Wachtel comments, "for many of us not having more has become equivalent to having less."[4] Perhaps the pastor as leader can help put these issues into perspective and take church members' minds off their wallets, reminding them of the larger reality in which these financial needs sit. At least according to our faith, we need not fear the future because, indeed, as Billy Graham has pointed out, God is already there. And the pastor can help church members restore their perspective on this point.

Fear

A similar need, also with an economic basis, that is surfacing in American society is the isolation and fear that comes from having more than others. As Proverbs 13:8 says, "A man's riches may ransom his life, but a poor man hears no threat." Author and teacher James Engel commented on this idea, "People would say, if you asked why they are not trying harder to impact world need in Jesus' name, 'Nothing can change the world.' They have fear of physical harm. They fear crime. The world has lost control, and they are in a private survival mode."

Craig Dykstra also commented on how the isolation so many feel in our society impacts the ability of church members to reach out with a global concern. "Insecurity and isolation feed each other. They build up over time. I think that the cycle of isolation, feeding insecurity, in turn feeding further isolation, and so forth is the greatest obstacle to anyone wanting to help the church minister to others' needs. At the same time, all of us know we can't live happily or well if we are trapped in this cycle. So we are floundering around for ways to overcome it—therapy groups, the whole small-group phenomenon—and to develop safe, structured ways to make contact with others."

Continuing to reflect on how the sense of isolation keeps many from supporting the larger mission of the church, Dykstra observed, "Another barrier is, people fear if they put their little toe into some need, it will just absorb them. The feeling is, if you go out to help others, you don't know that anyone will be with you, so it is dangerous to try. It takes a community to deal with overwhelming need, and we live in an age of personal autonomy."

Pastors face the difficult task of helping people move from an isolation reinforced by increasingly hostile social conditions and by a trend toward "cocooning" in front of five hundred cable television channels, interactive video games, and home entertainment centers toward the community of the church. Paul Wachtel observes, "The middle class in the United States, Western Europe, and other industrialized nations constitutes what one might call an 'asymptote culture,' a culture in which the contribution of material goods to life satisfaction has reached a point of diminishing returns."[5] He goes on to suggest that the increasing "decline in rootedness" in our society is directly related to the preoccupation with things. "Faced with the loneliness and vulnerability that come with deprivation of a securely encompassing community, we have sought to quell the vulnerability through our possessions."[6] Philip Slater explores how this preoccupation can then lead to greater isolation: "With wealth addiction, the harm lies less in wanting money or security than with the fact that our concern with these things deprives us of more nourishing human satisfactions—love, friendship, adventure, physical well-being, and so on."[7]

The cycle is one that is hard to break. We emphasize our individualism, which leads to a less rooted culture, which we compensate for by focusing on possessions, which isolate us from others, and the cycle begins again. In a society that promotes accumulation as the means to happiness, how can pastors counsel people to lose their lives in order to gain them? Pastors must help church members understand that, instead of using money in ways that provide for increasing isolation, sharing money can bring them true riches—of community interaction immediately and hope and satisfaction long-term.

For some people, church is still seen as a community—but sometimes from a survivalist mentality rather than with an openness to the broader world. Here again, pastors need to be equipped to counsel people in giving of themselves and taking risks instead of fearfully walling themselves off. Nordan Murphy, retired director of the National Council of Churches Stewardship Commission, observed, "So much results from a person who has learned to be generous. If they're not generous with money that they can control, that will affect their attitudes in other areas." So learning to give money is an important step in learning to open oneself to the broader world in general.

Closing a Congregation

When pastors find themselves guiding a community of faith that is operating with a maintenance/survival mentality, great insight is called for on the part of the minister as well as the national denominational leadership. In some cases, the congregation must be called to a new level of openness that includes not only the sharing of finances but also the willingness to welcome new members into what may have become a comfortably isolated congregation. This call will be more effective if the national denomination is promoting a broader vision than institutional survival.

In other situations, the pastor needs to be wise enough to recognize when a church's life and usefulness are at an end. The minister will need to sensitively guide church members through the process of grieving and release that comes with the closing of a congregation. Two stories may help illustrate these points.

One pastor we interviewed was serving a congregation that had decreased in membership. The church had recruited this particular minister, saying they wanted to grow. He was attracted to the possibilities he saw there and brought new ideas with enthusiasm. Yet the leadership resisted every suggestion the pastor offered. He finally decided to give them an ultimatum. This congregation needed to decide if they were going to be the last generation in that long-standing church, he told them, or if they would cooperate with him and grow. At a subsequent meeting, he asked for their answer. They responded that they were content not to change anything after all, and the few who would remain at the very end could close the doors and move to another congregation when it came to that point. The pastor, a particularly energetic and creative individual, left soon afterward. In this case, the pastor led the group to an increased self-awareness, although he did not endorse their conclusion.

It is for reasons such as this story illustrates that church growth experts suggest that starting new churches may be more productive than trying to grow established congregations. But from a purely economic point of view, that approach ties up the denomination's resources in not only starting new congregations to attract the unchurched but also supporting the currently churched who are unwilling to let go, even when there is little willingness to grow. It also abandons current communities of faith to what may at times be their own self-destructive tendencies. It is important to distinguish between a congregation that has potential and needs to be challenged not to turn in on itself from those churches that may have reached an end point. Unlike the congregation just above, which still had various options but chose not to pursue them, the congregation in the following story had a limited future but was unwilling to recognize it.

A retired regional official remembered one experience from early in his career. He met with five of the twelve members left in a congregation. After much discussion, it was agreed among those present that the church should close its doors and the twelve remaining members could join with another larger congregation nearby. The conference office went through the consideration process and approved the plan. The regional official then returned to a meeting for the final confirming vote from the congregation. That night, all twelve members showed up and asked him, "Why are you doing this?" Surprised at the resistance to what he thought was the will of the congregation, he responded with a question of his own. He asked one of the five who had previously agreed with the decision, "Why not close this congregation?" The man took the official to the window and, pointing to the graveyard outside, said, "Because of all those good church members out there."

A congregation such as this must evaluate its purpose for being. Is it to remember the dead or to serve the living? How can a pastor, a representative of the denomination both as an institution as well as an agent of change in the world, help a congregation work through this discussion in a logical way? This kind of discussion requires the gifts not of an institutional bureaucrat but of a trusted leader who can guide people through the inevitability of death and the grieving stages. Many pastors, though, find it hard to counsel in this area. So often, the decisions are promoted from an institutional or financial point of view. The lack of a compelling mission leaves congregations with little by which to gauge their actions other than what feels good to them. While church members may be willing to admit the truth of the financial bottom line, that perspective may not carry enough weight to overcome the desire to maintain the current comfortable patterns. What are church members giving up their comfort for? What goal is worth sacrificing the congregation? Indeed, what is the vision that will be large enough to convince congregation leaders who are perfectly comfortable now to be willing to risk involving new people in their fellowships?

Welcoming Strangers

Another pastor shared that the congregation she served had just completed renovation of the organ. The pastor knew an accomplished organist in a nearby town and arranged for a Sunday afternoon dedication recital. When the pastor announced these exciting developments at the next leadership board meeting, she was reprimanded. "If you have the recital in the afternoon," she was told, "that may encourage strangers to come to the church." The recital was rearranged for a morning service.

Congregations whose main goal is to pay the bills to keep the doors open need a limited number of members. Pastors striving to work with these congregations may find the task difficult. Is there a plan for training pastors to work with congregations more effectively so that they will be open to change?

Generational Differences

Another challenging area for pastors concerns the shift in generations. Many congregations lament that they have fewer young people; yet they are unwilling to let go of the power in the congregation—particularly to allocate resources for programming—that would allow younger people full involvement in the community of faith. One young layman had come to faith in a particular congregation and remained out of loyalty but he expressed frustration with some of the older members. They complained about the declining attendance, yet several young families had left because they were not allowed to introduce change in the program activities of the church.

Even where different generations have joined together in the same congregation, the transition of leadership may be anything but smooth. One pastor described a meeting of his leadership board where, for some reason, none of the older members were able to attend. Those of baby-boom age began to reflect on how resistant the older members were to change. A particular point of tension was the building and the financial commitment the older generation insisted the congregation make to it. The older members had seen the building take shape and now felt a responsibility to the community to maintain it as a local point of interest. The younger members had moved to the former agricultural community as commuters and felt no such obligation. Their goal was to tear the building down, construct a sanctuary that was more energy-efficient, and put more emphasis on programs that would attract other young families.

During the meeting that night, one middle-aged member complained that nothing would really happen until all the old members died. The next morning, the pastor received an irate call from one of the older members who had somehow heard a version of the previous night's meeting. This member was calling to see if it was true that the younger members were wishing them all dead! The pastor obviously faced a great challenge in holding these church groups together.

But are pastors trained to help congregations make the transition from one stage of existence to another? Once again, the nature of the church as a coalition of special interest groups comes to the fore. These disparate groups do not recognize an overarching vision that is larger than either of their immediate concerns, so the congregation is locked in a "matter/anti-matter" struggle (to use a *Star Trek* term) that keeps the church from fulfilling its potential.

In another case, the pastor's acceptance and awareness of the generational reality smoothed the way for the Stewardship Project staff to introduce the idea of the structured budget approach and the related educational activities with the goal of increasing missions giving. The introductory meeting was set for ten o'clock in the morning, a seemingly odd time for a leadership board meeting. When the staff walked in the room, they found the youngest person to be the pastor, who was over sixty. The presentation was given about the opportunity to increase giving in order to expand the mission outreach of the congregation. Questions were answered. Then one of the Stewardship Project staff asked whether this was indeed the leadership board. Oh no, they explained. Of the ten people present, only two had any official capacity. The pastor later explained that these individuals were the ones who really controlled the church. The leadership board could decide anything they liked, but if this group did not support it, it did not move forward. After this group decided it would be worthwhile for the leadership board to hear about the project, a second—evening—meeting was scheduled for the board, the majority of whom were employed during the day.

In that congregation's case, the older members had looked at the future of their congregation and decided they did not want to be the last generation. As a result, young people were willing to support the program financially and join with their older counterparts in working toward increased missions outreach. Yet the power continued to reside in the older members, and only with their approval was there room for the young to move.

No doubt there are very real differences among generations within the church. These very differences, however, can be a strength rather than a point of conflict. Just as attention is placed on racial reconciliation in the church, so should there be a ministry of generational reconciliation. Yet the church often reflects the world's attitudes toward age differences—and the world may have a different agenda for this issue. The secular focus on generational differences, for example, may well be a result of advertising and marketing efforts to target classes of buyers as potential consumers. Once again, the consumer society is setting the agenda for the church. Members come to church bringing an identity not as a member of Christ's body ("If the foot would say, 'Because I am not a hand, I do not belong to the body,' that would not make it any less a part of the body," 1 Corinthians 12:15, NRSV) but as a "baby boomer" or a "baby buster" or a Depression-era person, each defined not only by major social events but also by an advertising industry whose agenda is to build brand loyalty. How can a minister counsel church members to let go of the identity offered to them by the secular media and to embrace a oneness that transcends time?

To the degree that dividing a congregation into "cohorts," which had different national life-forming experiences—such as the Depression/World War II generation compared to the baby boom generation that came through the Vietnam War experience—can lead to bridges of understanding, such concepts may be very useful. Indeed, one regional official uses these identifiable distinctions in order to promote communication among groups that perceive life differently.

However, too often the differences are emphasized without a focus on building up the body of Christ. Previously the term *a generation* referred to a period of about twenty-five years. The baby boom generation, 1946–1964, consists of nineteen years. Douglas Walrath suggested as far back as 1979 that the definition was even decreasing then, as he writes, "College-age young people find their predominant attitudes and values very different from those of young people in high school; which, in turn, differ greatly from those of junior highs. . . . Thus, the generation gap is now a five-year matter."[8] What role do these age categories have in facilitating—or weakening—oneness in the body of Christ? The agenda of the church should be to explore what the generations have in common rather than focus with the world on what keeps them separate. Numerous passages in the Bible explore how these differences ought to be strengthening each other and present values that should be held in common regardless of age differences.

The experience of one church may illustrate the value of emphasizing oneness. A new building had been constructed. There was a sunny, attractive room at the front of the church that the older members wanted for their own. However, it was also perfectly suited for a nursery; and parents with young children thought they ought to have preference, since they represented the future of the church. The debate was quite heated until one night the church blew up, literally. Fortunately the explosion from a gas leak happened in the middle of the night and no one was hurt. However, the church was reduced to a hole in the ground. Insurance covered 100 percent of replacing the building, and *now* both the older group and the nursery parents were most solicitous about offering use of the room to the other. It is to be hoped that other churches could move toward increased harmony without the need of such dramatic motivation.

Traditions in the Church

Is there a way to recognize these generational differences and still demonstrate oneness in Christ's body? The present inward focus of many congregations tends to make such an exploration difficult. Without an external agenda, many great traditions of the church that bind congregations together are not being passed on. Denominations have not educated current younger members about the purposes these denominational channels serve; and in the absence of a clearly identified need for such organizations, financial contributions are declining. This decline leads to the dismantling of present structures, many of which have served a vital role in building global partnerships. These international counterparts may have been founded by a "mother church" based in the United States, but those relationships have shifted to the point that "sister church" is a more appropriate term. As church members direct their financial support away from both the regional and denominational levels to internal purposes, little thought is given to the future. Will some of these same structures be dismantled now, only to have to be reconstructed later at a greater cost (if it is even possible to rebuild them) and having interrupted valuable services globally in the meantime?

For example, it will be interesting to see whether the nondenominational Protestant megachurches will begin to grow beyond their generally internal focus and broaden to a mission vision. If so, what channels will they use to act on that vision? At a time when many congregations are dropping the denominational affiliation from their congregation names, the prototype megachurch Willow Creek Church in South Barrington, Illinois, has formed the Willow Creek Association to work with churches having similar aims. Currently about one thousand churches are affiliated and receive a newsletter as well as access to conferences and information. Willow Creek has largely emphasized debt reduction and building costs as a focus for contributions received since its founding. In 1994 the large offering at the end of the year was for the first time directed to external missions. What channels will Wil-

low Creek begin to use to act on that mission concern and perhaps recommend to its association members? Are we seeing the
rudimentary formations of a denominational network, whether or
not that language is applied to the structure? Members of denominational churches might do well to review and reevaluate the original need for their existing structures before deciding that such
denominational networks are completely outmoded.

In that evaluation church members need to consider a variety
of issues—and not only whether denominational channels meet
an immediate need. As others have commented, denominational
distinctives are important not only for the practical channels and
services they provide. They have also contributed to safeguarding
key elements of the faith within the various streams of Christian
thought. From this perspective the move toward fresh beginnings,
with no respect for the past, may not revitalize the church as much
as weaken it. "The Lutheran view of giving as thanksgiving for
grace or the Calvinist perspective of managing possessions that
ultimately are not our own or the Wesleyan position that giving is
part of the perfecting work of God—these historic understand-
ings are not widely known any more," commented Craig Dykstra.
Traditional practices of the church, he noted, are important elements of the faith. "The practices of prayer; of hospitality to
strangers; of repentance, confession of sin, forgiveness; of works
of justice and righteousness; of resistance to evil; and of reading
our local situations and personal lives in the context of all of that
and of bringing communal, critical discernment to the issues of
our time—if all those things are not being done in relationship to
each other, we will find we've lost touch with what it means to be
Christian at all. Practices like these can't be made up *ex nihilo*,
out of nothing. Only through recovery of gifts we've inherited from
previous generations can we continue to discover what it means
to be Christian. We do it in our own way in our own culture—but
our effort builds on the past."

So the pastor who is counseling church members on how to
make sense of their present challenges may do well to rely on the
vital traditions of the church. Church members may need to be
informed about these traditions as they face old problems that
appear in new forms. Therefore, denominational identity can
help the pastor formulate responses to life's questions. The move-

ment to localize can have broader theological ramifications than merely taking the denominational name off the sign in front of the building would suggest.

Ethics

Another area where economic concerns may merge with pastoral counseling may be in the realm of ethics, particularly as they interact with personal debt. In a survey of the American labor force, Robert Wuthnow found that "one person in three claims to have observed others at work doing unethical things," although only one in ten had a sense of having actually done anything unethical.[9] The M. J. Murdock Charitable Trust study of graduate theological education found that "90 percent of the laypersons surveyed reported that in their daily life as Christians, they feel unprepared for the ethical, economic, social, and leadership challenges confronting them. Most report they receive little helpful insight or even empathy regarding these challenges from their pastor."[10]

Fran LaMattina described how she read a book by Ron Blue and it had "turned her life around financially." She got out of debt and organized her personal finances—and she doubled her giving. She was also able to increase her savings as a result of her new financial approach. Sometime later she was asked to do something unethical at the place she was then working. She knew she could not comply with the request, and because her finances were in order, she felt she could walk away from the job. She also realized that a lot of people who are in debt cannot afford to respond to personal ethical challenges in such a decisive way.

How relevant are the ethics being preached from the pulpit when a church member may be facing great personal debt that compromises his or her ability to act on those ethics? Once again money is seen to interact with basic Christian principles. Can church members who are deeply in debt quite literally *afford* to act on their convictions, if to do so might threaten their incomes?

LaMattina's point may help explain another story shared by a church member. This person served as a volunteer financial counselor, using the principles of Larry Burkett and Christian Financial Concepts. His own household finances were in order, he had savings in the bank, and he was close to owning his home. At work one day, his boss asked his team to do something unethical. The person relating the story made sure he understood the request and then he explained to his boss, with his coworkers looking on, how he could not compromise his personal ethics and comply with the request. When he was home that evening, he received calls from two of his coworkers saying how much they agreed with the position he had taken with his boss and how glad they were he had spoken up. His question was, why hadn't they backed him up at the time? Is there a connection between the man's few personal debts and his willingness to stand up for his ethics at the risk of his job? Is it possible the two coworkers who called him that evening felt they could not afford to risk their jobs because of personal indebtedness?

Traditionally the church has served the purpose of providing a community, ideally allowing members to have a reference point that keeps them on track in their walk of faith. People have always confronted challenges to their individual ethics. The church has the potential to help people feel like they are not facing these challenges alone.

Wealth and Debt

In the first 150 years of U.S. history, the majority of Americans were struggling economically. Yet the church was able to raise its members' sights to the compelling needs of the urban centers and the western frontier, as well as to areas around the world. They cooperated through their church channels to establish helping and support networks domestically and globally.

Now the majority of the U.S. population is economically comfortable and has attained at least some version of the goals society promotes. Their very success, however, may have produced an increasing sense of isolation, a withdrawal from community. Don McClanen, founder of the Ministry of Money, strongly feels there is a role for reaching out to affluent people at this point of need. "How can we learn from the wealthy as we learn from the poor? There is a desperate cry. We hear the cry of the poor. But we don't hear the cry of the wealthy: emptiness, loneliness, fear, isolation, and death." McClanen further reflects, "People are going to laugh at that—'what in the world is he talking about?'

Wealth is so seductive, it's so enticing. There is pleonexia—the insatiable desire for more."

That desire, promoted so tantalizingly and relentlessly by many different types of media, can lead church members as well as others to mortgage their futures in order to fulfill it immediately. Pastors, though, have not been prepared to help church members develop spiritual disciplines to resist the pressures that lead to personal debt. Ron Blue has talked with a variety of pastors in his work. "My observation is, most pastors have been poorly taught and don't understand the area, so they feel guilty. They may feel they are not managing their own resources well, and so they may feel guilty. One of the concepts that must be involved is financial accountability between the pastor and congregation members." He suggested that there is a deep hunger on the part of a growing number of church members for increased financial accountability at the church level. "People want to bare their checkbooks. We almost can't handle all the people who want to become spiritually accountable in finances."

Given the reluctance pastors have regarding the discussion of money and the lack of support they have in the area, it is not strange that pastors such as the priest quoted at the beginning of this chapter would feel an uncomfortable sense of responsibility toward members who improve their financial stewardship at the pastors' urging.

Yet pastors should also feel a responsibility for the parishioners who have so indebted themselves that they are now slaves to the cruel master of debt. "Satan's bound up the boomer generation with credit cards and interest," lamented David Wheeler. "Some younger families really don't feel they can give. As a result, some are dropping out of church. I believe much of this is the result of credit card debt. People have spent themselves into bondage. It's a case of misplaced priorities in terms of their relationship with Christ."

Robert Wuthnow observed, "Despite enormous evidence of religious belief and attendance in the U.S., it's a very secular culture. Consumerism has increased enormously. People feel strapped, under the gun."

How the church will respond to this increased economic pressure is a serious challenge. "People are having a lot of financial problems," observed Robert Welsh, president of the Church Finance Council of the Christian Church (Disciples of Christ). "Divorces, suicide, alcohol—the reason time and again is a financial mess. People do not know what to do with a consumer society and are overrun in debt. Pastors are beginning to hear that. Regional ministers in our denomination are beginning to counsel with pastors on this subject that is just coming into focus."

Ron Voss believes that sometimes only pain or emptiness will bring people to an acknowledgment of their spiritual needs. And pastors need to be ready to respond. He described one couple who were typical of many people today. "They were raised in homes where they went to church every Sunday. He's one Protestant denomination, she's another. They believe in God, but their belief is more deistic than personal or orthodox Christian. They don't feel they need organized religion—would rather pick and choose, cafeteria Christianity. Anything with discipleship, challenge, and a cross is inconvenient. They don't want to invest in a disciplined way in their faith. The only way to reach them is when the pain settles in or they experience emptiness in their day-to-day lives. They're thirty-seven years old, have a $250,000 home, two new cars, and find themselves asking, 'Is there more to life?' They find emptiness and lack of meaning."

What Voss described has been termed "mammon illness" by John C. Haughey. He suggests three key symptoms: (1) "running after things" (see Luke 12:30); (2) numbness: "One begins to serve mammon rather than mammon serving one's chosen purposes and values"; and (3) "the split consciousness" between the spiritual and money.[11]

Philip Slater likens the preoccupation with the material world to an addiction. He finds (1) "money addicts" who like to make and accumulate it; (2) "possession addicts" who like to spend it in visible ways; (3) "power addicts" who use it in ways to gain influence over others; (4) "fame addicts" who use it to gain a sense of acceptance with the "right people" or focus on what posterity will think of them; and (5) "spending addicts" who "travel, entertain, amuse themselves."[12] In this latter category, he points to the remarkable situation of people who pore over catalogues. He describes the situation as, "Having decided 'I need money' . . . I now have to consult a book to discover what I need it *for!*"[13]

There may be more people recognizing that having everything begins to feel a lot like having nothing. Will the church be there to offer a real alternative that answers the larger questions in life and point to the larger meaning that comes with the paradox of losing life to gain it? Consultant David Schmidt suggested that there are always exceptional people who respond to the church's values quite apart from societal pressure. "But for the mainstream, they need the pastor to come along and say, 'I care.' He has to care so much that he'll serve them with guidance as to what it will take to bring their checkbook before God."

Karl Menninger believed that pastors are in a unique position to address the ills of society in a preventive manner. "Clergymen have a golden opportunity to prevent some of the accumulated misapprehensions, guilt, aggressive action, and other roots of later mental suffering and mental disease. How? Preach! . . . Cry comfort, cry repentance, cry hope."[14]

At the turn of the last century, Josiah Strong put forth a similar call when he wrote, "No, there is no lack of wealth in the churches, even in hard times. When the rod of conviction and consecration smites the flinty rock of selfishness, it will break asunder and send forth abundant streams of benefaction, which shall make glad the waste places and prove the water of life to the multitudes."[15]

John Haughey described the process that must take place in these terms: "A conversion is, finally, a change at the level of one's loves."[16]

It takes a heroic commitment on the part of pastors and priests to hold on to a broader vision worth sacrificing for, even as they sort through on a personal level the questions of designer clothes requested by nieces and nephews or family vacation destinations. Their own struggles with such lifestyle choices can provide the pastor-counselor with empathy for the challenges facing the parishioner.

In addition to these issues, however, the job of the clergy has become even more difficult because of some paradigmatic shifts or changes in the very framework of American society that have placed the church in a totally new environment in which to pursue its eternal goals.

13

Paradigmatic Shifts

But we never can prove the delights of His love
Until all on the altar we lay;
For the favor He shows and the joy He bestows
Are for them who will trust and obey.

John H. Sammis, 1887
"Trust and Obey"

The church in the United States was an experiment. Immigrants landed and conquered a country that would reflect their origins yet produce strikingly different results in the form their faith institutions would take.

The relative equality of the new social order (in contrast to societies in Europe where roles were determined by birth) corresponded to religious trends that included the vitality of multiple denominations (in contrast to established church structures that were present in their homelands). The immigrants who came to North America brought with them hopes for a better life and centuries of Christian traditions.

Most new settlers were not formally church members; they came from countries with state-established churches, but they often did not evidence individual commitment. One estimate suggests that by 1750 only 5 percent of the population claimed formal membership in a religion; and by 1800, only 6.9 percent. By 1914 church membership reportedly was 43.5 percent.[1] Even considering the effects that easing membership requirements over the years within some denominations would have produced on the statistics, the numbers suggest a remarkable level of activity. As historian Sidney Ahlstrom writes,

260

The end of the Civil War with its great burst in American population growth and accelerated westward expansion led to a resurgence of missionary activity. Baptist, Methodist and Presbyterian churches were most successful in these efforts, in large part because so many of them migrated, and because they were the most natural affiliation for the average unchurched but nominally Protestant American. But all denominations continued to extend themselves.[2]

The evangelistic activity in the nineteenth century that contributed to this increase in membership reflected the conviction that the church would rise to the challenge of the emerging nation and secure a place for the Christian perspective in its future.

The break with England during the American Revolution and the forming of a new country meant that there were limited numbers of trained clergy to minister to the new population. The formal church structures were concentrated on the East Coast, while the frontiers expanded west. The frontiers tended to be lawless compared to their Eastern counterparts. These conditions combined to produce a fertile field for sowing new religious organizations to complement those brought from Europe.

As the American experiment continued, an emphasis on personal experience in religion developed in the United States, in contrast to the communal experience of state-established churches in Europe. Revivals and evangelistic meetings occurred. Focusing on the frontiers, preachers who had less education than was traditionally expected but were able to produce conviction in listeners began to appear. Their followings grew. The individual freedom to pursue economic goals in the new country was accompanied by a vitality in religion. Personal responsibility in government, in one's economic condition, and in religion was expected.

By the nineteenth century, the Roman Catholic Church in the United States—up to that point representing a relatively small portion of church members—found itself challenged by the influx of immigrants, many of whom settled in cities and were Roman Catholic by background. The vitality that was an earmark of the Protestant church in the United States produced an intentional response in the Roman Catholic Church as well. As Latourette describes the response of the Roman Catholic Church as it faced the massive immigration wave of the nineteenth century: "It was no easy task to make provision for the religious education and spiritual care of these millions. They were in danger either of drifting entirely away from the faith or of being assimilated to the prevailing Protestantism."[3]

A high degree of volunteer activity marked the church in the United States. By the nineteenth century, various denominations were cooperating in the Home Mission Society, the American Bible Society, the American Tract Society, and the American Sunday School Union. The goal was to make sure the settlers on the frontiers of the expanding country were establishing the Christian faith at the same time they were establishing new cities.

Several denominations grew up indigenous to the frontiers, their founders feeling that the structure on the East Coast did not understand the needs of those in the West, even as the colonies one hundred years before felt that the European church was no longer relevant to their new surroundings.

Mission societies were organized to evangelize Native Americans. Further, once slavery was no longer the law of the land, the abolition societies continued their concern for African Americans through education and aid societies.

The strong trend in individual experience unique to the United States was accompanied by a trend to reform society so as to reflect Christian moral ideals.[4] These efforts focused on the abuse of alcohol, the role of women, the conditions in prisons and mental hospitals, and child welfare leagues.

While all this activity was directed toward the constantly changing frontier and urban areas, global missions were also on the church's agenda. The American Board of Commissioners for Foreign Missions was organized by Congregationalists in response to an appeal from students who were attending the newly established Andover Seminary. It received support from other Protestant denominations as well, particularly Presbyterians. One of the first missionaries recruited was Adoniram Judson. Responding to his conviction to become a Baptist, he removed himself from the American Board of Commissioners sponsorship and appealed to American Baptist congregations to support him. They organized a mission society to do so. Eventually all the denominations in the United States included global missions as a component of their cooperative congregational efforts.[5]

Denominations provided ministerial training, enforced discipline among the affiliated congregations, promoted particular theological perspectives, and coordinated cooperative outreach efforts on the part of the congregations—both on the home frontier and on a global scale. The emphasis on personal conviction among the church members translated into a common agenda for the churches. There were souls to be won, justice to be pursued, lands to be reached in the cause of the gospel. What an individual congregation could not do alone could be accomplished through association with like-minded groups of congregations. The fact that there were tasks to be accomplished was a given. The kingdom of God had as much of a destiny as the emerging country.

Today people talk of a post-Christian era in the United States. Although church membership remains relatively high, U.S. society may be similar to the colonies before the first Great Awakening, with a general residual commitment to Christianity without the same personal vitality in many cases. Congregations continue to provide community services, such as funeral dinners, vacation Bible school, support for various local outreaches, improving the quality of life in communities in which they find themselves. Yet data indicates that the church, as an institution, is losing "market share." The church is commanding a smaller portion of member income across the theological spectrum. And of the money coming into the congregation, more and more is directed to operating internal programs that directly benefit the members themselves, with less going to what might be termed the larger mission of the church. As a strong majority of both the pastors and the regional officials responding to the Stewardship Project survey indicated, they do not sense an overarching vision in the church with which to challenge congregation members to improve stewardship. Instead, churches are turning inward, more concerned about services for present members than about any tasks to be accomplished in order to be faithful to kingdom demands. What larger paradigmatic shifts—changes in the framework of the church's environment—have contributed to this present condition?

Changing Relationship with Mission Churches

For one thing, the global independence movements after World War II challenged the traditional mission ties that had been established through denominational mission agencies. Denominational officials struggled to understand what the increasingly independent daughter churches were saying as they grew in strength and demanded status as sisters rather than offspring. Professional denominational executives made it their business to become sensitized to the concerns voiced by their international counterparts. Missions were no longer the simple task of "taking the gospel to the heathen." There were demands for mutual respect and understanding that had not been typical of colonial relationships.

The end of colonialism caused a focus crisis in the church. As noted earlier, on the domestic scene, older, white male pastors understood the need for affirmative action but resented being deprived of prestigious positions they thought were theirs by right. In a similar fashion, on some level people understood that the colonial relationships, which First World countries had imposed on other nations, were no longer right. But church members were left confused about how to approach a world that appeared in their living rooms via television news stories. Instead of feeling responsible for a particular area of the world as a result of longterm denominational commitments that sat in a larger colonial framework, suddenly the caring Christian was responsible for the entire globe. And past efforts throughout the globe, they learned from their denominational headquarters, had been faulty at points.

Many times, the information that came back to the congregations was about how much had been done wrong on the mission field. Angry international partners pointed to the lack of parity and, in some instances, even called for a moratorium on missions funding. Denominational mission education efforts aimed at sensitizing congregation members helped convince many of them that much of the missions activity had been a mistake in some vague way. James Hudnut-Beumler observed that many denominational magazines took a cue from Woodward and Bernstein, the journalist investigators who covered the Watergate scandal, by reporting often on what had gone wrong. There was also a residual feeling of rejection by and ingratitude from the international churches that had benefited from previous mission efforts and were now critical of that involvement. Thus, by the early 1980s, when, for example, the general secretary of the All Africa Conference of Churches "called for renewed financial support from Western churches"—in effect putting an end to the moratorium on U.S. mission involvement in Africa[6]—much of the congregational mission audience in the United States was at best confused.

For example, 60 percent of the pastors and even more of the regional officials responding to the Stewardship Project survey disagreed with the statement, "Most church members are very aware of the good that is accomplished through their denominational global mission activities," as shown in figure 9.

Figure 9: Survey Observation #76

Most church members are very aware of the good that is accomplished through their denominational global mission activities.

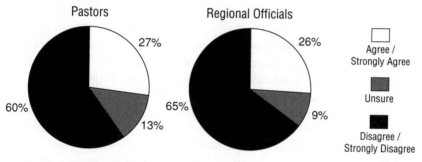

Details in the figures may not compute to 100% due to rounding.

The shift in focus among congregations from supporting denominational missions to sustaining an internal comfort agenda affected more than the church in the United States. One international church leader commented,

> A decline of Christianity in the West has had a negative effect on Africa in more ways than one. Take the case of African students in North America or Europe, for example. Many are they, once zealous for the Lord, who have capitulated, lost their faith and have been swallowed up by materialism and secularism. Back home, many point to the examples of the lukewarmness of the church in the West to legitimize their own nominalism.[7]

It may be that church members are receiving less of their information from their denominational agencies and more from secular media. The presence of global communications produced a profound effect on potentially mission-minded church members. As one national official suggested, "There are no romance countries anymore." Missions sounded exciting when the basic information church members received came from missionaries who had invested their lives in a country, learning to love the people and needing to inspire a similar love in those back home who were supporting their work. Television, on the other hand, provided news, which almost by definition was bad news. Stories of grain rotting on the docks or being misdirected were shown. Also the increased ease of travel took church members around the globe on business and pleasure, often seeing the sights prepared for tourists and rarely having reason to visit the mission sites that would convince them of the need to support the work financially.

William McKinney affirms the impact technological changes have had on mission support. "Our model for missions came into being when we didn't move far. To interact with China or Saudi Arabia wasn't on the screen. The church is not only local but is pulled to the universal dimension as well. There is a primacy to the local but the church can't be bound there. To express that broader dimension, the church created a mission movement."

However, in contrast to missionaries informing pastors who would interpret global reality to congregations, McKinney pointed out, "Now there is hardly a congregation in the U.S. that doesn't have people on a regular basis traveling to places that used to be exotic. I'm astonished where people go—Tunisia, Costa Rica, Bali—it's a global economy. We've broken out of our parochialism. But how does the pastor break out of parochialism? The pastor needs to try to keep up with the global experience of traveling parishioners when the pastor doesn't travel as much."

As a result of this influx of information from friends who had traveled or information through television and other media, many church members were educated to the position that the church had no business meddling in other people's affairs. Dean Hoge saw some of these issues as inevitable consequences of societal changes. The biggest challenge facing the church in the latter twentieth century is Christianity's specific identity. "There's a higher level of education, a higher level of affluence, greater cultural diversity, and a higher degree of pluralism—you can't keep old boundaries in place. The question is, do we have to keep the old boundaries in place to please Jesus Christ? That's where the acrimonious debate will be. It calls for theological discernment that's not going to be too easy. We live in a different world—kids are more urban, everyone is traveling all over the world. Why is it important? People's worldviews will shift under those circumstances. People's worldviews are changing. There's less stereotyping and there's interest in other religions." The role of global missions will be impacted by these major social shifts.

The distrust of Western money, which was part of the changing relationship between former sending and former receiving churches, confused missions leaders in the United States as well, and these leaders often passed on this ambivalence to congregation members. Mission agencies sent mixed signals. Mission agencies criticized themselves and church members in general for a lack of sensitivity; yet they still complained that the agencies were underfunded. Many mission personnel were confused because they saw bad examples of application of Western money and its negative impact in some areas. Yet they were surprised as agency funding decreased and programs had to be cut back. It seems difficult for those who are most in touch with the issues to hold the various sides together. For example, two national staff of one denomination explained in heated terms how more money from Western churches would only hurt the cause of the church in other countries. Their position sounded convincing until a third national staff person gently reminded them that these two were, nevertheless, trying to raise one million dollars from American Christians for a program they hoped to launch in another country.

The general ambivalence toward past mission activity became a widespread cultural phenomenon, fostered by news stories in the general media and fiction such as *The Ugly American*, so that even conservative churches that maintained a traditional approach to missions found support lagging at the congregational level.

Robert Niklaus of The Christian and Missionary Alliance Office for Communication and Funding noted that about 50 percent of their affiliated congregations do not give to the Great Commission Fund in their denomination. He noted, "There's a correlation between not giving a percentage to the Great Commission Fund and not seeing the theological framework in which that work sits."

Al Taylor, director of stewardship of the Church of God (Cleveland, Tenn.), feels that missions are still important in his communion, although the level of importance may have decreased. "Giving in missions has always been respectable, but when I was a kid it was the top priority. Now it's somewhere down the line. It shows we haven't discipled the new people. We've been growing so rapidly that we especially need to emphasize discipling. The old generation that understood the issues becomes a small minority." Taylor believes that this need for increased discipling has direct consequences for the role of missions in the church. "A missionary home from the field commented, 'I've seen Bible colleges and hospitals and churches worn around people's necks and on their arms and their hands.'" There is not the same compelling desire to share in a global context that motivated many church members formerly.

In the Stewardship Project survey, only a third of the pastors and just 21 percent of the regional officials were able to agree with the statement: "Global missions is just as important a topic as it used to be for most congregations."

Further, 91 percent of the pastors and 88 percent of the regional officials agreed with the idea: "When church members are asked to give funds for missions, in general, they want to know 'what their money will buy.'" This attitude on the part of church members is consistent both with the trend to pay the church for services rendered and also with an increasing distrust of mission involvement overseas.

In one workshop a retired scientist, who also served on his mainline Protestant congregational leadership board, summarized his view of missions. He noted he had always urged the congregation to support denominational mission activity. Yet he felt he could not continue to recommend that activity. "Sending money to missions," he said, "is like dropping a stone down a deep well and never hearing it splash." He ended his description with a concise plea: "I don't want payback. I want playback."

The fact that church members want more responsiveness in mission structures caused the leadership of The Christian and

Missionary Alliance to develop a more streamlined and efficient system, according to Bob Niklaus and other national Alliance leaders. The focus is now on "aggressive flexibility" rather than supporting traditional commitments. And the leadership plans to work on communicating more of a positive image. "In our total approach," continued Niklaus, "we're going to shift from emphasizing the 2 to 3 percent shortfall to talking about the 97 to 98 percent that's being accomplished."

International mission movements have also successfully resulted in maturing churches, which is a cause for celebration. This development has called for a readjustment in the relationships between churches in Western nations, including the United States, and these emerging national churches. In some cases, the emphasis changed from sending U.S. personnel to supporting indigenous efforts. David McCreath reflected on the strong mission tradition in the Presbyterian Church (U.S.A.) and its predecessor communions. "The traditions focus on education and medical missions. Church growth was pursued not through individual commitment but through congregational planting. Presbyterians were often the first on the U.S. frontier with schools, for example." McCreath also noted that a change took place from the 1960s to the 1990s. "By 1995 there was no place in the world where Presbyterians in mission were not in partnership with local outreaches."

Changing View of Missions

M. Douglas Borko, of the United Church of Christ, referred to the United States' system of sending missionaries as the surrogate system. "We're using a 150-year-old surrogate system when we freed up people to represent us in mission. Heifer Project [an interdenominational effort to purchase animals to be sent to poor farmers overseas] after World War II breached that surrogate system and introduced a new era of mission. People were giving themselves and not sending someone else. It was more than possible with the increased affluence, telecommunications, and travel. Traditional mission structures have not come to terms with the changes. Many denominational structures are still geared to an understanding of mission that's 150 years old."

As some denominations struggled to keep up with the changes and shift from an emphasis on sending U.S. missionaries to supporting projects planned by sister churches, they found their job of interpretation much more difficult. Dale Minnich is the executive for the Church of the Brethren General Services Commission. He described that communion's experience with congregational mission support during this transition. "The big adjustments came in the 1970s. It was a hard sell for us. There were a lot fewer missionaries in the field, which have always been attractive. Previously congregations would support particular missionaries. Now the focus became the support of new projects without tying that support to individual U.S. missionaries. As a promotional vehicle, that hurt us more than was helpful. It was in the late 1960s that we intentionally began pulling back personnel. It was an Annual Conference mission paper that really established that policy. Both the support of projects in the other country and the decrease in U.S. mission personnel are ecumenical and indigenous directions that were good. But they are tough sells at the congregational level."

Craig Dykstra and James Hudnut-Beumler noted in an article they coauthored that, while it was clear that denominations had valid reasons for changing the structures of both their global and domestic mission outreaches, "To speak in marketing terms, the national churches were divesting themselves of some of their most popular products."[8]

The relationships were also interrupted as the former colonies turned their attention to governing themselves. In addition, while moratoriums in some countries decreased U.S. mission agency involvement, Americans, who had struggled with isolationism throughout their history anyway, became preoccupied with the Cold War, the domestic civil rights movement, and their own economic expansion. In the interim, national church officials began to emphasize the need for missions "in their own backyard" as well as globally. Several national denominational officials found themselves in an ironic situation. After urging congregations to be more open to local needs, the national offices noticed a decline in giving. When asked about it, congregations responded, "You've been telling us to recognize the mission in our own backyard, and now that we are doing it, you are criticizing us for not supporting global missions"—and, by default, not supporting denominational structures.

Another factor affecting missions was that the financial success of more and more Americans occurred in a vacuum of a positive theological agenda for these increased resources. While global mission agencies sent mixed signals about the dangers of as well as the need for Western money, church members were being preached to from a different quarter. Lifestyle expectations steadily increased. Young families were not interested in starting simply but expected to begin their married lives where their parents had ended up after years of hard work. As wants were translated into needs, wives began to go to work, since it took double incomes to meet expanding expectations.

Changing Role of Women

The fact is, while women were traditionally in the home in the 1950s, they were in the workforce in far greater numbers by the 1990s. In 1950, 32 percent of women and 82 percent of men were employed, while by 1993, 54 percent of women and 70 percent of men were employed. Another way of looking at this issue is the change in the composition of the workforce. In 1950, 39 women were employed for every 100 men. By 1993, 77 women were employed for every 100 men.[9] With a smaller portion of men and a greater percentage of women working, a visible shift in the workforce has taken place. This development also had a direct impact on the external focus of the church in several ways.

First, women had long been the mission educators and promoters in the church. This perception was affirmed in the Stewardship Project survey, with more than 80 percent of the pastors and the regional officials agreeing, "Women have traditionally championed missions in the church," as shown in figure 10.

When a former national women's mission society president was visiting a local church, she was asked why it was that women were the ones who took care of global missions. She responded, "Because men were not doing them, and the men would not let women do anything else." So women gathered with prayers and pennies and focused on global missions. By the 1960s many of these denominational women's organizations had combined their

Figure 10: Survey Observation #119

Women have traditionally championed missions in the church.

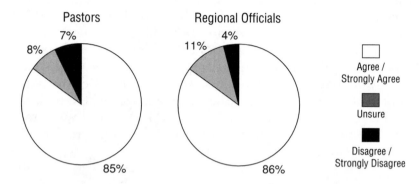

Details in the figures may not compute to 100% due to rounding.

pennies so effectively that they controlled hundreds of thousands, or even millions, of dollars. Women's mission groups continue to wield a degree of power at the congregational and denominational levels today. As Joan C. LaFollette has observed, women did not set out to create independent organizations, "but their exclusion from official leadership roles in the denomination in effect forced them into such alternative organizations."[10]

One writer noted:

> By the early decades of the nineteenth century, any attempt to keep women out of public ministry would have been futile. While it is true that women were not filling the command posts in the pulpits and seminaries, they had become a massive army of volunteers and professionals that were serving in the front lines of Christian ministry worldwide.[11]

In many denominations, these groups are now weakening, as younger women find it difficult to participate in daytime meetings and balance these commitments with work and family. This trend seemed to be obvious to the respondents in the Stewardship Project survey, with 90 percent of both the pastors and regional officials agreeing with the statement, "Women no longer have as much time as they did in past decades to volunteer as mission educators and promoters in the church."

In addition, whereas previously women were not allowed more traditional leadership roles in the church, that situation has changed in many denominations. Thus a younger woman can easily choose between being on the congregation's general leadership board or serving in the specifically women's mission group. Joan LaFollette comments, "The sense of unique purpose, so prominent in the early years when women's giving was essential to the survival of the mission movement, seems to have been lost in the intervening years."[12]

The women who were at home also had time to volunteer at the church. They were an invaluable communication source. One pastor noted that the level of stewardship participation of the family was often decided by the women in the home because they were more familiar with the church's needs. The women would know before the pastor that the curtains in the parlor needed to be replaced or that the utility bill was larger than expected that month. When the church was a social gathering place for women, the informal communications network that developed was invaluable for the smooth functioning of the church. Now the pastor has no such informal information system, since so many of the women in the church are busy in the workplace. The resulting communication void has been recognized, but no adequate alternative has been developed. One participant in a workshop commented, "As a woman, I feel the historic contributions of women in the church (and in mission) have been overlooked for so long; how sad and ironic that it's noticed only when it's no longer there."

The lack of volunteer time has also limited the activities the church can undertake. One pastor said she nearly had her "head bitten off" when she complained that some of the younger mothers in the church were coming to teach Sunday school and then not staying for church. "Look," one such mother told her, "I have one hour a week for church. You can have me as a Sunday school teacher or you can see me in worship, but you can't have both."

Pastors tell of the many community activities that demand parishioners' time. Concerts and sports activities and school meetings require that parents balance church commitments with other priorities. In one well-to-do metropolitan suburban church, there was a spiritual conflict over soccer practice. The practices had been scheduled for Sunday morning. Should the parents miss church to further their children's social standing that resulted from soccer participation? The issue was by no means easy to resolve for them.

While the time pressures on modern families may be one reason for less volunteerism in the church, another reason may be that laypeople are underchallenged. This problem seems to be generally recognized. Of the pastors in the Stewardship Project survey, 89 percent agreed with the statement, "The contribution of laypeople is underutilized in most congregations." The regional officials' response was even more pronounced, with 93 percent agreeing.

Changing Role of Laypeople

The role of laypeople in their congregations has also been impacted by societal changes. With more wealth and education, laypeople are less dependent on the church, and specifically the pastor, for their information. At the same time, churches that function at a maintenance/survival level have no need for the skills of a high-powered businessman. Howard Dayton quoted one businessman as saying, "I've never been given a vision big enough to challenge my entrepreneurial skills, so I've always been an usher." Would laypeople be willing to invest more quality time if the tasks they were given were more in keeping with their talents? In the study conducted in the early 1970s, which included more than three thousand interviews with both lay and ministerial leaders, Douglas Johnson and George Cornell concluded that many laypeople would like to be more involved but are waiting for an invitation from the minister to do a specific task. Further, pastors often voiced a wish that laypeople would be more involved, indicating a communication breakdown that kept the two groups apart.[13]

This dilemma may present positive opportunities to the creative minister, as represented in the following story. A young layman was resistant to a stewardship-mission effort his pastor was trying to introduce, and he successfully organized other church members against it. A year later, in a conversation, he came to understand the mission outreach in a different light. Missions was the goal of the church, in the same way that retirement security might be the goal of the individual. The church was not just arbitrarily giving money away but was trying to organize its finances in order to reach its goal. He connected that desire with the efforts of individuals who organize their personal finances to meet their family goals. A financial planner by profession, he began to see how his skills could assist the church to strengthen its outreach. He then became a promoter of the program he had been resisting.

Having a clear goal that is too large for the pastor to pursue individually might also assist him or her in seeing lay involvement as an asset—rather than a threat. One person described how threatened the pastor in the congregation he attended became when a layman successfully organized a group of congregation members to serve at a local homeless shelter. Loren Mead confirms his experience: "Many clergy are painfully ambivalent—even schizophrenic—about what they want the laity to be and do. If they really succeed in getting laity invested in the mission frontier, [they fear] it will disrupt the operation of the parish."[14]

Betty Lee Nyhus, director of Mission Giving for the Division of Congregational Ministries of the Evangelical Lutheran Church in America, said, "My swan song will be: The biggest untapped potential in the church is the laypeople who are just sitting there waiting to use the power of the Spirit to tell about Jesus."

Some among those interviewed believe that laypeople no longer have as large a role in church leadership as they had in the past. One church leader recounted how her parents, as lay leaders, held all the official positions in their small rural church in order to keep the congregation functioning. Yet now, her mother, who had served effectively as Sunday school superintendent in the past, refuses to pray in public because she feels she lacks adequate training to do so.

Andrew Greeley feels the church would benefit from an increased appreciation of the contribution that laypeople could make. "I think there's a much deeper spirituality in laypeople than clergy realize. We need to encourage clergy to be sensitive to lay as the Spirit speaks. We have to encourage/enhance spirituality of the laity. In my tradition, the clergy often feel the laity is spiritless and that they need to impose spirituality on them. I don't think they could be more wrong. When laypeople are asked to be involved, they swarm in to participate. The hard thing for clergy to do is to listen—and not to answer the question before we've heard it. Most of lay spirituality is focused at the individual and family levels. It will stay there unless the church figures out how to broaden opportunities. We need to create an opportunity for them to move into a more public domain. The task is to be freeing people to recognize their own spirituality and gently offering them opportunities. It is not ordering or demanding a response from them."

The very structures of most congregations make it difficult for the pastor to effectively develop lay leadership, suggested James Waits, executive director of the Association of Theological Schools in the United States and Canada. "At the core, there's a mind-set about the role of the minister. Everything in the church is the minister's role. One of the great resources in educating about stewardship is the laity—it's not just the giving. It's also the enabling of laity for giving.

"There is a theory of ministry that focuses all tasks of the church on the minister. When the pastor is uncomfortable and ill-equipped in the area of stewardship, you set yourself up for defeat. If a larger core of laity could be imagined, it would help. The pastor has to lead in equipping laity. There may need to be training on the issue: How do you avoid the pastor being alone at the center?"

Changing View of Religion

Another factor affecting the environment in which the church finds itself is the move toward making religion more private, resulting in pluralism and moral relativity. The relativism present in today's society had its roots in the Enlightenment of eighteenth-century Europe. The privatization of thought and the resistance to the idea that an authority higher than the individual existed were manifest in a variety of movements that affected world history for the next two centuries.

Yet the commitment to religion in the United States continued to resist the trend toward secularization such as that which appeared in communist countries, for example. If the church in the United States resisted the onslaught of relativism and secularism that had captured thinkers in Europe through the 1950s, what happened to bring the church to its present internal focus in the 1990s?

Success may have accomplished the weakening of the church that direct attacks on its existence could not.

By the 1960s several major social factors were present for the first time in history. One such factor was the post–World War II economic expansion. Before World War II a significant portion of urban residents were below what would have been the poverty line. Rural poverty was more difficult to measure but it is generally acknowledged that poverty in rural areas was more widespread than in urban centers. Thus it is not inappropriate to suggest that the majority of the U.S. population was at or below the poverty level before World War II.

By the early 1960s an economic phenomenon had taken place in the world. A number of societies, including the United States, were experiencing a situation in which the majority of members had more than they needed to meet their basic needs. While this development was good news in many ways—fewer people were hungry or worried about their basic needs—the changed situation brought with it a new set of challenges. Ronald Blue observed, "The threat of prosperity is a bigger threat than poverty. You tend to become self-sufficient when you have prosperity."

Indeed, Wade Clark Roof and William McKinney point to increased affluence, expanding media, and a greater emphasis on leisure as causing many Americans to seek "the realization of their 'potential' personhood. The breakdown of older religious norms of self-denial, the rise of more permissive child-rearing practices, and a thriving and expansive consumer culture all reinforced notions of self-gratification and enjoyment as ends in themselves."[15]

The editors of a seven-volume study on Presbyterianism and mainline religion in the United States suggest that U.S. churches may have been so internally focused that the major shift in the culture took them by surprise. As differences in theology were emphasized, church leaders missed an even greater problem, hidden by polls that continued to show Americans as a "religious" people. "If liberals and conservatives have stalked each other warily throughout the century, their obsession with combating each other has weakened themselves and depleted their resources for addressing a deeper and more fundamental problem: the challenge of secularity."[16] The increase of individualism, the emphasis on immediate needs, and the increasing resources to explore the related possibilities produced a cultural change at a deep level.

Accompanying the new affluence was an advertising industry that worked ever harder and more creatively to target these increasing resources of the *nouveau riche*. And advertising had a particularly effective selling medium in television.

Today television is a major preoccupation of American society. One study conducted by Robert Kubey of Rutgers University and Mihaly Csikszentmihalyi of the University of Chicago focused on Americans who all worked at jobs outside their homes. Participants in the study "reported feeling more passive, less alert, and experiencing somewhat more difficulty concentrating after television viewing than they did before viewing or after other activities." The authors of the study conclude that one factor in television viewing is loneliness, perhaps substituting for the basic human need of belongingness and love suggested by Abraham Maslow. The authors liken television watching to a hypnotic state: "In fact, a number of theorists have suggested that an involved television viewer is less defended and more suggestible—as in hypnosis." Advertisers who pay significant amounts of money to promote their wares use these trends to their advantage: "Television programs, after all, are carefully designed for dramatic action to peak immediately before the onset of advertisements that are so chock-full of special effects, flashy colors, movement, and sex" that even the most dulled psyche might become interested.[17]

The medium has changed the way Americans live. "In a variety of studies in different nations, television has been shown to decrease the amount of time spent with friends, doing housework and hobbies, sleeping, and reading." One expert suggested that no innovation, including the automobile, has had as much of an impact as television on the American lifestyle.[18]

The influence that television, with its evangelistic emphasis on lifestyle, has had on religious life in America is worth some reflection as well. In describing the choice of nineteenth-century immigrants to the United States to affiliate with a church, Latourette suggests these newcomers were willing to adapt to voluntary support of the church at least partly because of the important role it played in their communities. "The churches were social centres where the immigrant could find those of his native speech and cultural background." Latourette suggests that this cultural familiarity, combined with the vitality of the religious experience in the United States, led to the church's growth.[19] H. Richard Niebuhr also notes that religion served as the key unifying force and organizational center for immigrants newly arrived in this country.[20]

Today Americans may be finding that uniting bond through television instead. The authors of the study of television suggest that "before the advent of the electronic media, people living in different parts of the same country, or the world, would necessarily have had fewer commonly shared culture experiences. To the degree that one is shaped by prior experience, this means that the mass media will have homogenizing or mainstreaming effects on viewers."[21] As denominations become less a source of identity and personal faith is subject to greater privatization, people may be able to find an alternative bond with their fellow citizens through their televisions. Further, studies suggest that the experience of television watching is similar to that provided by religious ritual.[22]

> Perhaps no better proof could be offered of how television has come to absorb a significant proportion of the authority and power that the church, family, and school once held than the fact that television celebrities are now among those people most talked about, admired, and emulated in our culture. Television and its celebrities now compete with church leaders, parents, and teachers for the attention of children and are important sources of information for how one should live.[23]

In light of television's societal role, it is interesting to note several components of group dynamics, as presented by Dean Kelley in his book *Why Conservative Churches Are Growing*. Kelley presents a table of characteristics of "strong" groups and "weak" groups. If we use Kelley's categories to evaluate television, two of the "Weak Groups: Traits of Leniency" seem applicable: "relativism" of belief structure, including "that no one has a monopoly on the truth"; and "diversity," including "appreciation of individual differences (everyone should 'do his thing')." However, one point under "Strong Groups: Traits of Strictness" is "fanaticism (outflow [is greater than] inflow)." Kelley describes this charac-teristic as "All talk, no listen," and a combination of flooding the adherent or enforcing isolation if one is unwilling to absorb the input. In discussing religious movements, Kelley proposed, "Again, the high-demand movement will, by the urgency of its endeavor, seek to monopolize its members' every waking hour—and will frequently succeed!"[24]

Although interactive television may change the situation to some extent, television has traditionally provided hours of input, combining the relativism and diversity of Kelley's "weak groups" with a fanatical one-direction flow of information. Television may qualify as such a high-demand movement occupying its members' time when one considers that a conservative estimate suggests Americans, on average, watch 2.5 hours of television a day, or 17.5 hours a week,[25] and that at least one television is on in the aver-age American household for 7 hours and 34 minutes a day.[26]

Wade Clark Roof and William McKinney have pointed out that those who leave a church increasingly tend to switch not to another church but to no church affiliation, what they term the "secular constituency."[27] Are these people dropping out of traditional churches to find their spiritual needs met in the high-demand yet relative and diverse congregation of television watching?

It is not surprising, then, that almost two-thirds of the pastors responding in the Stewardship Project survey agreed or strongly agreed with the statement "Television and other media advertis-ing may influence church-member giving patterns more than the stewardship education they receive in church."

As people have committed more time to watching television, they have been told through advertising what they should buy, sometimes mortgaging their futures to buy promised happiness in the present. Easy credit began to become available during the early 1960s, and Americans used it to participate in the lifestyles brought into their homes each night. As Paul Dudziak said in an address at the National Catholic Stewardship Conference in November 1993, "The greedy materialism of the aristocracy is now the greedy materialism of the masses."

Many pastors are aware of the difficulty of providing a vision for a people so preoccupied with accumulation. Among the Stew-ardship Project survey respondents, 64 percent of the pastors agreed, "The way missions is presented in most congregations does not effectively compete with television for church members' time or money." Regional officials, whose job it often is to present the idea of missions to congregations, agreed even more strongly.

Yet, during the period of increasing affluence, and as church members along with other Americans were wooed by the compelling medium of television, the church leadership continued to approach congregations in the same manner they had when the majority of members were poor—comforting rather than challenging. The church also apparently assumed that shared common values would encourage financial and volunteer commitment that would enable it to continue at the same level that had existed in previous decades.

Giving did remain relatively high as a portion of income through the 1950s. Many denominations were able to expand their staffs and the services they could offer to congregations during that decade. However, as congregation members became more absorbed in their lifestyles, denominations have not continued to claim the same level of financial support.

Without a positive agenda for the widespread resources in the United States, in addition to a reluctance to bring a prophetic word to the lifestyle implications of affluence, the church leadership abandoned people to a consumer mind-set fostered and encouraged ever more creatively by the marketing industry.

The church in the United States exhibited a cause-oriented vitality from its earliest days. Confusion about the role of missions and an accommodation with pluralism, the pull of affluent lifestyles, and the resulting preoccupation of families with accumulation have resulted in an inwardly focused, comfort-seeking church that has little understanding of the need for the services provided by denominations.

Many have seen the church grow under persecution. Still, no one anticipated how thoroughly prosperity could sap the strength of the church in the United States.

14

Signs of Hope

Kyrie, eleison.
(Lord, have mercy.)
Christe, eleison.
(Christ, have mercy.)
Kyrie, eleison.
(Lord, have mercy.)

From the Order
of the Mass

The previous pages have dealt with several challenges before the church in the United States. A more convincing theology of stewardship needs to be developed. Clergy need additional training, not only in financial management but also in dealing with congregational control dynamics, counseling, and priority setting. Not only must major shifts in American culture be identified but their implications for the church need also to be understood. In that context, denominational leaders and congregation members alike will find it necessary to rethink their structures in light of their goals—once they have figured out what those goals are.

Given all of these challenges, are there also signs of hope in the church today?

There does seem to be a variety of reasons to hope that the church in the United States is working and growing toward a vital future in these turbulent times. The institutional financial crisis itself may have been a catalyst for congregations and denominational structures to rouse from their familiar patterns and begin to rethink their priorities. Fred Hofheinz pointed out one example. It was probably the heightening financial crisis that initially led the Roman Catholic bishops to develop the pastoral on stewardship. The final document became a teaching tool that explores stewardship within the framework of the spiritual implications of discipleship.

Others also recognized the financial stress on institutions as a starting point for future discussions. "Our problems are not trivial," commented William McKinney. "The issue is not how to raise money. It is about what we are called to be and to do as the church in the United States."

There seems to be little fear that religion itself will pass away. Dean Hoge did not envision a totally secular society as a result of the changes currently taking place. "People have genuine needs, and there is a religious market. Human life has some inconvenient aspects. The totally secular person doesn't have much to go on—'Why are we here? How should we live?' The fact that boundaries are disappearing is a worldwide phenomenon. The big market is moral education of children. If the church gets out of that business, someone will sweep in and take over." He also acknowledged that present times may be stressful for the church as it is presently constituted. And yet he saw a positive aspect to that development. "Any time there's a crisis in the family, after the shock is over, people get to the question of what is really important. That will be true for the church in this case too."

Robert Wuthnow also believes it is too early to assume that the current trend of the marginalization of the church in the larger society cannot be reversed. "I'm seeing more awareness than ten or fifteen years ago among undergraduates, for example, that the church could be a player in society. Maybe that's because the faculty and leaders are beginning to acknowledge the potential of the church as a leader."

The renewed energy that some people are noticing in the church is taking a variety of forms. James Engel is encouraged by what he sees as a growing interest in personal holiness. "Let's get people praying and fasting and on our faces before God— pray for renewal. I sense a real growing interest in holiness. I'm glad to see it. Lots of people are seeking. They fall down on their faces and say, 'God, where is it? It's pretty barren. If this is all there is, it's not very abundant.' What was different in ancient Rome from present American society? What is Christianity to do in the current culture? It should be the authentic salt and light—really making a difference."

M. Douglas Borko even sees potential in the oft-maligned baby boom generation. "The civil rights movement was a defining moment for my generation. I remember wanting to go be involved and being forbidden by my parents. The Vietnam War and the resistance to it was a defining moment—our personal engagement in making a difference. What it helped us to do was to come out from under the desk—we were taught in elementary and junior high school to protect ourselves from the bomb by hiding under our desks. We were to hide from nuclear radiation. We were raised that the world was going to end, and we hid out of hopelessness. Our experience with the Vietnam War resistance movement taught us that if we got involved, things didn't have to play out the way we had been taught they would."

It was the baby boomers who were described in glowing terms by Douglas Johnson and George Cornell in their report on the three thousand interviews with lay and ministerial church leaders in the early 1970s. "They also take heart in the young people, a generation dubious of church organization, but disenchanted with materialism and hungering for the transcendent."[1] While this age group seems to have overcome its initial distaste for materialism, it is intriguing to remember those earlier impulses and wonder if they have been lulled into a napping stage rather than totally eliminated by the dominance of mammon.

Borko now sees another social change developing, and this one may involve the church more directly. "Even the term 'yuppie' may be an apocryphal view. Now people are leaving rampant materialism. They are 'out from under the desk' and they realize they can influence and build. This may be a moment of hope as my generation comes out from that mind-set. Advertising is changing. Beer commercials show people sitting on the porch of the house they're renovating. This could be a major moment of hope and a reaction to the hopelessness and despair of being raised on the fear of the bomb. Enough of us are beginning to talk about this that it may be a moment of hope. Of course, it may not come. But if we can recapture what was ours in the '60s and '70s. . . . Now we have the wealth. The potential is there."

Wade Clark Roof and Sister Mary Johnson, in a study of trends related to baby boomers, conclude, "Many are looking not only for insights, but also for ways to be of service, for opportunities to give of their time and support to causes and projects that seem worthwhile."[2]

Seeing Change as an Opportunity

National denominational leaders are coming to terms with these changes. Their first response may have been to try to keep everything the same. But the shifts taking place are so convincing—and perhaps the financial downturn so consistent—that many have begun to rethink the future. James Hudnut-Beumler was encouraged by the attitudes present among a group of denominational leaders at a conference he addressed. "I was surprised and gratified how far people have come from a few years ago. Then it seemed as though people were beating their heads against a wall and saying, 'We've been done a dirty deed—it's political.' Now they have bottomed out, and they are trying to make the best of their situations. They're thinking creatively."

One denominational leader who looks at the shifts taking place as an opportunity rather than a threat is Timothy Ek. He observed, "The most strategic question as a denominational leader is: What kind of person are we seeking to deploy in the world? What kind of church produces those people? What kind of leadership board? What kind of pastor? What kind of denominational leadership helps those pastors?"

There is growing interest in an approach being pursued among Roman Catholic parishes called "sacrificial giving." This is an emphasis that Monsignor Joseph Champlin describes as "biblically based and essentially delivered by committed laypeople. It simply seeks to inform consciences, provide spiritual motivation for giving, and hold up a specific norm as an ideal (5 percent for the parish, 5 percent for the poor)." The effort has been implemented in more than one thousand parishes in the United States and Canada.[3]

The Presbyterian Church (U.S.A.) has also taken stock and started to make some changes in the ways it approaches the denomination's relationship to the congregations. As David

McCreath explained, "We've taken account of the fact that many Presbyterian congregations do planning annually. Each year there's a new committee, a fall campaign. We're hoping to change that. We want to train congregations for a three-to-five-year effort, where they can see significant growth in three to five years, unlike the episodic annual approach." They also plan to review some of the resources they make available to congregations. "There's a shift from the national office serving as grant-making or material resource agencies to the task of stewardship education/discipleship growth. Then we'll see what types of materials we need to accomplish that. The discipleship growth idea has been emerging for the past three years."

James Austin, vice president of the Stewardship Commission, pointed out that the Southern Baptist Convention has had a catalogue of stewardship materials for many years. The catalogue now contains more than 120 items, from calendars to tithing posters to books on responsible Christian lifestyle. A new area of development for the denomination is materials on individual finances titled *Live Wisely*. There is also a family budget computer program that includes the tithe automatically in expenses. James Powell of the SBC Cooperative Program office pointed out, "One of the strongest trends is the greater need today and more acceptance for Christian money management. People are more interested in learning how to manage money today. A person in our Commission is developing this area. We've been talking about lifestyle for years, and few have heard it. Now we're still talking. People are told they should increase their gifts to their church. How do they do that when they want to spend more and more on themselves? Until you can help them understand what they need and what they should want—and how to tell the difference—it will be a challenge. Teach people to manage money better and they will give more to the church—usually."

Changes at the seminary are also taking place. For example, North Park Theological Seminary of The Evangelical Covenant Church has had a core curriculum course on stewardship for some years. One Evangelical Lutheran Church in America seminary has an endowed chair for stewardship. Also, David Heetland, vice president for development at Garrett-Evangelical Theological Seminary, feels that development officers may be starting to take some leadership in the area in order to help seminaries come to terms with the topic of money and the church. "It is development officers rather than academics who are urging the seminaries to consider the topic. Development officers have a foot in both doors, in the seminary atmosphere and also with pastors who are actually in ministry. Development officers will have to model and teach on the topic." Heetland was aware of a handful of seminary development officers who have begun offering courses to ministerial candidates.

Some denominations have made a point to become more involved in congregation-level interaction. Dale Minnich described the "Face of Mission" effort in the Church of the Brethren. "The national staff and General Board members are to go to at least two congregations a year in order to update and listen to people. They can explore various topics together. By two years ago, 205 congregations had been visited. That seems to be meeting with a lot of positive feelings. Congregation members can know both the struggles and joys at the national level. And it elevates the information they receive about the General Board in their minds. They can know what the church is doing. Often people will say, 'I just didn't know what was going on.' The personal face-to-face encounter brings a dynamic that no other approach does."

Bishop William McManus also saw both the challenge and the potential before the church as it works to come to terms with the issue of financial stewardship. "The challenge is the nonchurchgoers or the irregular givers—we need to discover how to encourage them to pay a fair share. The key is to discover, to experiment. Of course you have to be careful," he added. "Any experiment runs the danger of creating an illusion that you can buy your way into heaven."

McManus continued, "On a bright note, I've been a priest for fifty-five years. Charity has improved vastly from when I was first ordained. We're approaching a time when an active Roman Catholic will be one identified as involved in some service to others. This is a spectacular departure from fifty-five years ago, when the main idea was to attend mass on Sunday and not eat meat on Friday. The stress was on obligations: 'Do this, or you'll be in trouble with the Lord.' Now the stress is on opportunities: 'Don't pass them by!' The mood now is, you are an authentic Catholic if you are trying to help someone."

The fact that more than a million copies of a summary of the bishops' pastoral on stewardship have been purchased and distributed indicates real interest in the topic of an authentic understanding of stewardship.

One example of a Catholic parish that is enthusiastic about stewardship is St. Francis of Assisi Church in Wichita, Kansas. The priest, Thomas McGread, addressed a group of participants one afternoon at the 1993 National Catholic Stewardship Council Conference in Nashville, Tennessee. McGread pointed out that in a congregation of two thousand, 85 percent of the members attend mass every week. "They get a sense of belonging, and then they get a sense of responsibility." He chooses to work with couples on the parish Stewardship Committee. "I select them. I choose positive people, Eucharistic people—people who believe in the mass. Through his blood, we have forgiveness of sin. We must be thankful people. The stewardship life is thanksgiving to God and is an example to all those around us who don't believe in God."

Other congregations throughout the United States join St. Francis of Assisi Church in being excited about stewardship. For example, Brian Kluth, president of the Christian Stewardship Association of the National Association of Evangelicals, described the priority setting that needs to go on in congregations in the United States. In that context, he mentioned the church he attends in Milwaukee. He feels that churches need to move away from their "materialistic agendas. I've learned firsthand the value of not using bank mortgages and bonds to fund God's work. For example, the church I attend met in a movie theater for three-and-a-half years, saving money toward a building purchase. Land and a new building were going to cost 1.5 to 2 million dollars. But God led us to a twenty-two-thousand-square-foot racquetball club we are purchasing for five hundred thousand dollars cash. Meanwhile, as we were saving for our own building, we also helped finance ministries and churches in India. Recently our congregation gave six thousand dollars to build two churches there. They were being persecuted and chased out of other facilities. God's agenda is bigger than our agenda. We could say we need to get our own needs met first. But we're trying to build things on a God-given agenda. Hopefully the pastor and mature leadership in the congregation will set a God-given agenda and let personal agendas follow."

The Positive Aspects of Affluence

As the Stewardship Project continued, having a positive agenda for the great affluence that has developed in American society emerged as one of the key challenges before the church. So many of the great cathedrals were built earlier in this century by communities of faith, whose majority of people did not have indoor plumbing or central heat, let alone central air conditioning. People saw the church as worth sacrificing for because they were not afraid of sacrifice in their own lives. Now, after factoring out taxes and inflation, Americans' incomes are, on average, well over 200 percent larger than incomes in the Great Depression. Yet church members are giving a smaller portion of their incomes to their churches than they did back then. While per member giving in a set of twenty-nine denominations increased 23 percent in inflation-adjusted dollars between 1970 and 1991, Americans' per capita recreational activity expenditures increased 130 percent. And between 1975 and 1990, it is estimated that total credit card interest payments increased 550 percent.[4]

If the church is not presenting a convincing challenge to church members about what to do with their money, it is clear people will find other ways to spend it. That is why the work of various Christian financial management counselors makes a vital contribution to the church. Larry Burkett, for example, has a widely syndicated radio program, *Money Matters,* in which he discusses practical details of organizing one's financial resources in a larger faith context. Through his organization, Christian Financial Concepts, he has trained hundreds of volunteers who work with individuals trying to get control of their incomes.

Another leader active in this area is Gary Moore. An investment counselor as opposed to a financial planner, he wrote *The Thoughtful Christian's Guide to Investing.* Through the book and workshops, he advises concerned church members on both practical investment plans as well as ethical and responsible investing concerns.

A third person involved in this area is Ron Blue. He began work in the financial planning area because he wondered why Christians were not giving more of their incomes. He had previously been a CPA and a banker. After coming to faith in Christ in 1974, his first response was to join a ministry outreach. In that context, he traveled to Africa eleven times in just a few years. He was struck with how creatively money was being put to use there and how many resources were not being tapped in the United States. He left the ministry with which he was associated to come at the problem from a different angle. His goal was to help people "plan and manage their finances so they can do what they want to do—to give."

Today his company receives inquiries from people all over the United States. His national office in Atlanta, Georgia, has expanded into fifteen other cities. The calls he receives are not usually from people with debt but people with large incomes who feel a vague necessity to be responsible with it. He described his ideal client. The man, a physician, is younger than forty-five, married and with children. "He established a 'finish line' on his lifestyle, is providing for his children's college educations, his housing needs, and retirement. But he is also saying 'enough is enough.' He now gives away 50 percent of his income."

It often takes two to five years of discipleship lifestyle for his clients to grow toward increased giving, he noted, and the majority do not reach the 50 percent level. However, among his clients, the average charitable contribution is 15 percent. Interestingly, the percentage tends to increase even as income goes up, so that the average in the second-highest income category among his clients is 28 percent in charitable donations.

Ron Blue's approach is to acknowledge that some people are talented at making money and then to give them the opportunity to integrate that talent with their spiritual priorities. One man who had heard Blue speak was ready to sell his one-hundred-million-dollar business as a result. Blue said he quickly counseled the man, "Don't kill the chicken—give away the eggs!" Today clients who have organized their finances are giving away tens of millions of dollars to Christian causes. And Blue, not one to think small, has set a goal of one billion dollars a year to be given away by his clients by the year 2000.

Requested to give input to a U.S. congressional subcommittee, Blue was asked what he would tell the American family. He offered the following advice: (1) Spend less than they earn, (2) avoid the use of debt, (3) build some liquidity, and (4) set long-term goals. When one senator commented that it sounded like good advice for the average family, Blue responded that it would work for the U.S. government as well.

While American families could benefit from the four principles cited by Ron Blue, it is not likely they have the means to hire a financial planner to aid them in organizing their finances. One source of possible assistance in this area would be small groups. "Small groups can have an enormous impact," observed Robert Wuthnow. "They can get people to talk about their concerns, provide an opportunity for being accountable, provide counterculture support to make decisions rather than basing those decisions on the values of the workplace or on advertising."

Howard Dayton also saw the potential of small groups when he founded Crown Ministries in the Orlando, Florida, area. In the early 1970s he saw a group of individuals developing independent ministries in the area of financial accountability. "God moved on them," was Dayton's description. Yet, when follow-up was done with people who had been touched by these ministries, it seemed that they made little long-term impact. After reflecting on the issues involved, Dayton left his real estate business to begin a network of small groups that focus on a series of lessons designed to help people change their lifestyles in the context of their faith. A congregation is able to offer the group to members once a leadership core has been trained. His experience also led him to conclude that the pastor is a key element in lay members feeling free to pursue such a small-group agenda.

Dayton also believes that people can be challenged to greater giving and an increased responsiveness to the promptings of their faith. He mentioned that he had talked to three or four men who were gifted at making money and who had recently decided to use those talents specifically to generate money that will be used to fund Christian endeavors. The challenge will be developing a large enough picture to be able to absorb people's interest. "I don't think the average church has yet articulated a vision that could captivate baby boomers," he remarked.

The Church in the Future

As the church enters the future, the role of money seems intertwined with the development of ministry in the world that is taking shape. The situation is not entirely new in the church; there have always been wealthy church members who have had various degrees of success with being generous. The new unknown in the ongoing story is what current church members' responses to the challenge will be. Al Taylor observed, "In history, when people got right with God about money, then revival happened. In the U.S., we won't have revival until people come clean about money and align ourselves and our affections with God's priorities. Until then, it won't happen in the U.S. And people won't come clean unless the church tells them the truth. The people proclaiming the truth about money need to live out that truth or people will say, 'This is another docudrama.'"

The prospects for the church in the United States are both exciting and scary, which is not uncommon when people venture out in faith. The current bleak picture facing many congregations who struggle with a maintenance mentality, as well as denominational structures facing reevaluation, sits in a much larger context. Loren Mead, author of *The Once and Future Church* and *Transforming Congregations for the Future,* shared his views on the church's current situation. "I do have hope—I know Who's in charge. The church is called to be more than ever before and invited into partnership with God's plan. During the worst section of Israel's history—the period described by Jeremiah and Isaiah—people found out who they were. Suffering produces understanding. I think it really is getting out of one paradigm and finding a new one that is compelling. We are getting out of an empire-building mind-set, and we must learn what it means to be a serving community."

Craig Dykstra is also hopeful that the current stress on church structures is more of a transformation process than a permanent structural breakdown. "It's kind of like a forest fire—huge old trees burning down and scrub brush is growing up. On the broad historical landscape, it's been happening over and over again. This type of experience is nothing new in Christian history. As both a personal faith statement and a traditional tenet of the faith, I would affirm that the sovereignty and purpose of God will out. I have no doubt the truth of the gospel will draw people to it, and they will drink living water and build new institutions shaped by it."

As current institutions face the challenges before the church, they are gathering together and looking for points of agreement. The Stewardship Project National Advisory Committee gathered in March 1995 for the second of two meetings over the life of the project. One goal of this diverse group—representing an estimated 55 percent of church members in the United States and the theological spectrum from Roman Catholic to evangelical, Pentecostal to mainline Protestant, Anabaptist to Holiness—was to see what areas related to financial stewardship they could affirm as a group. Seven points of consensus resulted. The conclusions were not "word-smithed" as Tim Ek pointed out, since the goal was not to develop a final version but to identify starting points for further dialogue. The points were as follows:

1. Owning the gap between beliefs and practice.
2. Recognizing creative tension between reality and vision.
3. Need for conversion/formation, which is part of the process.
4. Leadership needs conversion and formation in personal stewardship and to be given a level of confidence and courage in terms of corporate leadership.
5. A whole-life response to the Great Commandment of Jesus,[5] to be disciples who are stewards.
6. The church needs a positive agenda for the great affluence in our society.
7. Healthy churches produce generous people.

The discussion that led to these seven points focused on stewardship as a whole-life response to the gift of life. The following paragraphs summarize some of the highlights of the national church leaders' dialogue.

Stewardship was recognized as an important indication of where a person is on his or her personal journey, as indicated by the phrase, "Stewardship is what results from who you are." In this sense, stewardship is a by-product of one's spirituality, both on an individual basis and in the gathered congregation, rather than resulting from some high-powered technique.

Stewardship may involve sacrifice, but that word has changed in meaning, now referring to the painful giving up of things wanted. In its original definition, the term was "to make sacred." Thus stewardship involves an act of worship through the offering of oneself.

The word *co-responsibility* was offered for use. When the Catholic Pastoral was being translated into Spanish, there was no Spanish word for *stewardship,* so the term *core-sponsibilidad* was used. The word implies that stewardship involves a person in shared responsibility with other Christians, with those in need, and with God Almighty—the one attribute of God provided in the Apostles' Creed. Co-responsibility points toward a partnership in the mission and vision of God's plan.

The motivation for pursuing stewardship can be seen as based in the Great Commission, since the church is entrusted with the work of God on earth. Even more, that commission leads to an acknowledgment that stewardship involves the just administration of the responsibility invested in the church, leading to an association of justice with stewardship.

However, the church in general has moved away from the intentional effort to develop disciples. A key element, then, is for the leadership at all levels of the church—local, denominational (both regional and national), and seminaries—to model true stewardship, both individually and corporately. One element that may help at the local level is for national offices to develop an integrated approach. Those that have evangelism sections, stewardship sections, mission sections, etc., sometimes do not coordinate their contacts with the congregation. Thus the end users at the congregational level are left to integrate the various streams of the church into a holistic approach.

There was strong affirmation for the point that stewardship is at the level of spiritual conversion and formation. Although too often it is relegated to the level of "paying the bills," its proper place is at the level of converted hearts and renewed

minds. The word *idolatry* is perhaps the most apt description of the problem facing the church, but it is a word that
does not easily translate into modern people's experience. A
key challenge is how to define the idolatry of wealth in contemporary terms so it connects with people at a deep level.
Idolatry points to the worship of self, either on an individual level or in the preservation of an institution at any level,
in contrast to a living faith response to God. What is needed
is a turning from the almighty dollar to God Almighty.

Thus there needs to be a change at the level of values, since
behavior follows values. This change may lead people to
(1) an acknowledgment that there is a gap between the
spoken affirmations and the way we act, (2) confession followed by repentance, leading to (3) forgiveness/absolution
and healing.

Small groups may be one method of bringing people to such a
spiritual acknowledgment. Leadership—from lay leaders to
pastors, from denominational officials to seminary officials—
need to be supported as they guide others and given confidence and courage in their corporate leadership. The situation is serious and does not allow for continued timidity.

Part of the healing is to give those with changed hearts and
renewed minds a positive agenda for their resources, which
result from their responsible application of their time and
talents. Pursuing that positive agenda will involve the
church leadership at all levels in applying their gifts for the
glory of God.

Obviously, it was quite a task to summarize even these few
highlights of the discussion into the seven consensus points. The
process was a testimony to what God can accomplish among a
committed group of followers who have come together in Jesus'
name!

The positive agenda referred to in the seven points will no
doubt continue to involve a global as well as local component.
Ralph Winter of the U.S. Center for World Mission continues to
hold out the possibility of evangelizing the globe by the year 2000.
The late James Grant, formerly executive director of UNICEF,
never stopped issuing a call for an increased response on behalf

of the world's children. Many denominational structures continue to reevaluate, rethink, and revamp their approach in order to help Christians in the United States be part of a believable vision that allows them to be faithful to the call on their lives.

The Mennonite World Conference, representing Mennonite and Brethren in Christ churches, has developed one exciting approach. Their idea takes into account the need for increased partnership among both the giving and receiving churches while acknowledging the abundant resources on the part of church members in the United States. It is called the Global Church Sharing Fund. A committee includes representatives of Mennonite World Conference Churches, at least two-thirds of whom are African, Asian, or Latin American. Mennonites from around the world are invited to donate to this fund, confident that all distribution, scheduled to begin in 1997, will be with the guidance of committed Christians who are working together to apply the abundant resources of some for the good of all.

The church in the United States faces a great challenge in coming to terms with money, but there is evidence that the church continues to possess creativity and vitality with which to respond to these serious issues and craft its role in the future.

15

Looking Ahead

The kingdom of this world is become the kingdom of our
   Lord, and of His Christ,
And He shall reign for ever and ever.

George Frederick Handel
"The Hallelujah Chorus"

Money.

The church can't seem to come to terms with it. And yet the church cannot function without it.

Part of the problem before the contemporary church is that so many things have apparently changed so quickly. For one thing, society used to embrace a civil religion, meaning not only religion in the public sector but religion that knew how to conduct itself in polite society. The system maintained a certain effective status quo: Democracy depends on mutual cooperation for the good of the whole, and religion promoted both public and private responsibility.

Some suggest that this equilibrium was blindsided in the 1960s by the equivalent of an NFL middle linebacker in the Super Bowl. The general good gave way to the generally accepted elevation of the individual. By the 1960s people had been exposed to much more than previous generations through increased education, travel, and the medium of television. As a country, we were feeling powerful enough to shoot for the moon—literally—and we provided the funds to do it. Public constraints were previously reinforced by the private poverty of the bulk of the population who couldn't afford to indulge themselves. But now the individual whose wages were growing relatively steadily since World War II could follow almost any dream, and if people could not pay for what they wanted today, there were plenty of companies willing to allow them to have it today and pay for it tomorrow.

The church had been warned about the dangers that money can produce. Jesus talked a great deal about money and possessions. The Bible comes back to the topic again and again. One of the first problems in the early church was with the problem of fair distribution among the widows.

In America there were those who foresaw the outcome of the Industrial Revolution and tried to raise the alarm. But the alarm went largely unheeded, back then as well as more recently. The church was benefiting from the rush to the suburbs. Religion's place seemed secure, and so it was assumed the rising tide would raise the old ship of Zion along with it. But as some of those quoted on the previous pages pointed out, while the waters of affluence rushed about it, the church seemed to hit a sandbar.

Today religion does not have the hallowed place in our culture that it once enjoyed. For more people, no religion is now as good a condition as a little religion used to be. Further, the rush to help the individual reach his or her full potential has produced an atmosphere where issues of right and wrong are skewed. How can it be wrong if it feels good to me is a question asked with all sincerity. And money can buy a lot to make us feel good. There is no lack of new products or new adventures to pursue for those who can afford them.

And those who have absorbed the new good news about the value of the individual and all the related expectations—the "You deserve a break today" litany—have brought those expectations to the church.

How did this state of affairs come to be? Here was a problem. The only way to come to terms with the changes taking place after World War II was to talk about them. However, many of these issues involved the responsible use of money in light of scriptural demands. And pastors, perhaps above all things, did not—and still do not—like to talk about money. This standoff did not create problems as long as the church's residual cultural effect retained its hold on the populace. The collective memory produced a willingness to maintain many of the old patterns, including church giving, among those who remembered the times before. However, massive changes were taking place that would affect the next generation. Colonial frameworks were breaking down due to international independence movements. While the changes were to be celebrated, the church lost a framework it had depended on to focus the church's attention outward. Not only that, new information through global communications presented many with the shortcomings of past mission efforts. The news often led to confusion on a broader scale than ever before about whether it was even appropriate for the church to be involved "in other people's business"—a far cry from feeling a responsibility outlined in the Great Commission. Many women who had been the backbone of the volunteer network in the church, as well as a vital internal communication network, now entered the marketplace—in some cases to support their family and in others to support their family in the lifestyle to which they wanted to be accustomed. They learned about these lifestyles from a steady stream of input that came daily into their living rooms through television.

People became mobile, with a resulting breakdown in long-standing relationships and the associated mutual accountability. They were told their individual needs and desires were of primary importance, and anything that interfered with fulfilling their own potential was bad by definition.

Church members did not escape this new orientation. When membership began sagging in some quarters in the mid-1960s, studies were done to see how to make churches grow. The earliest theories recognized the spiritual needs that lead people to decision. But they were soon applied in ways to identify needs that lead people to consume offered services. With the biblical approach to the topic of money not having been included in most pastors' training, financial stewardship was reduced to fundraising, and church leadership hoped people would have some sort of spiritual experience that would then make their attitude toward their resources come out right.

The result was congregations turning inward, receiving confusing signals from their denominational offices. Organized in a cultural framework that existed before these dynamic changes occurred in the 1960s, the denominations themselves in some cases went through a reevaluation process when that framework began to erode. However, it was difficult to communicate their emerging perspectives to those at the congregation level. Church members knew that the old order wasn't what it used to be, but it was not exactly clear what the new order was. What was clear was that the church up the block was now adding a family life center, and we'd better think about our own after we've paid for the air conditioning. Some of the money that used to be sent far away was redirected to local mission outreach that could be more immediately recognized: soup kitchens, shelters, day care for the poor. American society still benefits from the involvement of churches in their communities in many vital ways. But some of the money was redirected to attract more people, and if they didn't come, well, we don't mind new carpeting anyway, if we can ever agree on the color.

Without a compelling reason to focus outward—indeed, having become convinced that focusing outward was far more complex than anyone had thought before—churches turned more and more of their budgets inward. This development created a crisis for the denominational structures, both national and regional. Some responded by increasing their pleas for more money. Others tried the use of regulatory force. In almost every case, however, the situation was viewed as an institutional support problem rather than a growing spiritual crisis.

And spiritual crisis it seemed to be. As a nation, divorce rates went up. Teen suicide became a tragic phenomenon. Crime escalated. Isolation ensued. These deeply affecting conditions made the pastors' job only more challenging, as people wondered why the church was not still making everything all right.

Further, congregations struggled in an atmosphere that degraded the idea of common consensus. You like to support that mission in Africa, and I think we ought to have a new baptismal font. No problem. We can each do our own thing. You give your money to Africa, and I'll recruit the money for the font, and we'll see each other in church on Sunday at 11:00. The idea that the church as an entity might have a particular role that superseded individual agendas seemed somehow inappropriate, even smacking of power politics.

Yet in the absence of such a large agenda to draw people out beyond themselves, pastors find themselves involved in all kinds of these dynamics. Again, these aspects of the church are nothing new. Stories about the pastor having to come to terms with a wealthy individual are as old as the church itself. It's just that now, with the general affluence available to so many more, this old problem is multiplied many times. Such individual power dynamics are only one aspect of the human condition. But unless pastors recognize and encounter them when they occur, even if only a few people are the source, these dynamics can rule by default. Here too, pastors have not been prepared through their educational experience. Also, many have not felt strong support from their denominational structures. So they do their best, making it up as they go along, trying to minister to the spiritual needs and balance the more material agendas that proliferate at the congregational and denominational levels.

These are some of the findings that resulted from several years of interacting with congregations about the church and its relationship to money. In light of all these factors, what are we to conclude?

First, we find ourselves still having a deep respect for the church. When all the changes that society has gone through in just the past thirty years become clear, the present state of the church can be described as heroic. One image that comes to mind is a group of people grasping a cliff's edge as wave after wave of a sudden storm tries to sweep them out to sea. You find yourself cheering them for their courage rather than criticizing them for having chosen that spot for a picnic.

And the church has done a remarkable job. Many people continue to find spiritual comfort. People who have not attended services for years come to the church at moments of crisis, and in a loving manner, the church is there waiting for them. Much of the international work that continues—and the little-known progress that has been made in global conditions—benefits from the faithful, if decreasing, contributions of the church. Local communities count on the church as a stabilizing influence. One example was offered: How would you feel if you saw a crowd of noisy teenage boys in T-shirts and torn jeans coming your way on the sidewalk? And how would you feel if you knew they had just come from a Bible study?

Many congregations continue to make valuable contributions in outreach activities. Countless homeless people and working poor would not be able to survive without the faithfulness of these

Behind the Stained Glass Windows

communities of faith. Further, churches perform the important spiritual task of guiding people through Bible studies, weekly worship, and personal counseling. Many continue to discover new joy in knowing God better through the ministry of the church.

Yes, the church continues to be the body of Christ, reaching out in the name of Jesus and doing great work.

However, there are signs that this ministry may not be on a par with what the situation demands. The declines in giving patterns are just one important symptom. General social conditions worsen. Having no belief is the fastest growing faith category. Individuals feel under siege. Like the mythical King Midas, gold dripping from one's fingers can also mean increasing isolation from other things one loves.

Still we do not want to be overly critical of the church. History is always easier to read than to make. Perhaps now enough knowledgeable people have reflected on the changes in the past thirty years so we can begin to recognize some of the themes that have impacted the church: the increasing emphasis on individualism; the definition of values as private opinion rather than public knowledge; the pleonexia, or insatiable desire for more, that can truly have no limits except those imposed by the credit company. These are factors that have hit the church full force, and of course it would take time to sort them all out.

But now quite a bit of time has passed. In another context, we likened the church since World War II to children in a candy store after hours. We've been able to try out new varieties and eat our favorites in an unrestrained way. However, after several decades, we are developing the toothaches and stomachaches that wiser counselors had warned us about. Our preoccupation has been understandable. But at some point a more constructive approach needs to be developed.

The church is the institution that has an authentic alternative to offer. Interestingly, the answer lies in the very place that much of the problem lies—with the individual. Jesus talked about the value of the individual in the parable of the single lost sheep. Our individual identity is so treasured that it is eternal: Jesus promises in Revelation 2:17 to give each of us a new name that only we and He will know forever. Jesus wants us to maximize our potential; His wish for us is to have life and have it more abundantly.

So the solution is where the problem is situated—with the individual. One national leader pointed out, "The devil is so tricky, he leads us to worship ourselves." Therein lies the crux of the problem. It's one thing to be faithful to a belief system when you don't have any better choices than the hope and long-term possibilities it offers. It's another to be faithful when you can easily drive off to a vast assortment of alternative entertainments that also promise to make you happy.

Money can accomplish great things. To kill the goose laying the golden eggs hardly makes sense. The point is, as one leader advised, to give more of the eggs away. Many talented, creative people are rewarded with money for pursuing their careers. What is the virtue in asking them to deny these talents or avoid the positive consequences of applying them diligently? Instead, the church is charged with the task of providing a broad, sweeping, vital vision that allows these talented people to also apply the fruits of their labor in magnificent ways.

Such a vision is not likely to develop without a sincere return to the roots of the faith. No limited strategy or technique is going to solve the present problem of money in the church. If too many competing agendas dissipate the church's ability to reach out, the solution is to find the one agenda that supersedes them all.

A good place for Christians to start looking is at the foot of the cross. God loved. How do we respond? Will we open our hearts to more of what God wants? Are we willing to try?

Confession and *repentance* sure are old-fashioned words. *Absolution* and *forgiveness* are too. Yet these words surfaced repeatedly at the Stewardship Project National Advisory Committee meeting. The discussion kept leading back to the heart of the matter being in the heart of the individual.

The old story remains the same. The path leads to a point of decision for each of us. The church in the United States may finally come to terms with the great opportunities presented by the tremendous, widespread affluence now available when we decide we want to try to love God with all our heart, soul, strength, and mind. Then, with the renewed vision with which God graces us, we may recognize in our neighbor our opportunity for loving God.

Historical Background and Description of the Stewardship Project

Introduction

The Stewardship Project included a congregation-level, programmatic structure. Designed to help congregations increase their missions outreach while at the same time meeting their own needs, the structure was not initially designed as a test instrument that would catalyze dialogue at the congregation level. Rather, empty tomb, inc., staff had begun an analysis of denominational data that suggested church-member giving was declining as a percentage of income. Further, the data indicated that the portion of congregational income going beyond the local congregation for denominational support, seminary support, international missions, and so forth was declining faster than the portion being spent on the congregation's own programs.[1] Thus in the late 1980s empty tomb staff designed an integrated vision and budgeting approach for churches to use in achieving what was assumed to be the goal of every congregation: to improve financial giving levels and congregational organization in order to be more faithful followers of Jesus Christ in pursuing the broader mission vision of the church.

However, interactions with congregations about the designed project from 1989 through 1991 produced remarkable feedback. The opinions expressed by church leaders were pronounced and began to suggest attitudes that might well be affecting giving patterns in negative ways. Also, some of the attitudes verbalized about church operations in specific did not correspond to the more general, abstract pronouncements made by church leaders about the value of stewardship, individual faithfulness, and increased mission commitment. Therefore,

305

in 1992, the project design was incorporated into a more formally constituted exploratory effort: "Congregation-Level Field Observations and Denominational Giving Reports Stewardship Analysis Project," or the Stewardship Project. The goal was to encourage dialogue with leaders at all levels of the church by presenting the structured budgeting approach designed to increase missions giving and inviting feedback about the ideas involved. In this way the leaders' feedback on various aspects of the church's ministry could be accumulated and analyzed in order to better understand some of the dynamics that might be affecting church giving patterns.

Description of the Structured Budgeting Approach

The structure offered to congregations was named The National Money for Missions Program. It was presented as an approach the congregation could adopt to address programmatically the area of church finances in the context of a comprehensive vision of congregational life. Aspects of that vision included the congregation's own needs, the congregation's specific denominational affiliation and commitments, and the congregation's role in the historically Christian church's potential for addressing both global and domestic need in word and deed, particularly in relationship to poverty-related child deaths. Congregations were invited to implement an organizing structure for their operations and activities that took these various aspects of the congregation's life into account. The key components of the structure were as follows.

1. Congregation-Wide Average of 10 Percent Giving

A majority of the congregation members in attendance on a specific Sunday must accept as a goal moving toward a congregation-wide average of 10 percent giving through the church over a three-year period.

2. Congregational Base Budget

If a sufficient number of congregation members agreed that the congregation should implement The National Money for Missions Program structure, the congregational leadership would develop a Congregational Base Budget (CBB) with the assistance of the project staff. This budget would be based on the past annual income and expenditures of that congregation. The budget would be all-inclusive.

Line Items Account for All Expenditures

Treasuries that were previously separate—such as the youth group, Sunday school classes, special offerings, memorials—were included as a line item in the overarching CBB. The exception to the independent treasuries was the historically established women's mission group, which would continue to conduct its business independently. The CBB would also include a capital reserve line item. The cash equivalent of a predetermined percentage of the CBB would be allocated to the capital reserve. The percentage was based on whether the congregation was carrying a mortgage or not. If the congregation was paying on a mortgage, the mortgage payment would also be a separate line item. Full denominational commitments were also to be included as a line item. Finally, the cash equivalent of 3 percent of the CBB was to be included as a contingency fund line item, to account for any unusual expenditures that were not anticipated based on the congregation's past financial patterns.

A "Finish Line" for Internal Expenditures

The CBB would function as a "finish line" for the congregation's own needs. Any expenditure the congregation made would have to be attributed to a line item in the CBB. Such expenditures could not expand the CBB total. Certain standard expenditures, such as salaries, utilities, and other ongoing operation expenditures could easily be attributed to regular line items. If an item were unusual, congregation leadership could reallocate funds from other line items to provide for that expenditure, decreasing one line item and expanding a second, to absorb the unusual expenditure. Another approach would be to decrease the contingency fund and increase another line item to absorb the unusual expenditure. However, if such an unusual expenditure could not be absorbed without affecting the total cap on congregational expenditures as represented by the CBB total—and this included expenditures that would be funded by special cash gifts from individual church members—the expenditure could not be made.

Annual Update

The CBB would be changed by a formula from one year to the next. The formula took into account changes in membership and attendance in the congregation, as well as changes in the economy, both inflation and real growth or recession. The congregation agreed to allow the formula to determine the total of the revised CBB for the next year and to allocate the line item amounts within that total.

Exceptional Circumstances

Provision was made for unusual circumstances, such as unexpected denominational appeals or for an unexpected building emergency that required immediate attention and for which reserve funds were not available.

3. *All Income Is Included*

All income to the congregation, including gifts, special offerings, memorials, fees and rents, interest, dividends and other income, and undesignated bequests would be viewed as Available Income. The first application of Available Income was to meet the CBB. When the CBB had been funded to date, Available Income would be applied to expanding the congregation's missions outreach within the guidelines of the structure. Designated bequests could be honored. Designated gifts from living donors for specific expenditures would have to be attributed to a line item without affecting the CBB total, or such gifts could not be accepted as designated.

4. *Mission Outreach*

Receipts in excess of the CBB would expand the mission outreach of the congregation in keeping with the accepted guidelines. The CBB would serve as a "finish line" for the congregation's internal operations. Church members would know that any money received in excess of the CBB total in a given year would be used in predetermined ways. That outline was as follows.

Overseas Ministry, 60 Percent

Of the money in excess of the CBB, 60 percent would be channeled through the congregation's own denominational channels for overseas ministry. A target country for the congregation's involvement was defined by a Yoking Map provided by The National Money for Missions Program.[2] The congregation could choose which denominational activities in the "yoked" country to fund. These funds would be in addition to the regular denominational commitments funded through the CBB line item and in addition to any previous ongoing missions commitments of the congregation already funded through a CBB line item.

Local Outreach, 20 Percent

The congregation would develop an ongoing personal relationship with a family in need in their locale, providing monthly cash assistance as well as social interaction.

CONGREGATIONAL STEWARDSHIP AND MISSION ACTIVITIES, 10 PERCENT

The congregation would apply 10 percent of the money in excess of the CBB to funding activities in the congregation that encouraged increased stewardship and mission awareness on the part of its own members, in keeping with the goals outlined in the structure. Suggestions included funding trips to the "yoked" country or bringing in special speakers.

SUPPORT GROUP OVERHEAD, 5 PERCENT

The denominational international channel and the local agency assisting with the local family relationship would receive a portion of 5 percent of the money in excess of the CBB in order to help with their related overhead expenses.

ORGANIZATIONAL OVERHEAD, 5 PERCENT

The National Money for Missions Program would receive 5 percent of the money in excess of the CBB for its own expenses and to expand the project into other congregations. The congregation was not charged by The National Money for Missions Program for education materials or training events leading up to the congregation's implementation of the program nor for ongoing support services. The congregation would only forward money to The National Money for Missions Program if the congregation's own needs were first met by fully subscribing to the CBB to date.

Presentation of the Budgeting Approach to Church Leaders

Appointments were made with regional denominational officials, either individually or in small groups, to present The National Money for Missions Program outline. In some cases, introductions to regional denominational officials were provided by members of the Stewardship Project National Advisory Committee. If the regional official was favorable to the structure, he or she would introduce the Stewardship Project staff to individual pastors or to groups of pastors. Notes were taken of conversations with the regional officials.

In some instances, the regional official arranged for a group presentation to pastors in the region. This presentation would include a slide set that presented research about current giving patterns, about major cultural changes such as the increase in credit card debt and leisure spending, and then a brief outline of The National Money for Missions Program structure. Pastors would be offered an opportunity to schedule a similar presentation to their individual congregation's leadership board. Stewardship Project staff took notes of the comments made by the pastors in response to the presentation.

In other cases the regional official would write a letter to individual pastors or provide a list of individual pastors for the Stewardship Project staff to contact. In these cases an in-person visit was scheduled with the pastor, if the pastor was willing to meet. Stewardship Project staff took notes of the pastor's comments regarding stewardship attitudes in general and The National Money for Missions Program in particular.

If possible, the Stewardship Project staff would then schedule a presentation with the individual congregational leadership board. Stewardship Project staff took notes of the comments made by congregational leaders during the presentation.

Notes were also taken during telephone interactions in setting up meetings or in follow-up to meetings with pastors, regional officials, and congregational leaders.

In addition, two regional officials in two denominations arranged for group conversations between sets of pastors and the Stewardship Project staff. In these instances, Stewardship Project staff presented questions for discussion, and participating pastors shared their thoughts.

Stewardship Project staff interacted with thirty-eight national denominational officials, including the National Advisory Committee members, who were each interviewed usually in their home offices. Finally, selected national church authorities, in a variety of settings such as academic institutions and church-related organizations, were interviewed by the Stewardship Project directors.

Table 1 provides the number of contacts made with various levels of congregational church leadership and regional officials during the period of March 1989 through May 1995.

Table 1
Stewardship Project Interactions[3]

Type of Interaction with Individual Congregations	Number of Congregations
In-person encounters with individual congregations: Stewardship Project staff met in person with the pastor or the pastor and the congregational leadership	203
Small-group discussions and presentations: Individual pastors who participated in small-group presentations and discussions where they interacted with the Stewardship Project staff	96

Type of Interaction with Individual Congregations	Number of Congregations
Telephone conversations with individual pastors: Telephone interactions with pastors who did not schedule an in-person encounter	207
Total number of congregations with which Stewardship Project staff interacted directly	506

Type of Interaction with Individual Regional Officials	Number of Regional Officials
In-person interactions with individual denominational regional officials	66
Telephone conversations with individual denominational regional officials	24
Denominational regional officials who participated in a small-group discussion with Stewardship Project staff	15
Total number of denominational regional officials with whom Stewardship Project staff interacted	105

If the congregational leadership board agreed, the next step was to implement a four-month education campaign to provide information to the whole congregational membership. That education campaign ended in Enrollment Sunday. At least 50 percent of those members registering attendance in church on that Sunday needed to agree that the congregation should implement The National Money for Missions Program structure, and at least 10 percent of those agreeing to go forward with The National Money for Missions Program structure also needed to agree to be in an ongoing small-group structure.

History of the Structure's Development

When The National Money for Missions Program was first presented to congregations between 1989 and 1991, it was not seen as a test instrument. Rather, it was designed as a strategy to help congregations act on their oft-stated desire to increase church-member giving and to involve people in missions more deeply. Of the sixty congregations contacted in this earliest phase, the leadership boards of ten congregations from five denominations decided to become involved in the first phase of the structure in 1989. The idea of a congregation-wide education campaign to inform the entire membership had not been developed at this time. The first program year of actually implementing the structure began January 1, 1990, and the congregations' leaders expressed enthusiasm about the changes they expected. Project staff stayed in contact with the congregations by telephone and through the mail, providing newsletters and a variety of activity materials. The staff also processed weekly financial reports from the congregations. An in-person interview with the pastor and a lay leader was conducted after six months of involvement, during the summer of 1990, to gauge the activities undertaken by the participating congregations in implementing The National Money for Missions Program.

Returning from the interviews, the project staff concluded that the effort was a failure. The staff knew that the weekly financial reports had indicated no noteworthy change in giving patterns in the first six months. It was hoped that this lack of change in giving patterns was due to a lag between the implementation and promotion of the project vision and a resulting change in behavior. However, it became clear from the interviews that there was another reason for the lack of improvement in giving patterns. On the whole, the variety of educational activities and materials developed by the project staff to help change church member attitudes toward their giving patterns had not been used. Further, in most cases, the congregational leadership, both pastors and lay, had not even informed the general membership about the congregation's participation in the program. Instead, in two cases, as the congregational leadership responsible for implementing the project began to understand more fully the disciplines required in the budgeting structure, they decided to end involvement with the project.

Once again at the empty tomb, inc., office, with lots of notes and low spirits, the project staff began to organize a report. The purpose was to try to make sense of why the congregational leadership who had approved involvement in the project had not followed through on that commitment. Why had the project failed? With that question in mind, staff began to categorize the comments made by the congregational leadership. As they categorized these comments, staff started to notice that certain themes reappeared in different interviews. Regardless of the congregational form of governance or theology of the speaker, pastors and lay leaders described specific dynamics again and again. Among the most striking observations were that it was difficult to talk about money in an intentional fashion, that it was difficult to rally congregation members around a common purpose, and that church members did not seem to understand stewardship as having to do with mission or faithfulness but saw it as having to do with paying the bills to keep the doors of the church open or to receive certain services.

At this point, project staff began to hypothesize that identifiable dynamics were defining stewardship patterns for many churches in the United States. These dynamics produced behaviors that often interfered with the congregation achieving its altruistic, stated goals. Further, these similar explanations began to suggest possible reasons why lay church leaders—who were often successful individuals in their private endeavors—were so ineffective in producing a similar level of success in their congregational financial activities. Such success was defined as, for example, fulfilling their stated desire to support fully their denominational commitments or to expand their missions activities. An early summary of these findings was included in a report circulated as "The National Money for Missions Program Congregational Pilot: Findings from the Six-Month Implementation Report."[4]

In 1992 empty tomb, inc., received a grant from Lilly Endowment Inc. The purpose was twofold: empty tomb, inc. would continue its annual *State of Church Giving* reports. These were the annual reports that analyzed congregational data for 31 denominations representing 30 million full or confirmed members and 100,000 of the estimated 350,000 religious congregations in the United States. The reports numerically established and monitored the negative giving trends in church member contributions.[5]

The project staff would also continue to interact with national, regional, and congregational leaders in the context of The National Money for Missions Program, which now began to function in the additional role of a test instrument. The staff would listen carefully and intentionally to the comments made by those contacted about the budgeting structure. The goal would be to accumulate enough information to confirm the initial hypotheses the staff had formed about stewardship patterns or to replace those hypotheses with more generally applicable theories.

Because the project staff was committed to working with congregations on an ongoing basis, if a congregation wanted to continue participation in The National Money for Missions Program beyond the life of the three-year Stewardship Project, the project staff were committed to supporting that congregation in implementing the strategy. However, if the congregation was not interested in implementing the structure, the interaction was still valuable, based on the dialogues about stewardship dynamics with groups of pastors, individual pastors, and individual leadership boards considering the structure. All the interactions, regardless of whether The National Money for Missions Program was implemented, would expand the observation base about dynamics affecting giving patterns.

Participation was sought from national denominational structures to facilitate the contacts with congregations. The goal was to involve a cross section of the historically Christian church in the United States. By involving a variety of denominations, it was hoped that the Stewardship Project could shed light on which areas the group had in common and where differences might exist. See appendix B, "Development of the Survey Instrument," for additional information about the National Advisory Committee.

Since most of the in-person contacts with regional officials, pastors, and congregations were conducted in Illinois and Indiana, a national elite sample survey was also distributed through the National Advisory Committee. The purpose of the survey was to gain additional feedback on the observations that were made in the context of the in-person encounters at the congregational and denominational levels. The survey is described in appendixes B and C.

Appendix B

Stewardship Project Survey Distribution and Analysis Methodology

Development of the Survey Instrument

The Stewardship Project Survey Observations summarize findings that resulted from in-person contacts within the context of the Stewardship Project (see appendix A). The goal of the survey was to obtain additional feedback on a number of the preliminary field observations made in the course of the Stewardship Project contacts and interviews.

The instrument was developed in consultation with Dr. Seymour Sudman, Walter Stellner Professor of Business Administration and Deputy Director, Survey Research Laboratory, University of Illinois at Urbana-Champaign, who provided helpful advice on the framing of the observations and organization of the survey presentation.

In order to provide for both negative and positive hypotheses directions, the observations were sometimes intentionally stated in negative terms that would, according to the hypothesis, produce a "disagree" answer, and sometimes the observations were intentionally stated in positive terms that would, according to the hypothesis, produce an "agree" answer. As stated in the first-page introduction to the survey as it was distributed to participants, "For the purposes of this Survey, the observations are sometimes stated positively and sometimes negatively. There are no 'right' responses. The response you circle should most closely describe your own opinion of the observation as stated in the survey."

The observations were presented in random order within four general categories. The 123 observations were developed as a result of the Stewardship Project encounters. The 123 observations were assigned

315

a random number and were then independently divided into four types of general categories: I. Pastors; II. Church Members; III. Congregational Leadership; IV. Miscellaneous. The observations were first sorted by category (I through IV), and then sorted by their random number within each of the four categories. This final sort provided the order in which the observations were presented in the survey.

The response range for each observation was "strongly agree" (valued at "1" for evaluation purposes), "agree" (valued at "2"), "unsure" (valued at "3"), "disagree" (valued at "4"), and "strongly disagree" (valued at "5"). In addition, a check box was provided to the right of each observation, inviting the respondent to check the box to indicate that any comments about that specific observation were written in the space provided at the end of the survey. A total of 123 observations were offered. Blank lines were also provided on the last two pages of the survey form for general comments or for comments keyed to specific observations.

The survey was distributed through the National Advisory Committee members. In forming the National Advisory Committee, the goal had been to assemble a group of communions that represented a cross section of the historically Christian church in the United States. The National Advisory Committee was made up of national stewardship staff from fourteen Protestant denominations, a Roman Catholic Archbishop who had chaired the National Conference of Catholic Bishops pastoral on stewardship committee, and a seminary vice president for development who also edited a national seminary development officers periodical. Although invitations were extended to two additional Protestant denominations, one Orthodox communion, and two African American denominations, no representatives of these denominations participated. The fourteen Protestant national denominational stewardship officials and the seminary vice president distributed the survey.

The denominational stewardship officials who served as National Advisory Committee members were asked to distribute the survey to one regional official they selected in each of ten regions in the United States, who would then select a practicing minister to complete a copy as well. In the case of the seminaries, the seminary vice president who served as a National Advisory Committee member was asked to distribute the survey to selected seminary development officers, who would then ask a faculty person at the same seminary to complete a copy of the survey. Therefore, the survey was designed as an elite sample of selected church leaders rather than a randomly selected representation. The role of the survey was to test the preliminary observations made in the Stewardship Project encounters and to highlight which areas might prove valuable for further research.

As noted, the groups targeted for the survey were pastors and regional officials. Smaller groupings of national denominational officials, seminary development officers, and seminary faculty were also surveyed. Because of the stratification in categories of laypeople that became evident during the Stewardship Project—e.g., income and giving levels, level of official involvement through boards and committees, level of unofficial involvement in administrative and policy matters, and membership and attendance patterns—the reactions of laypeople to these observations were not sought through this exploratory survey instrument.

Distribution Methodology Details of the Survey Instrument

A box of surveys was sent to each national denominational stewardship official in April 1994. Each survey was coded according to: (a) denomination (each denomination receiving a three-letter alphabetical code); (b) a number 1 to indicate that the National Advisory Committee member had distributed the survey (a 0 would have been placed on a survey code had any surveys been distributed other than through the National Advisory Committee); (c) region of the United States (0 for national; 1 through 10 for a specific region of the country); and (d) rank of respondent (0 being a national denominational official; 1 being a regional denominational official; and 2 being a pastor in a congregation). The code appeared on the bottom right-hand corner of each page of the survey.

Thus the National Advisory Committee member from the XYZ denomination would have filled out the survey coded "xyz.1.0.0." The regional official in Region 1 from that communion would have filled out "xyz.1.1.1" and the XYZ pastor in Region 1 would have filled out "xyz.1.1.2."

In addition, on the first page of the survey respondents were asked to provide their name, their title, their institution, and their address as a confirmation that the code matched the title and region of the respondent.

The ten regions of the United States selected for the survey distribution (and a major city in that region) were:

Region 1:   New England: Boston, Mass.
Region 2:   Middle Atlantic: New York City, N.Y.
Region 3:   South Atlantic: Atlanta, Ga.

Region 4:	East South Central: Jackson, Miss.
Region 5:	West North Central: Minneapolis, Minn.
Region 6:	West South Central: Houston, Tex.
Region 7:	Mountain: Denver, Colo.
Region 8:	Pacific 1: Los Angeles, Calif.
Region 9:	Pacific 2: Seattle, Wash.
Region 10:	Midwest: Illinois or Indiana[1]

The National Advisory Committee member was asked to send the surveys to a city closest to the city named in each region if the denomination did not have a regional office in the specific city named for each region. Region 10 comprised the two states in which most of the Stewardship Project in-person contacts were made. Rather than suggesting a specific metropolitan area in Region 10, the denominational leaders were asked to distribute the survey within this region.

In the box of surveys sent to each National Advisory Committee member, instructions on color-coded paper for each category of respondent were included.

A survey was included for the national denominational official to fill out.

In addition, ten envelopes were included to be mailed to regional denominational officials in each of ten regions of the United States. The national denominational official was asked to write a cover letter, asking the regional official to, first, ask a pastor in that region to respond to the survey and, second, fill out a survey. A sample letter, to serve as a prototype for the national denominational official's letter to the regional officials, was enclosed with the packet (see page 324).

When the regional official had filled out the survey, he or she was to seal the completed survey in a white confidential envelope provided for that purpose and place the sealed confidential envelope in a larger, stamped return brown envelope. Likewise, the pastor was asked to complete the survey, seal it in a white confidential envelope provided, and then return the sealed survey to the regional official. The regional official was to return both sealed confidential envelopes to the national official.

A large, stamped return envelope had been provided to the national denominational official, who was asked to place the sealed confidential envelopes that had been received into the large, stamped return envelope, along with the national official's own completed survey in its own sealed confidential envelope, and return all the surveys to the empty tomb, inc., office.

The procedure was similar for the seminaries. The National Advisory Committee member representing seminaries was asked to distribute the surveys to seminary development officers in the ten regions of the United States noted above. Each development officer was asked to fill out a survey. In addition, each development officer was asked to arrange for one faculty member to fill out a survey. Once again, white confidential envelopes were provided in which each completed survey was placed and sealed. The two completed surveys in their sealed confidential envelopes were returned to the National Advisory Committee member, who sent the returned surveys in their individual sealed confidential envelopes, along with the National Advisory Committee member's completed survey in a sealed confidential envelope, to the empty tomb, inc., office.

Survey Analysis Methodology

The analysis of the survey responses was carried out in consultation with Professor Stephen Portnoy of the University of Illinois Statistics Department, a Fellow of the American Statistical Association, and a Fellow of the Institute of Mathematical Statistics; as well as Dr. Kenneth Qing Zhou, then a graduate student in the University of Illinois Department of Statistics. Additional assistance was provided by Dr. Douglas Simpson, director of the Illinois Statistics Office, and graduate student Olga Geling, statistical consultant of the Illinois Statistics Office.

Of the 315 survey forms distributed with the cooperation of the 14 Protestant denominational stewardship officials and one seminary development officer, 244 were returned, for an overall return rate of 77 percent.

Within the specific categories, 97 of the 140 surveys distributed to pastors were returned, for a return rate of 69 percent. Table 2 lists the membership sizes of the responding congregations. Among the regional officials, 112 of the 140 surveys distributed were returned, for a return rate of 80 percent. Fourteen surveys were returned from the 15 national denominational officials who served on the National Advisory Committee, for a return rate of 93 percent. Among the seminary professionals, 11 of the seminary development officers, including the individual who served on the National Advisory Committee, returned surveys, for a return rate of 100 percent for that category. Ten seminary faculty returned the 10 surveys distributed, for a return rate of 100 percent.

Table 2
Membership Size of Congregations with Pastors
Responding to the Stewardship Project Survey

Size of Congregational Membership[2]	Number of Congregations
100 and Under	17
101–250	24
251–500	31
501–1,000	14
More than 1,000	11

Table 3 lists the number of responses from each region of the United States.

Table 3
Number of Respondents from Each Region of the United States

Geographical Region (including City or Area)	Number of Respondents (Regional Officials and Pastors Combined)
Region 1, New England: Boston, Mass.	18
Region 2, Middle Atlantic: New York, N.Y.	21
Region 3, South Atlantic: Atlanta, Ga.	23
Region 4, East South Central: Jackson, Miss.	16
Region 5, West North Central: Minneapolis, Minn.	20
Region 6, West South Central: Houston, Tex.	24
Region 7, Mountain: Denver, Colo.	17
Region 8, Pacific 1: Los Angeles, Calif.	24
Region 9, Pacific 2: Seattle, Wash.	28
Region 10, Midwest: Illinois/Indiana	18

When the surveys were received in the empty tomb, inc., office, each confidential envelope was opened by a staff member, the survey was stamped with the date received, and the original survey was photocopied without the identifying first page (each page of the survey had been coded upon printing and thus provided identification by respondent categories). The survey coded for rank 1 (regional official) had been copied on white paper. The survey coded for rank 2 (pastor) had been copied on ivory paper.

A Stewardship Project staff person compared the rank code on each returned survey with the title provided by the individual respondent in order to confirm that an individual from the coded rank had, in fact, completed the survey. In nine instances, the title provided by the responding individual did not match the rank code on the survey, e.g., the title indicated the individual was a regional official rather than a pastor, although the survey was on ivory paper and the code was rank 2. In those nine instances, the title provided by the respondent, rather than the code on the completed survey, was used to determine the rank of the respondent. In one instance, the responding pastor also indicated he carried out regional official duties in his denomination. This respondent's survey was ranked as a regional official rather than as a pastor.

After this review procedure was conducted on each returned survey, the original survey including the identifying cover sheet was replaced in its confidential envelope and filed.

The respondents were asked to circle one opinion for each of the 123 observations. As noted above, "strongly agree" was ranked as 1; "agree" was ranked as 2; "unsure" was ranked as 3; "disagree" was ranked as 4; and "strongly disagree" was ranked as 5.

If a respondent circled one answer and then drew an arrow toward the right or left, the answer was changed by .25. For example, if a respondent circled "agree" (value 2) and drew an arrow toward "unsure" (value 3), the answer was ranked at 2.25.

If a respondent drew a circle that included two answers, the answer was changed by .5. For example, if a respondent drew one circle around both "agree" (valued at 2) and "unsure" (valued at 3), the answer was valued at 2.5. Similarly, if a respondent drew a circle around each of two answers that were next to each other, for example, "agree" and "unsure," the answer would be changed by .5, in this case being valued at 2.5.

The combined frequency of a respondent either circling one printed option and drawing an arrow toward another, or circling two printed options occurred 43 times out of a possible 30,012 responses.

If a respondent did not circle an answer for an observation, the response was valued as a "blank" and was not included in the calculation of the total number of responses for the analysis of that specific observation.

If a respondent crossed out one of the offered opinions and wrote in an alternative word and circled it, for example, marking out "agree" and writing in the word "somewhat" and circling it, the answer was regarded as a blank and was not included in the calculation of the total number of responses for the analysis of that specific observation.

Again, if a respondent qualified the printed options by writing in an additional word and circling both the word that the respondent had written in and the printed option—for example, writing "somewhat" and making a circle around both the written and printed words to read "somewhat agree"—the answer was regarded as a blank and was not included in the calculation of the total number of responses for the analysis of that specific observation.

An average response by category of respondents was obtained for each question. For example, the mean response for observation number 1 for the combined answers of pastors and regional officials was 3.07. In addition, the mean response for specific categories was also calculated. The mean response for observation number 1 for the pastor category was 2.74; for the regional official category, 3.35; for national denominational officials, 3.86; for the combined responses of seminary development officers and faculty, 3.43.

In addition, a percentage was calculated for each level of opinion provided for each observation by category. For example, for observation number 1, 1 percent of the regional officials marked "strongly agree," 29 percent marked "agree," 10 percent marked "unsure," 56 percent marked "disagree," and 4 percent marked "strongly disagree." To determine the percentage of respondents who answered at each option level, the 43 instances where fractions occurred throughout the 30,012 possible responses were handled as follows. If the response was at the .5 level, half of the response was accrued to each of the whole number responses on either side of the fraction response. If the response was measured at a quarter fraction, .75 was accrued to the whole number closest to the response, and .25 was accrued to the whole number on the farther side of the response. Consider a simple hypothetical case. Suppose there were ten responses to an observation, and five were at the 3.0 level, four were at the 4.0 level, and one was at the 3.75 level. The fraction response would be divided as .75 to the 4.0 level as the closest whole number to the response, and .25 to the 3.0 level as the whole number on the farther side of the response. To determine the percentage of responses at each level, one can add the number of responses at the 3.0 level, that is five, to the .25 fraction to equal 5.25, which is then divided by the total of ten responses to produce a 52.5 percent response at that level. Similarly, one can add the number of responses at the 4.0 level, that is four, to the .75 fraction to equal 4.75, which is then divided by the total of ten responses to produce a 47.5 percent level of response at the 4.0 level.

Analysis of variance, using the General Factorial Analysis of Variance model in the SPSS package, was carried out to test whether responses to the observations significantly differed at the .005 level by rank (between regional officers and pastors; between seminary development officers and faculty); by region; and by denomination. Due to the small sample size, interaction effects are not reported. Although .05 is generally taken to be a level at which significance can be determined, the more stringent level of .005 was used in this analysis in order to keep from finding a small difference and inappropriately regarding it as a major difference. The survey contained 123 observations, providing a large number of possible responses. Also, the survey was an elite sample survey with a selected, limited number of respondents. The more stringent .005 level was used to identify differences between the two ranks of regional officials and pastors in order to increase confidence that any differences between these two ranks were due to real variation in opinion and not likely due to sampling method or the number of observations. The same level was also applied to the denomination and region categories, as well as the comparison between seminary development officers and faculty. Finally, for those observations for which the categories of denomination and region had a significant effect at the .005 level on the mean responses, a further General Factorial ANOVA with deviation contrasts was conducted. This allowed identification of those particular denominations and regions that differed significantly at the .005 level in their responses from the overall mean response of the combined regional officials and pastors responses to a specific observation.

Comparison of the combined regional officials and pastors mean responses with the mean responses of the national denominational officials as well as with the mean responses of the combined seminary development officers and faculty was carried out using the SPSS One-Way ANOVA procedure. Again, the conservative measure of .005 for the specific respondent category was used to determine the variation of the means of both denominations and regions from the overall mean of the combined regional officials and pastor responses, as well as the means of the national denominational officials and the combined seminary responses from the overall mean of the regional officials and pastors responses combined.

It should be noted that, because the sample was of a smaller size (particularly for the seminary personnel and the national denominational officials) and was not randomly selected, the significance tests were used to highlight marked differences on an exploratory basis within the response categories rather than to determine the applicability of the responses as representative of some larger population.

The statistical analyses were carried out using SPSS procedures MEANS and General Factorial Analysis of Variance.

The survey items and results are provided in table 4 in appendix C, with the mean value of the response to each observation for each of the categories surveyed: national denominational stewardship officials, denominational regional officials, practicing ministers, and the combined mean for seminary development officers and seminary faculty. The hypothesis for each observation is also provided. Further, the percentage of responses at each response option level is noted below the mean for each category.

Sample Letter to the Regional Officials

Date
Inside address

Dear Name:
Enclosed please find the empty tomb, inc. Stewardship Project Survey packet which you and I have previously discussed.

I am asking you to identify one Practicing Minister in your region who will complete one of the copies of the Survey enclosed. Please be sure you have selected the Practicing Minister before you review the materials, to avoid selecting the Practicing Minister with any expected reactions in mind. A gray stamped mailing envelope for you to address to the Minister is included in this packet. Also included is a gold stamped return envelope which you should address to yourself, for the Practicing Minister to return the completed Survey to you.

In addition, I am requesting that you complete the other copy of the Survey enclosed in this mailing.

Please be sure to send the enclosed Survey packet to the Practicing Minister by April 22. Also, I will appreciate receiving both your completed Survey and that of the Minister, each in their white sealed confidential envelopes, no later than May 10. A dark brown stamped, addressed return envelope has been included for your convenience.

Thank you for your cooperation in this project.
[Closing]

First Page of Survey, Containing Instructions

empty tomb, inc.
Congregational-Level Field Observations and Denominational Giving Reports
Stewardship Analysis Project
Survey

Thank you for your willingness to fill out this Survey. You will be assisting this effort to understand stewardship and missions support dynamics at the congregational level in a more comprehensive fashion. The summary findings from this Stewardship Project are scheduled to appear in a book, *Behind the Stained Glass Win-*

dows: Stewardship Patterns in the Church [working title], due from Baker Book House in late 1995 or early 1996.

The following pages contain observations about stewardship patterns. These observations summarize findings resulting from many interviews with church leaders at the local, regional and national levels. You are asked to circle one response for each observation. For the purposes of this Survey, the observations are sometimes stated positively and sometimes negatively. There are no "right" responses. The response you circle should most closely describe your own opinion of the observation as stated in the Survey.

If you have additional comments about a particular observation, please check the box next to that observation and then use the space at the end of the Survey to note your comments. Be sure to note the observation number your comments are keyed to. You might use the space at the end of the Survey to:

a) Provide a real-life anecdote or illustration that expands our understanding of your response to the particular observation.

b) Comment on a word, term or phrase which is not clear as you read the observation.

Also at the end of this Survey, there is a space for you to note any other dynamics or patterns which you feel might be affecting church member giving and which are not addressed in the Survey observations.

Please feel free to use additional paper as necessary.

It is important that you fill in your name, position title, your institution, your address and your phone number below. Your responses will be held in confidence by empty tomb, inc. Your comments will not be attributed to you by name unless we contact you and receive your permission prior to such use. Your comments may be used in a generic way designed to share the insight and yet protect confidentiality at the same time, such as, "One regional official commented . . ."

Upon completion, place the Survey in the enclosed white envelope labeled "Confidential" and seal it. A stamped, addressed return envelope is also enclosed. Please return this completed Survey, with any additional written comments, to the address on the return envelope no later than **the date on the white confidential envelope**.

Thank you in advance for your assistance.

Your name: _____

Your position: _____

Your institution: _____

Your address: _____
                    Street

                    Town/City   State   Zip
Your phone: _____

Appendix C

Stewardship Project Survey Results

Survey Observations and Responses by Category

The Stewardship Project survey consisted of 123 observations, which are presented in table 4. These observations were developed as a result of encounters with church leaders in various settings. The survey drew on an elite sample of 97 practicing pastors and 112 denominational regional officials. In addition, 14 national denominational stewardship officials, 11 seminary development officers, and 10 seminary faculty also completed the survey.

As noted, the elite sample nature of the survey does not represent some larger population. However, it is hoped that the sample was broad enough to provide an exploratory measure to indicate what observations may merit additional research on the emerging area of studying financial giving patterns.

Survey participants were asked to rank their response to an observation on a scale from one to five, with 1 being strongly agree; 2, agree; 3, unsure; 4, disagree; and 5, strongly disagree.

With each observation in table 4, a hypothesis is presented that was formed by the study directors as a result of interactions with church leaders, as described in appendix A. The hypothesis was not designed to reflect the study directors' opinion but the opinions that were frequently expressed during in-person encounters. The numerical value of the answer indicates the direction of the proposed answer and is not intended to indicate the expected strength of the opinion. Therefore, a 1 given for the hypothesis indicates merely that the study directors proposed that the response would be in the agree direction, rather than that the responses would specifically be "strongly agree." In several cases, the hypothesis was a 3, indicating an "unsure" response. The 3-

level response was proposed as the hypothesis in six instances where, based on the varied feedback received in in-person encounters, it was difficult to predict responses to observations asking whether the denominations' national stands in general or specifically on abortion or homosexuality would affect either church-member giving to the congregation or congregational giving to the denomination.

In contrast to the hypothesis, the means for the survey responses do indicate the strength of the answer given by the survey participants. Thus, the closer to 1 the mean of an answer, the more "strongly agree" describes that response, and the closer to 5 the mean of an answer, the more "strongly disagree" describes that response.

The values 1 through 5 are given with each observation in the table. The percentage of responses at each value level are given in the four columns to the right of each value, indicating how the people in each group responded.

The pastors column provides the mean and response percentages for the pastors; the regional officials column provides the mean and response percentages for the regional officials; the national denominational officials column provides the mean and response percentages for the national denominational officials; and the all seminary column provides the mean and response percentages for the seminary development officers and faculty responses combined. Details in each column may not compute to 100 percent due to rounding.

In the pastors and the regional officials columns, an asterisk indicates that the mean response of the regional officials and that of the pastors were significantly different from each other (at the .005 level). There were twenty-two instances in which this was the case. As noted earlier, the more stringent significance test of .005 was selected, rather than the .05 level, because of the method of selection of respondents, in contrast to a random selection, and because of the limited number of responses that had been solicited. Also, because many comparisons were being made, the .005 level reduces the likelihood of chance differences being called significant.

For the columns presenting the national denominational officials, and the seminary development officers and faculty combined data, an asterisk after a response indicates that the mean value of the response to that observation varied from the combined mean of the regional officials and pastors at the .005 level. There were no responses among the national denominational officials that differed at the .005 level from the mean of the combined regional officials and pastors responses. For five observations, responses provided by the seminary development officers and faculty combined were significantly different at the .005 level from the mean of the combined regional officials and pastors responses.

The survey responses are valuable in that they provide initial insight into the dynamics affecting church giving. They are not presented as being a scientific sample of all pastors, regional officials, national denominational officials, or seminary personnel in the United States. However, the responses do explore the attitudes that may be affecting giving patterns. The following responses suggest directions for further study as well as provide initial insight into the perspectives church leaders are bringing to their tasks.

Table 4
Stewardship Project Survey and Response Means

		Pastors	Regional Officials	National Denominational Officials	All Seminary
1. Most pastors feel they can effectively challenge their members about spiritual attitudes toward money	Mean:	2.74*	3.35*	3.86	3.43
	1:	7%	1%	7%	0%
	2:	48%	29%	7%	19%
	3:	10%	10%	0%	19%
	4:	31%	56%	64%	62%
	5:	3%	4%	21%	0%
Hypothesis: 5					
2. A pastor who uses a consumer oriented, "felt-needs" approach will have no more difficulty introducing traditional spiritual disciplines to new members than the pastor who uses more conventional approaches.	Mean:	2.99	3.27	3.08	2.95
	1:	4%	0%	0%	0%
	2:	32%	28%	33%	30%
	3:	29%	25%	25%	50%
	4:	31%	39%	42%	15%
	5:	4%	8%	0%	5%
Hypothesis: 5					
3. Pastors like to provide their congregational membership mailing lists for use in solicitation by denominationally-affiliated entities.	Mean:	4.09	4.21	4.64	4.10
	1:	1%	2%	0%	0%
	2:	7%	3%	0%	5%
	3:	6%	5%	0%	10%
	4:	53%	54%	36%	57%
	5:	33%	37%	64%	29%
Hypothesis: 5					

		Pastors	Regional Officials	National Denominational Officials	All Seminary
4. Most pastors who do not want to know what individual members give to their church, do not want to know because they feel such knowledge might influence the way they minister to individual members.	Mean:	2.33	2.21	2.29	2.38
	1:	12%	9%	14%	10%
	2:	62%	73%	64%	62%
	3:	8%	5%	0%	10%
	4:	15%	13%	21%	19%
	5:	2%	0%	0%	0%
Hypothesis: 1					
5. Most pastors feel they would receive strong support from their denominational structure if they were to challenge perceived selfish patterns among their congregation members.	Mean:	3.07	2.95	2.57	3.33
	1:	3%	2%	0%	0%
	2:	30%	37%	50%	24%
	3:	27%	30%	43%	19%
	4:	37%	28%	7%	57%
	5:	3%	4%	0%	0%
Hypothesis: 5					
6. Most pastors feel it is best not to know what individual members donate.	Mean:	2.58	2.52	2.64	2.75
	1:	9%	9%	0%	5%
	2:	47%	55%	64%	40%
	3:	22%	12%	7%	30%
	4:	20%	23%	29%	25%
	5:	2%	1%	0%	0%
Hypothesis: 1					
7. The pastor's knowledge of what individual members give to the church can be a helpful assessment tool of individual members' spiritual health.	Mean:	2.13	1.98	1.64	2.48
	1:	26%	31%	57%	19%
	2:	53%	52%	29%	48%
	3:	5%	7%	7%	0%
	4:	15%	11%	7%	33%
	5:	1%	0%	0%	0%
Hypothesis: 1					
8. A pastor described the situation very well when he said his congregation was a group of widows and orphans when discussing the pastor's salary, although the parking lot was filled with new-model cars.	Mean:	3.11	2.77	2.46	2.70
	1:	5%	6%	8%	0%
	2:	29%	42%	62%	60%
	3:	19%	19%	8%	15%
	4:	44%	32%	23%	20%
	5:	3%	0%	0%	5%
Hypothesis: 1					

(continued)

(Table 4—continued)

		Pastors	Regional Officials	National Denominational Officials	All Seminary
9. Most pastors enjoy preaching about money.	Mean:	3.92	4.16	4.43	4.24
	1:	0%	0%	0%	0%
	2:	6%	1%	0%	0%
	3:	8%	4%	0%	0%
	4:	73%	72%	57%	76%
	5:	12%	22%	43%	24%
Hypothesis: 5					
10. Most pastors are afraid their members would become angry if the pastor were to challenge the way members spend their family incomes.	Mean:	2.81*	2.08*	1.71	2.19
	1:	7%	14%	29%	10%
	2:	39%	74%	71%	71%
	3:	20%	5%	0%	10%
	4:	33%	7%	0%	10%
	5:	1%	1%	0%	0%
Hypothesis: 1					
11. Pastors would like more continuing education opportunities from seminaries in effectively challenging their church members about their financial stewardship.	Mean:	2.46	2.48	2.29	2.52
	1:	9%	4%	0%	10%
	2:	53%	62%	79%	48%
	3:	22%	19%	14%	29%
	4:	15%	15%	7%	10%
	5:	1%	1%	0%	5%
Hypothesis: 5					
12. Most pastors are afraid to hear the phrase, "The church is always talking about money."	Mean:	2.73*	2.15*	1.86	2.19
	1:	2%	15%	14%	5%
	2:	55%	65%	86%	81%
	3:	11%	9%	0%	5%
	4:	32%	11%	0%	10%
	5:	0%	0%	0%	0%
Hypothesis: 1					
13. Pastors would like more continuing education opportunities from their denominations in effectively challenging their church members about their financial stewardship.	Mean:	2.29	2.49	2.29	2.52
	1:	10%	5%	7%	10%
	2:	63%	62%	64%	48%
	3:	14%	14%	21%	24%
	4:	12%	20%	7%	19%
	5:	0%	0%	0%	0%
Hypothesis: 5					

		Pastors	Regional Officials	National Denominational Officials	All Seminary
14. Most pastors prefer a consumer-oriented approach to ministry than a more traditional approach to the spiritual disciplines of the church.	Mean:	3.29	3.25	3.45	3.20
	1:	0%	1%	0%	0%
	2:	23%	22%	14%	15%
	3:	30%	31%	27%	50%
	4:	42%	45%	59%	35%
	5:	5%	2%	0%	0%
Hypothesis: 5					
15. Most pastors know what individual members give to their church.	Mean:	3.43	3.51	4.07	3.38
	1:	1%	1%	0%	0%
	2:	19%	20%	0%	14%
	3:	20%	13%	7%	38%
	4:	58%	60%	79%	43%
	5:	3%	6%	14%	5%
Hypothesis: 5					
16. Most pastors feel they have no choice but to meet the consumer-oriented demands of potential church members in order to effectively compete with other congregations in town.	Mean:	2.92	2.69	3.06	3.05
	1:	0%	2%	0%	0%
	2:	47%	52%	40%	38%
	3:	20%	22%	21%	19%
	4:	28%	24%	31%	43%
	5:	5%	0%	8%	0%
Hypothesis: 1					
17. Most pastors feel they have had adequate training about stewardship at the seminary level.	Mean:	3.93	4.10	4.36	3.90
	1:	0%	0%	0%	0%
	2:	9%	3%	0%	10%
	3:	7%	9%	0%	10%
	4:	65%	64%	64%	62%
	5:	19%	25%	36%	19%
Hypothesis: 5					
18. Pastors feel pressure to be balancers among the various special interest groups in their congregations rather than strong leaders.	Mean:	2.67*	2.23*	2.07	2.29
	1:	3%	4%	7%	14%
	2:	59%	79%	86%	62%
	3:	9%	7%	0%	5%
	4:	26%	10%	7%	19%
	5:	3%	0%	0%	0%
Hypothesis: 1					

(continued)

(*Table 4–continued*)

		Pastors	Regional Officials	National Denominational Officials	All Seminary
19. To some extent, pastors perceive denominationally-affiliated entities as competitors for their congregation members' money.	Mean: 1: 2: 3: 4: 5:	2.70* 5% 55% 7% 31% 2%	2.08* 9% 80% 4% 6% 0%	2.00 21% 64% 7% 7% 0%	2.29 5% 76% 5% 14% 0%
Hypothesis: 1					
20. Pastors would like more assistance from their denominations in effectively challenging their church members about their financial stewardship.	Mean: 1: 2: 3: 4: 5:	2.37 7% 63% 15% 14% 0%	2.45 4% 63% 19% 13% 1%	2.21 7% 79% 0% 14% 0%	2.43 5% 57% 29% 10% 0%
Hypothesis: 1					
21. Pastors are concerned that if they avail themselves of denominationally-sponsored stewardship training, it may open the door for, and facilitate, future attempts on the part of denominationally-affiliated officials to solicit funds from individual members of the pastors' congregations for denominationally-affiliated purposes.	Mean: 1: 2: 3: 4: 5:	3.60 2% 13% 18% 57% 10%	3.38 0% 21% 22% 54% 3%	3.64 0% 14% 7% 79% 0%	3.24 0% 33% 10% 57% 0%
Hypothesis: 1					
22. Most pastors find it easy to secure broad support among the majority of congregation members for denominational programs.	Mean: 1: 2: 3: 4: 5:	3.44 0% 29% 6% 57% 8%	3.65 0% 18% 7% 67% 8%	3.63 0% 15% 6% 79% 0%	3.76 0% 5% 14% 81% 0%
Hypothesis: 5					
23. Most pastors feel that identifying large donors for solicitation by denominationally-	Mean: 1: 2:	3.77 1% 8%	3.70 0% 7%	4.00 0% 0%	3.21* 0% 19%

		Pastors	Regional Officials	National Denominational Officials	All Seminary
affiliated entities may be help-ful to their career.	3:	18%	21%	21%	40%
	4:	59%	67%	57%	40%
	5:	14%	5%	21%	0%
Hypothesis: 1					
24. Many pastors find it difficult to preach about financial stewardship because their salary and benefits are such a large part of the budget.	Mean:	2.90*	2.42*	2.14	2.80
	1:	3%	7%	7%	5%
	2:	47%	65%	79%	45%
	3:	9%	8%	7%	15%
	4:	37%	20%	7%	35%
	5:	3%	1%	0%	0%
Hypothesis: 1					
25. Pastors are concerned that it may be more difficult to meet their congregation's financial goals if they identify large donors for solicitation by denominationally-affiliated entities.	Mean:	2.90*	2.38*	2.29	2.48
	1:	1%	4%	0%	0%
	2:	44%	66%	79%	71%
	3:	21%	19%	14%	10%
	4:	32%	12%	7%	19%
	5:	2%	0%	0%	0%
Hypothesis: 1					
26. Church members above 50 years old are the best givers in most congregations.	Mean:	2.21	2.05	1.57	2.48
	1:	19%	18%	57%	0%
	2:	56%	67%	36%	67%
	3:	11%	7%	0%	19%
	4:	13%	8%	7%	14%
	5:	1%	0%	0%	0%
Hypothesis: 1					
27. Increasingly, church members are content to have the church meet a specific need rather than have the church lead them into a deeper under-standing of discipleship.	Mean:	2.18	2.09	2.21	2.71*
	1:	14%	15%	7%	5%
	2:	69%	68%	79%	52%
	3:	4%	10%	0%	14%
	4:	14%	7%	14%	24%
	5:	0%	0%	0%	5%
Hypothesis: 1					
28. Whether congregation mem-bers agree or disagree with the national office's handling of the	Mean:	3.65	3.71	3.07	3.38
	1:	1%	1%	7%	5%
	2:	19%	14%	43%	19%

(continued)

(*Table 4–continued*)

		Pastors	Regional Officials	National Denominational Officials	All Seminary
issue of abortion will have no effect on the congregation meeting its denominational commitments.	3:	10%	14%	0%	10%
	4:	54%	54%	36%	67%
	5:	16%	16%	14%	0%
Hypothesis: 3					
29. Church members today demand a higher level of comfort and services from their congregations than did previous generations.	Mean:	1.90	1.88	1.64	2.57*
	1:	26%	22%	36%	0%
	2:	65%	71%	64%	62%
	3:	3%	3%	0%	19%
	4:	6%	4%	0%	19%
	5:	0%	0%	0%	0%
Hypothesis: 1					
30. There is an increasing tendency for church members to want to keep a larger portion of the congregation's budget within the congregation.	Mean:	2.09*	1.78*	1.64	1.95
	1:	17%	33%	36%	14%
	2:	68%	59%	64%	76%
	3:	5%	5%	0%	10%
	4:	10%	3%	0%	0%
	5:	0%	0%	0%	0%
Hypothesis: 1					
31. In instances where immoral behavior occurs on the part of the pastor, such behavior has no significant effect on the level of giving in the congregation.	Mean:	4.35	4.07	4.16	4.24
	1:	0%	2%	0%	0%
	2:	3%	4%	7%	5%
	3:	3%	9%	13%	5%
	4:	49%	57%	38%	52%
	5:	45%	29%	43%	38%
Hypothesis: 5					
32. Whether congregation members agree or disagree with the national office's stands on various issues will have no effect on church member giving to the congregation.	Mean:	3.68	3.91	3.50	4.00
	1:	1%	0%	0%	0%
	2:	17%	10%	21%	5%
	3:	10%	8%	14%	10%
	4:	57%	63%	57%	67%
	5:	15%	19%	7%	19%
Hypothesis: 3					
33. Most people view stewardship as paying the church for services rendered rather than	Mean:	2.90	2.70	2.95	2.71
	1:	4%	9%	7%	5%
	2:	42%	43%	43%	48%

		Pastors	Regional Officials	National Denominational Officials	All Seminary
returning a portion of their income to God.	3: 4: 5:	16% 38% 1%	18% 28% 2%	5% 38% 7%	19% 29% 0%
Hypothesis: 1					
34. Most congregations prefer their pastors to challenge them effectively about the level of their faith rather than have the pastor merely keep the congregation running smoothly.	Mean: 1: 2: 3: 4: 5:	2.71 5% 49% 19% 24% 3%	3.04 4% 38% 13% 43% 3%	2.71 7% 43% 21% 29% 0%	2.67 0% 62% 10% 29% 0%
Hypothesis: 5					
35. Global missions is just as important a topic as it used to be for most congregations.	Mean: 1: 2: 3: 4: 5:	3.31 4% 28% 5% 57% 5%	3.62 2% 20% 7% 57% 14%	3.21 7% 21% 14% 57% 0%	3.57 0% 24% 10% 52% 14%
Hypothesis: 5					
36. Percentage giving is not generally practiced by most church members.	Mean: 1: 2: 3: 4: 5:	2.38 10% 62% 9% 16% 2%	2.20 10% 72% 7% 10% 1%	1.93 7% 93% 0% 0% 0%	2.19 5% 76% 14% 5% 0%
Hypothesis: 1					
37. Most congregations have as strong a denominational identity as they did forty years ago.	Mean: 1: 2: 3: 4: 5:	4.24 3% 0% 1% 61% 35%	4.30 0% 2% 2% 61% 36%	4.29 0% 7% 0% 50% 43%	4.05 0% 5% 5% 71% 19%
Hypothesis: 5					
38. Whether congregation members agree or disagree with the national office's handling of the	Mean: 1: 2:	3.65 0% 21%	3.59 0% 19%	3.43 0% 36%	3.29 0% 29%

(continued)

(Table 4–continued)

		Pastors	Regional Officials	National Denominational Officials	All Seminary
issue of abortion will have no effect on church member giving to the congregation.	3:	10%	14%	7%	14%
	4:	53%	55%	36%	57%
	5:	16%	12%	21%	0%
Hypothesis: 3					
39. Given that denominational reports indicate church members across theological traditions have been giving a smaller percentage of their incomes over the last 24 years, any occasional drops in giving resulting from major national denominational disagreements would not account for the overall decline in giving.	Mean:	3.03	2.91	2.57	2.60
	1:	1%	3%	7%	0%
	2:	37%	41%	57%	60%
	3:	25%	23%	14%	20%
	4:	32%	30%	14%	20%
	5:	5%	4%	7%	0%
Hypothesis: 1					
40. People will stay away from church if they feel they can't respond to stewardship requests because they are deeply in personal debt.	Mean:	3.01	3.03	3.34	3.29
	1:	1%	1%	0%	0%
	2:	38%	38%	23%	24%
	3:	22%	21%	27%	29%
	4:	39%	40%	43%	43%
	5:	1%	1%	7%	5%
Hypothesis: 1					
41. Church members younger than 50 years old have less denominational loyalty than members over 50.	Mean:	1.74	1.78	1.43	1.95
	1:	33%	30%	57%	5%
	2:	61%	65%	43%	95%
	3:	5%	2%	0%	0%
	4:	1%	2%	0%	0%
	5:	0%	1%	0%	0%
Hypothesis: 1					
42. Whether congregation members agree or disagree with the national office's stands on various issues will have no effect on the congregation meeting its denominational commitments.	Mean:	3.82	3.96	3.64	3.90
	1:	0%	0%	0%	0%
	2:	12%	8%	21%	5%
	3:	7%	4%	7%	5%
	4:	66%	72%	57%	85%
	5:	14%	16%	14%	5%
Hypothesis: 3					

		Pastors	Regional Officials	National Denominational Officials	All Seminary
43. Given that denominational reports indicate church members as a whole are giving a smaller percentage of their incomes than previous generations did, this trend is because people don't have as much money as previous generations used to. *Hypothesis:* 5	Mean: 1: 2: 3: 4: 5:	4.31 0% 2% 1% 61% 36%	4.21 1% 4% 3% 57% 35%	4.43 0% 7% 0% 36% 57%	4.10 0% 0% 14% 62% 24%
44. Most people join congregations to help participate in a common purpose. *Hypothesis:* 5	Mean: 1: 2: 3: 4: 5:	3.41 1% 24% 14% 56% 5%	3.60 1% 17% 9% 67% 6%	3.36 0% 29% 7% 64% 0%	3.57 0% 19% 5% 76% 0%
45. Whether congregation members agree or disagree with the national office's handling of the issue of homosexuality will have no effect on the congregation meeting its denominational commitments. *Hypothesis:* 3	Mean: 1: 2: 3: 4: 5:	3.96 1% 10% 7% 55% 27%	4.12 0% 4% 6% 62% 27%	4.07 0% 7% 7% 57% 29%	3.85 0% 10% 10% 65% 15%
46. Church members generally believe that older people on fixed incomes can be expected to increase their financial commitments to the church. *Hypothesis:* 5	Mean: 1: 2: 3: 4: 5:	3.89 1% 5% 8% 75% 10%	3.86 0% 7% 7% 79% 7%	4.07 0% 7% 0% 71% 21%	3.76 0% 5% 14% 81% 0%
47. People who come into the church in response to their own "felt needs" soon grow into people more concerned about others' needs. *Hypothesis:* 5	Mean: 1: 2: 3: 4: 5:	3.08 1% 34% 24% 38% 3%	3.24 0% 27% 26% 44% 4%	2.93 0% 36% 36% 29% 0%	3.42 0% 11% 42% 42% 5%

(continued)

(*Table 4–continued*)

		Pastors	Regional Officials	National Denominational Officials	All Seminary
48. There is still strong support among church members for the traditional Christian spiritual disciplines of self-sacrifice and self-denial among church members.	Mean:	3.05*	3.49*	3.23	3.48
	1:	0%	0%	0%	0%
	2:	43%	23%	36%	24%
	3:	14%	12%	13%	14%
	4:	38%	58%	45%	52%
	5:	5%	7%	7%	10%
Hypothesis: 5					
49. Most church members do not want the pastor to know how much individual members contribute to the church.	Mean:	2.03	2.15	2.14	2.76*
	1:	18%	12%	14%	0%
	2:	65%	67%	64%	43%
	3:	13%	16%	14%	38%
	4:	4%	5%	7%	19%
	5:	0%	0%	0%	0%
Hypothesis: 1					
50. Most church members do not want to discuss personal finances in the church.	Mean:	2.13	2.10	2.00	2.33
	1:	13%	12%	29%	0%
	2:	74%	74%	57%	76%
	3:	2%	7%	0%	14%
	4:	12%	7%	14%	10%
	5:	0%	0%	0%	0%
Hypothesis: 1					
51. Congregations today, compared to 40 years ago, use more independently-produced, rather than denominationally-produced, Sunday school materials.	Mean:	2.17	2.25	2.27	2.67
	1:	12%	7%	7%	0%
	2:	67%	69%	66%	48%
	3:	15%	16%	20%	38%
	4:	5%	8%	7%	14%
	5:	1%	0%	0%	0%
Hypothesis: 1					
52. There used to be a more broadly-held common vision in congregations than there is now.	Mean:	2.58	2.32	2.29	2.60
	1:	3%	5%	14%	0%
	2:	58%	72%	57%	50%
	3:	19%	12%	14%	40%
	4:	18%	11%	14%	10%
	5:	2%	1%	0%	0%
Hypothesis: 1					
53. Television and other media advertising may influence church	Mean:	2.52	2.43	2.36	2.48
	1:	6%	7%	7%	0%

		Pastors	Regional Officials	National Denominational Officials	All Seminary
member giving patterns more than the stewardship education they receive in church.	2:	57%	59%	71%	71%
	3:	17%	17%	7%	10%
	4:	19%	15%	7%	19%
	5:	1%	1%	7%	0%
Hypothesis: 1					
54. Most church members want to know "what their money is buying" when sent out of the congregation.	Mean:	2.00	1.95	1.77	2.14
	1:	17%	17%	23%	14%
	2:	72%	77%	77%	67%
	3:	4%	1%	0%	10%
	4:	6%	5%	0%	10%
	5:	0%	0%	0%	0%
Hypothesis: 1					
55. Church members are not clear how their increased giving would be used if they gave more money.	Mean:	2.81*	2.33*	2.29	2.52
	1:	0%	9%	7%	10%
	2:	52%	63%	71%	52%
	3:	17%	13%	7%	14%
	4:	31%	14%	14%	24%
	5:	1%	0%	0%	0%
Hypothesis: 1					
56. There is an increasing tendency for church members to want to keep more of the church's money in the local community, rather than send it beyond the local community.	Mean:	2.20*	1.79*	1.71	2.10
	1:	14%	29%	29%	10%
	2:	65%	66%	71%	76%
	3:	8%	3%	0%	10%
	4:	13%	3%	0%	5%
	5:	0%	0%	0%	0%
Hypothesis: 1					
57. When church members are asked to give funds for missions, in general, they want to know "what their money will buy."	Mean:	2.04	2.04	2.00	2.33
	1:	12%	16%	7%	5%
	2:	79%	73%	86%	71%
	3:	3%	4%	7%	10%
	4:	6%	8%	0%	14%
	5:	0%	0%	0%	0%
Hypothesis: 1					
58. A congregation having an endowment usually does not discourage church members	Mean:	3.01	3.16	2.79	2.90
	1:	3%	4%	0%	0%
	2:	37%	27%	50%	48%

(*continued*)

(Table 4–continued)

		Pastors	Regional Officials	National Denominational Officials	All Seminary
from contributing to the congregation.	3: 4: 5:	22% 32% 6%	25% 39% 5%	21% 29% 0%	14% 38% 0%
Hypothesis: 5					
59. There has been an erosion in the giving habits of church members older than 50 years of age in recent years.	Mean: 1: 2: 3: 4: 5:	3.43 0% 14% 30% 54% 2%	3.29 0% 24% 25% 49% 2%	3.79 0% 7% 7% 86% 0%	3.43 0% 10% 38% 52% 0%
Hypothesis: 1					
60. In instances where immoral behavior occurs on the part of the congregational lay leader-ship, such behavior has no significant effect on the level of giving in the congregation.	Mean: 1: 2: 3: 4: 5:	3.65 0% 14% 16% 59% 10%	3.35 0% 25% 19% 51% 5%	3.50 0% 29% 7% 50% 14%	3.43 0% 14% 33% 48% 5%
Hypothesis: 5					
61. Church members have changed from stewards into consumers.	Mean: 1: 2: 3: 4: 5:	2.32 5% 66% 22% 6% 1%	2.32 7% 68% 11% 14% 0%	2.14 7% 71% 21% 0% 0%	2.55 0% 60% 25% 15% 0%
Hypothesis: 1					
62. The way missions is pre-sented in most congregations does not effectively compete with television for church members' time or money.	Mean: 1: 2: 3: 4: 5:	2.54* 5% 59% 14% 21% 1%	2.20* 13% 68% 7% 9% 3%	2.34 14% 59% 5% 21% 0%	2.45 0% 65% 25% 10% 0%
Hypothesis: 1					
63. Most congregation members in this denomination agree with the national office's	Mean: 1: 2:	2.73 10% 42%	2.75 12% 43%	2.36 21% 50%	3.20 0% 30%

		Pastors	Regional Officials	National Denominational Officials	All Seminary
handling of the issue of homosexuality.	3:	18%	10%	7%	25%
	4:	25%	28%	14%	40%
	5:	5%	7%	7%	5%
Hypothesis: 1					
64. Church members over 50 years old have less denom- inational loyalty than their parents did.	Mean:	2.96	3.07	3.21	3.14
	1:	0%	1%	0%	0%
	2:	45%	39%	29%	24%
	3:	18%	15%	21%	38%
	4:	33%	41%	50%	38%
	5:	4%	4%	0%	0%
Hypothesis: 1					
65. Most church members would give more to the church if they knew that their pastor were tithing to the church.	Mean:	2.95	2.62	2.21	2.90
	1:	6%	4%	14%	10%
	2:	31%	48%	57%	24%
	3:	30%	29%	21%	33%
	4:	28%	18%	7%	33%
	5:	5%	1%	0%	0%
Hypothesis: 5					
66. Most church members feel money is not an appropriate subject to be discussed in church.	Mean:	3.33	3.02	2.57	3.10
	1:	1%	1%	7%	0%
	2:	28%	40%	64%	38%
	3:	11%	15%	0%	19%
	4:	57%	44%	21%	38%
	5:	3%	0%	7%	5%
Hypothesis: 1					
67. Most pastors have at least one story in which congre- gation members have made it clear the pastor is not to preach more than once or twice a year about the topic of money.	Mean:	2.98*	2.55*	2.57	2.62
	1:	1%	3%	0%	5%
	2:	41%	60%	71%	43%
	3:	21%	17%	0%	38%
	4:	34%	21%	29%	14%
	5:	3%	0%	0%	0%
Hypothesis: 1					
68. Many church members wonder if money "gets where it's supposed to go" in the	Mean:	2.84*	2.38*	2.73	2.60
	1:	4%	8%	7%	0%
	2:	45%	65%	50%	60%

(continued)

(*Table 4–continued*)

		Pastors	Regional Officials	National Denominational Officials	All Seminary
global mission activities of their denominations.	3:	15%	9%	5%	20%
	4:	33%	17%	38%	20%
	5:	2%	1%	0%	0%
Hypothesis: 1					
69. Most congregations take the services which the denomination provides to them for granted.	Mean:	2.14	2.05	2.07	2.14
	1:	13%	13%	14%	0%
	2:	74%	76%	71%	90%
	3:	3%	6%	7%	5%
	4:	8%	4%	7%	5%
	5:	2%	1%	0%	0%
Hypothesis: 1					
70. Most people come to church for certain activities which the congregation provides to them rather than in response to God's call on their lives.	Mean:	2.59	2.38	2.80	2.81
	1:	6%	4%	7%	0%
	2:	54%	68%	36%	48%
	3:	15%	15%	27%	24%
	4:	25%	13%	30%	29%
	5:	0%	0%	0%	0%
Hypothesis: 1					
71. Church members of all ages give a smaller portion of their incomes to their churches than previous generations of church members did.	Mean:	2.31	2.44	2.86	2.33
	1:	5%	6%	7%	0%
	2:	73%	59%	43%	71%
	3:	8%	19%	7%	24%
	4:	14%	14%	43%	5%
	5:	0%	1%	0%	0%
Hypothesis: 1					
72. Most church members want to know what the pastor gives to the church.	Mean:	3.35	3.23	3.07	3.38
	1:	1%	1%	0%	0%
	2:	17%	20%	29%	14%
	3:	31%	37%	36%	33%
	4:	48%	41%	36%	52%
	5:	3%	2%	0%	0%
Hypothesis: 5					
73. Most congregation members agree with the national stands taken by this denomination.	Mean:	2.72	2.86	2.57	3.30
	1:	9%	3%	21%	0%
	2:	39%	48%	36%	20%
	3:	24%	16%	7%	30%

		Pastors	Regional Officials	National Denominational Officials	All Seminary
	4:	26%	27%	36%	50%
	5:	2%	6%	0%	0%
Hypothesis: 1					
74. Younger people, below 40 years old, are in too much personal debt to be able to be large contributors to their congregations.	Mean:	2.89	2.87	3.00	2.95
	1:	6%	4%	0%	0%
	2:	44%	48%	50%	29%
	3:	7%	9%	7%	48%
	4:	41%	37%	36%	24%
	5:	2%	3%	7%	0%
Hypothesis: 1					
75. Whether congregation members agree or disagree with the national office's handling of the issue of homosexuality will have no effect on church member giving to the congregation.	Mean:	3.86	3.77	3.73	3.63
	1:	0%	1%	0%	0%
	2:	13%	14%	21%	16%
	3:	5%	8%	5%	11%
	4:	66%	63%	52%	68%
	5:	17%	14%	21%	5%
Hypothesis: 3					
76. Most church members are very aware of the good that is accomplished through their denominational global mission activities.	Mean:	3.31	3.48	3.79	3.67
	1:	3%	0%	7%	0%
	2:	24%	26%	7%	5%
	3:	13%	9%	0%	24%
	4:	59%	56%	71%	71%
	5:	1%	9%	14%	0%
Hypothesis: 5					
77. Church members don't want to give the church one more dollar than it needs.	Mean:	3.33	3.03	3.36	3.52
	1:	0%	3%	0%	0%
	2:	26%	39%	21%	14%
	3:	17%	15%	29%	19%
	4:	55%	40%	43%	67%
	5:	2%	4%	7%	0%
Hypothesis: 1					
78. Church members above 50 years old give because they	Mean:	2.14	2.16	2.21	2.57*
	1:	4%	5%	7%	0%

(continued)

(Table 4–continued)

		Pastors	Regional Officials	National Denominational Officials	All Seminary
have been taught that it is the right thing to do.	2:	85%	80%	79%	62%
	3:	3%	7%	0%	19%
	4:	7%	7%	14%	19%
	5:	0%	0%	0%	0%
Hypothesis: 1					
79. Given that denominational reports indicate church members as a whole are giving a smaller portion of their incomes than previous generations used to, this trend is because people now have more ways to spend money.	Mean:	2.58	2.80	2.66	3.05
	1:	4%	2%	7%	0%
	2:	59%	53%	55%	33%
	3:	11%	12%	2%	29%
	4:	24%	31%	36%	38%
	5:	1%	3%	0%	0%
Hypothesis: 1					
80. Older members are anxious to turn over the leadership of the congregation to younger members of the church.	Mean:	3.33	3.54	3.36	3.35
	1:	1%	0%	0%	0%
	2:	29%	17%	21%	20%
	3:	14%	18%	21%	25%
	4:	48%	59%	57%	55%
	5:	8%	6%	0%	0%
Hypothesis: 5					
81. Congregations are more like coalitions of special interest groups than cohesive communities of faith.	Mean:	2.92	2.73	3.14	2.80
	1:	3%	1%	0%	0%
	2:	43%	51%	36%	50%
	3:	14%	23%	21%	20%
	4:	38%	24%	36%	30%
	5:	2%	1%	7%	0%
Hypothesis: 1					
82. Mission strategies and goals are as clear to the average church member today as they were 60 years ago.	Mean:	3.65	3.91	3.93	3.76
	1:	1%	0%	0%	0%
	2:	17%	7%	7%	10%
	3:	7%	8%	7%	14%
	4:	67%	71%	71%	67%
	5:	8%	13%	14%	10%
Hypothesis: 5					

		Pastors	Regional Officials	National Denominational Officials	All Seminary
83. Most congregation members in this denomination agree with the national office's handling of the issue of abortion.	Mean:	2.36	2.44	2.21	2.85
	1:	12%	9%	14%	5%
	2:	53%	56%	57%	30%
	3:	23%	20%	21%	40%
	4:	11%	12%	7%	25%
	5:	1%	3%	0%	0%
Hypothesis: 1					
84. In most congregations, one layperson or a relatively small number of laypeople often effectively control the decision-making, whether or not they hold formal leadership positions.	Mean:	2.56*	2.16*	2.14	2.90
	1:	7%	7%	7%	0%
	2:	59%	79%	79%	48%
	3:	6%	5%	7%	14%
	4:	27%	9%	7%	38%
	5:	1%	0%	0%	0%
Hypothesis: 1					
85. The concern stated by many congregations—that they cannot be expected to improve their financial stewardship because so many members have responsibility either for young adults in college or aging parents—is a valid concern for many congregations.	Mean:	3.19	3.03	3.30	2.81
	1:	1%	1%	0%	0%
	2:	36%	43%	21%	52%
	3:	11%	10%	27%	14%
	4:	46%	46%	52%	33%
	5:	5%	1%	0%	0%
Hypothesis: 1					
86. Many congregation leaders who say they do not want to challenge their membership to improve financial stewardship will say it's because those young families just establishing themselves will feel badly when they can't respond.	Mean:	3.49	3.28	3.21	3.19
	1:	0%	1%	0%	0%
	2:	20%	28%	36%	24%
	3:	14%	18%	7%	33%
	4:	63%	50%	57%	43%
	5:	3%	4%	0%	0%
Hypothesis: 1					
87. Congregations that are challenged too strongly by the pastor about a difficult topic	Mean:	3.12	2.98	3.00	2.76
	1:	0%	3%	0%	0%
	2:	35%	38%	36%	57%

(continued)

(Table 4–continued)

		Pastors	Regional Officials	National Denominational Officials	All Seminary
may show their displeasure by	3:	20%	20%	29%	10%
not raising the pastor's salary at	4:	43%	38%	36%	33%
budget time.	5:	2%	2%	0%	0%
Hypothesis: 1					
88. Many congregation leaders	Mean:	3.37	3.31	3.57	3.24
who say they do not want to	1:	0%	0%	0%	0%
challenge their membership to	2:	23%	27%	21%	29%
improve financial stewardship	3:	20%	18%	7%	19%
will say it's because those	4:	56%	52%	64%	52%
members who have responsi-	5:	2%	3%	7%	0%
bility both for young adults in					
college and for aging parents					
will feel badly when they can't					
respond.					
Hypothesis: 1					
89. Most congregations feel	Mean:	2.97*	2.54*	2.71	2.76
that maintaining their current	1:	1%	2%	0%	0%
programs is all they can expect	2:	43%	67%	64%	52%
to do as their stewardship goal.	3:	15%	8%	0%	19%
	4:	38%	22%	36%	29%
	5:	2%	1%	0%	0%
Hypothesis: 1					
90. In congregations where 20%	Mean:	3.30	3.17	3.14	3.48
of the people contribute most	1:	2%	2%	7%	0%
of the budget, that 20% may	2:	31%	34%	36%	19%
not want to stress improved	3:	8%	13%	7%	19%
stewardship because they	4:	53%	49%	36%	57%
believe they will be the only	5:	6%	3%	14%	5%
ones to respond to the					
challenge.					
Hypothesis: 1					
91. Most congregations are	Mean:	3.37	3.45	3.57	3.15
willing to risk disagreements	1:	1%	2%	0%	0%
rather than maintain them-	2:	27%	21%	14%	35%

		Pastors	Regional Officials	National Denominational Officials	All Seminary
selves at the lowest common denominator.	3: 4: 5:	15% 49% 8%	13% 62% 4%	14% 71% 0%	15% 50% 0%

Hypothesis: 5

92. The concern stated by many congregations—that they cannot be expected to improve their financial stewardship because so many members are young families just establishing themselves—is a valid concern for many congregations.	Mean: 1: 2: 3: 4: 5:	3.57 1% 18% 12% 62% 7%	3.38 0% 29% 10% 57% 4%	3.34 0% 16% 34% 50% 0%	3.00 0% 48% 10% 38% 5%

Hypothesis: 1

93. Often, the congregational leadership board may not know about one or more reserve funds being maintained by a well-intentioned treasurer or other financial officer for a "rainy day" in the congregation's future.	Mean: 1: 2: 3: 4: 5:	3.48 3% 20% 10% 60% 7%	3.17 0% 36% 13% 50% 2%	2.64 0% 64% 7% 29% 0%	3.00 0% 29% 43% 29% 0%

Hypothesis: 1

94. The concern stated by many congregations—that they cannot be expected to improve their financial stewardship because so many members are on fixed incomes—is a valid concern for many congregations.	Mean: 1: 2: 3: 4: 5:	3.24 0% 38% 5% 52% 5%	3.25 0% 35% 8% 53% 4%	3.36 0% 29% 7% 64% 0%	2.62 0% 62% 14% 24% 0%

Hypothesis: 1

95. Many congregational leaders may, for various reasons, be wary of or distrust strangers who visit their church.	Mean: 1: 2: 3: 4: 5:	3.33* 1% 29% 11% 54% 5%	2.85* 2% 48% 15% 35% 1%	3.36 0% 36% 0% 57% 7%	3.43 0% 14% 29% 57% 0%

Hypothesis: 1

(continued)

(Table 4–continued)

		Pastors	Regional Officials	National Denominational Officials	All Seminary
96. Congregations have effective ways of pressuring the pastor to stop if the pastor challenges them on a difficult topic.	Mean:	2.67*	2.15*	2.14	2.33
	1:	1%	5%	0%	0%
	2:	58%	82%	86%	76%
	3:	15%	7%	14%	14%
	4:	25%	6%	0%	10%
	5:	1%	0%	0%	0%
Hypothesis: 1					
97. In most congregations, the goal of stewardship is defined as meeting the budget.	Mean:	2.21	2.00	2.00	2.14
	1:	9%	18%	29%	10%
	2:	74%	72%	57%	76%
	3:	4%	5%	0%	5%
	4:	11%	6%	14%	10%
	5:	1%	0%	0%	0%
Hypothesis: 1					
98. Discussions related to the congregation can be cut short if one vocal person suggests the topic will "split the church."	Mean:	2.74*	2.35*	2.57	2.67
	1:	5%	5%	0%	0%
	2:	49%	70%	64%	62%
	3:	12%	12%	14%	10%
	4:	32%	14%	21%	29%
	5:	1%	0%	0%	0%
Hypothesis: 1					
99. In most congregations, being able to pay the bills is the definition of successful stewardship education.	Mean:	2.41	2.15	2.21	2.38
	1:	9%	10%	7%	0%
	2:	64%	75%	79%	76%
	3:	4%	5%	0%	10%
	4:	22%	10%	14%	14%
	5:	1%	0%	0%	0%
Hypothesis: 1					
100. Congregations that are challenged too strongly by the pastor on a difficult topic may pressure the pastor to leave the congregation.	Mean:	2.62	2.47	2.71	2.52
	1:	3%	3%	0%	0%
	2:	54%	68%	57%	62%
	3:	22%	10%	14%	24%
	4:	22%	20%	29%	14%
	5:	0%	0%	0%	0%
Hypothesis: 1					

		Pastors	Regional Officials	National Denominational Officials	All Seminary
101. Occasionally, a particular church member will be discouraged from increasing his or her contribution because one or more key leaders in the church may fear the increased influence that may accrue to that particular church member.	Mean: 1: 2: 3: 4: 5:	3.72 0% 10% 20% 58% 12%	3.51 1% 16% 16% 64% 3%	3.71 0% 7% 29% 50% 14%	3.52 0% 14% 24% 57% 5%
Hypothesis: 1					
102. For most congregations, it is more important to come to a broadly-held consensus than to avoid disagreement.	Mean: 1: 2: 3: 4: 5:	2.65 6% 51% 18% 24% 2%	2.53 2% 65% 14% 18% 2%	2.71 0% 57% 14% 29% 0%	2.48 0% 67% 19% 14% 0%
Hypothesis: 5					
103. The most vocal church leader is usually the largest financial contributor.	Mean: 1: 2: 3: 4: 5:	4.14 1% 7% 2% 57% 33%	4.05 0% 5% 10% 59% 25%	4.14 0% 0% 7% 71% 21%	4.05 0% 0% 10% 76% 14%
Hypothesis: 5					
104. Many congregation leaders who say they do not want to challenge their membership to improve financial stewardship will suggest it's because those on fixed incomes will feel badly when they can't respond.	Mean: 1: 2: 3: 4: 5:	3.32 0% 29% 14% 53% 4%	3.25 0% 30% 17% 51% 2%	3.29 0% 29% 14% 57% 0%	2.90 0% 43% 24% 33% 0%
Hypothesis: 1					
105. In congregations where 50–80% of the people give only token amounts, those who give only token amounts do not	Mean: 1: 2: 3:	2.28 10% 67% 8%	2.16 8% 76% 6%	2.14 14% 71% 0%	2.30 0% 80% 10%

(continued)

(Table 4–continued)

		Pastors	Regional Officials	National Denominational Officials	All Seminary
have a clear idea why they should give more.	4:	13%	9%	14%	10%
	5:	1%	0%	0%	0%
Hypothesis: 1					
106. In congregations where 20% of the people give most of the budget, this 20% may not want improved stewardship among other members because the large contributors fear a loss of the control and/or influence they now exert in the congregation.	Mean:	3.85	3.65	4.00	3.76
	1:	1%	1%	0%	0%
	2:	6%	11%	0%	10%
	3:	13%	17%	7%	14%
	4:	66%	65%	86%	67%
	5:	13%	6%	7%	10%
Hypothesis: 1					
107. In most congregations, 20% of the people give 50–80% of the budget.	Mean:	1.84	1.86	1.71	2.05
	1:	23%	17%	29%	10%
	2:	73%	80%	71%	76%
	3:	3%	2%	0%	14%
	4:	0%	1%	0%	0%
	5:	1%	0%	0%	0%
Hypothesis: 1					
108. The people who give the largest amounts in a congregation may not want improved stewardship among other members because the large contributors fear they would experience a loss of status in the congregation.	Mean:	3.90	3.75	4.07	3.81
	1:	0%	1%	0%	0%
	2:	3%	8%	0%	5%
	3:	14%	11%	7%	19%
	4:	72%	76%	79%	67%
	5:	10%	4%	14%	10%
Hypothesis: 1					
109. Congregations do not have a clear overarching vision with which to challenge their members to improve their stewardship.	Mean:	2.18*	1.87*	2.07	1.90
	1:	13%	22%	21%	14%
	2:	68%	72%	64%	81%
	3:	6%	4%	0%	5%
	4:	12%	3%	14%	0%
	5:	0%	0%	0%	0%
Hypothesis: 1					

		Pastors	Regional Officials	National Denominational Officials	All Seminary
110. Nationally-affiliated denominational officials on occasion seek to solicit funds for nationally-affiliated denominational purposes from individual wealthy members of congregations.	Mean:	2.27	2.10	2.50	2.29
	1:	9%	17%	7%	5%
	2:	68%	67%	71%	71%
	3:	11%	5%	0%	14%
	4:	9%	11%	7%	10%
	5:	2%	0%	14%	0%
Hypothesis: 1					
111. There is a lack of mission vision in the church.	Mean:	2.20	2.06	2.43	2.24
	1:	24%	23%	21%	10%
	2:	52%	60%	50%	71%
	3:	7%	5%	0%	5%
	4:	16%	11%	21%	14%
	5:	1%	1%	7%	0%
Hypothesis: 1					
112. Denominationally-affiliated seminaries on occasion seek to solicit funds for the seminary from individual wealthy members of congregations.	Mean:	2.34*	1.88*	2.00	1.95
	1:	8%	21%	7%	14%
	2:	66%	71%	86%	76%
	3:	11%	5%	7%	10%
	4:	12%	2%	0%	0%
	5:	2%	0%	0%	0%
Hypothesis: 1					
113. Denominational officials expect a pastor to be able to secure support for denominational programs from the congregation as a whole.	Mean:	1.97	2.05	2.27	2.14
	1:	14%	14%	7%	5%
	2:	78%	75%	73%	81%
	3:	4%	2%	5%	10%
	4:	2%	9%	14%	5%
	5:	1%	0%	0%	0%
Hypothesis: 1					
114. The contribution of laypeople is underutilized in most congregations.	Mean:	1.95	1.83	2.00	2.00
	1:	23%	25%	29%	10%
	2:	66%	68%	57%	81%
	3:	5%	6%	0%	10%
	4:	6%	1%	14%	0%
	5:	0%	0%	0%	0%
Hypothesis: 1					

(continued)

(Table 4–continued)

		Pastors	Regional Officials	National Denominational Officials	All Seminary
115. Percentage giving is not generally taught in most congregations.	Mean:	2.65	2.50	2.57	2.38
	1:	7%	15%	14%	0%
	2:	52%	47%	50%	76%
	3:	13%	11%	7%	10%
	4:	25%	26%	21%	14%
	5:	3%	1%	7%	0%
Hypothesis: 1					
116. While more women have taken on formal leadership roles in the main structure of the congregation, fewer younger women have joined the traditional women's groups to promote missions.	Mean:	1.99	1.94	2.29	2.05
	1:	14%	20%	14%	14%
	2:	74%	71%	64%	71%
	3:	9%	6%	7%	10%
	4:	2%	4%	7%	5%
	5:	0%	0%	7%	0%
Hypothesis: 1					
117. Most church members have received the following types of information through various church education sources:	Mean:	3.39	3.39	3.41	3.33
	1:	4%	2%	0%	0%
	2:	20%	22%	30%	14%
	3:	18%	23%	13%	43%
• UNICEF estimates that	4:	51%	42%	43%	38%
worldwide there are 13 mil-	5:	8%	11%	14%	5%

117. (continued)

• UNICEF estimates that worldwide there are 13 million annual child deaths, most from preventable poverty conditions, and that $2.5 billion a year could prevent most of those poverty-related deaths;

• U.S. based Protestant overseas word and deed ministry was estimated to be $2 billion in 1991;

compared to

• the annual U.S. soft drink budget is $44 billion;
• the annual cosmetic budget is $20 billion;
• leisure travel is estimated to be $40 billion a year.

Hypothesis: 5

		Pastors	Regional Officials	National Denominational Officials	All Seminary
118. Denominational officials tend to see congregations as cohesive communities of faith rather than as coalitions of special interest groups.	Mean:	2.59	2.65	2.71	2.95
	1:	2%	3%	7%	0%
	2:	54%	51%	43%	38%
	3:	27%	25%	21%	29%
	4:	16%	21%	29%	33%
	5:	1%	0%	0%	0%
Hypothesis: 1					
119. Women have traditionally championed missions in the church.	Mean:	2.12	2.04	1.86	1.86
	1:	10%	14%	14%	19%
	2:	74%	71%	86%	76%
	3:	8%	11%	0%	5%
	4:	7%	4%	0%	0%
	5:	0%	0%	0%	0%
Hypothesis: 1					
120. In-depth training of lay leaders has often turned them into "little preachers" rather than enhanced the contribution of their lay gifts.	Mean:	3.57	3.40	3.50	3.29
	1:	0%	2%	0%	0%
	2:	14%	20%	21%	24%
	3:	22%	16%	7%	24%
	4:	57%	60%	71%	52%
	5:	7%	2%	0%	0%
Hypothesis: 1					
121. Women no longer have as much time as they did in past decades to volunteer as mission educators and promoters in the church.	Mean:	2.07	1.98	1.71	2.10
	1:	10%	21%	29%	14%
	2:	79%	69%	71%	71%
	3:	4%	1%	0%	5%
	4:	5%	9%	0%	10%
	5:	1%	0%	0%	0%
Hypothesis: 1					
122. The professionalization of the clergy has increased the distance between the pastor and the laypeople.	Mean:	3.03*	2.50*	3.07	2.95
	1:	5%	12%	0%	5%
	2:	32%	49%	50%	43%
	3:	18%	17%	0%	10%
	4:	44%	23%	43%	38%
	5:	1%	0%	7%	5%
Hypothesis: 1					

(continued)

(Table 4–continued)

	Pastors	Regional Officials	National Denominational Officials	All Seminary
123. Regionally-affiliated denomina- Mean:	2.46	2.30	2.71	2.33
tional officials on occasion 1:	8%	6%	0%	10%
seek to solicit funds for 2:	58%	68%	64%	57%
regionally-affiliated denomina- 3:	14%	15%	0%	24%
tional purposes from individual 4:	19%	11%	36%	10%
wealthy members of 5:	1%	0%	0%	0%
congregations.				
Hypothesis: 1				

In the above table, details in each column may not compute to 100 percent due to rounding.
$^*p < .005$.

An indication of significance at the .05 level could be an artifact of the large number of observations included in the survey. The value of considering the findings at that level would be to consider on a purely exploratory basis whether any observations may merit additional research.

If one considered a crosswise comparison between the regional officials and pastors at the .05 level, sixteen additional responses are noteworthy. Those are observations 2, 8, 9, 31, 32, 34, 35, 52, 60, 65, 66, 77, 82, 93, 97, and 99. In every case but three, the response mean for the pastors and the regional officials were both on one side or the other of the agree-disagree dimension; the .05 level indicated a slight difference in intensity of the responses. The exceptions were observation 2, in which the regional official mean of 3.27 was different from the pastor mean of 2.99 at the .05 level, observation 8, in which the regional official mean of 2.77 was different from the pastor mean of 3.11 at the .05 level, and observation 34, in which the regional official mean of 3.04 was different from the pastor mean of 2.71 at the .05 level.

Variation in Denominational Responses

In addition to the seminary participants, fourteen Protestant denominations also distributed the survey. The denominations, and the three-letter code for each, are listed in table 5.

Table 5
List of Fourteen Protestant Denominations Participating in the Stewardship Project Survey and Their Three-letter Codes

Denomination	Three-letter Code
The Christian and Missionary Alliance	cma
Christian Church (Disciples of Christ)	ccd
Church of God (Anderson, Indiana)	cga
Church of God (Cleveland, Tennessee)	cgc
Church of the Brethren	chb
Church of the Nazarene	chn
The Episcopal Church	epc
The Evangelical Covenant Church	ecv
Evangelical Lutheran Church in America	elc
The Lutheran Church-Missouri Synod	lms
Presbyterian Church (U.S.A.)	pch
Southern Baptist Convention	sbc
United Church of Christ	ucc
The United Methodist Church	umc

In the General Factorial ANOVA, for sixteen observations, the denomination effect showed a p value of .005 or less, suggesting that denomination had a significant effect on responses to these observations. Table 6 lists response means for all denominations combined—i.e., the overall combined regional officials and pastors response means—as well as for the individual denominational means for these sixteen observations. Asterisks in table 6 indicate the individual denominational means that differed significantly (at the .005 level) from the mean response of the combined regional officials and pastors to that observation.

For observations 66 and 104, no individual denominational mean is followed by an asterisk. This is because, although variation of the .005 level is evident among denominational responses to the observation, no individual denominational mean varied from the combined regional officials and pastors response mean at the .005 level.

The fact that no more than 13 percent of the observations yielded strong variation (measured at .005) among the denominational responses was of interest.

In observations 63, 73, and 83, the hypothesis was 1, although variation in the level of agreement with the specific observation was expected among the various communions. In fact, in observation 63, the denominations that might be more closely identified with the term "evangelical" responded on one side of the 3.0 value, and those that might be more closely identified with the term "mainline" responded on the other side of the 3.0 value, although one denomination was close to 3.0, at the 3.08 level. If responses were equally likely above or below 3.0, then the possibility of this distribution of denominations being due to chance is $(1/2^{14})$ x 2, or 1/8,192.

Observation 73 was the only other response that indicated some degree of separation along the denominationally based theological categories of "evangelical" and "mainline" on either side of the 3.0 measure. Observation 73 displayed a distribution of denominational means along evangelical and mainline lines similar to the distribution in observation 63, with the exception of one denomination.

It is worth noting that the variation in the responses to the other fourteen observations that had a .005 or smaller p value in a denomination crosswise comparison did not produce a clearly defined pattern among the denominational responses along the evangelical and mainline dimension.

As noted earlier, variation at the .05 level could be an artifact of the large number of observations included in the survey. Thus, discussion of variation at the .05 level is of limited value. Yet, in an exploratory effort such as this survey, noting such variation may suggest additional directions for research.

At the .05 level, an additional twenty-three observations posted some variation among the denominational responses.

In nine cases—observations 7, 11, 13, 17, 29, 45, 56, 97, and 113— the variation was in the intensity of the mean responses that were all on the same side of the agree/disagree dimension.

In an additional ten observations—6, 20, 21, 28, 35, 48, 62, 71, 89, and 93—no more than three denominations were on the opposite side of the agree/disagree dimension from the majority. In observation 35, two denominations agreed, one was unsure with a 3.0 mean, and the rest disagreed. In observation 71, 13 agreed and one posted a mean of 3.0.

In observation 2, four denominations posted means on the agree side of the dimension, and ten on the disagree.

In observation 34, nine were on the agree side, with five on the disagree.

In observation 67, ten were on the agree side, two measured unsure with means of 3.0, and two were on the disagree side.

In observation 122, eight denominations posted means on the agree side, two had means of 3.0, and four posted disagreement.

Table 6
Variation in Stewardship Project Survey Responses by Denomination

Obs. No.	Obs. Mean	Denomination													
		cma	ccd	cga	cgc	chb	chn	epc	ecv	elc	lms	pch	sbc	ucc	umc
15	3.47	4.16*	3.67	3.29	2.46*	3.63	3.00	3.22	3.89	3.55	3.67	3.69	3.38	2.85	3.53
24	2.64	2.42	2.08	2.35	3.54*	2.32	3.17	2.44	3.00	2.52	2.92	2.15	2.62	2.85	2.80
33	2.79	2.84	2.33	3.06	3.62*	2.74	3.17	1.56*	3.16	2.50	3.17	2.81	2.81	2.50	2.40
36	2.28	2.53	1.83	2.71	2.92*	2.32	3.42*	2.11	2.26	1.85	2.08	2.15	1.94	1.92	2.00
49	2.10	1.84	2.42	1.88	2.77*	1.79	1.92	2.00	2.00	2.10	2.00	2.23	1.81	2.58	2.40
63	2.74	1.58*	3.75*	2.00*	1.46*	3.16	2.00*	4.22*	2.38	4.15*	2.00*	3.08	2.25	3.33	3.40*
66	3.16	3.63	3.00	3.53	3.77	2.63	3.67	2.44	3.58	2.80	3.25	2.54	2.56	3.46	3.27
73	2.79	1.79*	3.54*	2.12*	1.92*	2.94	1.83*	4.00*	2.28*	3.80*	2.17*	3.31	2.75	3.46*	3.67*
76	3.40	2.47*	3.67	3.65	2.92	3.39	2.92	3.67	3.16	3.85	3.67	3.77	3.44	3.54	3.80
82	3.79	3.63	4.33	3.53	2.85*	3.83	3.67	4.00	3.74	3.85	4.08	3.92	3.88	4.15	3.80
83	2.40	1.53*	3.00	2.06	1.69*	2.74	1.83	2.94	2.11	3.00*	2.33	2.62	2.44	2.54	3.07*
100	2.54	2.11	2.25	2.81	2.31	2.26	2.67	3.00	2.95	2.65	2.83	3.00	2.00*	2.77	2.27
104	3.28	3.63	2.83	3.38	3.54	2.74	3.58	2.78	3.79	3.05	3.83	3.00	3.50	3.31	2.87
110	2.18	2.89*	1.75	2.06	1.92	1.84	2.67	2.44	1.68*	2.15	2.00	2.54	2.06	2.00	2.60
115	2.57	2.58	2.17	2.94	3.54*	2.37	3.50*	2.89	2.89	2.30	2.00	2.15	2.62	2.00	2.13
119	2.08	2.00	1.75	1.94	2.62*	2.26	1.83	2.00	2.47*	2.15	2.25	2.15	1.69	2.08	1.73

*$p < .005$.

No patterns among the combinations of denominations were immediately evident in the responses.

A Comparison of Seminary Development Officers and Faculty

In a crosswise comparison between the seminary development officers and the seminary faculty response means, observation 1 was the
single mean that had a p value of .005 or less. The development officers had a mean response of 3.91 and the mean faculty response was
2.90. Otherwise, the variation between the responses of these seminary
personnel was not marked.

As noted before, discussion at the .05 level of significance has limited value other than to highlight possible directions for additional
research to determine if the differences noted are substantive or an
artifact of the large number of observations included in the survey.

Mean responses to eight additional observations varied at the .05
level between the seminary development officers and faculty. Of these,
five observations—3, 53, 71, 106, and 112—had means for both the
development officers and the faculty on the same side of the agree/dis-
agree dimension; the difference in the means was in the intensity of
the same response.

It may be of interest to note that three of the observations that indicated variation between the development officers and faculty means at
the .05 level were on opposite sides of the agree/disagree dimension.
In observation 6, the development officers mean was 2.36, and the faculty mean was 3.2. For observation 58, the development officers mean
was 2.45, and the faculty mean was 3.40. For observation 122, the
development officer mean was 3.45, and the faculty mean was 2.40.

A Comparison of Regional Responses

Strong regional differences did not emerge in an analysis of responses
as categorized by region. Observation 35 was the single observation
that produced a p value of .005 or less in the regional analysis, as noted
in table 7. The overall mean for observation 35 was 3.48 for the combined pastor and regional official responses. The geographical region
from which the responses came included the city noted in each column of table 7. The national official asked a regional official in that
geographical area to fill out a survey and to arrange for a pastor who
was located as close to that city as possible to fill out a survey. The one
exception was in the case of Region 10, which included the two states
of Illinois and Indiana rather than focusing on a single metropolitan

Table 7
Variation in Stewardship Project Survey Responses by Region

		Geographical Region (including the listed city or area)									
		Region 1	Region 2	Region 3	Region 4	Region 5	Region 6	Region 7	Region 8	Region 9	Region 10
Obs. No.	Obs. Mean	Boston, Mass.	New York, N.Y.	Atlanta, Ga.	Jackson, Miss.	Minneapolis, Minn.	Houston, Tex.	Denver, Colo.	Los Angeles, Calif.	Seattle, Wash.	Illinois/ Indiana
35	3.48	3.53	3.76	2.91	3.41	3.15	4.08*	3.81	3.42	3.52	3.17

*$p < .005$.

area. These two states were the site of the in-person congregational and regional contacts made during the Stewardship Project. Table 7 presents the overall observation mean for the combined regional officials and pastors responses, plus the mean for each region. The asterisk indicates the mean that varied from the overall observation mean at the .005 level.

Again, any variation at the .05 level may be a function of the large number of observations included in the survey. It is of interest to note that at the less conservative level of .05, the number of observations that indicated variation among the regions was six.

In three of these—observations 28, 52, and 84—the variation was in the intensity of responses that were all on the same side of the agree/disagree dimension among the ten regions.

In observation 2, the region 10 mean was 2.5, and the region 1 mean was 3.00. The other eight regions posted means varying from 3.06 to 3.47.

In observation 21, region 7 posted a mean of 2.82, while the other nine regions varied from 3.05 to 3.82.

In observation 44, region 5 posted a mean of 2.85, while the other nine regions varied from 3.17 to 3.76.

List of Interviews

Person Interviewed	Affiliation	Location of Interview	Date of Interview
James Austin	Vice President, Stewardship Commission, The Southern Baptist Convention	Nashville, Tenn.	July 15, 1993
Ronald W. Blue	Managing Partner, Ronald Blue & Co.	Atlanta, Ga.	July 27, 1994
M. Douglas Borko	Steward for Congregational Stewardship, United Church of Christ, Cleveland, Ohio	St. Louis, Mo.	July 17, 1993
Joseph M. Champlin	Pastor, St. Joseph's Church, Camillus, N.Y.	Nashville, Tenn.	October 19, 1993
Daniel Conway	Secretary for Planning, Communications and Development, Archdiocese of Indianapolis	Indianapolis, Ind.	December 20, 1994
Raymond P. Coughlin	Director of Development, Archdiocese of Chicago	Chicago, Ill.	November 14, 1994
Howard Dayton	Crown Ministries, Longwood, Fla.	Louisville, Ky.	September 26, 1994
Craig Dykstra	Vice President, Religion, Lilly Endowment Inc.	Indianapolis, Ind.	October 19, 1994
Timothy C. Ek	Vice President, The Evangelical Covenant Church	Chicago, Ill.	September 29, 1993
James F. Engel	Executive Director, The Center for Organizational Excellence, Eastern College	St. Davids, Pa.	October 10, 1994
Andrew M. Greeley	Department of Social Sciences, University of Chicago	Chicago, Ill.	December 28, 1994
D. Moody Gunter	Finance Division Director, Church of the Nazarene	Kansas City, Mo.	June 8, 1993
David Heetland	Vice President for Development, Garrett-Evangelical Theological Seminary	Evanston, Ill.	March 11, 1993
Fred L. Hofheinz	Program Director, Religion, Lilly Endowment Inc.	Indianapolis, Ind.	September 6, 1994
Dean R. Hoge	Professor of Sociology, The Catholic University of America	Washington, D.C.	July 21, 1994
Elsie Holderread	General Services Commission, Church of the Brethren	Elgin, Ill.	May 12, 1993
James Hudnut-Beumler	Dean, Columbia Theological Seminary, Decatur, Ga.	phone interview	October 21, 1994
Brian Kluth	President, Christian Stewardship Association, Milwaukee, Wis.	Louisville, Ky.	September 27, 1994
Fran LaMattina	Director of Marketing, Ronald Blue & Co.	Atlanta, Ga.	July 27, 1994
Robert Wood Lynn	Scholar in Residence, Bangor Theological Seminary	Portland, Me.	July 25, 1994

List of Interviews (*continued*)

Person Interviewed	Affiliation	Location of Interview	Date of Interview
J. Hugh Magers	Director of Stewardship, The Episcopal Church	New York, N.Y.	August 2, 1993
Herbert Mather	General Board of Discipleship, The United Methodist Church	Nashville, Tenn.	September 27, 1993
Don McClanen	Ministry of Money	Gaithersburg, Md.	July 20, 1994
David McCreath	Coordinator of Stewardship Education, Presbyterian Church (U.S.A.)	Louisville, Ky.	September 28, 1993
William McKinney	Dean and Professor of Religion, Hartford Theological Seminary	Hartford, Conn.	October 12, 1994
William McManus	Bishop, Roman Catholic Church	Mt. Prospect, Ill.	December 2, 1994
Loren B. Mead	President Emeritus, The Alban Institute	Washington, D.C.	July 26, 1994
Donald R. Michaelsen	Director of Congregational Support, Church of the Brethren	Elgin, Ill.	May 12, 1993
Dale E. Minnich	Executive, General Services Commission, Church of the Brethren	Elgin, Ill.	May 12, 1993
Mark Moller-Gunderson	Executive Director, Division for Congregational Ministries, Evangelical Lutheran Church in America	Chicago, Ill.	January 29, 1993
Nordan C. Murphy	Retired Director, Commission on Stewardship, National Council of the Churches of Christ in the United States	Butler, N.J.	July 23, 1994
Thomas J. Murphy	Archbishop of Seattle, Roman Catholic Church	Seattle, Wash.	August 9, 1993
Ronald Nelson	Assistant Stewardship Counselor, Lutheran Church-Missouri Synod	St. Louis, Mo.	June 7, 1993
Robert Niklaus	Assistant to the President, Office of Communications and Funding, Christian and Missionary Alliance	Colorado Springs, Colo.	August 10, 1993
Betty Lee Nyhus	Director of Mission Giving, Division for Congregational Ministries, Evangelical Lutheran Church in America	Chicago, Ill.	January 29, 1993

List of Interviews (*continued*)

Person Interviewed	Affiliation	Location of Interview	Date of Interview
E. Earl "Scoop" Okerlund	Congregational/Synodical Stewardship Services, Evangelical Lutheran Church in America	Chicago, Ill.	September 1, 1992
James Powell	Director of the Cooperative Program Office, The Southern Baptist Convention	Nashville, Tenn.	July 15, 1993
Joan Sanford	Office of Communications and Funding, Christian and Missionary Alliance	Colorado Springs, Colo.	August 10, 1993
David Schmidt	President, J. David Schmidt and Associates, Wheaton, Ill.	Louisville, Ky.	September 27, 1994
Thomas P. Sweetser, S.J.	Parish Evaluation Project	Des Plaines, Ill.	January 26, 1995
Al Taylor	Director of Stewardship, Church of God (Cleveland, Tenn.)	Cleveland, Tenn.	July 16, 1993
Mark Teresi	Executive Vice President for Development, Mercy Home for Boys and Girls	Chicago, Ill.	November 14, 1994
Ronald Voss	Pastor, Christ Our Savior Lutheran Church (ELCA)	Indianapolis, Ind.	June 28, 1993
James L. Waits	Executive Director, The Association of Theological Schools in the United States and Canada	Pittsburgh, Pa.	October 14, 1994
Robert K. Welsh	President, Church Finance Council, Christian Church (Disciples of Christ)	Indianapolis, Ind.	September 17, 1993
Waldo Werning	Discipling Stewardship Center, Fort Wayne, Ind.	Louisville, Ky.	September 27, 1994
David Wheeler	Director of Evangelism/Stewardship, State Convention of Baptists in Indiana	Indianapolis, Ind.	May 4, 1993
James E. Williams	Executive Director, Division of World Service, Church of God (Anderson, Ind.)	Anderson, Ind.	July 14, 1993
Phil Williams	Executive Director, Ecumenical Center for Stewardship Studies, Indianapolis, Ind.	Louisville, Ky.	September 27, 1994
Wesley K. Willmer	Vice President for University Advancement, Biola University, LaMirada, Calif.	Louisville, Ky.	September 25, 1994
Norma Wimberly	Director of Stewardship Education, Section on Stewardship, The United Methodist Church	Nashville, Tenn.	September 27, 1993
Robert Wuthnow	Director of the Center for the Study of American Religion, Princeton University	Princeton, N.J.	October 11, 1994

Notes

Introduction

1. John and Sylvia Ronsvalle, *The State of Church Giving through 1993* (Champaign, Ill.: empty tomb, inc., 1995), 9.

Chapter 1: The Challenge before the Church

1. "Americans Admire Religious Leaders," *Princeton Religion Research Center Emerging Trends* newsletter 17, no. 5 (May 1995): 5.

2. Stephen L. Carter, *The Culture of Disbelief* (New York: BasicBooks, 1993), 115.

3. Kenneth Scott Latourette, *A History of Christianity* (New York: Harper and Brothers, 1953), 1045, 1269.

4. Sydney E. Ahlstrom, *A Religious History of the American People* (New Haven: Yale University Press, 1972), 149.

5. Latourette, *A History of Christianity*, 952.

6. A. James Reichley, *Religion in American Public Life* (Washington, D.C.: The Brookings Institution, 1985), 359–60.

7. Carter, *The Culture of Disbelief*, 36–37.

8. Richard John Neuhaus, "A Voice in the Relativistic Wilderness," *Christianity Today* (February 7, 1994): 35.

9. Robert Wuthnow, *God and Mammon in America* (New York: The Free Press, 1994), 15.

10. Loren Mead, *The Once and Future Church* (Washington, D.C.: The Alban Institute, 1993), 13ff.

11. The Gallup Poll News Service, "Religious Trends," (August 1994): 2.

12. Mead, *The Once and Future Church*, 43.

13. Jacques Ellul, *Money and Power*, trans. LaVonne Neff (Downers Grove, Ill.: InterVarsity Press, 1984), 75.

Chapter 2: Congregations

1. Josiah Strong, "Money and the Kingdom," in *Our Country: Its Possible Future and Its Present Crisis* (New York: Baker and Taylor for the American Mission Society, 1885), quoted in Robert Wood Lynn, ed., "Document 9," *Documentary History* (Portland, Me.: Bangor Theological Seminary, 1994, computer disk), 5.

2. H. Richard Niebuhr, *The Social Sources of Denominationalism* (1929; reprint, Gloucester, Mass.: Peter Smith, 1987), 104–5.

3. Wade Clark Roof and William McKinney, *American Mainline Religion: Its Changing Shape and Future* (New Brunswick, N.J.: Rutgers University Press, 1992), 8.

4. Ibid., 65.

5. Dean R. Hoge, "National Contextual Factors Influencing Church Trends," in Dean R. Hoge and David A. Roozen, eds., *Understanding Church Growth and Decline: 1950–1978* (New York: Pilgrim Press, 1979), 99.

6. *International Encyclopedia of the Social Sciences*, vol. 3 (New York: The

Macmillan Company and The Free Press, 1968), 340.

7. Rudolph Chelminski, "Any Way You Slice It, a Poilâne Loaf Is *Real* French Bread," *Smithsonian* (January 1995): 58.

8. Douglas W. Johnson and George W. Cornell, *Punctured Preconceptions: What North American Christians Think about the Church* (New York: Friendship Press, 1972), 119.

9. David A. Roozen and C. Kirk Hadaway, "Individuals and the Church Choice," in David A. Roozen and C. Kirk Hadaway, eds., *Church and Denominational Growth* (Nashville: Abingdon Press, 1993), 242.

10. Penny Long Marler and David A. Roozen, "The Gallup Surveys of the Unchurched American," in Roozen and Hadaway, eds., *Church and Denominational Growth*, 275.

11. Roof and McKinney, *American Mainline Religion*, 67.

12. Ronsvalle, *The State of Church Giving through 1993*, 9, 13.

13. Participants identified themselves using categories provided on a handout as follows: "Pastor," 82; "Pastoral Team Member," 20; "Parish Administrator or PLC," 8; Parish Council or Stewardship Committee," 104; "Other," 47.

14. R. Gustav Niebuhr, "Where Shopping-Mall Culture Gets a Big Dose of Religion," *New York Times,* 16 April 1995, sec. A, p. 14.

15. This estimate is based on information regarding the National Pastoral Life Center data regarding the number of Catholic parishes in the United States with 5,000 or more members as included in Joseph Claude Harris, *An Estimate of Catholic Household Contributions to the Sunday Offering Collection during 1991* (Washington, D.C.: Catholic University of America Life Cycle Center, December 1992), 29, combined with the estimate that 51 percent of Catholic members attend weekly services in Robert Bezilla, ed., *Religion in America, 1992–1993* (Princeton: Princeton Religion Research Center, 1993), 43.

16. R. Gustav Niebuhr, "Mighty Fortresses: Megachurches Strive to Be All Things to All Parishioners," *Wall Street Journal,* 13 May 1991, sec. A, pp. 1, 6.

17. Douglas A. Walrath, "Social Change and Local Churches: 1951–75" in Hoge and Roozen, eds., *Understanding Church Growth and Decline,* 250.

18. C. Peter Wagner, "Church Growth Research: The Paradigm and Its Applications," in Hoge and Roozen, eds., *Understanding Church Growth and Decline,* 270.

19. James F. Engel and Wilbert Norton, *What's Gone Wrong with the Harvest?* (Grand Rapids: Zondervan, 1975), 28.

20. Ibid., 55.

21. Robert A. Evans, "Recovering the Church's Transforming Middle: Theological Reflections on the Balance between Faithfulness and Effectiveness," in Hoge and Roozen, eds., *Understanding Church Growth and Decline,* 302–3.

22. William J. McKinney Jr., "Performance of United Church of Christ Congregations in Massachusetts and in Pennsylvania," in Hoge and Roozen, eds., *Understanding Church Growth and Decline,* 225.

23. Dean R. Hoge, "A Test of Theories of Denominational Growth and Decline," in Hoge and Roozen, eds., *Understanding Church Growth and Decline,* 216.

24. Mead, *The Once and Future Church*, 28.

25. Herbert Welch, ed., *Selections from the Writings of John Wesley* (Nashville: Abingdon Press, 1942), 208.

26. Niebuhr, *The Social Sources of Denominationalism*, 22.

27. Roof and McKinney, *American Mainline Religion*, 40, 33.

Chapter 3: Pastors

1. Roof and McKinney, *American Mainline Religion*, 187.

2. Bezilla, ed., *Religion in America 1992–1993*, 24, 23.

3. Loren Mead, *Transforming Congregations for the Future* (Washington, D.C.: The Alban Institute, 1994), 80.

4. *Clergy Well-Being, Fair and Just Compensation*, prepared by the Senate of the College of Professional Christian Ministers of the Christian Church in Illinois and Wisconsin (Bloomington, Ill.: Regional Office, February 1995): 31.

5. "Many Believe in Hell (Far Fewer Expect to Go There)," *Princeton Religion Research Center Emerging Trends* (February 1995): 3.

6. Karl Menninger, *Whatever Became of Sin?* (New York: Hawthorn Books, 1973), 188.

7. Ibid., 198.

8. Dean R. Hoge and David A. Roozen, "Some Sociological Conclusions about Church Trends," in Hoge and Roozen, eds., *Understanding Church Growth and Decline*, 324–25.

9. Douglas John Hall, *The Steward* (New York: Friendship Press, 1982), 2.

10. Menninger, *Whatever Became of Sin?*, 193.

Chapter 4: Pastors and Denominations

1. Roger J. Nemeth and Donald A. Luidens, "Congregational vs. Denom-

inational Giving: An Analysis of Giving Patterns in the Presbyterian Church in the United States and the Reformed Church in America," *Review of Religious Research* 36, no. 2 (December 1994): 116.

2. Robin Klay, "Changing Priorities: Allocation of Giving in the Presbyterian Church in the U.S.," in Milton J Coalter, John M. Mulder, and Louis B. Weeks, eds., *The Organizational Revolution: Presbyterians and American Denominationalism* (Louisville: Westminster/John Knox Press, 1992), 137.

3. *A Report to the Church: Discerning the Spirit, Envisioning Our Future*, Presbyterian Church (U.S.A.) General Assembly Council, Louisville, Ky., a report of the October 30–November 1, 1992, Chicago convocation, 248–50.

4. Craig Dykstra and James Hudnut-Beumler, "The National Organizational Structures of Protestant Denominations: An Invitation to a Conversation," in Coalter, Mulder, and Weeks, eds., *The Organizational Revolution*, 318–28.

5. Bradley F. Watkins II, "Let's Quit the United Methodist Church?" *The United Methodist Reporter*, Central Illinois Conference edition (January 27, 1994): 1.

6. McKinney, "Performance of United Church of Christ Congregations in Massachusetts and in Pennsylvania," 227.

7. R. Stephen Warner, *New Wine in Old Wineskins: Evangelicals and Liberals in a Small-Town Church* (Berkeley: University of California Press, 1990), 168.

8. Dykstra and Hudnut-Beumler, "The National Organizational Struc-

tures of Protestant Denominations," 317–18.

9. See, for example, Bruce A. Greer, "Strategies for Evangelism and Growth in Three Denominations (1965–1990)," in Roozen and Hadaway, eds., *Church and Denominational Growth*, 101–2, 107; and Richard W. Reifsnyder, "Managing the Mission: Church Restructuring in the Twentieth Century," in Coalter, Mulder, and Weeks, eds., *The Organizational Revolution*, 77.

Chapter 5: Congregations and Denominations

1. Johnson and Cornell, *Punctured Preconceptions*, 110.

2. General Council on Finance and Administration, The United Methodist Church, "Summary Report on the Annual Conference Listening Project (1993–1994)," 2.

3. Reifsnyder, "Managing the Mission," 94–95.

4. See, for example, Dykstra and Hudnut-Beumler, "The National Organizational Structures of Protestant Denominations," 327; and Warner, *New Wine in Old Wineskins*, 17.

5. Mead, *The Once and Future Church*, 79.

6. Paul Baard, "A Motivational Model for Consulting with Not-for-profit Organizations: A Study of Church Growth and Participation," *Consulting Psychology Journal* (Summer 1994): 22.

7. One member of the Stewardship Project National Advisory Committee mentioned that discussions surrounding Federal Accounting Standards Board Procedures, Regulations 116 and 117, may have a major impact on how both congregations and denominational structures organize their accounting and allocation procedures in the future.

8. Charles H. Fahs, *Trends in Protestant Giving* (New York: Institute of Social and Religious Research, 1929), 63–64.

9. Robert Wood Lynn, *Faith and Money* (Portland, Me.: Bangor Theological Seminary, 1994, computer disk), 55.

10. Reginald W. Bibby, "Religion in the Canadian 1990s: The Paradox of Poverty and Potential," in Roozen and Hadaway, eds., *Church and Denominational Growth*, 290.

11. Mead, *Transforming Congregations for the Future*, 54.

12. Milton J Coalter, John M. Mulder, and Louis B. Weeks, *The Re-Forming Tradition: Presbyterians and Mainstream Protestantism* (Louisville: Westminster/John Knox Press, 1992), 237.

13. Daniel V. A. Olsen, "Congregational Growth and Decline in Indiana among Five Mainline Denominations," in Roozen and Hadaway, eds., *Church and Denominational Growth*, 220, 224.

Chapter 6: Organizing Money and the Church

1. Luther P. Powell, *Money and the Church* (New York: Association Press, 1962), 115.

2. Ibid., 139-42.

3. Fahs, *Trends in Protestant Giving*, 6, 30.

4. Gordon McAlister, empty tomb, inc. Stewardship Project National Advisory Committee Working Papers (December 28, 1992).

5. See Alicia D. Byrd, "The Philanthropy of the Black Church: Historical and Contemporary Perspective," *Philanthropy and the Religious*

Tradition, Spring Research Forum Working Papers (Washington, D.C.: Independent Sector, 1989), 5; Gerald Jaynes and Robin M. Williams Jr., eds., *A Common Destiny: Blacks and American Society* (Washington, D.C.: National Academy Press, 1989), 173–76; C. Eric Lincoln and Lawrence H. Mamiya, *The Black Church in the African American Experience* (Durham, N.C.: Duke University Press, 1990), 242–43.

6. See, for example, Lincoln and Mamiya, *The Black Church in the African American Experience,* 140, 260, 273, as well as C. Kirk Hadaway, "Church Growth in North America: The Character of a Religious Marketplace," in Roozen and Hadaway, eds., *Church and Denominational Growth,* 354.

7. Norman M. Green and Paul W. Light, "Growth and Decline in an Inclusive Denomination: The ABC Experience," in Roozen and Hadaway, eds., *Church and Denominational Growth,* 113, 117, 122.

8. Ibid., 123–24.

9. John C. Haughey, *The Holy Use of Money: Personal Finance in Light of Christian Faith,* rev. ed. (New York: Crossroad, 1989), 102.

Chapter 7: Money as a Topic

1. Haughey, *The Holy Use of Money,* 1.

2. Wuthnow, *God and Mammon in America,* 141.

3. Ibid., 140.

4. Ellul, *Money and Power,* 77.

5. Tom Precious, "Money Talk Makes Stern Walk," *Albany (N.Y.) Times Union,* 5 August 1994, sec. A, p. 1.

6. Phil Sudo, "Ads All Around," *Scholastic Update* (May 7, 1993): 2.

7. Wesley K. Willmer, "Stewardship: A Key Link to Commitment and Ministry" (address given at Talbot School of Theology chapel, La Mirada, Calif., April 5, 1994), 1.

8. Randall Balmer, "Churchgoing: Mount Olivet Lutheran in Minneapolis," *The Christian Century* (November 16, 1994): 1074.

9. *Hoop Dreams,* produced by Fred Marx, Steve James, and Peter Gilbert; directed by Steve James, New Line Home Video distributed by Turner Video, 1994.

10. Johnson and Cornell, *Punctured Preconceptions,* 144.

11. Haughey, *The Holy Use of Money,* 44.

12. Timothy Morgan, "Re-Engineering the Seminary," *Christianity Today* (October 24, 1994): 75.

13. Daniel Conway, *The Reluctant Steward: A Report and Commentary on the Stewardship Development Study* (St. Meinrad, Ind.: Saint Meinrad Seminary and Christian Theological Seminary, 1992), 14–15.

14. Johnson and Cornell, *Punctured Preconceptions,* 51, 54.

15. Powell, *Money and the Church,* 94, 102.

16. Julio de Santa Ana, *Good News to the Poor* (Maryknoll, N.Y.: Orbis Books, 1979), 62.

17. Ibid., 77, 78.

18. *Clergy Well-Being,* 25.

Chapter 8: Pastors and Seminary Training

1. Jerilee Grandy and Mark Greiner, "Academic Preparation of Master of Divinity Candidates," *Ministry Research Notes: An ETS Occasional Report,* Fall 1990, 7.

2. Charlotte Allen, "Our Mother, Who Art in Heaven," *Washington Post Magazine* (December 10, 1995): 36.

3. *Review of Graduate Theological Education in the Pacific Northwest* (Vancouver, Wash.: The M. J. Murdock Charitable Trust, December 1994), 33.

4. Paul Wilkes, "The Hands That Would Shape Our Souls," *The Atlantic Monthly* (December 1990): 61, 66; see also *Review of Graduate Theological Education*, 5, 61.

5. Jerry Filteau, "Major Study Shows U.S. Nuns' Efforts Focusing on Needy," a Catholic News Service article appearing in *The Peoria Diocese Catholic Post*, 15 November 1992, sec. 1, p. 3.

6. *Review of Graduate Theological Education*, 15, 21, 22.

7. Wilkes, "The Hands That Would Shape Our Souls," 86.

8. *Review of Graduate Theological Education*, 64.

9. Ibid., 24.

10. Haughey, *The Holy Use of Money*, 41.

11. James L. Waits, "Stewardship in the Curriculum of Theological Education," in Conway, *The Reluctant Steward*, 51.

12. Conway, *The Reluctant Steward*, 17.

Chapter 9: What Is Money?

1. Philip Slater, *Wealth Addiction* (New York: E. P. Dutton, 1980), 5.

2. Paul L. Wachtel, *The Poverty of Affluence* (Philadelphia: New Society Publishers, 1989), 85.

3. *Forrest Gump*, produced by Wendy Finerman, Steve Tisch, and Steve Starkey, directed by Robert Zemeckis, script by Winston Groom, Paramount Pictures, 1994.

4. Mike Peters, "Mother Goose and Grimm," *Champaign (Ill.) News-Gazette*, 4 December 1994.

5. Lyman Beecher, "Resources of the Adversary and the Means of Their Destruction," in *Sermons Delivered on Various Occasions* (Boston: T. R. Marvin, 1828), quoted in Lynn, "Document 2," *Documentary History*, 11.

6. Strong, "Money and the Kingdom," 3.

7. Washington Gladden, "The New Idolatry," in *The New Idolatry and Other Discussions*, (New York: McClure, Phillips and Co., 1905), quoted in Lynn, ed., "Document 7," *Documentary History*, 3.

8. Lawrence W. Reed, "As Americans' Moral Values Erode, So Do Their Freedoms," *Champaign (Ill.) News-Gazette*, 5 June 1994, sec. B, p. 3.

9. Marc Allan, "D-Funk Mob Musik," *Indianapolis Star*, 6 September 1994, sec. C, p. 1.

10. James H. Smylie, "Church Growth and Decline in Historical Perspective: Protestant Quest for Identity, Leadership, and Meaning," in Hoge and Roozen, eds., *Understanding Church Growth and Decline*, 83.

11. Roof and McKinney, *American Mainline Religion*, 71.

12. Ibid., 96.

13. Mead, *The Once and Future Church*, 62.

14. Patrick Brennan, address given at the National Catholic Stewardship Conference annual meeting, Nashville, October 20, 1993.

15. Brian Kluth, "Common Stewardship Views Contrasted," Christian Stewardship Association, Milwaukee (September 1994), revised in correspondence received 5 June 1995.

Chapter 10: Coming to Terms with Money

1. Powell, *Money and the Church*, 72, 73.

2. Johnson and Cornell, *Punctured Preconceptions*, 152.

3. Haughey, *The Holy Use of Money*, 106.

4. Al Taylor, *Proving God: Triumphant Living through Tithing* (Cleveland, Tenn.: Pathway Press, 1991), 74–76.

5. Nan Duerling, "Part 1, Tithing Our Tradition," in Norma Wimberly, *Putting God First: The Tithe* (Nashville: Discipleship Resources, 1992), 7.

6. Ministry of Money newsletter (Gaithersburg, Md., April 1995), 3.

7. Elizabeth Greene, Stephen G. Greene, and Jennifer Moore, "A Generation Prepares to Transfer Its Trillions," *The Chronicle of Philanthropy* (November 16, 1993): 1.

8. Dave Barry, "1994: It Went by Like a Slow Bronco," a Knight-Ridder Newspaper feature appearing in *Champaign (Ill.) News-Gazette*, 1 January 1995, sec. E, p. 1.

9. Anne Willette, "No Savings Means More Work Longer," *USA Today*, 8 May 1995, sec. A, p. 1.

10. Strong, "Money and the Kingdom," 11.

11. Andrew Carnegie, "Wealth," *North American Review* 148 (June 1889), quoted in Lynn, ed., "Document 8," *Documentary History*, 6.

12. Adam Rogers and Jennifer Tanaka, "Your Own Private Collection," *Newsweek* (February 13, 1995): 10.

13. Letter from James L. Payne, *The Chronicle of Philanthropy* (April 6, 1995): 46.

14. Johnson and Cornell, *Punctured Preconceptions*, 187.

15. See Hoge, "A Test of Theories of Denominational Growth and Decline," 202; and Kenneth W. Inskeep, "Giving Trends in the Evangelical Lutheran Church in America," *Review of Religious Research* 36, no. 2 (December 1994): 240–42.

16. D. Scott Cormode, "A Financial History of Presbyterian Congregations Since World War II," in Coalter, Mulder, and Weeks, eds., *The Organizational Revolution*, 189.

17. *Calvin: Institutes of the Christian Religion*, John T. McNeill, ed., vol. 1 (Philadelphia: The Westminster Press, 1960), 800.

18. Hermann Rauschning, *Hitler Speaks: A Series of Political Conversations with Adolf Hitler on His Real Aims* (London: Thornton Butterworth Ltd., 1939), 58, quoted in "The New Light: 'German Christians' and National Socialism," presented by P. Larry Thornton to the Conference on Faith and History Fall Meeting (October 19, 1984), Fort Worth, Texas.

19. Niebuhr, *The Social Sources of Denominationalism*, 22.

20. Slater, *Wealth Addiction*, 184.

Chapter 11: Control Dynamics

1. Peter A. Zaleski and Charles E. Zech, "Economic and Attitudinal Factors in Catholic and Protestant Religious Giving," *Review of Religious Research*, 36, no. 2 (December 1994): 160–61.

2. Mead, *Transforming Congregations for the Future*, 100, including footnote 13 on 137.

3. Dean R. Hoge, Michael J. Donahue, Charles Zech, and Patrick McNamara, "Preliminary Report #2: American Congregational Giving Study" (delivered to the annual meeting of the Religious Research Associ-

ation, Albuquerque, N. Mex., November 4, 1994), 11–12.

4. Johnson and Cornell, *Punctured Preconceptions,* 78.

5. Coalter, Mulder, and Weeks, *The Re-Forming Tradition,* 248.

6. Wagner, "Church Growth Research," 277.

7. Baard, "A Motivational Model for Consulting with Not-for-profit Organizations," 22.

8. Dean M. Kelley, *Why Conservative Churches Are Growing: A Study in Sociology of Religion* (New York: Harper and Row, 1972), 123.

Chapter 12: Needs for Pastoral Counseling

1. Menninger, *Whatever Became of Sin?,* 154.

2. LynNell Hancock et al., "Putting Working Moms in Custody," *Newsweek* (March 13, 1995): 56.

3. Wuthnow, *God and Mammon in America,* 136.

4. Wachtel, *The Poverty of Affluence,* 20.

5. Ibid., 39.

6. Ibid., 65.

7. Slater, *Wealth Addiction,* 37–38.

8. Walrath, "Social Change and Local Churches," 248.

9. Wuthnow, *God and Mammon in America,* 82.

10. *Review of Graduate Theological Education,* 47.

11. Haughey, *The Holy Use of Money,* 11–14.

12. Slater, *Wealth Addiction,* 34–35.

13. Ibid., 10–11.

14. Menninger, *Whatever Became of Sin?,* 228.

15. Strong, "Money and the Kingdom," 13.

16. Haughey, *The Holy Use of Money,* 45.

Chapter 13: Paradigmatic Shifts

1. Latourette, *A History of Christianity,* 954, 1230.

2. Ahlstrom, *A Religious History of the American People,* 860.

3. Latourette, *A History of Christianity,* 1235.

4. Ibid., 1258.

5. Ibid., 1047.

6. *The United Methodist Reporter,* 4 September 1981, 5.

7. Tokunboh Adeyemo, "From Africa: An Open Letter to the North American Mission Community," in John A. Siewert and John A. Kenyon, eds., *15th Mission Handbook* (Monrovia, Calif.: MARC, 1993), 41.

8. Dykstra and Hudnut-Beumler, "The National Organizational Structures of Protestant Denominations," 319.

9. The 1950 employment rate in the civilian noninstitutional population 16 and over was 32 percent for females compared to 82 percent for males. Thus, adjusting for male and female percentages of the population, it was calculated that 39 women were employed for every 100 men (United States Bureau of the Census, *Statistical Abstract of the United States: 1970* [Washington, D.C.: 1970], 213). Those numbers were compared to the 1993 employment level of 54 percent for females and 70 percent for males (United States Bureau of the Census, *Statistical Abstract of the United States: 1994* [Washington, D.C.: 1994], 396). Therefore, 77 women were working for every 100 men employed.

10. Joan C. LaFollette, "Money and Power: Presbyterian Women's Organizations in the Twentieth Cen-

tury," in Coalter, Mulder, and Weeks, eds., *The Organizational Revolution,* 199–200.

11. Ruth A. Tucker, "A Historical Overview of Women in Ministry," *Theology News and Notes* (Fuller Theological Seminary, March 1995), 6.

12. LaFollette, "Money and Power: Presbyterian Women's Organizations," 232.

13. Johnson and Cornell, *Punctured Preconceptions,* 178–79.

14. Mead, *The Once and Future Church,* 35.

15. Roof and McKinney, *American Mainline Religion,* 47.

16. Coalter, Mulder, and Weeks, *The Re-Forming Tradition,* 279.

17. Robert Kubey and Mihaly Csikszentmihalyi, *Television and the Quality of Life* (Hillsdale, N.J.: Lawrence Erlbaum Associates, 1990), 71, 172, 164, 116, 102, 139.

18. Ibid., 150.

19. Latourette, *A History of Christianity,* 1235.

20. Niebuhr, *The Social Sources of Denominationalism,* 223.

21. Kubey and Csikszentmihalyi, *Television and the Quality of Life,* 176.

22. Ibid., 35.

23. Ibid., 197.

24. Kelley, *Why Conservative Churches Are Growing,* 84, 101.

25. Kubey and Csikszentmihalyi, *Television and the Quality of Life,* xi.

26. Ellen Gray, "Former Television Fans Organize First National TV-Turnoff Week," a Knight-Ridder article appearing in *Champaign (Ill.) News-Gazette,* 23 April 1995, sec. F, p. 3.

27. Roof and McKinney, *American Mainline Religion,* 180–81.

Chapter 14: Signs of Hope

1. Johnson and Cornell, *Punctured Preconceptions,* 183.

2. Wade Clark Roof and Mary Johnson, "Baby Boomers and the Return to the Churches," in Roozen and Hadaway, *Church and Denominational Growth,* 307.

3. Joseph M. Champlin, "Can We Patch the Hole in the Collection Basket? Yes, If We Put Our Money into Sacrificial Giving," *The Catholic Voice* (April 9, 1993): 4.

4. John and Sylvia Ronsvalle, *The State of Church Giving through 1992* (Champaign, Ill.: empty tomb, inc., 1994), 11, 47–48.

5. In the discussion leading to this point, the Scripture referred to was "Jesus answered, 'The first is, "Hear, O Israel: the Lord our God, the Lord is one; you shall love the Lord your God with all your heart, and with all your soul, and with all your mind, and with all your strength." The second is this, "You shall love your neighbor as yourself." There is no other commandment greater than these'" (Mark 12:29–31 NRSV).

Appendix A: Historical Background and Description of the Stewardship Project

1. See *The State of Church Giving* report series published annually by empty tomb, inc., Champaign, Ill. Also see John and Sylvia Ronsvalle, "The State of Church Giving through 1991," *Yearbook of American and Canadian Churches 1994* (Nashville: Abingdon Press, 1994), 12–16.

2. For a description of the Yoking Map and its development, see John and Sylvia Ronsvalle, *The Poor Have Faces* (Grand Rapids: Baker, 1992), 55–90.

3. Each congregation is represented in only one category in table 1. For example, there were telephone conversations with the pastors of congregations with which Stewardship Project staff met in person. However, for purposes of this table, such congregations would be included only in the "In-Person Encounters with Individual Congregations" category. The list excludes pastors who participated in large-group presentations but with whom there was no further follow-up, as well as multiple interactions with the same congregation, pastor, or regional official.

4. John and Sylvia Ronsvalle, "The National Money for Missions Program Congregational Pilot: Findings from the Six-Month Implementation Report" (Champaign, Ill.: empty tomb, inc., January 22, 1991).

5. This analysis began with the publication of *A Comparison of the Growth in Church Contributions with United States Per Capita Income*, John and Sylvia Ronsvalle (Champaign, Ill.: empty tomb, inc., 1988).

Appendix B: Stewardship Project Survey Distribution and Analysis Methodology

1. The ten regions follow the nine United States Census Regions, with the following modifications. The Pacific Region was divided into Pacific 1 and Pacific 2. The East North Central Region was referred to as Midwest and was limited to Illinois and Indiana, the two states in which the majority of in-person Stewardship Project contacts were made. The purpose of including the Illinois and Indiana area specifically was to check whether the answers in this area varied from other regions.

2. Each National Advisory Committee member was asked to fill out a form that asked for the "Number of Members" for the responding congregations. The denominational information provided, including any changes (in italics below) made to the form category of "Number of Members," was as follows: cma: Number of Members *Sunday A.M. attendance*; ccd: Number of Members; cga: Number of Members; cgc: Number of Members *Attendance, morning worship*; chb: Number of Members; chn: Number of Members: *Membership*; epc: Number of Members; ecv: Number of Members: *Members*; elc: *Baptized* Number of Members; lms: Number of Members; pch: Number of Members: *Total (Active + Inactive)*; sbc: Number of Members; ucc: Number of Members; umc: Number of Members. See table 5 for a list of denominations and the three-letter codes.

Bibliography

Adeyemo, Tokunboh. "From Africa: An Open Letter to the North American Mission Community." In *Mission Handbook*. Edited by John A. Siewert and John A. Kenyon. 15th ed. Monrovia, Calif.: MARC, 1993.

Ahlstrom, Sydney E. *A Religious History of the American People*. New Haven: Yale University Press, 1972.

Baard, Paul P. "A Motivational Model for Consulting with Not-for-Profit Organizations: A Study of Church Growth and Participation." *Consulting Psychology Journal* (Summer 1994):19–31.

Beecher, Lyman. "Resources of the Adversary and the Means of Their Destruction." In *Sermons Delivered on Various Occasions*. Boston: T. R. Marvin, 1828. Included in Robert Wood Lynn, ed. "Document 2." *Documentary History*. Portland, Me.: Bangor Theological Seminary, 1994. Computer disk.

Bezilla, Robert, ed. *Religion in America 1992–1993*. Princeton: Princeton Religion Research Center, 1993.

Bibby, Reginald. "Religion in the Canadian 1990s: The Paradox of Poverty and Potential." In *Church and Denominational Growth*. Edited by David A. Roozen and C. Kirk Hadaway. Nashville: Abingdon Press, 1993.

Byrd, Alicia D. "The Philanthropy of the Black Church: Historical and Contemporary Perspective." In *Philanthropy and the Religious Tradition: Spring Research Forum Working Papers*. Washington, D.C.: Independent Sector, 1989.

Calvin, John. *Calvin: Institutes of the Christian Religion*. Edited by John R. McNeill. 2 vols. Philadelphia: Westminster Press, 1960.

Carnegie, Andrew. "Wealth." *North American Review* 148 (June 1889). Included in Robert Wood Lynn, ed. "Document 8." *Documentary History*. Portland, Me.: Bangor Theological Seminary, 1994. Computer disk.

Carter, Stephen L. *The Culture of Disbelief*. New York: BasicBooks, 1993.

Coalter, Milton J, John M. Mulder, and Louis B. Weeks. *The Re-Forming Tradition: Presbyterians and Mainstream Protestantism*. Louisville: Westminster/John Knox Press, 1992.

Conway, Daniel. *The Reluctant Steward: A Report and Commentary on the Stewardship and Development Study*. St. Meinrad, Ind.: Saint Meinrad Seminary and Christian Theological Seminary, 1992.

Cormode, D. Scott. "A Financial History of Presbyterian Congregations Since World War II." In *The Organizational Revolution: Presbyterians and American Denominationalism*, edited by Milton J Coalter, John M. Mulder, and Louis B. Weeks. Louisville: Westminster/John Knox Press, 1992.

de Santa Ana, Julio. *Good News to the Poor*. Maryknoll, N.Y.: Orbis Books, 1979.

Duerling, Nan. "Part 1, Tithing Our Tradition." In Norma Wimberly. *Putting God First: The Tithe*. Nashville: Discipleship Resources, 1992.

374

Dykstra, Craig, and James Hudnut-Beumler. "The National Organizational Structures of Protestant Denominations: An Invitation to a Conversation." In *The Organizational Revolution: Presbyterians and American Denominationalism*. Edited by Milton J Coalter, John M. Mulder, and Louis B. Weeks. Louisville: Westminster/John Knox Press, 1992.

Ellul, Jacques. *Money and Power*. Translated by LaVonne Neff. Downers Grove, Ill.: InterVarsity Press, 1984.

Engel, James F., and Wilbert Norton. *What's Gone Wrong with the Harvest?* Grand Rapids: Zondervan, 1975.

Evans, Robert A. "Recovering the Church's Transforming Middle: Theological Reflections on the Balance between Faithfulness and Effectiveness." In *Understanding Church Growth and Decline: 1950–1978*. Edited by Dean R. Hoge and David A. Roozen. New York: Pilgrim Press, 1979.

Fahs, Charles H. *Trends in Protestant Giving*. New York: Institute of Social and Religious Research, 1929.

Gladden, Washington. "The New Idolatry." In *The New Idolatry and Other Discussions*. New York: McClure, Phillips and Co., 1905. Included in Robert Wood Lynn, ed. "Document 7." *Documentary History*. Portland, Me.: Bangor Theological Seminary, 1994. Computer disk.

Greeley, Andrew, and William McManus. *Catholic Contributions: Sociology and Policy*. Chicago: Thomas More Press, 1987.

Green, Norman M., and Paul W. Light. "Growth and Decline in an Inclusive Denomination: The ABC Experience." In *Church and Denominational Growth*. Edited by David A. Roozen and C. Kirk Hadaway. Nashville: Abingdon Press, 1993.

Greer, Bruce A. "Strategies for Evangelism and Growth in Three Denominations (1965–1990)." In *Church and Denominational Growth*. Edited by David A. Roozen and C. Kirk Hadaway. Nashville: Abingdon Press, 1993.

Hadaway, C. Kirk. "Church Growth in North America: The Character of a Religious Marketplace." In *Church and Denominational Growth*. Edited by David A. Roozen and C. Kirk Hadaway. Nashville: Abingdon Press, 1993.

Hall, Douglas John. *The Steward*. New York: Friendship Press, 1982.

Harris, Joseph Claude. *An Estimate of Catholic Household Contributions to the Sunday Offering Collection during 1991*. Washington, D.C.: Catholic University of America Life Cycle Center, December 1992.

Haughey, John C. *The Holy Use of Money: Personal Finance in Light of Christian Faith*. Rev. ed. New York: Crossroad, 1989.

Hoge, Dean R. "National Contextual Factors Influencing Church Trends." In *Understanding Church Growth and Decline: 1950–1978*. Edited by Dean R. Hoge and David A. Roozen. New York: Pilgrim Press, 1979.

———. "A Test of Theories of Denominational Growth and Decline." In *Understanding Church Growth and Decline: 1950–1978*. Edited by Dean R. Hoge and David A. Roozen. New York: Pilgrim Press, 1979.

Hoge, Dean R., and David A. Roozen. "Some Sociological Conclusions about Church Trends." In *Understanding Church Growth and Decline: 1950–1978*. New York: Pilgrim Press, 1979.

Hoge, Dean R., Michael J. Donahue, Charles Zech, and Patrick McNamara. "Preliminary Report: American Congregational Giving Study." Delivered to the annual meeting of the Religious Research Association. Albuquerque, 4 November 1994. Photocopy.

Innskeep, Kenneth W. "Giving Trends in the Evangelical Lutheran Church in America." *Review of Religious Research* 36, no. 2 (December 1994): 238–44.

Jaynes, Gerald David, and Robin M. Williams Jr., eds. *A Common Destiny: Blacks and American Society.* Washington, D.C.: National Academy Press, 1989.

Johnson, Douglas W., and George W. Cornell. *Punctured Preconceptions: What North American Christians Think about the Church.* New York: Friendship Press, 1972.

Kelley, Dean M. *Why Conservative Churches Are Growing: A Study in Sociology of Religion.* New York: Harper and Row, 1972.

Klay, Robin. "Changing Priorities: Allocation of Giving in the Presbyterian Church in the U.S." In *The Organizational Revolution: Presbyterians and American Denominationalism.* Edited by Milton J Coalter, John M. Mulder, and Louis B. Weeks. Louisville: Westminster/John Knox Press, 1992.

Kubey, Robert, and Mihaly Csikszentmihalyi. *Television and the Quality of Life.* Hillsdale, N.J.: Lawrence Erlbaum Associates, 1990.

LaFollette, Joan C. "Money and Power: Presbyterian Women's Organizations in the Twentieth Century." In *The Organizational Revolution: Presbyterians and American Denominationalism.* Edited by Milton J Coalter, John M. Mulder, and Louis B. Weeks. Louisville: Westminster/John Knox Press, 1992.

Latourette, Kenneth Scott. *A History of Christianity.* New York: Harper and Brothers, 1953.

Lincoln, C. Eric, and Lawrence H. Mamiya. *The Black Church in the African American Experience.* Durham, N.C.: Duke University Press, 1990.

Lynn, Robert Wood. *Faith and Money.* Portland, Me.: Bangor Theological Seminary, 1994. Computer disk.

The M. J. Murdock Charitable Trust. *Review of Graduate Theological Education in the Pacific Northwest.* Vancouver, Wash.: M. J. Murdock Charitable Trust, December 1994.

Marler, Penny Long, and David A. Roozen. "The Gallup Surveys of the Unchurched American." In *Church and Denominational Growth.* Edited by David A. Roozen and C. Kirk Hadaway. Nashville: Abingdon Press, 1993.

McKinney, William J., Jr. "Performance of United Church of Christ Congregations in Massachusetts and in Pennsylvania." In *Understanding Church Growth and Decline: 1950–1978.* Edited by Dean R. Hoge and David A. Roozen. New York: Pilgrim Press, 1979.

Mead, Loren B. *The Once and Future Church.* Washington, D.C.: The Alban Institute, 1993.

———. *Transforming Congregations for the Future.* Washington, D.C.: The Alban Institute, 1994.

Menninger, Karl. *Whatever Became of Sin?* New York: Hawthorn Books, 1973.

Moore, Gary D. *The Thoughtful Christian's Guide to Investments.* Grand Rapids: Zondervan, 1990.

National Conference of Catholic Bishops. *Stewardship: A Disciple's Response, A Pastoral Letter on Stewardship.* Washington, D.C.: United States Catholic Conference, 1992.

Nemeth, Roger J., and Donald A. Luidens. "Congregational vs. Denominational Giving: An Analysis of Giving Patterns in the Presbyterian Church in the United States and the Reformed Church in America." *Review of Religious Research* 36, no. 2 (December 1994): 111–22.

Neuhaus, Richard John. "A Voice in the Relativistic Wilderness." *Christianity Today*, 7 February 1994, 35.

Niebuhr, H. Richard. *The Social Sources of Denominationalism*. 1929. Reprint, Gloucester, Mass.: Peter Smith, 1987.

Olsen, Daniel V. A. "Congregational Growth and Decline in Indiana among Five Mainline Denominations." In *Church and Denominational Growth*. Edited by David A. Roozen and C. Kirk Hadaway. Nashville: Abingdon Press, 1993.

Powell, Luther P. *Money and the Church*. New York: Association Press, 1962.

Presbyterian Church (U.S.A.) General Assembly Council. *A Report to the Church: Discerning the Spirit, Envisioning Our Future*. Louisville: General Assembly Council Office, 1992.

Rauschning, Hermann. *Hitler Speaks: A Series of Political Conversations with Adolf Hitler on His Real Aims*. London: Thornton Butterworth, 1939.

Reichley, A. James. *Religion in American Public Life*. Washington, D.C.: The Brookings Institution, 1985.

Reifsnyder, Richard W. "Managing the Mission: Church Restructuring in the Twentieth Century." In *The Organizational Revolution: Presbyterians and American Denominationalism*. Edited by Milton J Coalter, John M. Mulder, and Louis B. Weeks. Louisville: Westminster/John Knox Press, 1992.

Ronsvalle, John and Sylvia. *A Comparison of the Growth in Church Contributions with United States Per Capita Income*. Champaign, Ill.: empty tomb, inc., 1988.

———. "The National Money for Missions Program Congregational Pilot: Findings from the Six-Month Implementation Report." Champaign, Ill.: empty tomb, inc., 22 January 1991.

———. *The Poor Have Faces*. Grand Rapids: Baker, 1992.

———. *The State of Church Giving through 1992*. Champaign, Ill.: empty tomb, inc., 1994.

———. *The State of Church Giving through 1993*. Champaign, Ill.: empty tomb, inc., 1995.

Roof, Wade Clark, and Mary Johnson. "Baby Boomers and the Return to the Churches." In *Church and Denominational Growth*. Edited by David A. Roozen and C. Kirk Hadaway. Nashville: Abingdon Press, 1993.

Roof, Wade Clark, and William McKinney. *American Mainline Religion: Its Changing Shape and Future*. New Brunswick, N.J.: Rutgers University Press, 1992.

Roozen, David A., and C. Kirk Hadaway. "Individuals and the Church Choice." In *Church and Denominational Growth*. Nashville: Abingdon Press, 1993.

Slater, Philip. *Wealth Addiction*. New York: E. P. Dutton, 1980.

Smylie, James H. "Church Growth and Decline in Historical Perspective: Protestant Quest for Identity, Leadership, and Meaning." In *Understanding Church Growth and Decline: 1950–1978*, edited by Dean R. Hoge and David A. Roozen. New York: Pilgrim Press, 1979.

Statistical Abstract of the United States: 1994. 114th ed. Washington, D.C.: United States Bureau of the Census, 1994.

Strong, Josiah. "Money and the Kingdom." In *Our Country: Its Possible Future and Its Present Crisis*. New York: Baker and Taylor for the American Mission Society, 1885. Included in Robert Wood Lynn, ed. "Document 9." *Documentary History*. Portland, Me.: Bangor Theological Seminary, 1994. Computer disk.

Sweetser, Thomas, S.J., and Patricia M. Forster, O.S.F. *Transforming the Parish: Models for the Future*. Kansas City, Mo.: Sheed and Ward, 1993.

Taylor, Al. *Proving God: Triumphant Living through Tithing*. Cleveland, Tenn.: Pathway Press, 1991.

Tucker, Ruth A. "A Historical Overview of Women in Ministry." *Theology News and Notes* (Fuller Theological Seminary, March 1995).

Wachtel, Paul L. *The Poverty of Affluence*. Philadelphia: New Society Publishers, 1989.

Wagner, C. Peter. "Church Growth Research: The Paradigm and Its Applications." In *Understanding Church Growth and Decline: 1950–1978*. Edited by Dean R. Hoge and David A. Roozen. New York: Pilgrim Press, 1979.

Waits, James L. "Stewardship in the Curriculum of Theological Education." In Daniel Conway. *The Reluctant Steward*. St. Meinrad, Ind.: St. Meinrad Seminary and Christian Theological Seminary, 1992.

Walrath, Douglas A. "Social Change and Local Churches: 1951–75." In *Understanding Church Growth and Decline: 1950–1978*. Edited by Dean R. Hoge and David A. Roozen. New York: Pilgrim Press, 1979.

Warner, R. Stephen. *New Wine in Old Wineskins: Evangelicals and Liberals in a Small-Town Church*. Berkeley: University of California Press, 1990.

Welch, Herbert, ed. *Selections from the Writings of John Wesley*. Nashville: Abingdon Press, 1942.

Wilkes, Paul. "The Hands That Would Shape Our Souls." *Atlantic Monthly*, December 1990, 61.

Willmer, Wesley K. "Stewardship: A Key Link to Commitment and Ministry." Address given at Talbot School of Theology chapel, La Mirada, Calif., 5 April 1994. Photocopy.

Wuthnow, Robert. *God and Mammon in America*. New York: The Free Press, 1994.

Zaleski, Peter A., and Charles E. Zech. "Economic and Attitudinal Factors in Catholic and Protestant Religious Giving." *Review of Religious Research* 36, no. 2 (December 1994): 158–67.

Index